Old Ontario

Essays in Honour of J.M.S. CARELESS

edited by
David Keane & Colin Read

Frederick H. Armstrong
associate editor

Published with the assistance of the
Ontario Heritage Foundation,
Ministry of Culture and Communications

DUNDURN PRESS
Toronto and Oxford
1990

Copy editor: Curtis Fahey
Design and Production: Andy Tong
Colour film: Colour Link
Printing and Binding: Gagné Printing Ltd., Louiseville, Quebec, Canada

The writing of this manuscript and the publication of this book were made possible by
support from several sources. The publisher wishes to acknowledge the generous assistance
and ongoing support of The Canada Council, The Book Publishing Industry Development
Programme of the Department of Communications, and The Ontario Arts Council.

In addition, the editors and publisher are particularly grateful to the Ontario Heritage
Foundation, an agency of the Ontario Ministry of Culture and Communications, for a grant
in aid of publication.

Care has been taken to trace the ownership of copyright material used in the text (including
the illustrations). The author and publisher welcome any information enabling them to
rectify any reference or credit in subsequent editions.

J. Kirk Howard, Publisher

Canadian Cataloguing in Publication Data

Main entry under title:

Old Ontario

Includes bibliographical references.
ISBN 1-55002-060-9

1. Ontario - History - 19th century.* 2. Ontario - Social conditions. 3. Careless, J. M. S., 1919-
. I. Keane, David Ross, 1946-   . II. Read, Colin Frederick, 1943-   . III. Careless, J. M. S.,
1919-   .

FC3072.053 1990   971.3   C98-090669-6   F1058.053 1990

Dundurn Press Limited
2181 Queen Street East, Suite 301
Toronto, Canada
M4E 1E5

Dundurn Distribution Limited
73 Lime Walk
Headington, Oxford
England
OX3 7AD

Old Ontario

Essays in Honour of J.M.S. CARELESS

edited by
David Keane & Colin Read

Frederick H. Armstrong
associate editor

Table of Contents

MAPS

Preface

Maurice Careless joined the faculty of the Department of History at the University of Toronto in 1945. For the next 39 years he shared his growing knowledge of Canadian and Ontario history with many thousands of appreciative students through his efforts as a lecturer, seminar leader, thesis supervisor and author. Now retired from teaching duties, he continues to research and publish in Canadian regional and urban history.

As instructor and author, he has promoted three distinct yet compatible approaches to the study of Canadian history. First, since the early 1950s he has urged students and colleagues to view Canadian development within a framework of metropolitan-hinterland relationships. Second, beginning in the later 1960s he has directed attention to the growth of urban centres in nineteenth- and early-twentieth-century Canada. Third, also since the later 1960s, he has argued for a broadening of the profession's agenda to include those "limited identities" which most directly and powerfully conditioned the mentalities and activities of the individuals and communities Canadian historians study. By this he means the nature and impact of regionalism, ethnicity, class and gender.[1] Throughout his career he has demonstrated the remarkable utility of these ways of looking at Canada and Canadians. His early *Brown of the Globe* (1959), later *Union of the Canadas* (1967), and recent *Toronto to 1918* (1984) illustrate why these approaches are often most potent when applied in combination. As well, they demonstrate why Maurice Careless has long been acknowledged as *the* specialist both of the Queen city and of Old Ontario from its Loyalist beginnings to the close of the nineteenth century.

A member for many years of the Ontario Historical Society, the Ontario Heritage Foundation, and the Historic Sites and Monuments Board of Canada, Maurice Careless has met, worked with, and become much admired by, hundreds of Canadians with no university connection who share with him a passionate interest in the history of Canada's communities and regions. They respect him for his fair-mindedness and conciliatory nature, his capacity for hard work and critical appraisal, and, not least, his talents as a public speaker. But Maurice Careless has touched a still wider professional and lay audience across Canada and in, for example, the United States, the United Kingdom and Australia, through guest lectures before local historical societies and academic gatherings or, as likely, by his books and essays. There is even a Japanese edition of *Canada: A Story of Challenge*.

Consequently, Maurice Careless is today probably English Canada's best-known academic historian, both within and beyond the Dominion. Certainly his writings on the development of Canada, the province of Ontario and the city of Toronto, have had a pervasive influence over the past three decades on the course of Canadian historical inquiry. Students and colleagues alike have invariably moved toward their own diverse approaches to national, regional, ethnic, class and community history from a background that includes familiarity with his scholarship. They may have been influenced by his skillfully crafted textbook contributions to the study of pre-Confederation British North America; his examination in *Brown of the Globe* of Toronto's metropolitan ambitions and rise to regional dominance; his numerous essays on nineteenth-century urban centres or regionalism in Canada; or his masterful reviews of national historiography and proposals for future agenda. Whether embracing or rejecting his approaches, interpretations and suggestions, the members of the Canadian historical fraternity have all been touched by Maurice Careless and his distinguished record of scholarship.

The contributors to this volume have perhaps been touched more deeply than others. Like ourselves, nearly all had the privilege—and pleasure—of being a student of Maurice Careless. A few knew him only or in addition as a colleague in the University of Toronto History Department. To the former he was an instructor or supervisor whose exceptional patience, sound editorial advice and moral support were greatly appreciated. To the latter, he was a colleague who willingly assumed more than his fair share of departmental chores and by his skills as a mediator helped carry the faculty through some particularly rough times. Yet, whether former teacher, colleague or both, Maurice Careless has become and remains a special friend—a mentor—inspiring us with his gentle humour, generosity of spirit, extensive knowledge and impressive breadth of vision.

After Maurice Careless retired in 1984, we thought something should be done to honour him and to celebrate his exceptional record as teacher, researcher, author, and spokesperson for historic sites and the preservation of Canada's material culture. A *festschrift* seemed the appropriate instrument by which to express our affection and appreciation. The result of our labours is this volume of original essays. Two of the twelve papers, a biography by Frederick H. Armstrong and a discussion by Kenneth McNaught of Maurice's historical scholarship, describe the personal and intellectual foundations of our friend's scholarship. The remaining ten apply one or more of the three interpretive frameworks he has promoted to topics in the history of nineteenth-century Ontario, the period and region to which Maurice has given his closest attention as a teacher, researcher and writer. Some of the ten deal with economic or social structures and social groups while others examine significant individuals and their circumstances within a political, social or ideological context. That they differ in both subject matter and methodology is assuredly appropriate, given Maurice's range of interests and, too, the flexible pragmatism and suspicion of both doctrine and monocausality characteristic of his work. Thus, shared approaches rather than a single topic or method are the thematic cement of the volume—another instance, perhaps, of that unity in diversity which informs Maurice Careless's view of Canadian nationality.

Collectively, these ten papers deal with a period in which the major material and intellectual dimensions of life in Old Ontario were changing, often dramatically. Half the papers recall and explain some of these hitherto neglected, fundamental transformations, tracing them through three or four decades, revealing the varying impact of domestic and external factors, of the urban world on the rural and vice versa, of values and perceptions upon behaviour and of the material world upon the ideological. The other half explore character and circumstance within much narrower temporal bounds, portraying aspects of life which were decidedly important to Old Ontarians of a particular class, ethnicity or gender, and about which our current knowledge or understanding is plainly deficient. In doing so our contributors illustrate the continuing vitality of the basic approaches advocated by Maurice Careless and which underpin his work. As well, they demonstrate in a convincing manner the analytical strengths that result when more than one of Maurice's fundamental approaches or concerns are applied in a single study.

The essentials of Maurice Careless's scholarship and what we celebrate with these essays are his faithful adherence to the documentary record, his sensitivity to both contexts and particulars underlying motivation and behaviour, his wide range of interests, and his determined flexibility of mind— especially regarding the value of any single methodology, theory or approach to the researching and writing of history. Whether building a synthesis from a number of studies or writing with original sources in hand, our contributors have been faithful to these most appealing elements in his teaching and writings.

David Keane   Colin Read
McMaster University   Huron College
Hamilton, Ontario   London, Ontario

1 August 1989

1   Maurice Careless's seminal paper, "'Limited Identities' in Canada" *Canadian Historical Review* 50 (1969), began as an address to the American Historical Association in December 1967. The text for the *Review* was drafted early in 1968. He recalls that by the time it was published, he was already annoyed at himself for omitting consideration of gender. With characteristic humility, he points out that he had not previously given serious consideration to the gender bias in Canadian historical studies, including his own work. He credits chiefly Alison Prentice, then one of his doctoral students, and her dissertation researches for his growing sensitivity during 1968 and 1969 to the dimension of gender and particularly to the enormous opportunities, and need, for research into the history of women in Canada. Thereafter, while not himself entering the field of women's history, he sought to make clear to his students and readers that gender was very much one of the "limited identities" historians might adopt as a framework for understanding past Canadians. J. M. S. Careless, personal interview, 15 May 1989.

Acknowledgements

A number of Maurice Careless's former students contributed to the making of this book. Jacques Monet was a generous host who helped launch the project. Barrie Dyster, Margaret Evans, Henry Klassen, Heather MacDougall, Francis Quealey, David Sutherland and Michael Cross were not in a position to offer chapters but provided much appreciated encouragement when we were getting started. Others, friends and colleagues of Maurice or ourselves, including Donald Akenson, Carl Berger, Robert Fraser, Robert Gidney, Elwood Jones, Douglas Leighton, Douglas McCalla, Brian McKillop, Michael Piva, Donald Smith and Donald Swainson, gave generously of their time and impressive expertise in the history of Old Ontario. Sandra McRae, Aurelia Shaw, and Daphne and Charles Maurer, respectively, made valued financial, editorial and technical contributions. Louis Gentilcore and Carolyn King ensured that our maps were done well and on schedule. Curtis Fahey laboured long and well, as copy editor, to make the rough edges smooth. Among our contributors, Fred Armstrong and Ken McNaught deserve special praise for completing difficult chapters at short notice. In addition, Fred was responsible for our decision to collaborate and as our associate editor provided advice and moral support throughout the course of the project. As well, his efforts to secure funding for the volume proved most timely and effective.

Without the help of these many individuals we would never have been able to bring this book to completion. We were touched by their unfailing generosity towards us and by their admiration and affection for Maurice. To them all we extend a heartfelt thanks.

The Ontario Arts Council and Ontario Heritage Foundation provided indispensible financial assistance. More than a few words of appreciation are owed to our ever-cheerful publisher, Kirk Howard, who kept faith with us despite unexpected difficulties and delays. Finally, we thank our wives and children. They have put up with our late hours and weekend labours with patience, understanding and good grace.

David Keane   Colin Read

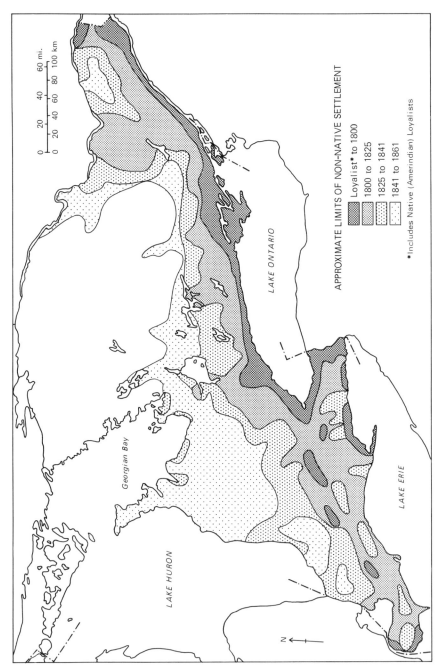

Limits of Settlement in Old Ontario to 1861

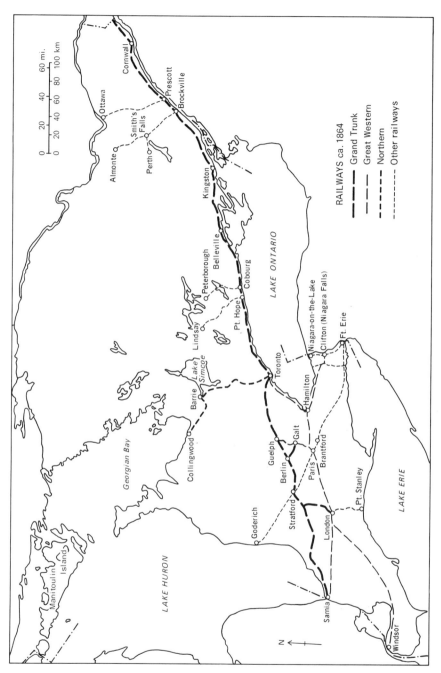

Settlements and Railways in Old Ontario ca. 1864

Maurice Careless

FREDERICK H. ARMSTRONG

James Maurice Stockford Careless's family came to Canada about 1910. His father, William Roy Careless, had been born in England, raised in Ireland and trained in engineering at Faraday House, London, where he specialized in the development of electrical equipment. Maurice's mother, Ada de Rees, was of Welsh descent and born in Monmouthshire (now Gwent). As well as Maurice, born in Toronto on 17 February 1919, there was his elder brother Denis, who in 1927 at the age of 17 went to Malaysia to work on an uncle's plantation and was rarely at home afterwards.

In Toronto the family lived mostly in the Moore Park and other north Toronto areas. Roy Careless, after service in the Canadian army and with the Imperial Munitions Board during World War I, was employed by various engineering companies handling electrical equipment. During the Depression, he was briefly jobless when his employers, English Electric of Canada, scaled down their business. Fortunately, the family suffered no real hardships for Roy soon joined the firm of R. H. Nichols, agents for several major British and European electrical firms. Roy's work for Nichols involved considerable travel as he designed special instruments, such as electric-control mechanisms for paper plants. When schoolwork permitted, Maurice accompanied him on trips to Quebec and the Maritimes. Thus, while yet in high school, he developed a feeling for the eastern half of Canada: its vastness, the lay of its lands and the society of its cities. With the outbreak of World War II Roy joined the hard-driving C. D. Howe's federal Department of Munitions and Supply as a chief inspector. The pressure of these duties broke his health and he died just as the conflict ended in March 1945.

Because the family moved frequently Maurice attended several schools and a variety of churches, including St. Paul's (Anglican) on Bloor Street where Canon Henry John Cody, later president of the University of Toronto when Maurice was an undergraduate there, presided at his christening. A bicycle-bus accident during his senior year in public school resulted in the loss of his right arm. It took time to learn to write well with his left hand—a year later a teacher told him that his writing was then as bad as it had been earlier with his right hand—but his education was not appreciably set back.

Following a four-month summer visit to England which opened his eyes to the Old World, Maurice entered North Toronto Collegiate. A year later he transferred to the University of Toronto Schools. At UTS his interest in cultural history was first awakened by Joe Gill, whose Shakespeare lessons brought Elizabethan society to life. Beyond Shakespeare, Gill's classes stimu-

James Maurice Stockford Careless

lated his interest in a broad sweep of history which came to include medieval, Islamic and Byzantine historical studies, as well as architecture, railways and shipping. Among his earliest writings, which appeared in the UTS journals, *Phoenix* and *Twig*, was an essay on Byzantine history and a story entitled "Dinner with Borgia"—a most appropriate investigation for any future university department head. More seriously, he studied sufficient Latin, French and German to stand him in good stead in his later work.

Several student friends at UTS went on to active roles in Canadian historical and literary fields, including Mavor Moore, who sat with him on the editorial board of the *Twig*. Both enjoyed drama and bridge, and the latter, along with badminton, became Maurice's favourite means of relaxation in his school years. He also read widely in historical fiction, for he found that this medium opened his mind to the complexities of both history and the human personality. His favourites included the romances of William Stearns Davis, which he regards as underrated today, and the many slow-paced books of G. A. Henty, with their wealth of social and military detail.

Away from school, Maurice and his father were avid fans of the new hobby of electric model trains, a diversion which he has passed on to his own children. Painting occupied him too; in his teenage years he enjoyed doing pen-and-ink sketches of ships, particularly those of the sixteenth to eighteenth centuries. Later he came to prefer landscapes in oils. Whatever the merit of these early landscape efforts—and within a year of his accident he had won a drawing prize—he now finds that his painted backdrops greatly enhance a grandson's model railway layout.

At UTS his interests were divided between history and literature, partially because he found his teachers in physics and trigonometry less stimulating. Entering the University of Toronto in 1936, he planned a double major in English and history; however, just as he arrived the joint program was abolished, and he chose modern history. Maurice selected Trinity for his college largely for its congenial atmosphere and small number of students. Although much of his university work was not closely connected with that college, he gained greatly from such courses there as Wilson Knight's Shakespeare and the program in religious knowledge. The latter was mainly a history of the Jews, Hellenistic Greece and the Middle Ages, thus reinforcing his earlier interests. Along with many of his friends he belonged to Phi Kappa Sigma, partaking in its lively dances and cheap lunches. An unexpected bonus came when, as a delegate to its annual convention at New Orleans in the late 1930s, he experienced the Old South, with its distinctive culture, society and, above all, jazz. As a result he stayed on a week after the conference ended, leaving only because his funds had been totally drained.

The small History Department at the University of Toronto in the immediate pre-war years provided an intimate atmosphere which had already gone when Maurice began his own teaching in the burgeoning university of the post-war boom era. There he met several professors who both influenced his thinking and later became friends and colleagues. Surprisingly to later-day observers, Toronto did not then provide great scope for studying Canadian history. In the 1930s, the small staff concentrated on England and Europe, the Canadian history offerings being limited to a combined Canadian-American survey and fourth-year seminars conducted by Chester Martin and Frank Underhill. Generally, too, the program in Canadian history had a certain British "evolution to freedom" outlook: what Careless later characterized as the "Political Nationhood School of History."

Despite its small size and Old World leanings, Toronto had stimulating teachers and provided an ideal atmosphere for a future historian's training. Dick Saunders, then a freshman instructor, further whetted Maurice's interests in the rise of Islam and in Middle Eastern and medieval European cultures. His dramatic but well-ordered approach to teaching held students spellbound, while at the same time providing them with an opportunity to take good notes. This was a combination of talents that is all too rare in any discipline. Later, in a second-year course, Saunders introduced Maurice to the use of documents through the medium of French newspapers. In "Bertie" Wilkinson's fourth-year seminar, Maurice studied further documents, such as the medieval English chronicles, which made him feel that history was both exciting and worthwhile in itself. Also, Wilkinson's treatment of social and intellectual movements in the "Age of Wycliffe," with its extensive examination of the Peasant Revolt of 1380, gave him his first sense of the pervasive influences of the feudal social order.

Donald McDougall, with his magnificent command of his lecture material and encyclopedic knowledge of sources, despite his blindness, taught him constitutional history. He was admired, but held in awe—and viewed with not a little trepidation. George W. Brown's kindness was respected by Maurice as much as it was by an ever lengthening line of students. A trip with Brown (who was not related to George Brown of the *Globe*) to St. Lawrence University at Canton, New York, for the latter's annual Canadian-American conference, gave Careless his first taste of Arthur Lower's forceful personality, quite different from those of his teachers at Toronto. Delivering the banquet speech Lower abruptly asserted, for effect, that it was "wrong to say that Canadians do not like Americans; they hate Americans." His bluntness intrigued Maurice and turned him to a further consideration of his works.

That other great proponent of the staples thesis, Harold Adams Innis, whose lecture style was often as dull and interjectory as his writings could become, left a particularly sharp impression through such memorable events as his "codfish" lecture, illuminated by faded sepia slides of stacked cod slabs. These all looked alike regardless of the angle from which they were photographed—and they were depicted from every angle. The lecture was marked by a constant shuffling sound. When the lights went on, Maurice—seated immediately below the lectern—looked around to discover that of the original 100-odd students only about 10 who were trapped at the front remained. Another teacher, Chester Martin, long-time head of the department, was influential with his firmly held views on the ordered growth of

Canadian autonomy. Although his opinions on Commonwealth glories were already rather a voice from the past, he did much to instill in his students a respect for documents.

Lectures at the University of Toronto also included courses from two very different Canadian historians: Donald Creighton and Frank Underhill. Creighton was a good teacher and, as departmental practice at that time was to have professors teach in almost any field, he lectured to Maurice first in medieval history, then in Tudor studies and finally on the French Revolution—all fields far removed from that in which both teacher and student were to become prominent. Creighton was then much less anti-American than he became later, regarding the Americans as associates who had left the Empire. Basically, he appeared as rather an advocate of Canadian national self-recognition. Underhill, still on reasonably good terms with Creighton in the late 1930s, had a much greater effect on Maurice's thinking as an undergraduate. A witty, provocative lecturer, especially with large audiences, he seemed to believe that if students left his classes frustrated and boiling it was all to the good, since extreme statements would force them to think things out for themselves.

His teaching led to something of a contrary reaction in Careless's political thinking, for while he liked Underhill's lively personality, nevertheless, he was bothered by his sweeping statements, which seemingly needed qualification and documentation. Then, too, he was little impressed with some of the speakers Underhill sent his students to hear—their theories seemed just too cut-and-dried. As a result, he began to rethink his own outlook and, while he had left high school fairly well to the left, he had gradually moved to the right of the CCF party by his fourth year at Toronto. Politically, he became, and remains, an independent. This was a stimulation of thought with which Underhill would have been pleased, though the direction in which it led might well have surprised him. In later years the advice of both Creighton and Underhill was to be of great assistance in Careless's graduate work; they became friends with whom he worked as a member of the History Department.

At Toronto one of Maurice's closest student friends was Bill Rolph, who later taught at the University of Western Ontario and then in Australia. Like Maurice, he was an American Civil War buff, and he particularly enjoyed inventing strategy games for that conflict. About 1938 Rolph conceived the idea of starting a "History Course Club," the Modern History Club of later years. The department was agreeable and such professors as Saunders and Brown acted as advisers. Careless was elected to the executive, which first brought him into contact with long-time future colleagues: Gerald Craig, who was a year ahead; and Harold Nelson, from the year behind. Paul Cornell, who was to make his career at the University of Waterloo, was another member; he and Maurice became great friends, as later did their wives Peggy and Betty. Another close associate at Toronto was Freeman Tovell who, like Careless, went on to Harvard after graduation.

With his B.A. completed, Maurice was duly admitted to the graduate body at convocation with the help of Canon (now also President) Cody, who personally hooded Maurice when the Beadle failed to appear, thus giving the impression that this student must be some sort of VIP. Now it was time to begin graduate work, a decision which flowed easily from his love of history. With Britain locked in war, advanced studies in Canada relatively undeveloped, and the American universities ready to welcome Canadian graduates, Careless applied to several institutions in the United States. His final choice was Harvard, not because the money was the best, for Pennsylvania and Columbia had each offered more, but because Harvard presented him with what he felt was the best overall opportunity.

While Maurice liked Canadian studies, he had as yet no strong bent for it; in his love of history, he was initially attracted to another field. Saunders had reinforced his high school leanings by rousing his interests in the Middle Ages and Near Eastern history; Creighton had helped him develop an interest in the Yorkist period of English history from 1461 to 1485, and McDougall had further bolstered this inclination. Maurice saw Harvard, with its renowned European and English specialists, as an ideal place at which to prepare a thesis on fifteenth-century medieval European history. Specifically, he wanted to follow up on Wilkinson's Age of Wycliffe seminar at the University of Toronto, taking a broad approach which set political and social institutions in an intellectual framework.

Harvard was at first daunting to a student coming from the relative coziness of his home-town university. Among the virtual mob of graduate students a newcomer felt himself reincarnated as a sort of "unknown freshman." There were, however, other Toronto graduates at Harvard to help ease the transition, including Freeman Tovell who was his roommate for the year-and-a-half before Maurice's marriage. In about three weeks Careless and Tovell were settled in at Conant Hall, the graduate residence. Although the A.M. year was to be a sort of freshman experience all over, they adjusted quickly. The transition was helped by the fact that the Harvard faculty regarded Toronto history students as well prepared, though rather narrow in their range and in need of wider grounding. To Toronto graduates, with their experience in the British-based essay system, the writing of papers came easily. Their workload was no heavier than it had been during their undergraduate years, and the Canadian tutorial system, then little used in most American universities, had provided a good undergraduate preparation. The city of Cambridge, mentally isolated as it was from Boston by its academic outlook and physically by the sweep of the Charles River, provided a comfortable base. Careless enjoyed the life of Cambridge, although it was not a place in which he would have chosen to settle.

In all, however, adjusting to Harvard and a new life was probably more of a problem than the selection of new fields of study. Harvard's history program at that time was divided into two sections: American, and everything else. As part of the British Empire, Canada came in the latter category. The Master's degree, in itself, was not regarded as important; rather it was either a rubber stamp along the way or a terminal dismissal for those who proved unsatisfactory. Graduate students had to provide evidence of a thorough background and could be required to take undergraduate surveys to fill gaps. As part of their preparation they were required to take one major field and two minor fields, plus one outside field. This last did not necessarily call for course work and involved a written examination only.

While Maurice's first choice of the Late Middle Ages as his major field was remote from his long-term area of productivity, the themes which he already planned to explore—such as the rise of towns and regionalism versus centralization—were ones that would be crucial to his later written work. And, even while concentrating on late medieval history, he was also, indirectly, laying the background for his future Canadian studies through such American subjects as "The Westward Movement," a lecture course taught by Frederick Merk, who had succeeded the great frontier historian Frederick Jackson Turner at Harvard. Merk's excellent classes, with their special maps, charts and slides, gave Maurice a completely new outlook on the art of teaching. Although Merk did not turn him to American history, he did much to direct his interest to the problems of frontierism and the social questions raised by expanding settlement.

In his planned major field of study, Maurice found medieval French history as presented by Charles Taylor a stimulating course, moving as it did from a study of medieval French regionalism to the examination of the history of such cities as Toulouse. His paper on the southern French province of Languedoc in the years before 1400 helped him re-examine and expand these regional interests. Medieval constitutional and political history from Charles McIlwain, however, proved somewhat disappointing. Though McIlwain was a likable teacher, his rather legalistic approach, closely following such collections of documents as Bishop William Stubb's medieval charters, proved much less stimulating than Wilkinson's seminar had been. This kind of arid approach to medieval history, combined with the necessity of his developing a much greater capacity for medieval Latin, began to lead Maurice away from his original interest. Gradually he decided that "medieval history is not for me." This was to be his crucial career decision.

While his interest in the Middle Ages was waning, he was becoming increasingly attracted to Victorian England, thanks to David Owen, Harvard's specialist in the field. Not yet known as a great writer, Owen was an excellent teacher. His seminar, which in Careless's year emphasized social and party élites, had become almost *de rigeur* for students with a Canadian background. The weekly meetings at Owen's house added a relaxed, informal and more personal side to the discussions. Careless's choice of field and thesis supervisor was now in view. The course began a relationship that was to last until 1967, when Maurice, arriving in Boston to lecture at Owen's request, found that his mentor had died suddenly, and that he also had the sad task of delivering an impromptu eulogy.

One of Maurice's greatest difficulties in becoming acclimatized to Boston during his first term at Harvard had been parting from his future wife, then Betty Robinson, whom he had met while holidaying at Lake Simcoe in July 1939. Although not yet engaged when Maurice left Toronto, they decided during the fall to arrange their marriage at the Christmas 1941 break. The ceremony, with Freeman Tovell acting as best man, was performed by Canon Cody at Hart House on New Year's Eve—and the Carelesses quickly returned to Harvard for the mid-year examination period. It was a very rushed beginning for a happy partnership that has continued for forty-eight years and raised five children.

Maurice's second year at Harvard saw the completion of his course work and his decision to move into the Canadian field. Again there were studies with leading scholars, including a reading course on Canada with Merk and a course on economic history with A. P. Usher which, while not lively, provided some new ideas. More influential was a seminar with Crane Brinton on British romanticism and intellectual history, which involved wide-ranging investigations of group biography, climates of opinion, social perceptions of revolution and English political ideas in the nineteenth century. Careless's paper on the Victorian liberal Richard Cobden, which included an investigation of newspapers, quarterlies and reviews, drew on some of the bibliographies and ideas which he later utilized in his work on George Brown. Also, Arthur Schlesinger Sr.'s lectures on the rise of the American city provided many valuable insights into urban society, violence, and the overall relationship of the city and countryside, which were later to help clarify his thinking about Canadian development.

He was also introduced to teaching, becoming an instructor in the third-year course on English history from 1688 which was taught by Elliott Perkins in the fall and by Owen in the spring. His duties included grading the work of about 100 students and giving a lecture just before Easter on the English Labour Party in the 1920s and 1930s. The course greatly deepened his understanding of the English social structure and clarified his ideas on the development of middle- and upper-class liberalism. At Christmas he was excused from taking his general or comprehensive examinations because he had a straight-A standing. The only hurdles remaining were the written examinations in his minor fields and the oral examination in his major concentration, or special area. Harvard's fairly old-fashioned view of his major field, officially termed British history from 1760, was that it included Canada and the rest of "the British Empire." This special area examination was not required, however, until the doctoral thesis was submitted. Thus for the time being he could go ahead with settling plans for the thesis itself.

It remained to define a topic. Some combination of Victorian liberalism and newspaper studies seemed appropriate. Since the war made it impossible to go to England for research, a Canadian theme most neatly fitted his needs and interests. Soon he was focussing on some combination of the ideas obtained from his work with Brinton on Cobdenism and environments of opinion, Usher's teaching on transportation and communications networks, and his own general interest in the North American frontier. Somehow it all came together when, home for Christmas in 1941, he raised the matter with Underhill, who suggested turning to the plentiful newspaper documentation on George Brown of the *Globe*. Maurice soon developed this into a formal proposal, a study of "Victorian liberalism in the Canadian colonial environment," which Owen accepted. Although the subject was outside his field of special knowledge, he proved to be a good supervisor, providing excellent direction while giving his students opportunities to develop ideas on their own. These were methods Careless himself applied to his own students with great success in later years.

With his residence completed at Harvard, Maurice was granted a Sheldon Travelling Fellowship of $1,500 for research, and the Carelesses moved to Toronto in July 1942, making their home at the Cawthra Apartments at College and St. George Streets. There they were conveniently located near both the central Toronto Public Library and the Legislative Library in which much of the thesis research could be done. The latter possessed a near complete set of the *Globe*. Some work was also necessary in Ottawa. While proceeding with his research, Maurice audited Donald Creighton's new seminar on Canadian federal-provincial relations. He was, of course, familiar with Creighton's *Commercial Empire of the St. Lawrence*, which he felt was too romantic and too closely modelled on Innis's staples-based approach to Canadian development, particularly in respect to Creighton's treatment of geographical settings and power groups. Still, although he disagreed with many of his ideas, Creighton's perspectives began to affect his thinking. While not founding or subscribing to the metropolitan approach, Creighton did testify that developments of great significance happened at the centre, and believed that metropolitanism could equate with imperialism; although he realized that there was much more involved in metropolitanism than just imperial territorial control.

Thesis research, however, was soon interrupted when Maurice moved to Ottawa in the early spring of 1943 to become a wartime aide under Gilbert Tucker in the Naval Historian's Office, Department of Naval Service—at that time each service had a separate historical section. The work at Naval Headquarters enlarged his experience of teaching, his first lecture there—on the theme of sea power—being given to a class of Wrens. His duties also involved security and intelligence matters and thus membership on various joint committees. This in turn directed him toward the Department of External Affairs, to which he was transferred in the autumn of 1943; he remained with External until the end of the war. Officially, Maurice began in External as an odd-jobs man for Saul Rae. Considerably involved with exchanges of prisoners of war, he worked as well on a great variety of other, often secret matters: some routine, some quite exciting, and some truly alarming because of the insights they presented into the progress of the war.

The Naval Headquarters' records on ship destruction were particularly disturbing. In the fall of 1943, as a result of the efficiency of German spotter planes, the rate at which merchant ships in convoys were being sunk seemed well ahead of the rate at which they could be replaced with new vessels. From Maurice's perspective it looked as if the war was all but lost. Then the tide turned as the Allies succeeded in extending the range of air cover through the use of short-service aircraft capable of downing enemy spotters. Still, there were some bad months in 1944. At the other end of the scale were such ludicrous tasks as the drafting or answering of appropriate "high-level" telegrams of official praise on such momentous occasions as a victory (real or supposed) of Generalissimo Chiang Kai Shek's forces or the due congratulating of Marshall Stalin on some Red Army Anniversary.

His duties frequently brought Maurice into contact with the great and near great. On one such occasion in 1944 he was working in an attic on the third floor of the East Block of the Parliament Buildings, where the pre-war signals from Tokyo were stored. The task at hand was a grubby one that required wearing his old clothes, including a bilious green sweater. Suddenly, he was interrupted by a call from Saul Rae to come and take the notes at a press conference called to proclaim the elevation of Canada's Washington legation to the rank of an embassy, our first. There, though he tried to hide, he was seated directly in front of the desk from which an impeccably attired (and, Rae later reported, disapproving) Prime Minister William Lyon Mackenzie King made the momentous pronouncement. This was hardly the way to come to official attention!

Press conferences also brought Careless into contact with Hume Wrong. Son of long-time head of the History Department at the University of Toronto, George M. Wrong, Hume gave regular External Affairs briefings to the members of the Parliamentary Press Gallery. The reporters included Bruce Hutchinson, whom Maurice came to know well in later years in Victoria. Maurice kept the minutes of these meetings, essentially to ensure that there was no cheating on off-the-record statements. The minutes were also circulated to External Affairs posts as official reports on public policy headed "WRONG and CARELESS." (Later, when lecturing at Toronto, Careless would open his survey of Canadian history by noting that the students should not be concerned at having a lecturer called Careless, for a former head of the Department had been a Professor Wrong.) These reports and other related materials subsequently evolved into a published External Affairs journal.

But the most notable part of Maurice's work as a wartime assistant in External Affairs involved the exchange of Canadian and Commonwealth prisoners-of-war for German prisoners in Canada, the interviewing of exchanged Allied personnel to obtain information on conditions within Germany, and the assessing of intelligence data gathered from German prisoners held in Canada. The exchanges took place in Sweden or Spain, a Swedish liner, *Gripsholm*, being used to transport Axis and Allied personnel across the Atlantic. They were not conducted on a per capita basis; rather, any "sick and wounded" were eligible for exchange once they had been certified as medically unfit. In 1944–45, as their shortages of able-bodied men and of foodstuffs for their civilian and military populations worsened, the Germans grew increasingly ready to make such exchanges. From the Allied viewpoint, mounting evidence of the progressive breakdown of the German communications system raised the spectre of inadequate care for Allied prisoners in a collapsing Germany, and emphasized the need to get as many of the sick and wounded out as soon as possible. And so the *Gripsholm* sailed under a safe-conduct agreed to by the warring sides, carrying around 1,200 repatriates both coming and going. Jerry Riddell, later Canadian ambassador to the United Nations, dubbed Careless "The Cruise Kid" for, in the course of his duties as a diplomatic exchange officer, he sailed to Algiers, Barcelona, Belfast, Liverpool, Kristiansand (Norway) and Gothenburg, among other destinations.

Maurice especially remembers cocktails at sunset off the Azores on the afterdeck of the *Gripsholm* when the tracks of two torpedoes from some ill-informed U-boat ran all too close to the ship's stern; the embarking of the captured second-in-command of the German *Afrika Korps* at Algiers in the midst of a cloud of huge yellow locusts; and wandering through the dockside of Gothenburg with a case full of some 2,000 British pounds in pay for returning prisoners—without knowing a word of Swedish. Possibly the worst was the grim day spent while the *Gripsholm* was impounded by the German navy at Kristiansand; the Gestapo came aboard armed with enormous pistols, searched the crew's quarters, and took away two reputed agents of the Danish underground. But he also recalls much less excitement and far more routine work in Ottawa in the last months of the war.

With the end of the conflict in 1945 and a multitude of veterans preparing to complete their education, the University of Toronto History Department invited Maurice to become a member of the faculty. Although the personnel remained much the same as in the late 1930s, the numbers of students, the pace of life, and the whole atmosphere were to be very different from that of the relatively intimate department of his undergraduate days. Shortly after he arrived, the garden of the department's long-time St. George Street home, Baldwin House, which stretched south to College Street, was torn up to make way for a new chemistry building—a harbinger of the unceasing construction activity that surrounded him at Toronto throughout his career. Maurice was the first post-war junior appointed, followed by Jim Conacher the next year. They found themselves amidst the coterie of long-established elders, who were friendly but augustly different. The newcomers were soon joined by several others, including Gerald Craig, Harold Nelson and Michael Powicke. A few of them passed through quickly; but several remained at Toronto as colleagues for the next 30 to 40 years, building on the base established by their elders and sustaining the department's pre-eminent position among those of the Canadian universities.

In the mid 1940s and indeed for another two decades, faculty members were still teaching survey courses in any area where they were required; for instance, in his early years Maurice often taught in British surveys with Underhill or Creighton. As he said himself in his "Appreciation" of Jim Conacher in that colleague's *festschrift*, "we taught as generally needed and had to take time to develop our own special historical interest."[1] Thus,

"The Cruise Kid" on leave: at home with Betty, Ottawa 1944

during his first year at Toronto in 1945–46, Maurice was busily engaged with seven tutorials in medieval history and participation in the British survey from 1485. Such diverse assignments in tutorials or lectures (sometimes extending from the decline of Rome to the Reconstruction Era in the United States) were part of his standard fare until he became chairman in 1959. In 1947 his duties expanded into Canadian history tutorials when the honours Canadian-American survey was split. Only when Chester Martin retired five years later did Maurice begin lecturing in Canadian too, sharing the honours course with Creighton. All this constituted a heavy load, and an especially frustrating one when it involved preparing courses that were given only once or twice. As a result it was 1952 before he began his own fourth-year undergraduate seminar in Old Ontario to which graduate students were later admitted. In 1956 he commenced his Old Ontario graduate seminar, which has trained as many Canadian historians as any graduate course in Canada.

Meanwhile, research for the thesis had been progressing despite all the interruptions and finally, in December 1949, Maurice boarded the train to Boston to undergo the defence. Inevitably, given his workload, he had had inadequate time for preparation, so he took a sleeper to ensure a good rest for the anticipated ordeal ahead. But he was used to sitting up on trains and sleep proved elusive. The next morning he tottered off the train and into his examination in anything but a rested state. Harvard's doctoral orals for "special" fields were designed to be grueling. There were two sessions totaling some four or five hours: a morning examination of the thesis itself and an afternoon cross-examination on the general background. For those who had earlier been excused from the comprehensives, as Maurice had, the afternoon session could be especially wide ranging.

His examiners were Owen, his supervisor, and Robert Albion, the economic historian whose study of the rise of the port of New York remains one of the great classics of urban history. The morning session went well; Albion later observed that he had had "a good time" and, indeed, "had never enjoyed an exam more." Lunch with Professors Owen and Albion followed, a human touch mitigating the rigorousness of the format. In the afternoon session, as he modestly explains, Maurice "deflected the discussions masterfully," leading his examiners into a review which he had just read, managing to deliver a half-hour lecture on the Whig Supremacy, and following that with an analysis of late-nineteenth-century British social history. At five p.m. it was all over and he and Albion proceeded to supper at the Owens'. Afterwards friends from his graduate student days escorted him to a less formal celebration that broke up at four a.m. His final triumph was catching the noon train to Toronto! The Ph.D. was duly awarded by Harvard in 1950. Toronto had already promoted him from lecturer to assistant professor in 1949; he received his associate professorship in 1954.

The structure of the Toronto History Department in those years was still basically monarchical with a head appointed for life, advised by a committee of seniors (full professors) and with a departmental secretary, later executive officer, doing the administrative work. When Martin's long reign ended with his retirement in 1952, Ralph Flenley took over for three years and then Donald Creighton became chairman with Maurice as his executive officer. In this post he sat on the senior committee, and his expanded duties included more planning than recording. In addition, he was progressively engaged in committee work. As he sums it up himself, he was "chairman of innumerable forgotten faculty and departmental committees over the years— or member, who isn't?" He was also active in the rejuvenation of the Faculty Association and helped organize the Canadian Association of University Teachers' constitution.

One of the most controversial and time-consuming matters with which Careless was involved, both then and later, was curriculum change. Throughout his entire teaching career Ontario universities were in a state of flux as a series of waves and troughs in registration flooded and abated through their halls. The post-war boom was followed by a drastic decline in the 1950s; by the 1960s numbers rose again, only to decline throughout the 1970s and begin yet another increase in the 1980s. These surges invariably had a destabilizing effect on the number and variety of courses needed and the size of the staff. Coupled with the 1940s influx was the growing feeling that the curriculum had been locked in place first by the Depression and then by the war years and that change was overdue. The post-war years thus witnessed demands for reform, which the radical student movements of the 1960s were to intensify.

During the post-war expansion even Chester Martin—who gloried in the orderly evolution of the British Empire—said that "what we need is a revolution," though one doubts that his heart was strongly behind such an idea. Many of the younger members of the staff, however, were quick to recognize that the increasing number of students, combined with the growing size of the faculty, presented an opportunity to expand into a greater variety of fields. Suggestions for change were soon rampant. Surprisingly, Creighton, though subsequently renowned as a protagonist of conservatism, was among those ready to take an active stance in favour of reforms, particularly in curriculum matters. Some major reforms were opposed by Edgar McInnis, and Frank Underhill was quite ready to leave things the way they had been at Oxford when he was a student there. Underhill also felt that American models were none too suitable, while Creighton was prepared at least to look at them.

Two plans for reform gradually and painfully emerged. The first built on the existing programs with the creation of more surveys and more seminar courses as options afterwards. The second was a much more radical departure foreshadowing the sweeping reorganizations of the 1960s. Ultimately, moderation prevailed—in the main supported by Maurice—and the radical changes were put aside, only to resurface during his chairmanship.

It was during these years, the late 1940s and early 1950s, that Careless laid the basis of his scholarly reputation. With Conacher and Craig he was co-editor of the *Canadian Historical Review*, then virtually a departmental operation. In one laudable attempt to broaden the journal's social and anthropological perspectives they accepted an article on the medieval awareness of the Arctic, as evidenced by the trade in polar bears and various animal skins, which elicited dubious reactions from the more narrow-minded members of the historical community. It had the salutary effect of providing the editors with an in-house system of classifying submissions under the headings of one, two, or three polar-bear quality—the increase in numbers not indicating an increase in desirability.

Careless even found time to contribute to the *Review* himself, his "The Toronto Globe and Agrarian Radicalism" appearing in 1948. It was followed in 1954 by "Frontierism, Metropolitanism and Canadian History," which has lighted the way for urban historians in Canada for over thirty years. At this time too his long connection with the Macmillan Company of Canada began with the publication of *Canada: A Story of Challenge*. The volume won the Governor General's Medal in 1954, has been reprinted many times and has appeared in Japanese editions. Working with Macmillan proved to be a pleasant experience; Careless "never thought of leaving" and John Grey, Macmillan's head for so many years, became a good friend. Other projects included a popular social-science series of high school texts published by Dent from 1953 to 1955. Written with his colleagues George Brown, Gerald Craig and others, they discussed Canada's relations with the Commonwealth, the Americas and the World.

As well, there were travels to Britain and Europe. With the death in 1953 of George Brown's son, George Mackenzie Brown, who had intended to write a biography of his father, the George Brown papers became available for research. That Maurice gained access to them was more the result of a typically thorough research strategy than of luck. Somewhat earlier, he had contacted members of the family to see what material, if any, had survived and George M. Brown had advised him that only a small amount of family material was extant. But after Brown's death, on the suggestion of a great-grand niece, Dr. Katherine Ball, Careless contacted Ted Brown, George Brown's grandson, in Scotland. He was immediately granted access to the papers in Ted Brown's possession and went over to work on them in 1955 on a Rockefeller Foundation grant. Happily, the papers were far more extensive and far more valuable than he had earlier been led to believe. During 1955–56 Maurice and his family lived in Cambridge, England, while he organized the collection. The long-term result of the expedition was his two-volume study of Brown and eventually, through his efforts, the transfer of the Brown papers to the National Archives at Ottawa.

In 1958 he visited Australia for the first time on a Canadian Humanities Council research fellowship, crossing the country on a fascinating rail journey on tracks built to three different gauges, and lecturing at universities from Brisbane to Sydney to Perth. Although he was originally attracted to Australia by the idea of comparative studies of its cities and regions, the visit more broadly turned his attention to the possibilities of research on the Pacific Rim.

With Creighton's retirement as department chairman in 1959, Careless was offered the post by Dean Moffat Woodside. The term was indefinite, though it was understood that the appointment would be for at least five years. As he was an associate professor his selection was a departure from the tradition that the departmental head be chosen from among the full professors; however, he already had more than three years' experience as executive officer, was the most senior of the junior professors, and was acceptable to all the full professors. Maurice had mixed feelings about accepting the chairmanship during what would obviously be a trying era of transition and expansion. He felt, however, that such posts should be shared; as he phrases it himself, "In one's life one has to do these things." Also, with five growing children, funds were naturally tight and the offer carried with it both a promotion to full professor and a raise in salary.

His system as chairman was, in essence, one of anticipating problems and working for compromises in the string of delicate situations that constantly arose throughout his term, while simultaneously trying to keep things moving ahead. Departmental problems in the 1960s were solved neither quickly nor with ease; even when they seemed settled they had an unpleasant way of boiling up again. As chairman he was in a very sensitive position and Maurice frequently found his tasks rather daunting. To make matters more difficult, despite the size of the department and the magnitude of its problems, in those days the chairman was allowed only a small reduction in teaching load—one so slight it would overawe any present-day administrator. Careless still participated in the honours Canadian survey lectures and taught both fourth-year undergraduate and graduate seminars. Amazingly, he still found time to revise his courses somewhat, broadening out his Old Ontario undergraduate seminar and sometimes substituting a Canadian social history seminar (1815 to 1867) with considerable urban content.

Notwithstanding all these duties, his chairmanship marked one of his most active periods of writing. The first volume of *Brown of the Globe*, covering the years 1818 to 1859, had appeared in 1959; the second, covering the period from 1860 to 1880, followed in 1963. Further awards accompanied these publications. In 1962 he was elected a fellow of the Royal Society of Canada and received its prestigious Tyrrell Medal. A second Governor General's Award in 1964 followed completion of his work on Brown. Four years after *Brown* came the publication of *The Union of the Canadas, 1841–1857* in the Canadian Centenary Series, a worthy sequel to colleague Gerald Craig's superb history of Upper Canada. Simultaneously, he was engaged in editing a two-volume essay collection on Canadian history for Macmillan. The first volume, *The Canadians, 1867–1967*, co-edited with R. Craig Brown, appeared in 1967; the second, *Colonists and Canadiens, 1760–1867*, for which he was both the sole editor and one of the authors, was published in 1971.

Such writing came as a pleasant respite from departmental problems and the chaos of curriculum reform. His chairmanship began with preparations for the department's 1960 move from Sir Joseph Flavelle's opulent

Queen's Park Crescent mansion, where it had spent less than a decade, to the new, utilitarian Sidney Smith building. By that time, with its membership growing rapidly, the department was again changing its attitudes and there was an increasing demand for new systems and new courses, which echoed what was happening across the university. Professors were escaping from having to teach outside their own specialized fields, new scholars were joining the department, and new fields were being added: Latin America, Eastern Europe, the Spanish Empire, China and Japan are examples. Surveys seemed unnecessary to many of the faculty, and the growing American contingent felt that a switch to American forms of organization was badly needed, with more lectures, more options and abolition of a distinct honors program. Inevitably, radical ideas parallelling those of the 1940s were soon voiced. In response, the Canadians at Toronto seemed almost embarrassed by their own nationalism, when they dared to raise it. Some, particularly Creighton, whose ideas were always anchored in his deep love for Canada and his desire to protect its institutions, strongly opposed radical changes. Probably the majority of the faculty were against major changes, but circumstances rendered some changes necessary.

In the middle of this mêlée Careless strove, in his own words, "to save the essence of the system, including tutorials, while still bringing in needed curriculum changes." He guided the department through seemingly endless meetings which frequently dragged on until seven or nine at night. The infighting was often bitter, but with sensitive management he prevented the department from ripping itself apart. By 1966 a compromise was worked out. A less rigid pattern of courses was adopted which retained the surveys as prerequisites to seminars and kept a sense of a progression through four years in a structured honours program. While playing an integral role in these changes, Careless also did much to strengthen the old core sectors of the department; with the help of such colleagues as Conacher, Craig, John Cairns and Robert Spencer, he made new appointments and expanded the number of courses in the traditional British, North American and European fields.

Through this progressive diversification, Careless feels, the department established one of the best programs on the continent. Yet the new order was not to last, despite all the effort that went into it. Broader changes were afoot. In 1967–69 the Macpherson Commission on the reorganization of curricula for the entire university completed the trend that had begun in the 1940s by yielding, as Maurice and many others felt, to faddishness, student democracy and anti-élitism. The commission's report resulted in the abolition of Toronto's longstanding and successful honours program. A similar process was, of course, taking place in most Ontario universities.

As Careless says philosophically, he "missed the worst anyway," for with the debate over departmental curriculum apparently settled in 1966, he had decided to retire the next year after eight years as chairman. To state the matter simply, he had had enough. He had appointed "umpteen people"— the department had grown from under 20 to over 50—and a good core curriculum had been laid down. Now he felt that he had no more to offer. Further, with *Brown of the Globe* completed, he wanted to get on with new writing and other scholarly work. In fact, writing would be a great relief after the drudgery of administration.

In 1968, the year after stepping down as chairman, Maurice went to the University of Victoria on sabbatical leave. This was his second sojourn to Victoria, for in 1966 he had taught summer school there. Victoria's History Department was a smaller, more intimate scene than Toronto's and his tutorials had proved to be fun, taking him back to his early years at Toronto. Moreover, he and Betty had soon found they liked Vancouver Island. Thus the offer to return to Victoria was most welcome, not least because his proposed graduate seminar would allow him to explore with students his ideas on the frontier-metropolis relationship and to develop these into a new theme that he could alternate with his Old Ontario seminar.

Initially the Careless's went west this second time without planning to stay; but soon the whole family found themselves considering the possibility of leaving Toronto permanently, for Victoria offered Maurice a permanent post, good research funding, and the right to spend a year at major centers of study every four years. At the same time he was offered a permanent post by Dalhousie University in Halifax. With the possibility of returning to Toronto still open, Maurice was faced with a bewildering range of transcontinental choices. He loved Ontario but he also loved the sea and the prospect of working by the ocean was a tempting one. While a mid-January visit to Halifax somewhat weighed the balance against the east, the west coast still beckoned. Both Maurice and Betty, however, like big cities, with their varieties of restaurants, museums and art galleries. Opportunities for such diversions in Victoria in the later 1960s were limited, as was demonstrated by a long-running exhibition on "The Favorite Paintings of Our Dear Queen." (Victoria, naturally!) The Pacific coast also seemed very much at the end of their particular world; by February 1969 they had made their decision. Although they greatly liked the west coast and other parts of Canada, Toronto and Ontario were home. As Maurice notes, "This is the place where I belonged." Still, the year at Victoria was to prove pivotal, for while he and Betty were happy to remain Ontarians, three of their children fell in love with the Pacific coast and have since settled in British Columbia. And Maurice and Betty thus often return there, very gladly.

Back in Toronto, where his successors were wrestling with first the new curriculum and then the transition from expansion to slowdown, he was thankful to be able to concentrate on his own teaching and writing. With the new program in place, there were three surveys in Canadian history: an overview, a pre-Confederation course and a post-Confederation one. Maurice was always engaged with one or other of the first two, and as well gave either his Old Ontario or Metropolitanism and Frontier seminars. After 1971, with the decrease in enrolment, graduate and senior undergraduate seminars were often presented as combined meetings in which senior undergraduates sometimes comprised as many as a quarter of his students. The seminars were varied by the addition of new topics and material. He considered mounting one on Canadian intellectual history or a purely urban seminar, but found himself too occupied with his other work and, basically, quite happy with the material that he was already teaching. He continued to be kept very busy with theses, and to date has supervised no less than 24 Ph.D.s, 10 M.A.s and 5 Masters of Museology—a most impressive total— with a few more theses still under way. The variety and breadth of their topics reflects both the wide extent of his own interests and his willingness to encourage others researching a broad range of themes.

Even while chairman he had been involved with many boards and councils. After stepping down as department head he found this number rapidly expanding. He was president of the Ontario Historical Society from 1959 to 1960, fortunately, for once, a quiet year in the life of that organization. The presidency of the Canadian Historical Association came in Canada's centennial year and Maurice helped set up seminars on regional approaches to Canadian history to be held in Victoria, Winnipeg, Sudbury, Stanley House (Quebec) and St. John's. He also assisted Jim Conacher organize the first joint meeting of the Canadian and American Historical Associations in Canada since 1932, which was held in Toronto in December 1967. Careless's scholarship and support for historical societies was recognized by the American Society for State and Local History in 1965 and in 1968 he received the Ontario Historical Society's Cruikshank Gold Medal for his services to Ontario history.

Maurice's centennial activities also included a two-week series of George Brown Lectures in Edinburgh to help celebrate the Ontario government's gift of some 45,000 books on Canada to Scottish universities. Again he was able to visit Brown's home town of Alloa where he unveiled an appropriate plaque. Then in 1971 Gerald Graham, the Rhodes Professor of Imperial History at the University of London, whom he had met while at the Naval Historical section, arranged for him to give a special Commonwealth lecture in London, which he and Betty combined with a tour of Greece and Italy. A second visit to Australia came in 1978, this time as a senior visiting research fellow at the Australian National University in Canberra. There he expanded his research on comparative ideas on the frontier and considered combining it with Pacific Rim studies. But time never permitted him to pursue this goal—there was just too much work to be done on Canada.

Increasingly, he was involved with government-appointed boards as well as academic councils, and also with consulting on Canadian Broadcasting Corporation and National Film Board epics. From 1961 to 1972 he was co-chairman of the Archaeological and Historic Sites Board of Ontario, and from 1975 to 1981 was called back as a director of its successor, the Ontario Heritage Foundation. From 1972 to 1985, years which saw a major breakthrough in public support for heritage preservation, he was also on the Historic Sites Board of Canada, serving as its chairman for his last five years. As well as improved public support, strong appointments were needed in order to build up boards that would be valuable, independent and impartial bodies. This meant members who were neither "yes" men for government projects nor "local heroes" who could not see beyond their own communities. With regard to the Historic Sites Board of Canada, there was also the need to view matters from a nation-wide perspective in designating historical sites, as opposed to an approach based on a quota system requiring that a set number or proportion of sites of various types, for instance lumber camps or fortifications, be distributed regionally across the country. Greater success was achieved in overcoming the designation problem than the appointments. Another project that has long occupied Maurice's time is the government-supported Ontario Historical Studies Series. Originally established to commission biographies of the major premiers, the series quickly expanded its efforts to add an extensive group of thematic studies. He became a trustee initially in 1971 and has been chairman since 1982.

Maurice also played a major role on two other Ontario boards. The first was the Commission on Post-Secondary Education, which sat from 1969 to 1973 investigating the obdurate problem of curriculum reform as well as the broader issue of how to secure both quality and mass participation in higher education. A major difficulty, given the mood of the time and the problems of accessibility, was the avoidance of accusations of élitism. Careless felt that universities should be seen as only one route in educating the community, and that community colleges could help by expanding the range of their programs and making post-secondary education accessible to greater numbers, including workers who could be allowed to phase in and out. He was particularly worried about providing for the distinctive needs of northern Ontario where, he felt, more could be done by spending dollars on technical education than on new or overly-ambitious existing universities. As a member of the editorial committee writing the commission's report, he had to be sure that it reflected the fact that the years of seemingly endless expansion and budget increases were over, and thus did not make recommendations for reforms based on money that was not going to be available. Altogether it was a frustrating and exhausting, albeit necessary, task. Unfortunately, it produced few results.

Another, rather unexpected, post was a trusteeship on the Ontario Science Centre from 1963 to 1973, the years when the planning and construction of that remarkable complex took place. The appointment arose out of his work on the Archaeological and Historical Sites Board; the original intention was to include an historical component in the Science Centre and someone was needed to provide historical judgments. He was most heavily involved in the original planning, which encompassed arranging for the design reports, choosing the present site and selecting a director. There were difficulties over the expansion of the plans to increase accessibility for school children, and some of the public were critical of Raymond Moriyama's radical design; but the centre has become a renowned success.

Writing and teaching continued along with this round of committee work. His pamphlet for the Canadian Historical Association, *The Rise of Cities in Canada Before 1914*, appeared in 1978 and has been a boon to both teachers and students ever since. He edited *The Pre-Confederation Premiers: Ontario Government Leaders, 1841–1867* for the Ontario Historical Studies Series, published in 1980, in which he wrote both a general theme chapter and one on Robert Baldwin. For many years he has also been working on articles and papers dealing with urbanization in specific cities and areas, all in preparation for his planned history of the city in nineteenth-century Canada. As part of this study he wrote *Toronto to 1918: An Illustrated History*, which was published in 1984 just as he retired.

Throughout his last years at the University of Toronto and since his retirement numerous honours have come his way. In 1977 he was elevated to the rank of University Professor, a rarely granted dignity that has been awarded to only two other members of the department: Donald Creighton and Charles Stacey. The first of his many honorary degrees was granted by Laurentian University in 1979 and in 1981 he was appointed an officer of the Order of Canada. Most recently, in May 1987, he became one of the initial members of the new Order of Ontario. With his characteristic zest for life Maurice says that he thoroughly enjoys such occasions, whether he has to speak or not, for he likes meeting people and attending a good party. Beyond this, helping his last students finish their theses, reading articles, papers and book manuscripts from students of more ancient vintage—sometimes very ancient vintage—as well as outside requests for lectures, advice and plaque dedications, have left him little time to get on with rounding out his work on nineteenth-century Canadian urbanization.

Maurice Careless has been active in so many fields, has published so extensively and has advised so many students, that others must wonder how he managed to accomplish so much. Maurice feels his success came from establishing clear priorities and carefully organizing his time. Teaching always came first; this was his most important duty. He never took on extra work to its detriment or skipped a class to meet the demands of an outside organization. Odd jobs were fitted between classroom hours. Meetings were scheduled at non-teaching times and as far as possible outside work was relegated to the summer, when he could adjust his schedule. Research was fitted into weekends and the summer months. As well, he arranged his timetable to provide one free day a week even if doing so filled in some other days quite heavily. Writing time came in the evenings. After dinner he would relax with his family, read or watch television and then go upstairs and write until one or two in the morning. After another session of television to unwind, often for up to an hour, he would turn in—yet be up by eight ready to head off for another day, with morning lectures at ten. It was a remarkable demonstration of both discipline and stamina, and, as he says, "of the understanding and damn hard work of a wholly supportive wife, whose capable management of the family enabled me to keep up such a program."

Sightseeing in sunny Santorini (now Thira), Greece, in 1971

Whenever possible, Maurice has combined travel, research and conference papers. For example, the Canadian Historical Association's annual meetings could be combined with research at the local archives, and he would stay on at his own expense for a week if possible. His visits to cities were not limited to universities and libraries. Like Sir John Summerson, the English planner who has stressed the need to view cities as a whole in order to understand them, he would savour the streets, public buildings, galleries and museums during such a sojourn, trying to absorb what constituted the society of the place, what was scruffy and what made it beautiful. His investigations encompassed not only Canadian cities but extended to others stretching from Tokyo and Manila to Delhi, Philadelphia, Venice and Ephesus.

In concluding the biography of a scholar one should record his views on his own work and note the criteria he has used to govern his writing of history. Careless regards the biography of George Brown as his major work because "it says more about the important aspects of Canadian life and history than anything else I have done." When uttered by an historian whose metropolitan approach has played such a directing role in Canadian historiography over the past 30 years this statement may come as a surprise; but it must be remembered that Brown was at centre stage during a pivotal era in Canadian history. Moreover, beyond his part in the negotiations for Confederation, Brown's activities provide Canadians with an important study in the rise of our leading metropolis. His career tells the story of the establishment of the nation that was to become the metropolitan hinterland of Toronto and Montreal. Careless's topic is thus not just the biography of a man; it is also the story of the consolidation of Canada around its central metropolitan foci. This soaring theme provides us with something of the acuteness of Careless himself and gives another insight into his imaginative outlook and sweeping interests. Thus, on the one hand, it shows how he has inspired his students to undertake theses on so many, varied topics, and on the other, how, through his own writing, he has come to investigate the intertwined themes of nineteenth-century Ontario history that the editors have attempted to reflect in this volume.

Careless asserted his feelings on the need for flexibility in historical writing in 1970 in his reflections on Donald G. Creighton in that scholar's *festschrift*: "History seeks to be a science as far as possible but...remains an art."[2] That is how he sees his metropolitan approach to Canadian history—a method within the pursuit of an art. To make it into a more formal or rigid thesis would be to make it into something else, something different, something uncharacteristic of the man and his ideas. Maurice also realizes that historians can never completely remove themselves from the picture they paint; as he noted in the same article, "an historian's value judgments may vary...but they are always there."[3] For himself, he has taken the broad, liberal approach that will least slant the judgments in his interpretations. The success of his ideas shows not only in the major role he has played in

Canadian historical writing and the Canadian historical profession, but also in the careers of his many students, who today are to be found in governmental and museum posts throughout the nation, and who occupy chairs of history and teach in high schools across Canada from sea to sea.

In retirement Maurice Careless retains an office at the university where he works almost daily. Beyond the completion of his urban study, he looks forward to the much lighter and equally enjoyable task of writing about the social life of the Brown family. Meanwhile, he and Betty are reasonably free to visit Toronto's galleries and museums, and to relax over extended dinners in the wide variety of good restaurants available in the city.

This biography is based on a series of interviews with Maurice Careless, as well as discussions with Betty Careless, Gerald Craig and a number of Dr. Careless's former students. Naturally, it includes some of my own recollections over the many years since I first met Maurice Careless as one of my undergraduate lecturers in 1948. As well, reference has been made to biographical notices in such works as *The Canadian Who's Who* and to Careless's own curriculum vitae. Particularly valuable sources were Careless's articles in a similar vein: "Donald Creighton and Canadian History: Some Reflections", in John S. Moir, ed., *Character and Circumstance: Essays in Honour of Donald Grant Creighton* (Toronto, 1970), 8–21, and "J. B. Conacher: A Personal Appreciation", in Bruce L. Kinzer, ed., *The Gladstonian Turn of Mind: Essays Presented to J. B. Conacher* (Toronto, 1985), ix-xv. There is a Careless interview by Paul Bator, taped in 1983 for the University of Toronto Oral History Programme, at the University of Toronto Archives. As well, the editors of this volume and Professor Peter F. Neary, my colleague in the History Department at the University of Western Ontario, have made many helpful suggestions.

1 Careless, "Conacher", x.
2 Careless, "Creighton", 15.
3 Ibid.

"Us Old-Type Relativist Historians": The Historical Scholarship of J. M. S. Careless

KENNETH McNAUGHT

I propose in this essay to sketch an intellectual portrait of a complex and gifted historian. It is a tall order; for Careless is that contradiction in terms, a quiet pioneer. His self-effacing demeanour belies the depth of his convictions, the acuity of his analyses and the extent of his accomplishments.

As the editors of this volume have noted, Careless has been a three-fold pioneer: in his teaching and studies on metropolis-hinterland relationships, in his work on urban development and life, and in his advocacy of "limited identities" as an approach to understanding Canadians and their society. My portrait of this man of many parts draws on his publications in each of these areas but mainly on the large body of his work on metropolitanism, his flagship from the beginning. However much he has captained the other supporting craft, metropolitan-hinterland studies remain the foundations of his thinking about Canada and its diverse communities. Moreover, both critics and admirers agree that these works include his most original and significant contributions to our historiography and that, of the three approaches Careless has considered or promoted, it is his treatment of metropolitanism that has stirred the most controversy. For all these reasons I have looked primarily to Careless's writings on metropolitanism and have found in them the most helpful sources for this modest sketch.

As I hope to explain, Careless has been a revisionist historian in almost all that he has written. At the same time he never strays far from the hard path of primary research, and from that research have sprung the books and articles which form such a large portion of the core reading in Canadian history—both for students and general readers. Intertwined with his ongoing "story" of Canada is always a rich mixture of hypotheses and guarded conclusions. It is tempting to lay these out in some deceptively clear academic pattern (from which notes for seminars might the more readily be lifted). But the simplicity of such an exercise would be illusory. The chronology would probably also be misleading. Careless does not call himself a relativist lightly; and if the reader of this essay perceives the contrapuntal

*Ontario Premier William Davis, Maurice Careless and OHSS Editor-in-Chief Goldwin French with **The Pre-Confederation Premiers**, Toronto 1980*

quality of his historical thought that reader will likely also reach a deeper understanding of the Canada in which Careless lives and works.

"Like any other history, that of Canada has been written within the framework of intellectual concepts, some of which have been consciously applied by historians, while others have shaped their work more or less indirectly through the influence of the surrounding climate of opinion."[1] In this opening sentence of his 1954 essay "Frontierism, Metropolitanism and Canadian History"—one of the most frequently cited articles in our literature—Maurice Careless raises two central and somewhat sticky problems for anyone attempting to analyze the body of his research and writing.

Initially, Careless seems to accept both the existence and validity of theses which purport to explain history and which historians do, in fact, employ. Certainly his article was the opening salvo in a long and frequently passionate debate about the nature, variety and utility of metropolitanism as an (or the) explanatory force in Canadian history. In the course of that unfinished series of skirmishes Careless occasionally presents a defence which verges on the sensitivity of a doctoral candidate enduring a thesis oral. That impression is entirely inaccurate. For all that he is attracted by "intellectual concepts" Careless remains essentially a relativist. "Beyond that..." is one of his favourite bridge phrases. Thus, to assess his position as the "godfather" of metropolitanism one must keep a sharp eye always to the endless nuances in his own discussions of the concept and also on the themes which wind their way through his extensive forays into biography and history, or biographical history.

Plainly (another favourite Careless word), metropolitanism is an aspect, rather than the *sine qua non*, of his scholarship. It is, in fact, an approach to the understanding of the Canadian experience, "a most instructive proposal,"[2] as Careless dubbed the Turner thesis. Canada and Canadians, however, and not some monocausal abstraction, are what mostly interest this quintessential Canadian. Careless's obituary article on Turner's frontierism, after all, sprang in part from his research on George Brown; that research was inspired by an intense interest in historical continuities, climates of opinion and the personal aspects of political-economic power.

Writing about Donald Creighton in 1970, Careless observed that "individual and collective biography" provide "the humanizing 'soft' data of quality, and make social history neither a set of formalized abstractions nor a mass of meaningless parochial chronicles."[3] There is no doubt that Careless, for all that his own writing features the heavy shading of many provisos and exhortations to shed doctrinal, absolutist blinkers, felt a cautious admiration of Creighton. In his own biography of the least flamboyant father of Confederation (but perhaps the most crucial), there are not a few touches of the master storyteller, of the Creighton who could "evoke individuals or groups of individuals in a living world of their own times," or provide "inferential reconstruction of personal conduct."[4] While there may be no lowering Laurentian storm clouds foretelling disaster, there is a fine evocative power in the Brown biography, which opens thus:

> For brief minutes the ships lay restlessly alongside, while several bags of potatoes and fresh meat were passed from the *Eliza Warwick*, eight days out of Liverpool, to the *Collingwood*, inbound from Calcutta. For the British emigrants aboard the New York-bound craft it was a last chance to send a message home. As they scribbled notes to put aboard the *Collingwood*, Peter Brown pencilled a few hurried words to the family left in Scotland: "Monday, 8 May, 1837. At sea for 8 days, made only 400 miles. All well—not a minute to spare. Every good wish attend you. God bless you." Then, with a rattle of blocks and the boom of filling sails, the vessels drew apart. Their wakes stretched out between them. The *Eliza Warwick* continued on her slow way westward, crammed to the legal limit of two passengers for every five tons of ship's burden: among them, the former Edinburgh merchant and his eighteen-year-old son, Peter and George Brown.[5]

In his depiction of individuals, and even of groups, Careless exhibits a non-judgmental balance which infuriates ideologues of whatever hue—but particularly those who charge him with being blind to the operation of class and élite power. He is undoubtedly prone to see the reasons for individual and group behaviour rather than to seek out social culprits, and thus has been dubbed a "consensus" historian.[6] Application of this class-war yardstick underlines the importance of Careless's historical imagination. A superb inferential talent enables him to stroll among Canada's eminent and less eminent Victorians in perfect ease. It has not made of him a pollyanna apologist of neanderthal capitalism; neither has it blinded him to the rugged initiative, optimism and personal virtue which flourished amidst the nineteenth-century promontories of hypocrisy and exploitation. If Creighton's aura recalls that of Anthony Trollope laced with Macaulay and Wodehouse, one finds in Careless a distinctly Dickensian flavour, an attention to foibles, convictions and courage rather than to visions, crises and heroics. Thus, the first volume of the Brown biography ends with a "letter to a political enemy" in which Brown offers help to a Malcolm Cameron "irretrievably embarrassed" in his "mercantile affairs." Careless lets the letter speak for itself, which it does with revealing eloquence. And having brought Brown through the political jungle of the 1840s and 1850s, through the construction of a strong Reform party and to the verge of Confederation, he sketches him in the setting from which he drew much of his strength:

> It was the Browns' sixteenth Christmas in Canada. It was their home; Scottish beginnings seemed far away. George himself had not been back to Edinburgh for over twenty years and would not make his first return for two years more. Outside, in the chill streets of Toronto and across the frozen countryside of Upper Canada, where farms were snuggled down to wait out the winter, was the land he had wholeheartedly accepted, as it had accepted him. But inside the warm parlour, behind shutters and drawn curtains, where the lamplight and the firelight softly contended on the ceiling, where George Brown sat, as ever, in happy contentment with his father, his family and good friends— it seemed that the Edinburgh household had hardly changed at all.[7]

In the life of Brown, Careless presented, of course, not just an illuminating biography. The two volumes contain, beyond the raw material for burying frontierism, the essential counterbalance to Creighton's enthronement of Macdonald; it remains a work indispensable to an understanding of Confederation. And Careless leaves no doubt about his own assessment of Brown's decisive role: "What of the institutions he had done so much to mould in Canada: the press, the Liberal party, Confederation itself?...He had shaped an irresistible sectional movement—and used it to achieve a great national purpose, federal and transcontinental union."[8]

If one takes only the articles and chapters in which Careless has tried to develop a "framework of intellectual concepts" it is very easy to misconceive his humanist concern to understand and express, rather than to devise an infallible causal structure. In his biography of Brown, as in his *Union of the Canadas, Story of Challenge, Toronto to 1918* and the stream of articles on regional and national themes, continuities and contingencies, people and decisions bulk as large as patterns and forces. "I can't see it as determinism," he wrote recently,

> to say that such technological agents [as ships and railways] made it possible to do such-and-such. What was done still paramountly engaged human choice and effort, while motivation was an intensely personal factor (which I first got from Usher's theory of novelty in mechanical inventions and their economic consequences)...as an unredeemed relativist, I can't accept the absolutes of any generalized determinism; for that would seem both intellectually unsound and practically stultifying to a historian who still thinks his subject is the high art of particulars.[9]

Another way of invoking "character and circumstance"? Very plausible. And like Donald Creighton, Careless undertakes his scholarly quests from a deeply felt Ontario milieu. More than occasionally the Old Ontario strand reflects a warm light across his writing, as when he observed in 1964:

> A too-easy tendency in Canada today to disparage the "little" War of 1812, and its glow in past tradition, ignores the fact that the very creation of heroes and legends out of this conflict reveals the impact that it made on popular consciousness. Has Canada since, after two world wars, found a military hero to equal General Brock?...The war acted as a screening process, straining out the most disaffected and leaving a community largely convinced of, or converted to, a vociferous provincial patriotism.[10]

In many of Careless's reviews, articles and shorter pieces he reveals a feeling for his native heath not short of love, and frequently tinged with a defensiveness entirely appropriate to a Torontonian.[11] Because of this and, as I will suggest, because of his particular approach to metropolitanism, some historians in the "rags and ends" of Confederation seem to feel that he sees Canada as Ontario writ large: like George Brown himself; and there may be a smidgen of truth in this.

But, like Brown, Careless sees the warts clearly, and especially that disfiguration which can be the outgrowth of bigotry. Firmly rooted in the study of Victorian liberalism, Careless's sympathies lie clearly with the essential tolerance of that credo. If he can laud the vigour and initiative of developers and voluntaryism, his predilections slant perceptibly toward reformers and, more cautiously perhaps, "regenerators." But above all, they lead Careless to a perception of compromise, adaptation and conciliation as the most characteristic political forces both in Ontario and in Canada. For the biographer of the man who made the most spectacular political concession in Canadian history this is perhaps entirely suitable. That Careless attributes Brown's ultimate compromise in substantial measure to the influence of his late-in-life marriage and designates Brown's wife "the Mother of Confederation" highlights also his sensitivity to the role of individuals.

Innate mistrust of absolutes combines with cautious tolerance of opposing views to engender in Careless a prudently nuanced approach to Canadian nationalism. He did not subtitle his survey history a "triumph," or a "rise," but a "story" of challenge. His endorsement of the Canadian experiment, especially when that enterprise is contrasted with "Republican Virtue," is unmistakable. Yet his avuncular pats on the head of the Beaver Patrol come with kindly warnings that original sin resides with us as with others.

Thus, Ramsay Cook's felicitous phrase of 1967, "limited identities," struck instant recognition and Careless borrowed it for his 1969 discussion of "one nation, eminently divisible." In that article,[12] an earlier version of which was read at the 1967 meeting of the American Historical Association, Careless extended the historiographical analysis which had been the context of his 1954 article on metropolitanism. "Canadian historiography," he asserted in 1969, "has often dealt too wishfully with nationalism—and *ergo*, with unification—thus producing both expectations and discouragements out of keeping with realities." He then elaborated a notion of Canada, building upon the themes of regionalism and ethnicity, "because the theme of nation-building has an unfortunately teleological cast. One looks for the end to be achieved…a strong united nation." Such a built-in purpose "neglects and obscures even while it explains and illuminates, and may tell us less about the Canada that now is than the Canada that should have been— but has not come to pass." No doubt he was recalling his own frequent reminders in his treatment of Brown and in the *Union of the Canadas* that Confederation was as much about separation as it was about union when he reasserted that the actual experience "did not focus greatly on Ottawa" and that Canada has been as much about "limited identities of region, culture and class" as about transcontinental federal union: "The union of 1867 was in large degree a coming together of regions and so has remained." There was "no all-embracing, sovereign people but rather particular societies of people under a sovereign crown." Moreover, those regional societies were defined as much by "social values" as by geography.[13] French Canada's "corporate authoritarian traditions of the seventeenth century" specified a community as surely as did English Canada's "organic, pragmatic Victorian liberalism of the nineteenth century." And such values "stressed the nearer corporate loyalties of religions and ethnic distinctions—Scots, English and Irish, as well as French—instead of broad adherence to a democratic state."

Seeking always, if with scruple, those features of Canada's experience which render the country different from the other federal union on this continent, Careless suggested irony in the functioning of the very evolutionary "sovereign crown." While the 1867 architects of union looked to that sovereignty to "obviate pretensions of founding power in the provinces," in fact the royal symbol cut two ways "so that, in the Canadian union of the twentieth century, one might almost witness the gradual victory of the long defunct Confederate States of America." With perhaps unconscious reverberations of Turner's treatment of antebellum sectionalism, Careless observed that with "the growing demands on government in an industrializing, urbanizing society," and the provinces' growth in status and function supported by their share of the royal dignity, "federal-provincial conferences have acquired something of the atmosphere of diplomatic exchanges between states."[14] Again, the roles of metropolitan centres in helping define regions in Canada and the United States differ. The scene is simpler in Canada, "where a few large cities dominate huge sweeps of territory, sometimes within one provincial jurisdiction, and that perhaps centered within the city itself." Such conditions and continuities of tradition ensure that one "can identify the west coast culture of Vancouver, for example, far more explicitly than the traits of national culture; just as one can more easily depict an Albertan or a Maritimer than a Canadian."

When Careless generalizes in this fashion, and he does so in not a few instances, it is plain to anyone who reads his more profusely supported research articles and books that he seldom strays far from the factual base he has accumulated. This is certainly the defence he offers against those who charge him with writing history from the top down, of minimizing the role of class and the life of the common people. Undoubtedly, matching his own studies and reflection with those of the maturing graduates of the 1960s, who often devote themselves to the "new social history," quantitative method and the self-perceptions of the working class, he has concluded that his formulation of regionalism, metropolitanism and limited identities should not be more deeply affected by class antagonism than by other active ingredients in the historical process. Our distinctive ethnic compositions, he argues, are greater than those in the United States. This may be seen in the formal distinction between "founding peoples" and later arrivals, and in popular culture by the conversion of "ethnic" into a noun. Thus,

> today, class discontents are still largely expressed in regional or provincial stances, as in the Martimes or in Quebec communalism....regional, ethnic and class identities have all tended to fit together more than to develop national identification in Canada. The ultimate conclusion, indeed, might seem to be that the true theme of the country's history in the twentieth century is not nation-building but region-building.[15]

Yet the positive cadence typical of Careless's writing may be detected also at the end of this overtly revisionist piece: "the whole may indeed be greater than the sum of its parts, producing through its internal relationships some sort of common Canadianism...the articulation of regional patterns in one transcontinental state."

That positive note, so evident amidst warnings about the skewing potential of the search-for-nationhood historical teleology, was made much more resonant when Careless commented a decade later on the reception accorded his 1969 article, and upon the explosion of research in local, regional, class and ethnic-cultural history in the 1970s.[16] In some respects the second piece appears to apply the brakes to what threatened to become an almost heedless rejection of the Canadian reality itself. Such a rejection, however implicit, could not, eventually, be accommodated to Careless's view of Canadian history. Shading in the contours of Canada's experience was one thing; ignoring its existence was quite another.

Just as Careless would adjust his approach to metropolitanism, so he endeavours to keep his perception of the Canadian fact clear-eyed. Thus, in the 1980 article he noted the immediate milieu of a "strenuous chorus of dissatisfactions voiced from Newfoundland to British Columbia" and observes that in the 1969 piece he was "after all, as an historian...only— typically—reflecting views and currents at work around me at the time." He then presented a concise review of research and institutional expressions of interest in various aspects of the theme he had earlier developed, all of which have "illustrated the strong socio-cultural emphasis of recent Canadian historiography" and a "quickening interest in limited identities." Cultural pluralism, he maintained, was "no less significant than the regional variety," and in this respect "the limiting presence of the French Canadians...provided the leeway for other ethnic groups to maintain some cultural separation of their own...the way to cultural pluralism was opened." But again he glances over his shoulder at a too-easily jettisoned past and seeks some kind of synthesis, some enriched continuity of perception and interpretation: "What is left of Canada if we display multiple identities in culture, class and region, but little overall?...finally, all these limited identities together are part of an interlaced, national mediating structure, which has an existence of its own as more than the sum of its parts."

The relativism, from which Careless does not swerve, forces him always to look for interaction amongst apparently discreet entities, influences, events, decisions. No matter how startling may be a fresh perception of any *identity* or *force*, let no person set it apart as a total explanation in itself. Referring to W. L. Morton's masterly work on Manitoba, and with more than a touch of Carl Berger's *The Sense of Power*, Careless hoisted the flag cautiously: "Manitoba's geography and history, like Canada's geography and history, 'were one and inseparable,' for each was the 'response to the challenge of the North.' These are truly themes that run through Canada, beyond particularisms, and the country itself is their total product...the history of Canada is an expression, an epitome of the whole."

The new research on regions, cities, class and culture can and should be woven into Canada-wide themes, Careless exhorted:

> The very "have" and "have-not" categories of Canadian
> history may have a rather dubious basis. Parts of central
> Canada, that is, could be better compared with sectors to
> west or east instead of treating the whole area as a unit, as
> one of those non-existent regional monoliths, the myths of
> shallow thinking. Thus disadvantaged eastern Quebec, or
> segments of eastern Ontario, might be more effectively
> examined alongside Atlantic regional communities in his-
> tory than the Atlantic regional communities with [the]
> all-too-different West.

Over-simplifications of regional identities, he argued, "ignore about as
many vital internal variations as the old national overview ever did," and
the same is true for class identities or ethnic identities: "we cannot assess the
facts of ethnic survival and diversity without weighing the equally significant process of ethnic integration and national assimilation...." It was time to
look around "so that once again we may discern the still vast Canadian
[nation] as an entity, or identity, in itself."

At the centre of his decennial reflection on limited identities Careless adverts
directly to the relationship between regionalist-cultural-class interpretations and metropolitanism. "I can immodestly affirm," he wrote, "that
during the past decade I have done a certain amount to elaborate and apply
ideas on the major significance of metropolitan centres—leading cities—in
historical developments across the regions of Canada." Indeed, the impact
of his formulation of a metropolitan approach to Canadian history, beginning with the 1954 article rejecting the Turner thesis, and continuing through
a series of papers, articles, reviews, chapters and a book on Toronto, and the
general study of metropolis and frontier in Canada on which he is now at
work, is difficult to exaggerate. Achieving "near doctrinal status," as Donald
F. Davis has put it, it helped stimulate a flowering of urban studies and
riveted the attention of geographers, sociologists, quantifiers, intellectual
historians and, indeed, of any scholar who investigated region, locality, class
or the whole country. It is not surprising that challenges, modifications and
even rejections should have generated a lively, if reasonably civil, debate.[17]
At the centre of this sometimes scholastic disputation, Careless sustains
splendidly detached involvement, a detachment rooted in the flexible pragmatism he brings to his investigation of any "intellectual concept" or "instructive proposal." Because of this it would be unseemly to docket him
simply as a metropolitanist. He has himself too often given reason for
avoiding such designation, not only by the breadth of his own work but also
in comments upon that work and upon historical schools and doctrines.
   "When individual historians are considered they do not always fit
neatly into one particular classification," wrote Careless at the outset of his
article on frontierism and metropolitanism. In the course of his analysis he

illustrated the point by showing the frequent overlapping among the "schools" or "general approaches" he perceives in Canadian historiography, to which he assigned the titles "Britannic", "Political Nationhood" and "Environmentalist". His whimsical subtitle for the third group—"North Americans All"—seems to me much more revealing than appears at first glance. Why? Because the most enduring, if not explicit, *purpose* in Careless's scholarship is to account for (and not infrequently to celebrate) those facets of our historical experience which render Canada distinctive—distinct, that is, not only from Britain and the United States, but also in the ways the country and its parts have been related to outside centres of power and influence. In his writing on Brown, on Upper Canada and the Union, he stressed heavily the flow and influence of British immigration and cultural-economic connections; in his discussions of limited identities he stressed the "socio-cultural values" which fostered "ethnic persistence" and thus greater pluralism in Canada than in the United States; in the development of the metropolitan approach he investigates an ecological explanation not only of the inner dynamism of Canadian history but quite specifically, again, of the differences between Canada and the United States. That is, of why we are not simply "North Americans All." As a replacement for frontierism, Careless's metropolitanism is quite consciously an expression of that sense of continuity: not the simple notion that history is just one damn thing after another, but that historians build upon each other's work, and that he, as a Canadian historian, derives something from each of the schools he depicts in his article; and, equally, that regions and countries do much the same thing. Thus, as a starter, it is absurd to argue that American or Canadian individualist democracy sprang parentless from the continent's forests and plains.

Examining the pervasive influence of Turnerian frontierism upon Canadian historians in the 1920s and 1930s, Careless observed that such environmentalism had produced much valuable research and writing. But he also noted the cautious reservations that some of the environmentalists expressed in the 1940s.[18] His own view of frontierism was jaundiced principally by its powerful monocausal explication, and by its "moral implications of a struggle between sound native democratic forces and elements that clung to privilege, exploitation, and empty Old World forms. In so doing they often oversimplified a conflict between West and East, or better, between pioneer agrarian interests and exploitative urban centres."[19] But especially, Canadian adaptions of Turner "tended to neglect the influence of the seas beyond, the 'maritime environment' that had always tied the continent to Europe. Canada might be treated as a northern extension of certain continental physiographic provinces, without due consideration of geographic and historic forces that had from the beginning of white penetration made the country an east-to-west projection from Europe." Careless then gently rapped the isolationist knuckles of those environmentalists who had seen Canada "as a number of disparate American regions held out of the American republic by mainly emotional forces and by the chance of history: in short, a loose grouping of less well-favoured, somewhat backward, American states. A rather paradoxical basis, this, for the nationalism environmentalists usually professed."[20] Such writing is as near as Careless ever comes to taking off the gloves, save in private, convivial circumstances. The unsignalled left jab doubtless enhanced the impact of his article, just as it underlined, once again, his pervading purpose of depicting Canada as it was and is.

The ground prepared, Careless launched his counter proposal of metropolitanism, albeit with minor obeisance to Laurentianism which he described as "in some ways a qualified version of environmentalism" and as resting upon a geographic given that "was as real a feature of the North American environment as the North American forest, and a good deal more permanent." As he mulled over the article, Careless was also in the midst of studying the work of the immigrant George Brown and the evolution of a Toronto-based region; there were two aspects of Laurentianism that struck him with particular force. First, the Laurentian interpretation revealed that the "huge communications and transport system could transfer immigrants, ideas and impulses in one direct channel from Britain deep into the heart of the continent." Second, "it looked not from the forest-born frontiers for its perspective of Canadian history but from developing eastern centres of commerce and industry. Indeed, it primarily studied the effects of the East on the West, and largely regarded businessmen and conservative urban political elements as agents of national expansion who might well be more far-sighted in their outlook than were their agrarian opponents."[21]

It is worth pausing here to remark upon the carefully fabricated context within which Careless originally discussed metropolitanism. That context was the interaction of ideas, climates of opinion and research, an evolving, interdependent body of thought with discernible linkages inside Canadian scholarship and also well beyond. Creighton's Laurentianism was closely related to the "monumental studies of H. A. Innis on the organization of the staple products trade of broad North American areas through costly and complex transportation systems controlled in large urban centres." While far-reaching in its implications, metropolitanism, as Careless introduced it, was "at root a socio-economic concept that [had] already seen some application in Canadian history" by A. R. M. Lower and by D. C. Masters in *The Rise of Toronto, 1850–1890* (1947).

As a general approach, metropolitanism grew naturally out of the widely accepted work of Innis, Creighton and Lower and was "the study of the role of metropolitan forces in this country, a vitalizing approach that may yet undergo considerable development." As a more definite theory it had been propounded by N. S. B. Gras in his *Introduction to Economic History* in the early 1920s and further elaborated by C. A. Dawson and W. E. Gettys in *An Introduction to Sociology.* Careless, noting these pioneer statements, observed that

> the rise of the metropolis in general is one of the most
> striking features of modern Western society. Briefly, this
> implies the emergence of a city of outstanding size to domi-

nate not only its surrounding countryside but other cities and their countrysides, the whole area being organized by the metropolis, through control of communications, trade and finance, into one economic and social unit that is focussed on the metropolitan "centre of dominance" and through it trades with the world.[22]

In a footnote, Careless outlines Gras's four precise stages by which a city achieves metropolitan dominance. But his own statement and especially its generality seems to me more important, since he had already made clear the route by which he himself came to see the inadequacy of frontierism.[23]

That route, and the possible direction of future fruitful investigation, he re-emphasized toward the end of his 1954 article:

> Frontiers may often supply grievances for political movements. Urban centres as often supply the intellectual leadership; so that frontier demands take form at the hands of urban journalists and professional men....For example, one might examine unrest in Upper Canada in the 1830s, when the frontier area was rapidly expanding with the tide of British immigration, as a result of the vigorous extension of powerful business interests into a broad new domain, and of the spread of educated men and stimulating ideas from older communities, displayed notably in the rising power of the press and the journalist on the Upper Canada scene.

Again, in the campaign to organize "the maturing western community around Toronto" against "the domination of the region by Montreal, Toronto supplied both intellectual leadership, in the form of the *Globe*, and strong party direction in the form of George Brown and other wealthy and prominent business or professional men: the urban element was critically important."[24] Finally, returning as he almost always does to his principal concern of explaining the nature and survival of Canada, Careless noted:

> the functioning of metropolitanism may do more to explain the course of Canadian history than concepts of frontierism borrowed from the United States and set forth before the significance of the modern metropolis was clear. For example, the greater conservatism of Canada as compared to the United States may be read as a mark of the much stronger influence exercised in this country by conservative-minded eastern urban centres—which were certainly far removed from any impulses of forest democracy. Moreover, the stronger influence of British ideas and institutions—and even of colonialism—must have been fostered in Canada by its long and close focussing on the British

metropolis itself....The metropolitan approach largely recognizes what is already going on in Canadian historiography and provides a new framework.[25]

In the years following publication of the 1954 article, Turnerian frontierism virtually disappeared from Canadian historical analysis while urban
and regional studies proliferated. At the centre of much of the writing in the
1960s and 1970s lay the question of the metropolis-hinterland relationship,
especially in the work of urban historians who acknowledged a particular
debt to Careless.[26] Yet, as urban history took off, Careless himself cast a wary
eye at some of its products. After all, he had enunciated the metropolitan
concept in large measure to make it clear that American environmental and
interpretative patterns are frequently inapplicable or misleading in the
Canadian milieu. Now, with "the new urban history" in the United States
casting long shadows northward—often substantial as young American
scholars flocked to expanding Canadian universities—he suggested caution
in adopting the quantitative method which seemed to dominate urban
historical studies south of the border:

> At times, one still feels doubts about the meshing of quanti-
> tative formulas and qualitative judgment, the validity of the
> sampling, however statistically adjusted and imposingly
> extrapolated (on the basis of what I say three times is true?).
> Sometimes there is the atmosphere all historical diehards
> apprehend in sociology, that of systemized tautology.[27]

Careless was particularly troubled by scholars who "paid little heed to
such historical data as 'contemporary observations, letters, political discourse,' in reaching hypothetical conclusions on the state of the community
consciousness from findings on external indexes of social position alone."[28]
Thus, while he acknowledged that Michael Katz's analysis of Hamilton's
mid-nineteenth-century social structure was helpful, he was much more
impressed by books such as John Cooper's *Montreal: A Brief History*. Cooper's
rigorously compressed study, he observed,

> falls within a more traditional category, urban biography,
> one still worthy of much development in Canada, where
> there are so few scholarly histories of our major cities. And
> there is nothing old about Professor Cooper's penetrating
> scholarship, his comprehension of the play of factors that
> have shaped Montreal.... It is a treat to read—clear, succinct,
> authoritative—but the footnotes and bibliography appended
> make plain the lifetime work of scholarship that lies behind
> this engagingly direct, short book.[29]

Such reiteration of the importance of people as opposed to numbers, of the
discrete event, of multiple causation and of literacy did not endear Careless

to those of a more scientific and numerate bent. Yet both in its humanism and its gentle reaffirmation of his own approaches to evidence and interpretation it was entirely characteristic.

Exactly 20 years after the article on frontierism, Careless read a paper at the annual meeting of the American Historical Association which epitomized his interim thinking and research.[30] An extensive, if selective, comparison of the differing character and effect of metropolitanism in the United States and Canada, "Two River Empires" is perhaps his most daring historical overview. Because it also moves exceedingly close to what might be called ecological determinism, its opening admonition is important: "there was no overmastering determinism at work, although environmental influences and potentialities for development were continually and pervasively significant." Tracing the political, economic and cultural influences operating in the St. Lawrence and Mississippi regions in the century following the 1760s, Careless stressed the crucial differences, noting also that they became focal points for "two quite divergent nationalist interpretations of history."

Within the American and British political frameworks after 1783, Careless argued, there were plainly two very different roles for the two rivers: for the St. Lawrence as "a unifying force in British North America"; for the Mississippi "as a potential source of disunity in the United States."[31] The inherent source of ethnic discord in the St. Lawrence valley "did not alter the essential role of the St. Lawrence in linking and binding the Canadas together...along a direct route that outflanked the Appalachian uplands" and then gave access "over low heights of land to western and northwestern rivers...and finally to the very Arctic and Pacific limits of the continental land mass." Moving close to Laurentian determinism, Careless then asserted that the St. Lawrence provided "the backbone for a Canadian political entity" and, as the Union came to a political deadlock, there also came "the recognition that the river empire could not be divided, but that its political framework must be revised instead." After Confederation, moreover, "by the opportunities it offered, the interests it built up, and the projects it inspired, the St. Lawrence...essentially served to develop a new national east-west power structure, one that was firmly rooted in its central valley...."[32]

With heavier ecological shading Careless then assessed comparatively the role of the Mississippi in the same period, a role which seemed "most notably to present major threats of disruption to another political system." The menace of "the men of the Western Waters" to "seek a different destiny than membership in an Atlantic-fronting republic" was met by the Louisiana Purchase and the repulse of the British at New Orleans. But these responses derived from outside the Mississippi domain; they were "the effective intervention of a Washington-based, seaboard imperium." Moreover, as the antebellum sectional crisis deepened, the Mississippi region "still remained at the very heart of the intensifying power struggle." In the Civil War "United States imperial strength, again based in Washington, overcame the forces of separatism in the river valley." The American union was maintained and the Canadian federation born in the same decade, "the first through overcoming grave obstacles athwart the Mississippi, the second through building along the line of the St. Lawrence."[33]

After an extended description of the rise of towns and cities together with their transportation-communications networks that "serviced [the St. Lawrence and Mississippi] territories and focussed their hinterlands about themselves," and noting the equal importance of "lines of metropolitan connection that stemmed from outside" significantly affecting "their traffic systems and course of regional growth," Careless observed that "so encompassing are the stories of the river domains, so profound their past influences, that it is not surprising that they have made deep imprints on historical thinking in Canada and the United States." This resulted especially in "Laurentianism and frontierism, both of which are strongly environmental in nature and may indeed be applied as environmental determinism."[34]

Rejecting again the "largely deterministic" purport of Turnerianism, Careless pointed to the growing emphasis in American research on the urban frontier. Plainly, he concluded, towns in the United States were "projections of the East, transplants set down, which proceeded to adapt and organize the environment, as well as necessarily adapting to it and being organized themselves by its land forms and water routes, climate and resources." So, also, Laurentian geographic determinism was still in need of modification, of some new ingredient. Creighton's "vivid presentation and strong commitment...may carry one further than intended....Those who recognize and conform to the demands and promises of the St. Lawrence are right; those who fail to do so, or work against them, are wrong—especially as they may thereby be working to destroy Canada. National treachery, indeed." But even while criticizing Creighton's later writing for neglecting the Liberal party's concern with "keeping together the all-important core of a national society, a working partnership in the old St. Lawrence heartlands between English and French Canadians," it is clear that he sought continuity, evolution of historical interpretation rather than some totally new departure: the Laurentian bathwater might be cloudy but it could be filtered. Thus, Careless claimed that Creighton

> underrates the rather paradoxical point that the success of a St. Lawrence-based economy from its early days rested partly on American connections in trade, finance, traffic and investment, and also, that recognizing these facts and the consequent need for repeated adjustments of north-south regional relations was no less an inherent aspect of Macdonald Conservatism than of Mackenzie King Liberalism—or of the policies of any national party that seeks to govern Canada for very long.[35]

Further, while Laurentian determinism must be rejected, the historical significance of the St. Lawrence environment remains: "If it was a part of North America, it was a special part of North America offering its own possibilities

and impediments for human use that made the resulting interaction histori-
cally distinctive, in both continental and national terms." A Laurentianism
which took *full* account of the human factor, then, was required. That the
east-to-west extension of Canada overcame "physical north-south align-
ments and regional tendencies to separatism, only suggests more strongly
that the environment *per se* did not determine the historic outcome."[36]

Summing up a subtle, intricate discussion, Careless asked if there was a
way to resolve these "divergent complexities.... I think there is, and would
say, without apologies, that it lies in the approach called metropolitanism....
There is nothing deterministic about the whole approach.... It is essentially
the power to control political and traffic systems that counts."[37] In this 1975
article he put forward his most persuasive and revealing explication of the
metropolitan organizing principle; persuasive because of its comparative
breadth and amplitude of illustrative material; revealing because it reiter-
ates his concern to circumvent both rigidity of doctrine and oversimplifica-
tion of analysis. When he wrote the article, Careless had already tested the
approach in several research pieces and reflective statements. He had, as I
have said, become the focal point of what has turned into an increasingly
precious dissection of the metropolis-hinterland categories of analysis. While
he rather enjoys the disputatious fray, he has left himself free to investigate,
with very few ideological shackles, the nourishing potential of metropolitanism.

In 1977 Careless suggested that regionalism in Canada could best be understood in the light of the "new" approach. Examining the regional roles of
Saint John, Halifax and St. John's, he commented that:

> Metropolitanism, the pattern of reciprocal relations whereby
> large urban communities focus broad areas on themselves,
> is intimately associated with regionalism. For regions usu-
> ally centre on metropolitan communities, which largely
> organize them, focus their views, and deal with outside
> metropolitan forces on their behalf. Indeed, much of what is
> often called regionalism may be better expressed in terms of
> metropolitan relations and activities.[38]

Moreover, the metropolitan-hinterland syndrome does not require cities
that are "huge and teeming by modern standards." The three Atlantic region
cities, he asserted, each showed the four stages of metropolitan growth
"broadly" recognized by expositors of metropolitanism.[39] But to these "economic characteristics," he added with fresh emphasis, went "political power
or military authority often centered in the metropolis; and, quite as frequently, the exercise of religious, educational, and intellectual leadership for
the general community, along with the press influence over its opinion." It
follows, he argued, that a metropolitan system is "inherently a system of

communications" which may well be "deeply affected by changes in technology."

Reviewing the ebb and flow of the three Atlantic mini-metropoli, their regional organizing functions, their concurrent dependence on external metropolitan centres, the Canadian continental pulls, the role of their "urban élites" and entrepreneurs and, especially, the impact of profound technological changes, Careless once again underlined the need to beware of monocausality. Thus, while technological change was clearly a force of particularly deep significance for the Atlantic metropoli, he had no intention of putting forward technological change "as a kind of simplified economic determinism." Characteristically, he concluded the article with a series of questions—questions which were already the staple of debate among increasingly sectarian congeries of urban-regionalist (or metropolis-hinterland) scholars. How far, asked Careless, did technological change

> relate to the decision-making process both of business and of government? How far was it the factor that made urban business élites in the Atlantic metropolitan centres aware of their own need to respond to change and make adjustments? How far did they use political influence to do so, and what were the reactions in their own regional communities? We need a great deal more study of the role of these urban élites, in the Atlantic region as elsewhere in Canada....[40]

The interplay of entrepreneurial élites, technological change and the relations of metropolitan centres both with their own hinterlands and with external metropoli Careless examined in a series of research articles and a study of Toronto to 1918.[41] In every case he places his research findings, finally, in a context of the Canadian whole; always, too, he hedges his emphasis on any particular element within the metropolitan-hinterland relationships. Thus, on the diminishing power of one small metropolis he commented that

> the island community of Victoria had been brought into a continental system, and now had little weight to bear against the whole thrust of Canadian metropolitan designs...it was not so much lack of enterprise as lack of situation and economic leverage that had placed it beyond the power of Victoria's businessmen to deal with changing patterns of trade.[42]

And on the character of regional metropolitanism in the West Careless's emphasis falls distinctly on those aspects which made it unlike America: "Hence, in the Canadian West—where, indeed, the railway instrument of eastern metropolitanism and industrialism often preceded the settlement of western land frontiers—society would be especially likely to exhibit not only the forms but also much of the content of eastern institutions, including the municipal." Pointing to the conservatism of western cities where "government was soon left in the hands of an élite in-group" by "a citizenry that normally preferred to be left alone," he suggested that our urban west quickly produced "a lifestyle none too different from the urban East." In the process, technological change was a major key:

> the technology of transport...was the prime mediating factor between environment and population in the ecology of the urban West, the most vital urbanizing force there. Sprung from and tied to eastern metropolitanism, railway technology essentially integrated the new western cities into a continent-wide metropolitan pattern. They would build their own regional metropolitan domains within this pattern.[43]

As Careless continued to test the validity of the "metropolitan approach" he acknowledged the stimulus provided by American urbanists,[44] but noted that he varied their conceptualization "to fit Canadian circumstances in the well-tried Canadian way of borrowing."[45] Analyzing nineteenth-century urbanization in Ontario, he noted Eric Lampard's "four primary factors involved in urbanization: environment, population, organization, and technology," and used them "as categories for examination." Environmentally, he emphasized, Ontario's urban communities were tied to the soil and waterways south of the Shield and thus no big towns sprang up in the interior prior to the railway era. "Urban Ontario," he wrote, "was originally oriented to its trunk water system, and really remained so during the nineteenth century, despite the spread of the railway net." Yet the east-west waterway orientation was sharply modified by another environmental factor: "close proximity and ease of access to the United States." The Erie Canal and its feeders became "an environmental force" and "the treaty of 1854 with the United States was a wholly consistent climax to the development." So, too, with railway-building by which Ontario cities benefited immensely. The north-south lines of contact were further enhanced by "the new national environment" of Confederation and the National Policy which brought "business connections, techniques and capital for branch plants" along with books, periodicals, road companies, lecturers and fashions. Summing up his Canadianized view of environmental influences on Ontario's urban growth, he wrote that "in one sense, urbanization and Americanization had proceeded together."[46]

With respect to the "population factor," Ontario's urbanization was clearly susceptible to Lampardian urban analysis. While smaller numbers were involved in comparison with the United States, Careless argued that "what matters is the size of the closely populated centre in relation to its whole society....in 1857, in a rural Canada West of some 950,000 people, Toronto could loom fairly large with 30,000—about the size, incidentally, of the highly important town of Bristol in the English Middle Ages." While all Ontario towns grew rapidly during the railway-building fever, after "the heyday of the country market-town" in the mid-nineteenth century, concentration of "fewer but larger manufacturing units in the chief centres" led to the beginning of rural depopulation and by 1901 Ontario's population was 40 percent urban. The move of the Massey plant from Newcastle to Toronto in 1879 was just one indicator of the process of metropolitanization. And as the population centres became increasingly concentrated, the capital city's domination of the political process meshed with its roles in financial, commercial, manufacturing and cultural activities to make it the principal locus of regional organization.

Metropolitanism in Ontario was further matured by a high degree of centralization in urban organization. Dealing with that organization, from the appointed district magistrates through the 1849 Municipal Corporations Act and beyond, Careless described it as

> a combination of North American circumstances and precepts of British Victorian middle-class liberalism. Based on rule by elected representatives, it by no means went as far as popular democracy. A still engrained conservatism, the set habit of looking to an élite, distaste for party politics in municipal affairs, the fear of 'Yankee' boss rule and corruption, all militated against any further move to full democratization.…the structure of public life in the towns, the kinds of places they became, continued to differ significantly from American counterparts across the border, in the lesser play of popular power, the greater degree of social control from above—and, one might add, in less evidence of confused and corrupt administration.

What is evident in his other articles and even in *Toronto to 1918* is prominent also here in his refusal to apply monocausal class analysis while, at the same time, laying heavier emphasis upon the role of élites:

> The degree of class polarization still must not be overemphasized. At one end of the social scale there continued to be an aristocratic social leaven…still further down the scale, the still numerous "respectable artisans" and tradesmen served to bridge and blur sharper class identification…the strong sectarian religious ties that cut across class lines were frequently the more in evidence, particularly when deep-rooted Protestant and Catholic antipathies divided the working class itself.[47]

Technological changes, apart from those in manufacturing which Careless stressed in his 1974 statement on urbanization in Old Ontario, were chiefly in transportation: the rail network which affected all towns as well as the lumber and mining hinterlands, and which enhanced Toronto's dominance at the expense of such cities as Kingston with its smaller hinterland and steadily lessening role in transshipment.

As one re-reads Careless's work, the extreme care he takes to avoid entanglement in a precise theory of metropolitanism, let alone of urban growth *per se*, becomes cumulatively evident. Rigid "stages" give way constantly to rephrasing of "patterns" and, especially, to emphasis laid upon particularities, individuals, ecology and communications. In *Toronto to 1918*, after examining the city's locational advantages, he observes that "site factors do not necessarily ordain the emergence of a city, but do enter deeply into shaping its growth. Yet that involves as well such human factors as interests, power and work, along with innovation, expectation, and what we consider luck. Out of this amalgam comes an urban community." Nevertheless, Toronto's expansion to metropolitan stature, first regional, then national, does conform to a rough pattern. That evolution

> essentially comprised several main stages...the process whereby a major city comes to dominate an extensive economic territory or hinterland by controlling its commerce, knitting the area into a transportation network, centering many of its industrial activities, and organizing financial services for it. The hinterland territory may well contain many smaller cities and towns with their own lesser tributary districts, but all are linked to the over-riding dominance of the master city. And this metropolitan-hinterland pattern of development, equally evidenced by other leading cities in Canada or in the world beyond, is an integral feature of the whole organization of human society.

But, having reiterated this basically Grasian formulation, Careless at once qualifies it by rejecting an exclusively economic set of criteria:

> The executive, parliamentary, judicial and administrative activities...established at Toronto gave it special distinction from even its youngest village days. And in subsequent periods, political functions that centered in the city kept it dominant as a prime place of decision for the public and private concerns of areas well beyond it. Moreover, Toronto's role as home of prominent élite groups, as a concentration point of major ethnic and religious bodies, and in time as well of popular movements or working-class organizations, also gave it widening social holds upon its hinterland. So did the city's influence on cultural developments, through its leading place in provincial education, publishing, professional and artistic life, and generally, over time, through

its becoming a central source of information, cultivation and opinion. In evident ways, Toronto's rise to metropolitan status proceeded in much more than solely economic terms.[48]

While the structure of *Toronto to 1918* conforms in a manner to the "received" stages of metropolitan growth, the content is also that of a vibrant city biography with relativistic stress upon human agencies. Careless fittingly concluded the volume thus: "From Simcoe to Jimmie Simpson, Berczy to Joseph Flavelle, was a very long way. Yet 1918 still marked only an end to the beginnings of what human action would do to transform a Lake Ontario locality into a world-scale city."

One of the main themes of Careless's version of metropolitanism is best summed up in the term *communications*: not just the evolving technology but, even more important, the personal relationships, the press, the educators, the writers and artists which formed the conduits transmitting ideas, techniques and decisions in a two-way traffic of benefit both to metropolis and hinterland. For this emphatic point of view he has been questioned by those metropolitanists who stress the exploitative aspects of the "thesis" and especially by those who see metropolitanism "as a relationship linking peripheral élites with the 'core groups' whom sociologists have identified at the centre of Canadian capitalism."[49] It seems to me that Donald Davis is wide of the mark when he also writes of Careless: "The fundamental evasion lies in the ascription of 'metropolitan ambitions' to cities rather than to the individuals to whom they properly belong. Ambitions, like dominance and power, are attributes of élites *not* cities. Nor do cities exercise economic control; entrepreneurs and business corporations do."[50] In any event, Careless returns repeatedly and with undiminishing emphasis to human agencies when analyzing multiple causality.

The significance of complex human communications and mutual advantages accruing to metropoli and hinterlands is implicit, for example, throughout his article on the early business relations of Victoria.[51] He clearly enjoys his research most when he can tie it down to people, as in his depiction of the Lowe brothers, "these two not untypical, nor unimportant, figures in the early development of trading activities between the main west coast trading centre [San Francisco] and its northern adjunct [Victoria]". And, with respect to ambitions and motives, while the Lowe brothers represent a commercial extension of San Francisco, "they were obviously not Americans, outsiders invading the Island market. Instead they sought to develop the Island's trade for its own sake as well as their private interests, and they never escaped their pro-British orientation." Moreover, the "core groups" of either British or American capitalism, are, for Careless, in fact interconnected individuals; they express legacies and continuities which are not to be understood by mere abstractions. Thus, the Lowes' ties with the Hudson's Bay Company were "plainly vital for a large part of their business operations." The Lowes were part of an "old boys' net" and Careless poses the suggestive question of how many others "in this era of rising commercial enterprise in the northwest coast might similarly find beginnings among Company men still present, and in veritable clan contact, long after their fur oligopoly had passed away?" Pursuit of the role of individuals within communications networks strongly suggested to Careless "that a view of San Francisco's dominance over much of British Columbia's earlier coastal development requires a wider perspective, for beside or behind the lines of growth from the Californian metropolis older British metropolitan forces were still significantly at work in the hinterland."

In an extended review of A. R. M. Lower's *Great Britain's Woodyard: British America and the Timber Trade*,[52] Careless adverts to some of the points just mentioned and, as well, to his fundamental insistence on mutuality within the metropolitan schema. Acknowledging that Lower "largely pioneered in applying metropolitan concepts to Canadian history," he questioned sharply Lower's stress on the exploitation of the hinterland supply centres by metropolitan demand centres. "Metropolitan communities," Careless argued, "are also supply centres in themselves, answering, in turn, the demands of the hinterland areas for goods and services, not to mention information, ideas and social standards." That is, the relationships are reciprocal even though "in most instances the metropolis calls the shot, amasses greater proportionate gains and generally exercises the final decision-making power that Lower rightly sees as lying at the core of metropolitanism." Further, hinterlands generate metropoli of their own and the relationships amongst metropolitan centres are never static; thus "the demand-metropolis and supply-hinterland dichotomy is too limited and rigid a pattern to cover the varieties of human experience." In the evolution of the metropolitan approach among Canadian historians, W. L. Morton was correct, according to Careless,

> in stressing that "no metropolis lives of itself, it is a function of its hinterland." He is wrong in inferring that metropolitan studies necessarily express "centrality" while minimizing "regionality"—the life of the hinterland itself....A metropolitan pattern involves the context of its regional associations: a regional pattern, as it develops, involves at least an emerging sub-metropolitan organization within its spatial limits, as well as external relations to greater foci of metropolitan power. It is frequent, indeed, that one has to speak of a regional metropolis...and in no way is metropolitanism foreign to regionalism....Metropolitanism by no means has to be identified with a centralist or Laurentian view.[53]

The review article on Lower's book came close, in fact, to defending a "school" of history; yet it is entirely characteristic that Careless loaded it with many codicils and provisos. Thus,

> if metropolitanism is not Laurentianism, neither is it to be
> equated with environmentalism, even as a later stage of
> that school of thought. It does not express the ruling power
> of environmental forces, but the interaction of the environ-
> ment with human organization and culture in an ecological
> relationship....what is being studied is a process of societal
> change, whereby a metropolitan system of related commu-
> nities emerges, exerts its influence, changes, and eventually
> declines, or is absorbed in still another pattern of metropoli-
> tan relationships.

Yet there remains the sequence of interpretative perceptions: "a staples
trade example [as in Lower] offers one illustration of the workings of
metropolitanism, often a very clear one, since, owing to the relative lack of
complexity in the functions of a staples system, the power of the directing
metropolis can stand out starkly indeed." What both Laurentianism and
staples trade analyses minimize, or even ignore, is interaction: a hinterland
"can shape responses, at least qualify outside purposes, and generate activities of its own—so that the logical outcome of metropolitan influence does
not have to be the ruined stump field, the ghost town or the total export of
resources under an unbridled capitalism." Further, a frontier is essentially
"a hinterland in an early stage of development [and] metropolitanism must
be seen as a persistent phenomenon, clearly evident in frontier stages and in
the simpler trading conditions of under-developed areas, but in no way to be
restricted as an interpretative approach to the terms set by those special
stages or conditions."

Careless's major criticism of staples theory, then, is that however illuminating it may be, it offers a too narrow interpretative base. And, equally,
metropolitanism, while a salutary broadening out, is to be used only with
great care and with a steady watch on the two-way streets. "In essence," he
commented,

> the metropolis-hinterland relation is a particularly influen-
> tial case of that classic relationship that runs through his-
> tory, that of town and country, of the concentrated human
> community to the diffused or extended community....the
> great city or metropolis is studied in the context of the
> hinterland; the outlying region in relation to the metropoli-
> tan centre. The result is neither urban nor regional history,
> but a combination of aspects of both. And the result is not
> the key to all history, or even to all Canadian history, but
> rather an approach to the interpretation of some of its
> significant themes. Accordingly I would disclaim and deny
> a metropolitan "thesis"....[54]

Small wonder that some urban and regional scholars are either infuri-
ated or frustrated, sometimes both, as they attempt to categorize Careless's

metropolitanism. Model-makers, especially, depreciating Careless's stimulus to research-writings which, more often than not, are designed more to raise questions and examine hypotheses than to erect watertight structures, fault him for imprecision. Representing this view, Donald Davis berates him for making mutuality rather than conflict his analytic focal point, and for not defining the primacy of either "natural processes" or "human agency." In attempting, writes Davis, "to cross-fertilize two historical models, one of which stressed the impersonal workings of nature [Gras], and the other the power of élites [staples-dependency theory], Careless has produced a relatively sterile hybrid."[55]

It appears to me that some critics are upset not by imprecision and caution in Careless's writings but rather by his quite constant assertion of a Canadian perspective—which is the obverse of his insistence upon mutuality and interaction. Dependency theory proponents perceive in him a strong tendency to downplay, excuse or even ignore exploitation of disadvantaged regions,[56] while those concerned more with class relationships charge lack of interest in the centralizing-oppressive role of the élites.[57] Relativists are more than likely to be imprecise; they lay seige to myths or models which appear to contradict evidence. Thus, discussing metropolitanism in maritime Canada, Careless stressed changes in technology and "continental pulls" in accounting for the relative decline of the Atlantic cities and suggested that "adjustment," which was only relatively successful in the twentieth century, came because of, rather than in spite of, Confederation.[58] There may be some imprecision here, but Careless also questions sharply the simplistic reiterations of heartless exploitation—sharply enough to draw the rebuke that he "absolved Confederation and central Canada of responsibility for the post-1867 regression of the region's principal cities." Unlike most recent historians of Atlantic Canada, he blamed the region's difficulties on "new forces of continental dominance," which he attributed to changes in communication technology.[59]

As "western alienation" once again became both academically trendy and a political force, Careless put into journalistic form some of the analysis and questions he had developed elsewhere, especially in his 1980 essay on "limited identities." In "The Myth of the Downtrodden West"[60] he exhibited forcefully his awareness of the political impact of historical interpretations. Careless knows well the role that such interpretations, both anglophone and francophone, have played in forming climates of political opinion, that *je me souviens* or *notre maître le passé* can be simultaneously translated across the country. He is, consequently, wary of any deliberate manipulation of historical evidence and of the potential for distortion inherent in an historian's lineage and milieu.[61] His attack on the western "myth," he would likely concede, was not (could not) be uninfluenced by his own Ontario base; its force, however, derives far more from his research and a perception of Canada itself, a perception which includes a most quizzical appreciation of republican metropolitanism. Thus he wrote in 1981 that the whole National Policy package of railway building, freight rates, tariff and resource control was "aimed at building the Canadian union, including the West, by promot-

ing a more diversified, higher-level economy with a broad home market—
one that would not be absorbed piece-meal by the highly protectionist
United States." Until that process was begun there was "virtually no western regional community....The achievement of this design, in fact, was the
rapid settling of the West, which then increasingly protested central domination."[62] Conceding the fostering of powerful vested interests, business-
political alliances and even inefficient industries, he maintained that industrial growth would have occurred in central Canada in any event: "central
economic ascendancy was based on far more than any tariff grip on the
West." Indeed, he continued, the Canadian West would have been much
worse off in a régime of free trade at the mercy of "even bigger American
firms."

While one might charge, correctly, a certain reluctance to assign an
order of precedence to the "forces" within this aspect of metropolitanism,
Careless clearly leans heavily upon geographical location and technological
change—as he did in his analyses of Victoria and the Atlantic region.
Equally, however, he does not shrink from some pretty definite conclusions.
And one cannot miss, again, his insistence upon keeping a pan-Canadian
perspective—particularly when he perceives one Canadian "myth" threat-
ening another which he considers more consonant with a complex historical
reality. Thus he reminded alienated westerners (and regional social historians) that under the National Policy Manitoba did, indeed, build up "decidedly valuable industries" and that "western cities in general did well on the
east-west flow of trade....It follows that there is no inherent crime in pursu-
ing a protectionist policy." Moreover, the "downtrodden" myth is far too
generalized: "campaigns for readjustment were more often concerned with
advantages for particular western interests or places than with equal justice
for all." As to the general cost-benefit sheet, "effectively the Canadian government (and taxpayers) have provided a western subsidy, huge over the
years, which has compensated for the higher charges the West has claimed
to suffer from tariff and rail subservience." Again, because of different
policies, American rates were higher and the Canadian western myth simply ignores geography, which was "the main factor." Just as growth, technological change and metropolitan mutuality had meliorated discordance in
the past, Careless asserted, so they may be expected to function in the
present: as population shifts westward "the centre's domination, not a
sinister plot but a joint product of history and geography, will be modified
and offset. The current metropolitan rise of Vancouver, Calgary and Edmonton, and the new wealth, diversity and energy of their own western hinterlands, proclaims as much." As the National Energy Policy came and went,
Careless may have looked back wryly at this prediction. Certainly, in 1981,
he did not doubt what was required: "We could also use a shrewdly
adaptable John A. Macdonald to wangle new combinations, even a skilfully
delaying Mackenzie King, rather than urgent confrontationists. If the Canadian genius (of seeing anything but genius) does come through, western
alienation could subside without explosions."[63]

When Careless finished the second volume of *Brown of the Globe* in 1963 he wrote in the Preface that his subject was "generally envisaged among the 'Fathers' of Confederation as a stern, white-headed Old Testament patriarch—instead of the vigorous, exuberant man of forty-five that he was at the time," and that he deserved "rescuing from the indifference and near ignorance that Canadians so often display about their past." He also observed that while Brown reached the peak of his achievement in the period from 1860 to 1867, the years from then until his death in 1880 "were by no means a mere epilogue....His continued influence in the Liberal party and his power on the *Globe* gave him an important role in the newly-created federal union." It is tempting to make a fanciful comparison, without, however, loading it unduly. Confederation, after all, was as much a means of understanding and expressing a Canada that, in many respects, already existed, as it was an act of political creation—an evolution so well explored in the *Union of the Canadas*. For Careless, understanding an existing Canada which, despite nationhood, remains in a fluid state of self-definition (a highly laudable condition, he might affirm) has been the theme connecting and even directing all his work. And like the notion of Confederation, that of metropolitanism has deep roots, is the work of no single person, and has been very much subjected to sharply varying interpretations.

Perhaps the best pad from which to launch a summation of Careless's historical scholarship is a remark taken from the 1954 article: "The metropolitan approach largely recognizes what is already going on in Canadian historiography and provides a new framework."[64] The implication is clear: "frameworks" which, after all, are simply the intellectualization of scattered facts, must be constructed out of existing material. New material, of the sort that Careless's own work has vastly augmented, requires modifications and, perhaps, reconstruction of frameworks. But the whole process is a continuum not to be comprehended by any single theory, model or ideology. Careless has himself provided a candid, retrospective view of that process. As he was finishing *Toronto to 1918* and about to buckle down to his present work on the metropolis and frontier in Canada, he prepared a careful response to the critical analysis of metropolitanism written by Donald Davis, the latter having sent him an advance copy.

"All I had in mind," wrote Careless, "when I initially came to [formulate a metropolitan approach] in the 1950s,"

> was to redress the then-current overemphasis on frontierism in Canadian history....others had already queried, "frontier of what?" Manifestly, frontiers or hinterlands did not just push themselves out of their own volition and clearly they fed back to major command centres, sometimes with clash and confrontation, but far more fully and broadly by ways of complementation. This was no major transmis-

sion from ecological social science or centre-margin staple theory, but stemmed just from reflections on the Canadian experience.[65]

At the same time, he observed, Creighton's Laurentionism "failed to cover the whole duality of the shared relations almost as much as frontier one-sidedness did." The path from frontierism to metropolitanism, then, was no road to Damascus but was strewn with cumulative perceptions. "In then taking up Gras," he reflected, "(first via Masters), to inform a metropolitan concept, I was also considerably influenced by my own background in medieval English and French social history, the former with Wilkinson in Toronto, the latter with Taylor at Harvard on medieval French regionalism."

Then Careless even more explicitly refuted the implication in Davis's article that his primary source of thinking about metropolitanism was the work of Gras and that of the Chicago school of sociology. More important, he wrote, "was feudalism":

> I got into it when I first planned to be a medievalist, not through Chicago's sociology. In fact, I only probed into the Chicago School later, working back from studies on metropolitanism, and found their ecology pretty arid compared to the communitas approach of medieval historians. The chain of mutually dependent relationships, the loci of power and responsibility, derived from the latter, as did my first real knowledge of urban history.[66]

Recalling that his first studies of the frontier had been with Frederick Merk, Turner's heir at Harvard, Careless reflected "So I got my two sides neither from Creighton or Innis—though I also studied under both at Toronto." The other principal route into metropolitanism, and this is certainly clear from the sequence of his research, Careless described thus: "Seminars with [Crane] Brinton at Harvard on 'climate of opinion' in British intellectual history, and with Owen on Victorian social élites, had further strangely led me into Canadian history."[67] The route followed was, of course, that to the *Globe* and a doctoral thesis on that "powerful Victorian opinion instrument." The urban élite, so closely related to the *Globe*'s power, was not unconcerned with the potential of technological change; Careless noted that work at Harvard had alerted him to "the role of technology and knowledge-control in economic history," while Arthur Schlesinger Sr. nourished his already distinct interest in urban history. Again, there was no single lineage:

> These various inputs, coming together with a perceived need, accordingly turned me toward metropolitan considerations. Chicago ecology wasn't a factor; I didn't wholly follow its Grasian offshoots either....social-élite complexes, attitudinal responses and information-flow themes had thus

far affected me more than any economic formulations. But Gras thereupon provided a very useful economic basis, to my mind, on which to structure general patterns of city-hinterland interplay within Canada itself.

In his article, Davis discerned five "schools of thought" within the metropolitan approach.[68] Although Careless complimented him for putting "a good deal into meaningful perspective," and judged the piece "schematically valid," he certainly didn't accept it as the obituary of metropolitanism, not at least as he understood it. Rather, it was "an invitation to more work." And, clearing the decks, as it were, for that work, he queried several specific aspects of Davis's analysis. Accepting that his own approach was broadly ecological, Careless disclaimed any "antique organicism" in his perception of the interaction of metropolitan and hinterland communities. Such social configurations he did not see as "super-biological organisms transferred from some obsolete natural history." As to slighting the element of *exploitation* in metropolitanism:

> ...it has always seemed to me that this is but part of the action, not its essence. That is, instead, the mutuality of metropolitan-hinterland relations....Granted, western town-lot grabbers and boosters might be greedy and make undeserved fortunes, if they didn't go broke, but what value does one ascribe to the town they worked to build up in their own interests?...As for the forests of New Brunswick or the Ottawa, what else might have been done with them in our colonial *cum* laissez-faire context of the earlier nineteenth century? This is not to absolve the apostles of enterprise and avarice, but to see them in their time and place, and concommitently within the overriding reciprocal system of relations.

Such insistence upon the importance of historical imagination is Careless's answer to economic determinists who accuse him of neglecting not just exploitation but also the role of class confrontation.[69] To the question of *dependency*, closely related to that of exploitation in metropolitanism, Careless responded in similar terms. Neither the dependency nor the exploitation of hinterlands is to be seen as a static condition—they exist and change within an interactive process over time:

> In an "old" country like Britain, the decline of a Glasgow from eminence, or the inroads of external finance on London, have scarcely marked the termination of metropolitan relations there. In a "new" country like Canada, the advance of Toronto hardly has proved that its ascendancy would last forever. Dependency scholars may perhaps be

led to more pre-fixed, non-temporal views, that favour
freeze-frame snapshots of how the model said it had to be.
Yet old-style ecologists might prefer a continuously running movie camera.[70]

Careless also proclaimed the need to retain a strong geographical, or
spatial, perspective in the developing, pragmatic analysis of metropolitanism, and particularly the expediency of stressing discrete aspects of the
theme wherever this seems appropriate. This he had done in discussing both
the Winnipeg and Victoria business communities. Further, should such
forays into the activities of entrepreneurial élites and power concentrations
in urban-metropolitan growth (or decline, as with Victoria and the Atlantic-
coast cities) suggest modification of an hypothesis, the question should be
met with flexibility. Thus, working with Jacob Spelt, and supervising Frederick Armstrong's thesis on Toronto, Careless accepted that Gras's sequential
stages of metropolitan growth were by no means holy writ—and he used the
Grasian prescription only with modifications in his *Toronto to 1918*. Not
regarding his approach as a thesis, he wrote,

> I pursue it where and when tracing out the operations of an
> interacting system seems perceptively enlightening, yet may
> not do so if the topic of inquiry suggests some other fram-
> ing. This could well be called impressionistic; but that's a
> term that will not necessarily upset us old-type relativist
> historians, though it may be a pronouncement of anathema
> for sociologists and Marxians.

To the criticism that metropolitanism is of little help in understanding
urban history, especially cities' social structures and power networks, Careless replies that "my own concept deals with *double-sided relationships* between dominant urban centres and hinterland expanses, *not with the totality
of urban phenomena.*" The metropolitan approach, he continued,

> must be integrally linked with inner urban conditions. But
> it will not necessarily tell much about internal neighbour-
> hood and power distributions (though at times it might),
> the civic society, its polity, culture, services and so on.
> When I wrote my own history of Toronto to 1918....I treated
> metropolitan factors where I deemed they applied, and not
> where they didn't in the story as a whole.

To be overwhelmed by one's dismay at the massive domination of hinterlands by main metropolitan communities, he pointed out, is equally distort-
ing when considering the life of regions. Thus, posed against the more
exuberant flourishes of a Lower describing the "universal, timeless concentration of power," or a Morton seeing "a blind destroyer" gobbling up its

hinterland, metropolitanism can establish the actual balance of metropolis-hinterland interaction—and thus describe each as a function of the other.

Apart from gently nudging Davis toward a more accurate mapping of the course he had followed to metropolitanism, Careless reacted with some warmth to the charge of determinism,[71] and I think that his explication in this respect serves well as a concluding focal point—not least because it conforms pretty closely to my own view of his historical scholarship. As the basis of his critique Davis had selected articles which, Careless observed, were "largely overviews and initial probes. There was little room to get down to persons at their level." Even so, he maintained, he had not ignored "human volition and policy making" in the articles on Victoria, Winnipeg and Atlantic metropolitanism; in the Toronto volume, he noted, "I have sought to give full play to entrepreneurs, business firms, social classes, political and attitudinal responses, quality of life, cultural and ethnic influences, etc., still linked with metropolitan associations wherever these bear." He might well have pointed to the Brown biography as yet stronger evidence of his understanding of "the human equation" and the interplay of political-economic élites. The following passage describes, if there ever was one, an urban-metropolitan élite, even "core group":

> In any case, Reform nominating conventions were in full swing by this time; the *Globe* was full of reports of them through March and April [1867]. The Reform Association of Upper Canada was reconstituted as well. On April 9 its Central Executive Committee was formed at a meeting in Toronto. The membership list included names as well established in the business community as George Brown, John McMurrich, William McMaster, John Macdonald and A. M. Smith, as well as newer names like Edward Blake, J. D. Edgar and Adam Crooks. The same group, it appeared, was to guide the Toronto branch of the Reform Association, along with Gordon Brown, H. S. Howland (brother of the cabinet minister), John Taylor, William Elliott and other owners of leading city firms. Nor was it without significance that when the first general meeting of the Bank of Commerce was held a week later, as Toronto's answer to the Bank of Montreal, George Brown was present as a prominent shareholder, while Howland, Macdonald, Elliott and Taylor were elected directors and McMaster was made president. For Toronto's leading Liberals were concerned with both political and economic control of the West. It was quite natural that the same men should be at the core of both the western Reform party and the big new western banking institution, each of which was dedicated to gaining power in the Dominion that was so soon to be established.[72]

One could argue that the whole of the metropolitan approach is in the foregoing, and especially in its human content. These men knew what power was and used it very consciously. They understood and forwarded the economic, cultural, transportation and communications interconnections with their hinterlands and most certainly welcomed the battles of inter-metropolitan competition. Their entrepreneurial taste buds salivated as they contemplated each new railway project, manufactory, bank, insurance company. Nor did they shy away from eleemosynary activity. Careless makes no bones about any of this and he certainly does not ignore it in favour of an overriding technological (or any other) determinism. Thus, when conducting hypothetical treks into the whys, as opposed to the hows of the Canadian experience, he can never become quite the social scientist.

Careless's perception of historical method has remained that of "the high art of particulars." His approaches to interpretation, beyond simply description, have been immensely stimulating; yet it is no surprise that they cannot completely seduce quantifiers or model-makers. His hypotheses are always subject to qualifications, to consideration of elements "beyond that...." If they veer away consistently from the monocausal, however, they everywhere exhibit a deep affection for the kaleidoscopic reality which is Canada. They will never be open to that vivid characterization which enlivened Frank Underhill's comments on the first volume of the Rowell-Sirois Report: "a ghostly ballet of bloodless economic categories."

All unattributed material is by J. M. S. Careless.

1   "Frontierism, Metropolitanism, and Canadian History", *Canadian Historical Review* [hereafter *CHR*] 35 (1954), 1.

2   "Two River Empires: An Historical Analysis", *American Review of Canadian Studies* 5 (1975), 45.

3   "Donald Creighton and Canadian History: Some Reflections", in J. Moir, ed., *Character and Circumstance: Essays in Honour of Donald Grant Creighton* (Toronto, 1970), 20.

4   Ibid., 4.

5   *Brown of the Globe*, I: *The Voice of Upper Canada, 1818–1859* (Toronto, 1959), 1.

6   Donald F. Davis, "The 'Metropolitan Thesis' and the Writing of Canadian Urban History", *Urban History Review* [hereafter *UHR*] 14 (1985), 95–113. Davis asserts that Careless's interpretation of the metropolis-hinterland relationship "fits the mould of 'consensus history'; it reflects the optimism both of Americans in the 1920's when Gras first expounded his thesis and of the postwar boom of the 1950's when Careless and Masters popularized it in Canada" (p. 102).

7   *Brown*, I, 328.

8   *Brown*, II: *Statesman of Confederation, 1860 to 1880* (Toronto, 1963), 371.

9   Letter to Donald Davis, 11 July 1983, in response to Davis, "Metropolitan Thesis" (prepublication draft), copy in possession of the author, courtesy J. M. S. Careless.

10   "Introduction", in Morris Zaslow, ed., *The Defended Border...* (Toronto, 1964), 2, 3.

11   See, for example, "In Praise of Vacant Lots", *Globe and Mail* (Toronto), 19 Feb. 1977, 7; "The Life of a New City: Toronto, 1834", Empire Club of Toronto, *Addresses 1983–1984* (Toronto, 1984), 285–97; "The Emergence of Cabbagetown in Victorian Toronto", in Robert F. Harney, ed., *Gathering Place: The Peoples and Neighbourhoods of Toronto,*

1834–1945 (Toronto, 1985), 24–45; "The Myth of the Downtrodden West", *Saturday Night*, May 1981, 30–34, 36.

12 "'Limited Identities' in Canada", *CHR* 50 (1969), 1–10.

13 Careless is not to be trapped into any pronouncement on the *relative* importance of such conditioners.

14 In emphasizing the monarchical structure of Canadian political history Careless shows a somewhat startling resemblance to the conservative W. L. Morton, a scholar whom he greatly admired despite their differing interpretations of the role of metropolitanism.

15 Careless offers no clear definition of class; but neither do those who write most about it, especially those who perceive a free-standing "working class culture."

16 "Limited Identities—Ten Years Later", *Manitoba History* 1 (1980), 3–9.

17 The most comprehensive review of that debate is Davis, "Metropolitan Thesis." Davis's critique concludes that, like the earlier frontierism, metropolitanism should now be abandoned "for it impedes rather than promotes understanding" (p. 109).

18 "Frontierism", 10–11. The reservations and some fresh approaches by people such as A. R. M. Lower, A. L. Burt, G. F. G. Stanley and J. B. Brebner reinforced his own cavils stemming from his work on Brown and the Grits. By 1946, notes Careless, even Frank Underhill accepted that "the original frontier agrarianism of the Clear Grits had subsequently been qualified by urban and business leadership introduced to the party by George Brown and other Toronto worthies."

19 Ibid., 12.

20 Ibid., 13. He added that "these latter factors [ideas, traditions and institutions transferred from Europe] were particularly important in a portion of North America that did not undergo a revolutionary upheaval, emotional as well as political, to break ties with Europe, and which continued to place a special premium on the word 'British' as applied to institutions and ideas. In fact, it is these very things which chiefly mark off the development of Canada from that of the United States. They give validity to the study of a separate Canadian history, one which is not just a counterpart of United States history in having a similar North American content" (p. 14). W. L. Morton, again, must have appreciated this particular passage.

21 Ibid., 16.

22 Ibid., 17. It is worth noting that manufacturing is not mentioned as an essential characteristic of a metropolis.

23 Careless cites Masters's book for the formulation of the four stages and probably did not read Gras until later.

24 "Frontierism", 18–19.

25 Ibid., 20–21.

26 Davis, "Metropolitan Thesis", 96, states that Careless's articles on metropolitanism "marked in some ways at least the self-conscious beginning of urban history" in Canada. See also Gilbert Stelter, "A Sense of Time and Place: the Historian's Approach to Canada's Urban Past", in his and Alan F. Artibise, eds., *The Canadian City: Essays in Urban History* (Toronto, 1977): "in the research of J. M. S. Careless and his students, city growth is generally seen as the interaction of the decision-making of dynamic individuals or groups and technological and population change" (p. 425).

27 Review of *Montreal: A Brief History* by J. I. Cooper, and other urban studies, *CHR* 52 (1971), 178.

28 Ibid.

29 Ibid.

30 My discussion is based on the published version of his paper, "Two River Empires" (see note 2).

31 Ibid., 31.

32 Ibid., 31–33.

33 Ibid., 33–34.

34 Ibid., 41.

35 Ibid., 43.

36   Ibid., 43, 45–46.

37   Ibid., 46–47.

38   "Aspects of Metropolitanism in Atlantic Canada", in Mason Wade, ed., *Regionalism in the Canadian Community, 1867–1967* (Toronto, 1969), 117.

39   Ibid., 118. Careless restated these attributes thus: "first, the provision of commercial facilities for the import and export trade of the city's dependent region or hinterland (on which, of course, it in turn depends); second, the establishment of industries to process the products of, or import for, the hinterland; the development of transport services to channel traffic to and from the urban centre; and fourth, the creation of financial facilities for investment and development in the region."

40   Ibid., 129.

41   See especially "The Lowe Brothers, 1852–70: A Study in Business Relations on the North Pacific Coast", *BC Studies* 2 (1969), 1–18; "The Development of the Winnipeg Business Community, 1870–1890", Royal Society of Canada, *Proceedings and Transactions*, 4th ser., VIII (1970), 239–54; "The Business Community in the Early Development of Victoria, British Columbia", in David S. McMillan, ed., *Canadian Business History: Selected Studies, 1491–1971* (Toronto, 1972), 104–23; "Aspects of Urban Life in the West, 1870–1914", in Anthony W. Rasporich and Henry C. Klassen, eds., *Prairie Perspectives*, II: *Selected Papers of the Western Canadian Studies Conferences, 1970 and 1971* (Toronto, 1973), 25–40; "Some Aspects of Urbanization in Nineteenth-Century Ontario", in F. H. Armstrong et al., *Aspects of Nineteenth-Century Ontario...* (Toronto, 1974), 65–79; "Metropolis and Region: The Interplay between City and Region in Canadian History before 1914", *UHR*, no. 3–78 (1979), 99–118; *Toronto to 1918: An Illustrated History* (Toronto, 1984).

42   "Early Development of Victoria", 120.

43   "Urban Life in the West", 125–41. Emphasizing the regional organizing power of the West's "instant cities," Careless wrote (p. 126): "In short, in these large jurisdictions the town grew more than the country in the classic era of the rise of the West" and, in fact, Winnipeg, Edmonton, Calgary and Vancouver was each more populous and powerful in proportion to its hinterland than was the case with either Montreal or Toronto.

44   Especially an article by Eric Lampard, "American Historians and the Study of Urbanization", *American Historical Review* 67 (1961), 49–61. Careless's use of Lampard's four factors was as experimental and undulating as was his similar use of Gras.

45   "Aspects of Nineteenth-Century Ontario", 65.

46   Ibid., 66–68.

47   Ibid., 73–75.

48   *Toronto to 1918*, 17.

49   Davis, "Metropolitan Thesis", 108.

50   Ibid., 108. I suppose it might equally be argued that *élites* and *corporations* do not, *per se*, exercise power or possess ambitions.

51   "Lowe Brothers."

52   "Metropolitan Reflections on 'Great Britain's Woodyard'", *Acadiensis* 3 (1973), 103–9.

53   Ibid., 104–6.

54   Ibid., 106–9.

55   Davis, "Metropolitan Thesis", 102.

56   See, for example, the Introduction to L. D. McCann, ed., *Heartland and Hinterland: A Geography of Canada* (Toronto, 1982), 1–62; S. D. Clark, "Canadian Urban Development", *UHR*, no. 1–74 (1974), 14–19.

57   Much of the criticism is implicit as, for example, in Wallace Clement, *Continental Corporate Power...* (Toronto, 1977). A very tangential criticism indeed is in James Lemon, *Toronto Since 1918: An Illustrated History* (Toronto, 1985). Lemon lays much heavier stress than does Careless upon public sector activity and class relationships, due only in part, I suppose, to the changed nature of the times.

58   "Metropolitanism in Atlantic Canada", 118ff.

59   Davis, "Metropolitan Thesis", 101.

60   "Myth of the Downtrodden West", 30, 36.

61 "Two River Empires", 47: "The Turnerian version [of the Mississippi empire] stemmed from an historian who came out of a Mississippi background; the Creightonian interpretation from one whose professional career was shaped in the Great Lakes-St. Lawrence milieu. Was each of them himself determined by his environment?"

62 In his 1973 paper, "Urban Life in the West", 130, in discussing the impact of railway technology on western cities, Careless observed that "City journalists extolled the wealth and progress it would bring to their community, then attacked its unjust rate structure, its selfish, greedy, heartless tyranny....Here was, in fact, a characteristic response to the metropolitanism inherent in the industrial technology of transport that was both shaping and mastering the West. Hence the significance of the reaction in the young western cities to railways, which had made them yet continually threatened to unmake them...."

63 "Myth of the Downtrodden West", 36. We are left to wonder whether blame should be distributed equally among the "confrontationalists." Apparently, however, there was more need of change at the centre than in the hinterlands.

64 "Frontierism", 21.

65 Letter to Davis. The Davis article was a revision of his paper presented at the 1983 Canadian Historical Association annual meeting and which incorporated one or two comments made by Careless in response to the advance reading. As evidence, Careless's letter seems to me rather better than, say, a taped interview whose contents have not received the sort of careful consideration one gives to the writing of a 15-page response to a comprehensive critique.

66 This question of derivation is obviously significant. A colleague has suggested that Careless, perhaps unconsciously, played down his debt to American sociologists in his 1954 article as well as in his response to Davis. This may have happened, it was suggested, because of "the historical profession's suspicions of sociology when he wrote in the early 1950s; it is also to be expected now that he has been accused of a certain determinism." I can see no good reason for reading this into Careless's letter; his own account of the intellectual evolution appears to be consonant with everything he has written, and especially with the sequence of that writing.

67 Donald Creighton also came "strangely" to Canadian history, having originally thought to become an historian of France. The reason for the shift in Creighton's case, however, was his failure to secure the necessary funds to study in Paris.

68 Davis, "Metropolitan Thesis", 97. He listed the schools and their "deans" as: entrepreneurial—Creighton; hinterland variant on the entrepreneurial—Artibise; ecological—Careless; dependency-exploitation—Lower; heartland-hinterland—Innis.

69 A good example of Careless's recognition of the difference between judgment and imagination in the writing of history is his treatment of George Brown's attitude to labour relations. Discussing the *Globe*'s position on unions, he wrote: "An adherent of mid-Victorian liberalism could hardly deny the principle of freedom of association. But—and it was a large but—labour associations could not infringe on another basic liberal principle, freedom of contract....Brown might acknowledge a union's right to exist—but very little more. It might function as a benevolent society; yet he would scarcely concede it the power it needed to ensure effective bargaining." *Brown*, II, 289-90.

70 He added: "Still, the relations are in a continuing open-ended process over time. And this metropolitan-hinterland process is not just a passing phase of nineteenth-century capitalism in a heyday of national states, but originated long before....It still continues in an era of super-states, multi-nationals, and no less in planned economies."

71 Davis, "Metropolitan Thesis", 103: "Indeed, the ecological approach has exhibited a strong technological determinism....Careless himself has stressed the influence of transportation technology...in developing the cities of western Canada and the Maritimes, and in determining their relative rankings. Yet the articles he wrote on these two regions were ultimately unsatisfactory since they largely omitted the human equation....the ecological interpretation of metropolitanism has had difficulty fitting the

human factor into the history of urban development....the ecological concept of dominance offers no guidelines for the study of power as wielded by élites."

72   *Brown*, II, 243–44. While he did not mention the biography of Brown, Careless did chide Davis for overlooking such items as "Metropolitanism and Nationalism", in Peter Russell, ed., *Nationalism in Canada* (Toronto, 1966), 271–83, and "Metropolis and Region" (see note 41). In both these pieces Careless stressed communications and even the "psycho-cultural" realm in a "metropolitan ambit" which was "far wider than just the materially economic."

Farms, Forests and Cities: The Image of the Land and the Rise of the Metropolis in Ontario, 1860–1914

ALLAN SMITH

Until the era of Confederation, those who saw the Upper Canadian encounter with the landscape in positive terms tended to concentrate on the land's capacity to sustain agricultural activity.[1] Poets, publicists, politicians, land company agents, farmers, teachers, historians, geographers, novelists, journalists and essayists—all argued that the province's abundance of good land permitted not only an important economic activity and a high material standard of living but also the emergence of a morally regenerate individual in a pure and undefiled community. "True independence"—Susanna Moodie's words were representative—"greets you here." In the fields of Canada West you "breathe a purer, freer air/...Indulgent heav'n has blessed

An early rural Ontario landscape after the pioneer phase of settlement: Adolphustown ca. 1830, by Thomas Burrowes

the soil,/ And plenty crowns the woodman's toil."[2] Inhabiting what Samuel Strickland called a "Garden of Eden,"[3] the farmer of that region occupied a place where "all can become the possessors of their own broad acres...where the invidious distinctions of rank and wealth are little known."[4] As the University of Toronto's Daniel Wilson put it, thanks to the fact that the province was "dowered with the inestimable blessing of a fertile soil,"[5] its people enjoyed a truly elevated status. Alexander McLachlan, farmer and rhymster of Amarantha Township, Simcoe County, summed up the argument with wit and conviction: "He's a king upon a throne/ Who has acres of his own!"[6]

Yet, even as this view of the land was arriving at the apex of its influence, new realities were beginning to erode the foundations on which it rested. The march north towards mineral-laden and timber-rich New Ontario in the 1870s and 1880s certainly threatened the understanding of the province as an agrarian and land-based community,[7] while so far as most Ontarians were concerned, the rise of the city and the industrial and bureaucratic patterns associated with it did even more to militate against the idea that their province was a place of sturdy and independent yeoman farmers.[8]

Awareness of these trends provoked a variety of responses. Some commentators rushed to define Ontario, with the rest of the Europeanized world, as increasingly urban and industrial. "This is," proclaimed a young student of politics at the University of Toronto in 1891, "an age of great cities."[9] Others insisted that Ontario's future lay in the north. For them, "the barren north suddenly became New Ontario and the province an empire."[10] Others still remained firmly attached to what they considered the conventional wisdom concerning the province's character. This link was, paradoxically, easiest to maintain in relation to the north, for the absence of a body of experience showing that farming was not in fact practicable there left the way open for the sort of simple and direct argument which could be made by assertion. In the clay belt particularly, settlement promoters claimed, the soil was excellent, the growing season more than adequate, and the prospects for upward mobility unlimited. "The penniless pioneer of a few years ago," insisted a government pamphleteer, "is the substantial, independent, farmer of today."[11] Indeed, as a later commentator put it, "much other evidence and testimony could be adduced, all going to indicate a magnificent future for this great belt, which will some day support millions of people on the land, and prove a considerable factor, not only in Canada's development, but in meeting the world's rapidly increasing demand for food and other products of the soil."[12]

The south, however, also continued to be seen in agricultural terms, for notwithstanding the gains being made in that area by town and city, the farm remained an obvious part of its landscape. But the arguments of the farm's supporters there now betrayed a clear sense that agriculture's supremacy could no longer be taken for granted. Particularly evident in what they wrote was a distinct feeling that, in light of the ever more prominent urban reality, the farm's retention of its favoured place would require constant and unrelenting emphasis on its virtues along with an equally forceful stress on the city's many and varied defects. One of agriculture's friends thus found himself not only exalting the rural life and the "happy farm" but also putting those joyful places in explicit apposition to the rising city, where, he remarked with distaste, one lived a distressing and unpleasant life hard by "the busy hum of machinery, the regal mansion of the capitalist, and a background of squalid tenements where vice, and penury, and dirt, produce a diseased and vicious population."[13]

By the beginning of the new century some four decades of rural depopulation, with its associated migration to the United States, the Canadian prairies and, of course, the cities of the province, had made much more acute the belief that the farm, though still society's seat of virtue, was steadily losing ground to the expanding metropolis. "Our farming community," as Ontario's deputy minister of agriculture said, might be retaining its capacity to act as a bulwark against the "decadence" being spawned by the new order. It had, however, also to be emphasized that the urban challenge was developing to the point where one could speak of the "national calamity" that would ensue "if our Ontario farms were to be deserted."[14] Indeed, thought poet and essayist William Wilfred Campbell, matters had gone so far that "the greatest cure for many of our modern ills and problems" was to be spoken of in terms of "a return to the land," a getting back to the farm-based kind of community which, he thought, had been so largely lost.[15]

These turn-of-the-century observers had no doubt that the farm retained its traditional qualities. As one 1912 commentator wrote, "the normal or natural life is living in the country. The man who does not touch the fresh-turned soil, tramp through the bush, fodder the cattle…or watch the garden grow, has missed the great charm of existence.…"[16] Yet also plainly evident in what they wrote was a recognition that decreasing numbers of people were exposed to these positive and uplifting influences and that in consequence of this sad reality the farm no longer worked its magic in the comprehensive and general way it once had done.

In these circumstances, the place occupied by the farm in the task of upholding the idea that contact with the land was beneficial and regenerative steadily diminished in importance. Now plainly necessary to the preservation of that conception was something that would permit definition of the link between landscape and regeneration in terms consistent with the kind of life increasingly being lived by the most characteristic members of the new kind of society. Maintaining the integrity of the general proposition that exposure to the land was good certainly required a step of this kind, for keeping that proposition dependent on a declining institution could only serve to lessen its own strength. Meeting the specific needs of the ever more prominent city dwellers also made it necessary, for those people, enmeshed in the city, were well past the point where anything other than a massive reversal of the historical process—something akin to Campbell's "return to the land"—could restore them to the life of the farm. Forcefully struck by these developments, as much persuaded as they had ever been that the well-being of society's inhabitants required exposure to the sort of pure and uplifting influences still widely associated with the farm, believers in the importance of that sort of contact began to look about them for a kind of landscape that would allow it to be sustained.

The process of locating a landscape capable of sustaining an image of itself as a source of regeneration for the members of a society which was increasingly urban was, as it happened, greatly aided by the very circumstance which had in the first instance made that search necessary. The rise of settlement and town not only threatened the ascendancy of the farm; it also changed the character of the forest. This was of immense significance. During the province's early years only a handful of observers had perceived the forest in positive, inviting terms. The poet Adam Kidd, for example, found in the 1820s "...On Huron's banks...that peace, that tranquil good/ which cheers the freeman of the bount'ous wood."[17] Another such early observer was Dr. William "Tiger" Dunlop, who pronounced the wilderness of Upper Canada to consist of "forests abounding in game, and lakes and rivers teeming with fish."[18] But more typical were those displaying a clear tendency to describe the forest in the dreariest and most unattractive terms. Novelist John Richardson thought it had a "thick, impervious, rayless"[19] aspect; another observer characterized it as simply "wild woods";[20] in the view of Catharine Parr Traill, it contained nothing even remotely resembling any of the elements of "picturesque beauty."[21] Once, however, large portions of it had come under the axe, been cut through by roads and railways, turned into farms, or consumed by expanding towns and cities, it ceased to invite consideration of itself in language of this unpleasant kind and began to attract attention of a sort involving images of an altogether different order.

The changes which might result from this process manifested themselves with special clarity in the new view of the forest developed as a consequence of its continuing exploitation by the timber trade. Seen in the early years of the century by lumbermen and politicians alike as a virtually limitless commodity to be harvested and marketed in as great quantities as practically possible, its destruction though several decades focussed increasing attention on it as a phenomenon which, far from being inexhaustible, was finite and in need of protection. As early as the 1860s this view began to develop,[22] by the 1880s systematic concern with forest conservation was being urged,[23] and by the turn of the century argument[24] was being enforced by action.[25]

For most Ontarians, however, it was the rise of town and settlement which affected the meaning of the forest most deeply. The impact of that process can hardly be overestimated. It first vanquished the sense that the land was covered by a terrifying and impenetrable overgrowth and then replaced it with the notion that what people now confronted—if they confronted anything—was a subdued and pleasant collection of quite manageable trees. Certainly, thought two 1882 observers, the change had been dramatic in the extreme. In the space of just 50 years, they wrote, "the dense forest, the silence of whose solitudes was broken only by the bark of the wolf," had been converted by the emergence of farm and village "into the fruitful field...rejoicing in thousands of homesteads, filled with the bounties of a veritable promised land."[26] One observer in fact found the process of bringing the forest to heel to have been so overwhelmingly successful that memory and imagination would soon offer the only way of sustaining contact with what he called "that grand old world of woods which the nineteenth century is fast civilizing out of existence."[27] If, however, few of those contemplating these events went so far in their assessment of what was happening, there was, nevertheless, a widespread view that the forest had come to be present in the province's life in a limited, controlled, vulnerable way which was fundamentally different from the manner in which it had earlier manifested itself. Even the farmer, long its principal antagonist, began to see it in this light. Where he had once viewed trees as things to be cleared away as quickly and thoroughly as possible, he now began to perceive them as did the forester, as objects to be cultivated. "Plant some trees," the *Canada Farmer* told readers in 1868, "stock the orchard and shrubbery; line the roadside and lane. The country is far too bare and shelterless."[28] "We must," agreed a Toronto observer of farm and country life in 1891, "preserve and plant more forest in Ontario than we have been in the habit of doing, or else we shall injure the productiveness of the land as other countries have done."[29]

If these changes in the forest's estate allowed it to be seen in terms of a need for care and cultivation, they also permitted it to be given meaning within the framework of familiar romantic conventions defining it as an alternative to civilization, a place where one could find solace, uplift, repose, tranquillity and regeneration in a withdrawal from the constraints imposed by the new urban order. That this important development could finally take place was owing directly to the delimitation of the forest by the forces of that same civilization, for it was not until this process was under way that an element essential to thinking of the woodland in these terms was actively in play. By itself, alone, untouched by the arts and techniques of man, the forest virtually compelled understanding of itself—*pace* the remarks of Richardson et al.—as a barbarizing place, withdrawal into which produced a Caliban-like state of degradation. When, however, the forces of civilization were at work, giving access to, supporting activity in, and providing a means of exit from, the forest, it could attract attention as an altogether less frightening entity. This, of course, was critical, for once it got that sort of attention, the sense of it as the venue of a terrifying encounter with an intractable force could be displaced by an understanding of it as the place where people might find a temporary, accessible and refreshingly different alternative to the kind of life they normally lived. The new order, in sum, might have created a special need for uplift and regeneration, but it also generated conditions which made it possible to seek those things in places once thought capable of providing only their opposite. Ontarians, at last able to confront the forest with confidence instead of terror, thus moved to consider glade and tree in terms consistent with the kind of pastoral and romantic discourse which had been present in western cultural life for centuries.

That Traill reacted to the forest of the 1870s in tones far different from those she had employed earlier—"How beautiful," she wrote in 1878, "how grand are the old pine woods"[30]—was one indication of how profoundly influential the new perspective became. Equally eloquent testimony to the force of its impact can be seen in the concern shown by a variety of observers to make the link between forest and regeneration absolutely clear. The woods, insisted Alexander McLachlan, were now to be seen as a place of literal rejuvenation:

> We'll throw off our years,
> With their sorrows and tears,
> And time will not number the hours
> We'll spend in the woods,
> Where no sorrow intrudes,
> With the streams, and the birds,
> And the flowers.[31]

"These fresh forests," proclaimed one of Toronto poet Isabella Valancy Crawford's characters, "make an old man young."[32] "In this brave new world"—a fictional Upper Canadian frontiersman asked the ultimate question—"where the odour of the woods is a tonic, and the air brings healing and balm, how can death exist?"[33]

Owing, then, to changes in the province's economy and society, it became possible to conceive of wood and forest in terms formerly associated with the agricultural landscape alone. It was this important development which, in finally permitting the emergence of something akin to a Wordsworthian conception of nature,[34] allowed acceptance of the farm's growing incapacity to sustain identification of itself as the place providing most of the province's people with their contact with the land. The forest, under control so far as the part of it with which most people had contact was concerned, but still wild enough to make city dwellers think they were in contact with nature uncontaminated, now stood ready to replace the farm. Having thus been taken in hand, the fundamental anxiety present in much of the commentary concerning the decline of the farm—that the loss by increasing numbers of Ontarians of their contact with it would deprive them of their access to the regenerating land—gradually grew less acute.

The simple and uncomplicated notion that the forest possessed the capacity to uplift and regenerate those exposed to it had great appeal in a society whose population was increasingly urban, since city dwellers, functioning within the framework of a highly structured system, seemed in particular need of escape from the constraints of routine and organization. This is not to say that the farm disappeared completely from the view of those concerned with these issues. It was, in fact, held by some observers to be capable of accommodating itself at least in some measure to the new and stringent requirements set by the need to flee the city. Lampman himself found respite from "the echoing city towers" in a field of timothy,[35] while a less accomplished versifier agreed that the relief provided by a sojourn on the farm was quite wonderful in its effects: "My folks, they say it's better far than paying needless doctors' bills/ So go and spend a holiday down on the farm at Uncle Will's."[36]

But if "great numbers of city families throughout Ontario spent their summers as guests on farms,"[37] those places were, nevertheless, very seriously limited in terms of what they could do for city dwellers. Their range of activities was usually narrow. More important, guests were always conscious of the farm's own routine and discipline, and of the fact that while it might not be their place of work, it nevertheless functioned as such for their host and hostess. Far, then, from giving them that measure of relief from proximity to the things of the workaday world which would allow them to feel "free at last from the city vast"[38] in some absolute sense, it left them very much in the midst of a regimen not so very different from the one they had left behind. It was, in consequence, hardly surprising that they took to the view that "one of the great pleasures of a holiday-outing is to abandon oneself to primeval nature,"[39] because in doing so they could in some real way be free and unconstrained. The requirement that there be a sense of freedom, joined with the farmer's own reluctance to risk disruption of the routine of his business and the privacy of his home, virtually ended any chance that the farm would play a significant role as a holiday destination for the urban vacationer.

As this preoccupation on the part of city dwellers with release and abandonment suggests, much emphasis was laid on the value of a forest

En route to the resort: the steamer **Nipissing** *on Lake Muskoka, 1888*

vacation in dissipating the routine-induced nervous debilitation which was becoming all too obviously a feature of city life. "Men and women cribbed in towns/ with nerves o'er wrought and weak,"[40] the "weary, over-worked toiler of the city,"[41] and even the children of that confining place "would find their nerves being turned to healthful music" as a consequence of their time spent midst the tranquil splendors of the woods. Physical well-being, too, would be enhanced. "By leaving an atmosphere tainted with sewer gas to inhale the tonic perfume of the pine bush" they would find "their cheeks flushing with freshened tints of purified blood."[42] "The healing sunshine" and "fresh air" of the woods and forest would, in fact, "work wonders."[43]

Closely linked to this celebration of the forest's regenerative powers was a clear emphasis on the variety of ways in which city-dwellers could get contact with it. Camping, noted one commentator, provided a sense of release that was almost palpable. Thanks to that activity, he continued, "the prudent man flies from all artificial conditions and yields himself to the soothing influences of nature on the shores of the lakes and rivers in the depths of our primeval forests."[44] For the growing number of city-dwellers who wanted more extensive contact with the woods, the acquisition of a summer cottage, thought other observers, would provide what was needful. By 1900, noted a Toronto journalist, "the neighbourhood of each city [contains] one or more special districts where the summer cottage is in increasing evidence and where the formalism and restraint of the city can be laid aside to the benefit of mind and body."[45] So intense, claimed a visitor to Muskoka, was this rush to the woods that it was producing something close to congestion. "It is really surprising," he pointed out, "the number of tents and small cottages that dot the shores of these beautiful waters."[46]

At the camp with Native guide and cooks, Parry Sound District ca. 1895?

The fishermen tell their tale, Muskoka or Parry Sound District ca. 1900?

To those to whom the delights of the woods did not encompass cooking for themselves or pitching tents, other means of gaining access to them were available. An Ottawa commentator was inspired to verse by his forest retreat—"I love this hunting lodge secluded far/ from that loud world that strives and toils in vain"[47]—while others merely turned up in ever larger numbers at such resort hotels as the Temagami region's Ronnoco, Temagami Inn, and Lady Evelyn.[48] There was, too, a particular interest in exposing children—boys especially—to the character-building influences of the woods. Joseph E. Atkinson of the Toronto *Star* established the "Fresh Air Fund" to get poor Toronto children in touch with them,[49] artist-naturalist Ernest Thompson Seton proposed the middle-class oriented Woodcraft Indian Club for boys,[50] and Arthur Cochrane, physical training instructor at Upper Canada College, established Camp Temagami in 1903, dedicating it specifically to "character building through vigorous outdoor living and wilderness appreciation."[51] Even a simple walk in the woods, claimed some commentators, could do what was necessary. "How soothing and refreshing it is," enthused a Kingston resident, "to withdraw awhile from the toil and turmoil of life to some shady nook in a retired wood."[52] "The bush," an old pioneer informed the readers of his memoirs in 1884, "has [n]ever lost its charms for me. I still delight to escape thither; to roam at large…forgetting the turmoil and anxieties of the business world."[53]

If what city dwellers did received attention, where they might go also came under scrutiny. For some observers, the Thousand Islands were a favoured spot.[54] Others celebrated the attractions of Algonquin Park.[55] Still others thought the Lake Temagami area was to be preferred.[56] Above all, however, was the Muskoka region. "Here," asserted one of its partisans, "the business and professional man finds rest from care and toil; [and] the feeble, health."[57] "To the worker," insisted another, "this [vacation] life [in Muskoka] is a seduction."[58] In that happy place, as a third put it, one could spend "cool, healthy, happy days, as unlike those of busy town life as civilized men and women can devise."[59]

The woods, then, were in the view of these commentators the ideal vacation place for urban dwellers. A variety of activities, no one on hand but other vacationers or employees unobtrusively serving the holiday-takers' needs, a regimen tailored to the exigencies of the short-term visit, and an abundance of fresh air, green trees and open skies were there before them. In these happy circumstances, how could they not find the opportunity for regeneration and uplift denied them in the midst of the city?

If some observers continued to see recreational space beyond the city as different than and distanced from the metropolis, implicit in the comment of others was a much different view. Far from seeing the forest isolated and apart, they defined it as being in the process of absorption into the metropolitan system. Subject, in their view, to the workings of urban-focussed transportation networks, the enthusiasms of planners and bureaucrats, and ultimately the imperatives created by the needs of the metropolis itself, the forest seemed in fact to be experiencing a complete loss of its identity as a place distinguishable in terms of distance, character and function from the world of the city.

The sense that what lay beyond the city was being integrated into the city's system manifested itself in a number of different ways. Evident in one commentator's focus on the manner in which transportation technology was placing recreational space very much within the city dweller's reach—the railway, he wrote, "in half an hour...Bears us from the stone-paved streets to quiet woods"[60]—it could also be seen in the attention another observer drew to the role the trolley might play in placing "the country, [with] its pure air, sunlight, and wholesome surroundings" so close to the "hosts of people who work in offices and shops" that they might actually be able to live there.[61]

An altered view of the land beyond the city was apparent, too, in observations which had as their thrust the notion that the forest was not something worth preserving as it stood, but a phenomenon needing the sort of improvement which could only come through the intervention of bureaucracy and system. Those who made these comments did not, of course, in any sense argue that the changes they favoured would blur the distinction between town and country so completely that it would disappear. Equally, however, their remarks betrayed a clear acceptance of the fact that the extension to the countryside of plan and organization would, in producing a triumph for the rational and systematic principles of the new order, represent a defeat for the spontaneity and distinctiveness of the old. This view of things was certainly to be seen in the remarks of one Ontario bureaucrat.

Taking the province's highways as his focus, Road Commissioner Archibald W. Campbell made it, in fact, more than clear that leaving nature on its own through failure to extend the improving hand of man to the highways, and, in particular, the countryside flanking them, had produced an exceedingly sad state of affairs. "Whatever beauty the country highways of Ontario possess has," as he put it, "been bestowed upon them by nature"—"we have been entirely deficient." Since what this gross negligence had yielded was plainly unsatisfactory, it was time to mould and reshape those highways in a manner consistent with the principles of balance, harmony and form—to undertake, in short, "the artistic treatment of roads" in a way that would order and present them as they should be seen.[62] What, claimed another observer, had been done with relatively large tracts of land in certain parts of the province gave special cause for belief in man's capacity to render nature at once more accessible and more attractive. Queen Victoria Niagara Falls Garden Park had been in a particularly unfortunate state until the provincial government stepped in to take over and regulate its operations. Thanks to this extension of control and administration, "it has a nature setting of rare charm, one that is best realized by a comparison with the unkempt condition of the Canadian shore territory prior to government control."[63]

Even clearer evidence of the new thinking was provided by remarks which, in essence, amounted to the following: the land beyond the city was not only linked to and capable of being tranformed by the metropolis; it was also a resource at the city's service. Here, too, what Road Commissioner Campbell had to say was of significance, for it offered a particularly graphic example of the manner in which this variation on the basic theme might be played. In arguing that "the artistic treatment of highways would be a constant reproach to the shiftless; neglected lawns would become fewer; ramshackle houses and barns would be less common; the eye [would not only be] refreshed [but also] educated at every point...,"[64] he in fact made obvious a belief that the highway beautiful was desirable not on aesthetic grounds or as a complement to the natural charms of the countryside but because, once in being, it would act to inculcate the very values of order, discipline and efficiency whose creature it was. Even ostensibly nature-exalting propositions conveyed the message that the good "Nature" might do was done very much in the city's interests. She might, to be sure, be showing her own power by restoring what one commentator called those "natural mechanical and inventive gifts" which had been "atrophied" by life in the city. The critical thing to note, however, was the fact that those gifts, blunted in the city and revitalized by nature though they might be, had a particular meaning for the technically oriented, machine-minded people of the town. Nature's action in restoring them could, in consequence, mean nothing other than that her powers were being directed specifically to the servicing of city dwellers' needs.[65]

The tendency to subordinate the countryside to the system, values and requirements of the city manifested itself with absolute clarity in the treatment given by different observers to the vacationers' encounter with what they visited. Freely conceding that encounter to be finite—vacationers, after all, were by definition doing what they did for a specific and limited time and a particular and well-understood purpose—these observers placed unambiguous emphasis on the fact that the land beyond the city permitted sojourners on it only temporary contact with what it offered them. They would, indeed, be in touch only long enough to restore their flagging energies and then, at least to a point refreshed, they would return to the city, the better able to do its work. The kind of regeneration that land provided was not, in consequence, to be understood in terms of the extravagant imagery of the new beginning, but in the more restrained language appropriate to description of a process by which those who did urban society's work were revitalized. City dwellers might, to be sure, sojourn amidst "woodland sights and fragrant breezes" and get "a stock of health and strength of body and mind," but they had to keep firmly in mind that these bounties must "serve for the rest of the year."[66] Their inevitable destiny was to pursue their fate as "cogs in the wheel of that mighty machine called [urban] humanity."[67] However successful a vacationer might be in forgetting "for the term of his sojourn the common mercantile interests that yield him his subsistence," however "refreshed" he found himself upon "awakening from his reverie," he must in the end "resume his daily avocation."[68]

Thus, while the city dweller's friends might join the partisans of the farm in using the Edenic metaphor,[69] their doing so in no sense signalled the founding of what was held to be a new kind of society. Instead, their emphasis on the quite extraordinary capacity for revitalization attributed to the resort areas by those who vacationed there did no more than dramatize the reaction of these short-term visitors to their temporary home. That the limited sojourn amid nature's wonders on the part of people tied firmly to the urban order had become, as an observer put it, "one of the characteristics of modern times,"[70] seemed, indeed, a proposition capable only of confirmation. So marked a feature of the new reality did it appear that, thought a contributor to a London journal, a definition of the person who best appreciated landscape and scenery now needed to be put in quite different terms from those in which it had formerly been framed. It was not, he wrote, the person in constant contact with a given terrain who best understood it. "Habitual association," it could now be seen, "dulls appreciation; a too-close focus blurs the picture." The person who would get the most out of contact with the land was the person who was always seeing it anew, whose powers of observation had been kept keen by the need to assimilate fresh sights and new information. The holidayer, the vacationer, the temporary sojourner was, it therefore followed with ineluctable force, the being to whom the land showed its most rounded face. "The picture"—nothing could now be clearer—"appears in perfection only to the thoughtful traveller."[71]

The land beyond the city thus found itself being conceived in terms that established it firmly in the city's orbit, rendered subservient to the need of the metropolis for a constantly refreshed and revitalized workforce. Put there most plainly by these commentators' emphasis on the railway, the trolley and the planner's function, it had also been moved to that place in the much more subtle sense that commentators now defined the most fulfilling sort of contact with it in terms only the city dweller could meet. Far, then, from being perceived—as in the days of the farm's ascendancy—as the foundation of an independent order and a phenomenon best appreciated by those in constant contact with it, the land had been reduced by these observers to the status of an adjunct to the metropolis, a thing most fully understood by those who spent the bulk of their time somewhere else.

The same attitude manifested itself even more clearly in the rhetoric of those concerned with the creation of green spaces within the city itself. Enthusiasm for this activity derived, of course, from a number of sources. It was, for example, plain that many urban dwellers had neither the leisure nor the income necessary to give them contact with nature on its own ground. There was as well an increasing tendency to emphasize the role that trees, boulevards and parks might play in making the city an aesthetically richer place, one capable of giving at least a measure of psychological satisfaction to its inhabitants. But whatever the reason for travelling in this direction, the destination was clear: an understanding of the land as a thing which worked its wonders to the benefit of, in ways permitted by, and now literally within, the metropolis.

Seeing the land in these terms did not, of course, always involve viewing it as altogether bereft of its traditional character as a place of naturalness and spontaneity. As late as the 1870s, recalled Ernest Thompson Seton, one could find more than a little of the old forest world in the mightiest Ontario city. "Not far," he remembered, "a quarter mile from our home, was Queen's Park, one hundred acres of virgin forest but little changed...[while] easterly was the Don Valley, a happy land of bosky hills and open meadows, abounding in bobolinks."[72] Even in the 1890s, reported clergyman and memorialist Henry Scadding, one could marvel at the noble survivors of the forest still to be seen in the midst of the metropolis.[73] The city dweller might even keep up his contact with agriculture and the farm. A 1910 observer noted:

> In Toronto, there is a large club for boys called the Broadview Boys' Institute....these boys have a field....and it is divided into farms of different sizes....you mustn't think that city boys know nothing about farming, even if they have never seen a threshing, or ridden on a hay rake.[74]

Yet, as the character of this contrived and artificial enterprise suggests, the city's voracious appetite for land made it increasingly necessary to see urban green spaces as capable of establishment, maintenance and preservation only as the result of a conscious and organized effort. Systematic activity of various kinds for the purpose of insuring the existence of such spaces was, accordingly, advocated by a number of commentators. Tree planting, thought some, was one way in which activity of this kind could yield a positive result. Such effort was, they explained, a particularly critical undertaking for reasons concerning the physical health of the city dweller. Cities, as one put it, fouled the air, giving off "carbonic gas" and other unpleasant excrescences. Trees, by contrast, absorbed these things while releasing life-giving oxygen. The "vitiation" of the air urban dwellers breathed could thus be avoided by bringing large numbers of these wonderful objects right into the heart of the city. There was, as a result, a clear "necessity of encouraging the growth of as much vegetation as possible within the limits of the cities themselves."[75] Indeed, enthused London's Park Superintendent, trees not only fostered physical health in the direct sense; they also did it by creating an atmosphere of calm and tranquillity. "What," after all, "can be more restful and refreshing to the tired limbs and weary eyes than when refreshed with green at every point?"[76]

If a concern with health moved these observers to support an organized approach to tree planting in cities, others were stimulated to propose similar action by a blend of aesthetic concern and a related desire to see Ontario cities evolve beyond a crude materialism. As early as 1865, one commentator pointed approvingly to the presence "in very many localities" of "choice lawns, flower borders, and even conservatories" as encouraging evidence that standards of taste and refinement were beginning to show themselves. There was, of course, some way to go before "these gratifying manifestations of elevated taste, and superiority to mere money-hoarding" achieved the standard set by "the splendid grounds and conservatory at Chestnut Park on Yonge Street," but that was all the more reason to encourage movement in the right direction.[77] By the first years of the twentieth century, reported another observer, much progress had been made. Developments had in fact become so marked, he thought—his flattery was intended to encourage its recipients to even greater efforts—that "citizenship had come to carry with it a noticeable tendency towards the pride in beautiful surroundings which brought fame to the cities of Greece for all time."[78]

The sense that a specific and planned place for trees, flowers, shrubs and grass must be made in city life was at its clearest in the arguments for parks. Not everyone, of course, thought that their place and function could be rigidly defined in terms absolutely consistent with the character and needs of their urban progenitors. Essayist and publisher G. Mercer Adam in fact considered the urban park to be a kind of refuge, a place—here he was speaking of Toronto's Queen's Park—of "escape from the hubbub and glare of the city," a means of retaining some of the naturalness and spontaneity of the old time.[79] Others, however, were plainly of the view that these spaces could be thought of as nothing other than deliberately created devices for enhancing the aesthetic dimension of urban life within the framework of a planned environment in a way that would produce a clearly intended effect. When, therefore, a spokesman for the City Beautiful movement, which was dedicated to making cities greener, better kept and more handsome places, called for "more park territory" for Toronto,[80] there was an expectation that it would take the form of "a great park system,"[81] a vast complex of planned spaces "integrated," as a recent student of the matter puts it, "into a system connected by parkways," all of this in its turn being done to facilitate the offering of "visual delight to vehicular traffic."[82]

The adoption by city dwellers of values consistent with the character of the new urban order—a world of planning, organization, systems, limits and confinement—could, it was occasionally thought, be explicitly encouraged by placing them in touch with a kind of green space specifically set up for that purpose. The establishment of urban playgrounds—again a qualification is necessary—was, of course, not always seen in these terms. One of their advocates linked his argument for them directly to pre-industrial times, asserting a need for a kind of "village green," "a few old-fashioned commons properly distributed within the city limits," where "growing lads and young men seeking healthful outdoor exercise near at hand" could get the sort of regenerating physical activity they needed.[83] Another, however, frankly framed his case in terms that took him far beyond this familar kind of concern with revitalization and uplift. This was so not simply in the sense that almost all of what he said was informed by assumptions reflecting a preoccupation with system and planning; it was a reality in the far more significant respect that his argument centered on the important role of recreational activity on these spaces in encouraging the development of principles of behaviour consistent with the needs of the new order. Exposure to recreational spaces in cities, Ontario's Superintendent of Neglected Children told a Toronto meeting of the Empire Club in 1907, would not only give contact with a healthy environment; the regulated, scheduled, competitive, skill-testing activities it involved would provide an "object lesson...of rational enjoyment." By thus encouraging a certain kind of outlook—here was the real point—it would build up the capacities of the urban child to be "successful in business, in school, or any other line."[84]

Understanding of the circumstances under which people came into contact with the land, not to mention the result expected from that contact, had thus changed in striking ways. That understanding now involved an extraordinary stress on planned action in the midst of the urban system. By defining the encounter between citizen and land in terms of order and regimentation, it fostered a way of thinking that was absolutely compatible with the structured nature of urban life; indeed, there were even indications that some kinds of activity were to be encouraged precisely because they inculcated values that would remove any lingering capacity the city dweller might have to be rather more a natural and spontaneous than a rational and controlled being. Confined and organized within the city system, the land as viewed by these observers thus lost, literally and figuratively, all vestiges of its position as the foundation of a separate and superior estate. There was, they thought, nothing in the quality of most peoples's contact with it to warrant seeing it as anything other than wholly subordinate to the new urban reality. First outpaced by the growth of that unpleasant phenomenon, then made its servant, and finally drawn into it altogether, the land at last had lost all capacity to sustain a community with a character and purpose of its own.

A striking illustration of this point can be seen in two attempts to restore the land to its once pre-eminent position. In neither case depending on an appeal to the kind of contact with the land experienced by most Ontarians— as the source of the problem the character of that contact could hardly function as part of the solution—these efforts turned instead on the creation of mental constructs which were, in principle, independent of the circumstances defining the experience of the people in whose heads they took shape. One of them, in the event, had only a limited success; the other, by contrast, established itself almost immediately in the depths of the Ontario consciousness. In combination, however, they made it clear that, so far at least as certain observers were concerned, any attempt to establish contact between man and landscape in a way that would allow it to be invested with the sort of comprehensive and general significance it had once possessed would now have to mean using methods of a quite unprecedented kind.

The first of these two devices functioned through the medium of memory. Whatever, insisted those who deployed it, might be true in the urbanizing present, man had had purifying contact with an abundant and uplifting landscape in the pioneer past. Looking back to the province's early days, savouring the details of the settlers' existence, accompanying them on their daily rounds, would thus, it followed, involve getting in touch—in the mind's eye at least—with a society most of whose people had lived the kind of authentic, innocent, elemental life which was now so plainly gone.

The picture of the pioneer past which was built up as a result of this attitude was, needless to say, highly romanticized. Pioneer men and women, their urban descendants were told, "lived near the beginnings of society" and had "to make, invent, adapt, and bear everything."[85] Theirs was, nonetheless, a "rude abundance"—"the virgin soil brought forth plentifully, deer roamed the forest, wild fowl swarmed in marsh and mere, and the lakes and rivers teemed with the finest fish."[86] Anything could be grown, and with almost no effort: "the seeds of melons when carelessly strewed upon the ground and covered, without any further attention attained a degree of perfection in size and flavour which sounds apocryphal."[87] "We had," as a Grand River pioneer remembered it, "a beautiful garden, a great abundance [of] roses, marigolds, hollyhocks, sunflowers, bachelor's buttons, violets and pansies, and an abundance of currant bushes, gooseberries, quinces, cherries."[88] It was, recalled another commentator, "a land flowing almost literally with oil, wine and honey,"[89] "a little bit"—here spoke a third—"of Arcadia."[90]

So long as this agreeable reminiscing was related to the present only in the sense that it permitted a kind of flight from it, it did its job in an effective and uncomplicated way. When the tie that bound it to the commentator's own time became more intricate and complex, however, matters began to go awry. Those who recalled the province's beginnings in order to do more than simply stimulate a journey in the mind did, of course, concede that the happy time of which they wrote was long ago and far away. But in also going beyond that point to celebrate the pioneer's possession of virtues— mostly associated with hard work and self-help—which had a place in their own day, they established a measure of common ground, a kind of bond, between their time and the pioneer past which by definition deprived that past of its separate, distanced, pure and innocent character. And when they went even further to imply that a full honouring of the pioneers' achievements required their descendants to be true to their sacrifice by working as they had worked, these commentators were encouraging a kind of behaviour which they considered to be fully relevant to the modern age. Thus, levered out of the past on the fulcrum of this presentist argument, lodged firmly at the centre of contemporary life, the pioneers became figures noticed for reasons precisely the opposite of those animating the commentators who had looked back to them and their time as a way of fleeing the urban order.

Emerging as early as the 1860s, when as one Hamilton newspaper put it, "the hardy pioneers" were "now disappearing from amongst us,"[91] treatment of the pioneer past in these terms almost always involved a focus on diligence, effort and sacrifice. Accordingly, insisted one journalist, the Huron Tract was settled by people who, "with no other capital than strong arms and stout hearts" had, "single-handed," cleared land and built homes while "struggling for years amid the privations of [the] pioneer's life."[92] The land in general, another was sure, could only have been brought under cultivation "by a class of settlers of strong purpose, unceasing industry, and indomitable perseverance."[93] Whatever form these utterances took, the basic message contained in them hardly varied: any failure by the present to cultivate the virtues of the pioneer past would be doubly unfortunate; bad in itself, it would also dishonour the memory and sacrifice of the founders.

If the pioneers found themselves pulled out of their simple past and made functioning parts of the age which had supplanted their own, their privileged and innocent status was abridged in other ways as well. All those who paid tribute to pioneer society as the harbinger of 'contemporary' values pointed with particular force—and an inescapable irony—to the very thing whose triumph had made recourse to the myth of the pioneer past seem necessary in the first place. Here, it should be noted, more was involved than such things as a simple stress on the farmers' role as "the forerunners of human civilization,"[94] or a general emphasis on the assertion that "the old Pioneers...found the country a wilderness, and by their toil and sweat have made it blossom like the rose."[95] Central to the argument was an explicit concern with the agriculturalist's place in generating what one observer of the Ontario scene called "an outburst of energy, that is building up factories, piercing the bowels of the earth, improving its cities and towns, and seeking new fields of venture."[96] It had been—the president of Toronto's National Club pressed the point home—"those lowly and obscure toilers in the midst of our trackless forest [who] laid broad and deep the foundations of Canada's position."[97] What, then, could be more obvious than that the pioneers, however tranquil and calm the existence they were held to have had in their own day, were also the first cause of the splendour, magnificence and energy now surrounding the urban observer?

Early Upper Canadians thus emerged from these rememberings as figures surrounded by doubt and ambiguity. They might, as many observers preferred, be conceived as innocent toilers in an idyllic age. Yet they were also seen as people who, in political economist Adam Shortt's words, "laid the foundation for our present...life,"[98] setting in motion the play of forces which would subvert the innocence and simplicity they themelves epitomized. In sum, even in memory the unambiguous virtue of wood and farm eluded capture. Gone in reality, it was proving itself beyond the reach of remembering as well.

If a concept built on memory and recollection turned out to yield results which were at best uncertain, perhaps, thought some Ontarians, an image fabricated in different ways with other materials would give a better return. Perhaps, they suggested, the people of the province could be confronted with a visual rendering of lake, forest, wood and rock so striking that contemplation of it would by itself excite the mind in a way which would lead directly to an apprehension of truth and beauty. This apprehension, indeed, might be so exalting and powerful that an altered state of consciousness—and, perforce, the uplift and regeneration of those experiencing it—would be produced.

The new vision of the north which began to emerge just before the Great War—culminating during and after it in the work of the Group of Seven—was, of course, the product of many influences, among which the new view of the forest, the thrust into New Ontario and the search for a uniquely Canadian landscape were central.[99] Yet it also reflected a mystical conviction, borne of a close familiarity with theosophy, transcendentalism and the work of the Scandinavian symbolist painters,[100] that imaginative contact with the land through exposure to a properly crafted symbolic representation would allow it to work its magic even more effectively than an actual physical presence in it. That this was so, these painters argued, derived from the fact that art must not simply imitate the externals of reality as a photograph did; its purpose was rather to expose to view the inner, essential, elements of that reality. It could, however, do this only if it managed to present what painters called the accidents—line, form, mass, colour and volume—of that reality in ways which made visible the inner truth whose existence they at once veiled and suggested. Since artists, thanks to their insight and sensitivity, had seen these accidents in the needed way, it fell to them to set them forth in a manner that permitted others to do so as well. What resulted—the work of art—thus presented the things which at once shrouded and gave access to this essential reality in a fashion that allowed viewers to see, as it were, through them so that they could have contact with what lay behind or beyond or within them. Contemplating the work, and the arrangement of line, form, mass, colour and volume of which it consisted, thus became the principal route of access to the higher truth and the special state that knowledge of it permitted one to experience. "Art"—the Group's Arthur Lismer summed up these notions years later—came out of

> a consciousness of harmony in the universe, the perception of the divine order running through all existence. The artist[,] sensitive to rhythm, the beat of life, creating in space and time the image of his reception of this order, projects his vision in the eternal language of line, tone, and colour, and creates not an imitative outward appearance of the common aspects of life, but an inner, more noble life than yet we all know.[101]

The elements of this credo were, of course, only vaguely in evidence before 1914. It was not, in fact, until 1913 that J. E. H. MacDonald and Lawren Harris travelled from Toronto to Buffalo, there to find reinforcement of what they were trying to do in the painting of the Scandinavian artists on exhibit in that city. That it was a work—A. Y. Jackson's *Terre Sauvage* (1913)—done by a friend who had not been with them which first succeeded in capturing something of the "mystic north"[102] suggests, however, that ideas of this sort were already very much at work in their circle. Harris, certainly, had been reading the American Transcendentalists as early as 1906.[103] And, he recalled years later, the exhibition's great contribution was not that it moved him and MacDonald in new directions but that it confronted them with "a large number of paintings which gave body to our rather nebulous ideas...Our purpose became clarified and our conviction reinforced."[104]

Whatever the precise character of the painters' doctrine in this early period, there can be no doubt that those who viewed their work underwent from the beginning an experience which was in all essentials defined by the impact on their sensibility and understanding of what they saw on the plane surface in front of them. This was true not simply in the sense that those who considered such paintings as Tom Thomson's *A Northern Lake* (1912–1913), MacDonald's *A Rapid in the North* (1913) or Jackson's *Terre Sauvage* might in consequence of their exposure to these works undergo the sort of mystical apprehension of an inner truth with which Harris was becoming increasingly concerned. Nor did it have merely to do with the fact that viewers would be using the power of intellect and imagination to assign their own meaning to a thing which was in itself the expression of a personal vision of the world, for they had always occupied a place of just that sort in relation to artists and their work.

What made the act of looking at these paintings so profoundly imaginative was the fact that it gave viewers their sole point of contact not only with the artist's vision but also with the thing depicted. Where gallerygoers considering a landscape by Homer Watson would be almost certain to have first-hand, and even extended, experience of Watson's settled and peaceful countryside, the same could not be said of viewers of the Group's work. Unless they were campers, cottagers or resortgoers—and even then their contact with forest, lake and shield would be severely limited—they would know what they were seeing thanks only to their exposure to the play of light and colour on the canvas before them. In eventually pointing out that these painters "did not live in the north...they lived in Toronto,"[105] the historian Frank Underhill thus managed to say only part of what needed noticing, for these were not simply paintings done by artists who themselves had little sustained contact with the land; they were—and the point is at least as important—produced for those who, having even less, were the more dependent for their sense of that land on what their minds and intellects could do with the artificial objects they found themselves confronting.

With the appearance of a device which turned on the assumption that the best link between man and landscape operated at the level of imagination rather than experience, a way of understanding that connection fundamentally different from those which had prevailed through much of the nineteenth century presented itself for the consideration of Ontarians. Distinguished from those others by its character as well as its content, in no way dependent for its validity on the fact that it reflected something of which its viewers would necessarily have sustained and close experience, the new configuration was exempt from the burden of having to be consistent with the style of life actually being lived by significant numbers of people in the present. In no way mirroring—as the imagery of farm, forest, park and playground had tried to mirror—the point of real and tangible contact between society's members and nature, and, therefore, in no way compelled to change as the nature of that contact changed, it found itself able to breast the constraints of time and decay in a way those others had been unable to do. Much more a thing of consciousness, idea and mind than they, it had a far larger capacity to stand forth in a fixed and permanent way, a vision projected—Lismer's phrase is worth repeating—"in the eternal language of line, tone, and colour,"[106] a phenomenon whose truth and appeal, unconnected to any sort of relationship it might have to the changing experiences of most Ontarians, could endure so long as there were minds to perceive it.

Over the course of a critical half century a substantial number of Ontario thinkers developed a set of images to explain their society's changing relationship to, and their own understanding of, the land. Each of these had at its core the idea that the encounter with the land—a source of well-being and uplift in both a figurative and literal sense—was to be seen in positive terms. Forced by constantly shifting circumstance gradually to concede that the land as most Ontarians experienced it was being drawn into the framework of a new kind of social, economic and geographical system, they never yielded on that central point.

With, however, the emergence of a belief that contemplation of the image rather than contact with the reality could do what was required, matters changed fundamentally. In leaving behind the nineteenth century's attempt to work out the relationship between landscape and regeneration in terms of the actual circumstances in which Ontarians lived, observers in the twentieth century would move increasingly to accomplish that goal in terms of the symbolic representation of a geographical mass which, while it made up almost all of the province, was wholly unknown to most of its people. They thus found themselves a far distance indeed from their predecessors, who had been able, albeit with difficulty, to celebrate the vitalizing power of the land on which they and their fellows actually stood.

1   Some historians have argued that early nineteenth-century observers also saw the forest in a positive light. Challenging the argument of literary critics such as Northrop Frye, they assert that, far from seeing the wilderness as harsh, intractable and overpowering, poets and writers were inspired by romantic modes of thinking to see it as sublime and uplifting. Some of these writers, as this study notes below, did see it in these terms. A comprehensive reading of texts produced in early nineteenth-century Upper Canada suggests, however, that enthusiasm for the land was most often manifest in relation to those parts of it which were perceived to have agricultural potential. For the argument of the literary critics, see Northrop Frye, "Conclusion", in C. F. Klinck et al., eds., *The Literary History of Canada* (Toronto, 1965); Marcia B. Kline, *Beyond the Land Itself: Views of Nature in Canada and the United States* (Cambridge, Mass., 1970); Margaret Atwood, *Survival: A Thematic Guide to Canadian Literature* (Toronto, 1972); and John Moss, *Patterns of Isolation in English Canadian Fiction* (Toronto, 1974). For some criticism of that argument, see Edward Dahl, *"Mid Forests Wild": A Study of the Concept of Wilderness in the Writing of Susanna Moodie, J. W. D. Moodie, Catharine Parr Traill and Samuel Strickland, c. 1830–1855* (Ottawa, 1973), who claims that the Upper Canadian reaction to the forest was both positive and negative, and M. L. MacDonald, "Literature and Society in the Canadas, 1830–1850" (Ph.D. diss., Carleton University, 1984), 321–55, who develops the view that it was almost entirely positive.
2   Susanna Moodie, "The Backwoodsman", in her *Roughing It in the Bush; or Life in Canada*, I (London, 1852), 123.
3   Samuel Strickland, *Twenty-Seven Years in Canada West...*, ed. Agnes Strickland, I (London, 1853), 65.
4   *Address Delivered Before the Provincial Agricultural Association at its Twelfth Annual Exhibition at Brantford, by George Alexander, of Woodstock, C.W.* (Toronto, 1857), 16.
5   Daniel Wilson, "The President's Address", *The Canadian Journal*, Mar. 1861, 119.
6   Alexander McLachlan, "Acres of Your Own", in his *Poems and Songs* (Toronto, 1874), 155.
7   See Morris Zaslow, *The Opening of the Canadian North 1870–1914* (Toronto, 1971), 147ff.
8   Beginning in the 1870s, "the province underwent tremendous urbanization and industrialization, developments that were promoted by considerable population movement and growth. This fundamental shift in the nature of Ontario society required major adjustments"; Donald Swainson, "Introduction", in his, ed., *Oliver Mowat's Ontario* (Toronto, 1972), 3.
9   Arthur H. Sinclair, *...Municipal Monopolies and Their Management* (Toronto, 1891), cited in Paul Rutherford, ed., *Saving the Canadian City: The First Phase 1880–1920* (Toronto, 1974), 6.
10 H. V. Nelles, *The Politics of Development...* (Hamden, Conn., 1974), 51.

11   *Ontario as a Home for the British Tenant Farmer Who Desires to Become His Own Landlord* (Toronto, 1886), 3.

12   "The Clay Belt in Ontario's Northland", *Farmer's Advocate...* [hereafter *FA*] (London, Ont.), 9 June 1910, 946; see also in *FA*: "The Ontario Pioneer Farm", 15 Sep. 1896, 370; "New Ontario Lands for Settlement", 15 Dec. 1898, 588; "The Opening of New Ontario", 1 Oct. 1901, 632; "The Golden Fleece in Canada", 8 Dec. 1904, 1,661; "Northern Ontario. Is it Suitable for Successful Agriculture?", 7 Dec. 1905, 1,731–32; "Agriculture in New Ontario", 29 Apr. 1909, 720–21; and also John Sharp, "New Ontario", *Queen's Quarterly* [hereafter *QQ*] 11 (1903), 76; Frank H. Newton, "The Northern Ontario Clay Belt", *Canadian Magazine* [hereafter *CM*] 35 (1910), 530.

13   Barry Dane, "National Health", *The Week* (Toronto), 30 Oct. 1884, 760.

14   C. C. James, "The Problems of a Farmer's Wife", *FA*, 9 Dec. 1909, 1,944.

15   William Wilfred Campbell, "Back to the Land", *FA*, 25 May 1905, 787.

16   "What Ails the Farm?", *FA*, 22 Feb. 1912, 313.

17   Adam Kidd, "The Huron Chief", in his *The Huron Chief and Other Poems* (Montreal, 1830), 34.

18   [William Dunlop], *Statistical Sketches of Upper Canada...* (London, 1832), 32.

19   [John Richardson], *Wacousta; or, the Prophecy. A Tale of the Canadas*, I (London, 1839), 7.

20   [J. L. Alexander], *Wonders of the West; Or a Day at the Falls of Niagara...A Poem, by A Canadian* (n.p., 1825), 23.

21   C. P. Traill, *The Backwoods of Canada* (London, 1852), 113.

22   "Forest Management", *The Canada Farmer*, 15 Jan. 1864, 1.

23   R. W. Phipps, "Forestry and the Necessity for its Practice in Ontario", in Canadian Institute of Toronto, *Proceedings*, 3rd ser., 3 (1884–85), 109–12.

24   Richard Lees, "Forestry Problems in Ontario", *QQ* 11 (1903), 110–11; Judson F. Clark, "The Forest as a National Resource", in Canadian Forestry Association, *Report of the Sixth Annual Meeting, Québec, March 9–10 1905* (Ottawa, 1905), 101. Clark was Ontario's provincial forester.

25   Nelles, 182–214.

26   A. Kemp and G. M. Grant, "From Toronto to Lake Huron", in G. M. Grant, ed., *Picturesque Canada: The Country as it Was and Is*, II (Toronto, 1882), 544.

27   J. Macdonald Oxley, "Through the Trackless Forest", *The Week*, 10 Oct. 1890, 713.

28   "The North", *The Canada Farmer*, 1 May 1868, 129.

29   R. W. Phipps, "Forestry", *FA*, 7 Jan. 1891, 17.

30   C. P. Traill, "Our Forest Trees", *Rose-Belford's Canadian Monthly*, July 1878, 95.

31   Alexander McLachlan, "May", in William Wilfred Campbell, comp., *The Oxford Book of Canadian Verse* (Toronto, 1913), 28.

32   Isabella Valancy Crawford, "Malcolm's Katie", in her *Old Spookses Pass, Malcolm's Katie, and Other Poems* (Toronto, 1884), 86.

33   Graeme Mercer Adam and A. Ethelwyn Wetherald, *An Algonquin Maiden: A Romance of the Early Days of Upper Canada* (Montreal, 1887), 13.

34   One result of which was the fact that poet Archibald Lampman could be described by his brother-in-law as "happiest when exploring new scenes in the forest land...[this] to him was the garden of nature"; Rev. Ernest Voorhis, "The Ancestry of Archibald Lampman, Poet", in Royal Society of Canada, *Proceedings and Transactions*, 3rd ser., vol. 15, sec. 2 (1921), 103. For another discussion of changing views of the forest and nature in this period, see George Altmeyer, "Three Ideas of Nature in Canada 1893–1914", *Journal of Canadian Studies* 11 (1976), 21–36.

35   Archibald Lampman, "Among the Timothy", in his *Among the Millet* (Ottawa, 1888), 14.

36   Lilian Ruth Milner, "Down on the Farm", *FA*, 31 July 1913, 1,330.

37   Roy I. Wolfe, "Ontario Summer Resorts in the Nineteenth Century", *Ontario History* 54 (1962), 159.

38   Alexander McLachlan, "The Pines", in his *Poems and Songs* (Toronto, 1874), 109.

39   W. R. Bradshaw, "The Georgian Bay Archipelago", *CM* 15 (1900), 16.

40   Crowquill, "Summer Holidays", *The Dominion Illustrated*, 3 Aug. 1889, 75.

41 William B. Varley, "Tourist Attractions in Ontario", *CM* 15 (1900), 29.

42 John Hague, "Aspects of Lake Ontario", *CM* 1 (1893), 263.

43 Varley, "Tourist Attractions", 29.

44 A. Stevenson, "Camping in the Muskoka Region", *The Week*, 13 May 1886, 382.

45 [The Editor], "Canada and the Tourist", *CM* 15 (1900), 4.

46 "Muskoka as a Summer Resort", *FA*, 3 Aug. 1905, 1,095.

47 W. R. Robson, "The Upper Ottawa", *The Dominion Illustrated*, 11 May 1889, 302.

48 Bruce W. Hodgins and Jamie Benedickson, "Resource Management Conflict in the Temagami Forest 1898 to 1914", in Canadian Historical Association, *Historical Papers* (1978), 162.

49 Ross Harkness, *J. E. Atkinson of the Star* (Toronto, 1963), 70–71.

50 Ernest Thomson Seton, *Trail of an Artist-Naturalist* (New York, 1940), 374–85.

51 Hodgins and Benedickson, 164; see also "A Boy's Camp in Temagami", *Rod and Gun* 10 (1908), 49–51.

52 K., "A Short Ramble in June", *Saturday Reader*, 14 July 1866, 289.

53 Samuel Thompson, *Reminiscences of a Canadian Pioneer...* (Toronto, 1884), 108.

54 Fidelis, "The Thousand Islands", *Canadian Monthly and National Review*, July 1874, 42-47; Frederic W. Falls, "The Thousand Isles", *CM* 4 (1894), 148–63.

55 Thos. W. Gibson, "Algonquin National Park", *CM* 3 (1894), 542–55.

56 See Hodgins and Benedickson, 161.

57 "Muskoka Summer", *The Dominion Illustrated*, 15 Nov. 1890, 326.

58 W., "Lotos-Eating in Muskoka", *The Week*, 30 Aug. 1889, 618.

59 Catherine Blinfield, "Muskoka Days and Doings", *CM* 5 (1895), 486; see also E. Maurice Smith, "Muskoka, The Summer Playground of Canada", *CM* 21 (1903), 33–38; William T. James, "Midsummer in Muskoka", *CM* 11 (1898), 225; and M. Forsyth Grant, "Camping in Muskoka", *The Dominion Illustrated*, 14 June 1890, 382–83.

60 Bernard McEvoy, "Prologue", in his *Away From Newspaperdom, and Other Poems* (Toronto, 1897), 9.

61 "The Eve of the Trolley Age", *FA*, 1 May 1901, 291.

62 A. W. Campbell, "Artistic Country Roads", *CM* 8 (1897), 214.

63 Frank Yeigh, "The Queen Victoria Niagara Falls Park", *CM* 39 (1912), 541.

64 Campbell, "Country Roads", 218.

65 W. Rideout Wadsworth, "With Rifle and Rod in the Moose Lands of Northern Ontario", *CM* 13 (1899), 262.

66 Fidelis, "The Thousand Islands", *Canadian Monthly and National Review*, July 1874, 44.

67 H. V. P., "A Three Weeks' Fishing Trip to Muskoka", *Rose-Belford's Canadian Monthly*, July 1880, 20.

68 Falls, 153.

69 Agnes Maule Machar, for example, extolled the Thousand Islands in her poem "The Happy Islands" in these terms: "Fair do they seem as Eden/ When Eden was newly made, To the weary city toilers,/ Who seek their grateful shade." See her *Days of the True North and Other Canadian Poems* (Toronto, 1902), 66.

70 Gibson, 543.

71 "A Holiday Jaunt: The Niagara District", *FA*, 21 June 1906, 1,001.

72 Seton, 62.

73 Henry Scadding, "Survivors of the Forest in Toronto", *The Week*, 8 Dec. 1893, 38.

74 "Farming in the City", *FA*, 31 May 1906, 897; see also Puck, "Some City Farmers", *FA*, 10 Mar. 1910, 413.

75 "Effects of Vegetation in Cities", *FA*, 1 Jan. 1875, 10.

76 John S. Pearce, "Value of Street Trees", *FA*, 9 Aug. 1906, 1,255.

77 "Hon. D. L. McPherson's Grounds and Conservatory", *The Canada Farmer*, 1 Dec. 1865, 364.

78 Horace Boultbee, "Toronto: A City of Homes", *CM* 32 (1909), 299.

79 G. Mercer Adam, "Toronto & Vicinity", in G. M. Grant, ed., *Picturesque Canada:...*, I (Toronto, 1882), 433.

80 Jean Graham, "The City Beautiful", *CM* 31 (1908), 177.
81 Byron E. Walker, "A Comprehensive Plan for Toronto", in Canadian Club of Toronto, *Addresses 1905–06* (Toronto, 1906), 134–39, cited in Rutherford, ed., 224.
82 This was an idea developed in the Toronto Guild of Civic Art's *Report on a Comprehensive Plan for Systematic Improvement in Toronto* (Toronto, 1909); see W. Van Nus, "The Fate of City Beautiful Thought in Canada, 1893–1930", in Canadian Historical Association, *Historical Papers* (1975), 197.
83 "A Plea for the Village Green", *The Week*, 16 Aug. 1895, 896.
84 J. J. Kelso, "The Play Spirit and Playgrounds in Toronto", in Empire Club of Canada, *Addresses 1907–1908*, (Toronto, 1908), 181.
85 Rev. W. W. Smith, "Backwoods Proverbs", *New Dominion Monthly*, Mar. 1877, 220.
86 William Henry Withrow, *A History of Canada for the Use of Schools and General Readers* (Toronto, 1876), 120.
87 Robina and Kathleen M. Lizars, *In the Days of the Canada Company, 1825–1850* (Toronto, 1896), 55.
88 Charles Durand, *Reminiscences...* (Toronto, 1897), 42–43.
89 C. O. Ermatinger, *The Talbot Regime, or the First Half Century of the Talbot Settlement* (St. Thomas, 1904), 1.
90 William Wye Smith, "Illustrations of Canadian Life—Part II", *Rose-Belford's Canadian Monthly*, Mar. 1882, 233.
91 "Prospectus", *Canadian Illustrated News* (Hamilton, 8 Nov. 1862); see also William Canniff, *History of the Settlement of Upper Canada (Ontario), With Special Reference to the Bay Quinté* (Toronto, 1869).
92 J. C. S., "A Summer Outing", *FA*, 28 July 1904, 1,024.
93 "The Romance of Ontario's Unexampled Agricultural Progress", *FA*, 13 Dec. 1906, 1,934.
94 Lizars, 375.
95 James Young, *Reminiscences of the Early History of Galt...* (Toronto, 1880), 73.
96 J. L. S., "Sketches in Upper Canada", *New Dominion Monthly*, Dec. 1867, 140.
97 William K. McNaught, "Pioneers of the Canadian Farm", in J. Castell Hopkins, ed., *Canada: An Encyclopaedia of the Country*, V (Toronto, 1899), 19.
98 Adam Shortt, "Life of the Settler in Western Canada Before the War of 1812", *QQ* 22 (1914), 88.
99 Douglas L. Cole, "Artists, Patrons, and Public: An Enquiry Into the Success of the Group of Seven", *Journal of Canadian Studies* 13 (1978), 69–78.
100 Roald Nasgaard, "Canada: The Group of Seven, Tom Thomson, and Emily Carr", in his *The Mystic North: Symbolist Landscape Painting in Northern Europe and North America 1890–1940* (Toronto, 1984), 158–202.
101 Arthur Lismer, "Canadian Art", *Canadian Theosophist*, 14 Feb. 1925, 178.
102 J. E. MacDonald, "Scandinavian Art", lecture, Art Gallery of Toronto, 17 Apr. 1931, cited in Nasgaard, 160, and reprinted in *Northward Journal*, no. 18/19 (1980), 9–35.
103 Dennis Reid, "Lawren Harris", *Artscanada*, 25 Dec. 1968, 13.
104 Lawren Harris, "The Group of Seven in Canadian History", in Canadian Historial Association, *Annual Report* (1948), 31.
105 Frank H. Underhill, "False Hair on the Chest", *Saturday Night*, 3 Oct. 1936, 1, cited in Mary Vipond, "Ideas of Nationalism in English Canada in the 1920's" (Ph.D. diss., University of Toronto, 1975), 517.
106 Lismer, 178.

The Quest for the Kingdom: Aspects of Protestant Revivalism in Nineteenth-Century Ontario

NEIL SEMPLE

A fundamental transformation occurred in Protestant religion in Ontario during the nineteenth century. Into an environment defined by Anglican and Calvinist ideologies came not only the Wesleyan churches but, equally important, a new personal commitment to vital religion spawned by Wesley's English revival and the American "Great Awakening." Anglicans, Baptists, Congregationalists, Lutherans, Presbyterians and many with no previous religious belief were caught up in the revival and either altered their church

The Camp Meeting at Grimsby, held 25 August 1859

affiliation or became active supporters of a personal, experimental spirituality within their own denominations. Inspired by the twin goals of converting the individual and spurring the community along the path of spiritual and ethical growth, revivalism became one of the pre-eminent concerns of the nineteenth-century, English-speaking world and redefined the very nature of religious expression.[1]

As the century wore on, however, neither the churches nor secular Ontario could withstand the social and intellectual changes associated with urbanization, by which is meant the growth of cities and their increasing ability to define society's norms. The city was not only a formidable consolidation of people; it also helped create individuals qualitatively distinct from those who remained outside its influence. Urbanization developed an ethos which came to be expressed in a bewildering range of traits—"progress, tolerance, culture, decay, sin, alienation"[2] as well as respectability and order—and all of these became associated with city living. Further, as the pattern of towns and cities became fixed and integrated through improved transportation and communication networks, new ideas and a new openness to ideas reshaped the entire cultural fabric of Ontario. Church leaders recognized this process, and, in various ways, introduced values and approaches to meet the perceived needs of the larger urban centres. Although the process was neither even nor universal, both the essence and the institutions of revival were altered by the geographical and intellectual changes triggered by urbanization.[3] Despite its transformation, however, revivalism has continued to fulfil a meaningful role in twentieth-century Protestantism.

What follows is an examination of the transformation of both revivalism and revival institutions in Ontario during the nineteenth century, especially as they adapted to suit the perceived needs of an urbanizing society. The focus will be on the Methodists since they were both the natural heirs of Wesley's spiritual revolution and the leading exponents of the popular techniques of mass evangelism. Nevertheless, it must be remembered that revivalism significantly influenced all evangelical Protestants irrespective of their denominational labels.

Methodism from its inception was religion in earnest.[4] John Wesley, however, had never intended to appeal exclusively to emotional experience and found the accompanying enthusiasm rather repugnant to good taste and healthy spiritual growth.[5] Conversion and sanctification involved discipline and this could be seriously weakened by the loss of control associated with a highly emotional state. Yet, while he was initially shocked by such conduct at Methodist gatherings, Wesley endorsed a pragmatic approach to revival[6] and came to accept enthusiasm as a legitimate expression of religion. Emotion was as much a part of man as reason; if God chose to work through this means, Wesley could not refute the beneficial results.[7]

Mass evangelism, the principal embodiment of revival in the nineteenth century, took various forms in Ontario but in all its manifestations it stressed a simple, straightforward, highly charged appeal to spiritual regeneration. Much of the subtlety of John Wesley's theology—with its four pillars of Scripture, Tradition, Reason and Experience[8]—was forgotten and there remained only a narrow body of doctrine and a powerful co-ordinating discipline. Revivals did not seek to elaborate theological debate nor to analyze denominational peculiarities; rather, they established absolutes to be obeyed. Methodist revivalism assured the individual that although salvation was not guaranteed, it was promised to all. However, it could only be achieved by a deep personal rebirth and a continuous struggle for a purer religious condition.

Mass evangelism was particularly effective in creating an environment in which the individual could "experience" his fallen state and seek Christ's forgiveness. Although the conflict had to be fought alone, the group could stimulate this personal decision. As Arthur Kewley points out:

> In this corporate setting a man's mind, heart and will are so
> strongly touched that he must make a personal decision one
> way or the other. The crowd is not the important factor in a
> man's conversion, but it has a significant place in helping
> man to that condition of loneliness in which he must seek
> God or die.[9]

Revivals thus utilized the social context of the group to break down the barriers imprisoning the free movement of the spirit and created the vital climate enabling man to break away from the corrupt world. In this way, the unbeliever became convinced of his sinfulness, the backslider sought to renew his religious pledge, and the new convert gained a fresh impulse toward a state of holiness.[10]

Revival services, especially, tended to stress mass emotional expression as the most legitimate basis for social conversion. Salvation clearly depended on reason as well as emotion, but past experience had shown that reason too easily abandoned faith for a godless, skeptical rationalism.[11] Furthermore, revivals naturally evoked earnest expression under the power of the Holy Spirit. J. Wesley Johnston, a prominent American preacher, claimed, "He inspires, He arouses, He stimulates; He awakens the dormant energies, He stirs up the latent faculties, He creates zeal, He calls forth enthusiasm".[12] Occurrences which might appear fanatical to the skeptical observer were not to be questioned since they were only the legitimate expression of that spiritual presence.[13] Early opposition was accordingly dismissed as the unsound criticism of the unsaved. The proof rested on the numerical growth in the congregations and the vitality of the normal church operations.

While the church sought this deep spiritual commitment in all its religious exercises, the most distinctive revival services in Upper Canada were the *camp meeting* and the *protracted meeting*. Since they were only rarely used by other denominations in the province, they became indissolubly linked to the various Methodist connexions. For those who acknowledged the positive attributes of the services, Methodism gained the credit; for those who scoffed at the strange conduct and questioned the validity of the salvation experience, Methodism was obliged to bear the stigma of a coarse, fanatical denomination.[14]

The camp meeting movement originated in the United States in the 1790s and was especially popular in what Whitney Cross has characterized as the "burned-over" district of upstate New York.[15] Camp meetings were large open-air gatherings which lasted for several days. Numbers of individuals and families would travel to a prearranged location and construct a temporary village of tents. The Reverend Samuel Coate of Montreal, one of the early organizers of camp meetings in Canada, witnessed a major gathering in New York and attempted to analyze the phenomenon:

> I attended a Camp meeting last June (1805) in [New] York State near the city of Albany where there were visible displays of the power and presents of God....On the sabbath day the rain was measurably over, and the number that attended was computed to be about four thousand...a number protest to be converted, and a great many more to have the work deepened in their hearts....A volume might be written to particularise every circumstance, however, it lasted upwards of three days, and upon the whole I believe great good was done. I impute the gracious effects of Camp Meetings partly to their novelty exciting different emotions in the mind—setting the passions a float and thereby rendering the heart more accessible—and partly to their nature, or continuance without intermission. The ears of the people being momently saluted with the sound of preaching, singing, and prayer; at length they are under the influence of these exercises so much, that when you speak to them, they melt down like wax before the fire. It is not an uncommon thing for them to imagine they hear the same noise in the woods a week or a fortnight afterwards. We had many flaming Preachers at the Meeting, more filled with faith and the holy Ghost.[16]

Drawing on such experiences, Canadian Methodists organized their own camp meetings in Upper Canada. In the absence of large, permanent buildings, they quickly recognized the value of camp meetings in assembling large crowds. John Carroll, a leading Methodist promoter of camp meetings, described the establishment of the first camp meeting he attended. It was organized in 1825 at Cummer's Mills just north of present-day Toronto. A week before the revival, a large board tent and preaching stand were erected; slab seats were arranged in a gentle slope ringing the stand; and the whole encampment was surrounded by a high stockade to keep out intruders. During the meeting guards would be stationed at the gates to minimize rowdyism. Finally, the site was cleared of brush and arrangements were made for a supply of water and firewood.[17]

Isolated from outside influences and temporal distractions, the camp meeting could create a deeply religious environment. A succession of preaching, exhorting, singing, prayer and confession stimulated the basic spiritual drives of the participants. Usually four or five itinerants and as many lay preachers alternated in rousing the listeners and leading them step by step until they became so emotionally and psychologically immersed that they had to acknowledge their own sinfulness and seek repentance. As well, the familiarity that tended to break down social inhibitions created an intense sense of community and a kinship of the spirit. Under these combined pressures, it was difficult to avoid being swept along with the tide of fervour.

Camp meetings in Upper Canada were vitally connected with the established organization of the Methodist church. They were neither spontaneous nor independent of institutional control; the discipline and authority of the church were always present.[18] In fact, success depended on detailed planning and skilled leadership both before and during the services. Though spiritual conduct was spontaneous, sermons, exhortation and prayer followed a regular timetable as the clergy sought to channel the release of spiritual energy into a responsible religious growth. Almost as essential, order was a major priority.[19] Nevertheless, despite their Methodist links, camp meetings still crossed denominational boundaries in their appeal and influence. Individual Baptists, Anglicans, Presbyterians, as well as members of the smaller denominations and, more critically, those who disdained organized religion altogether, joined in the quest for a new spiritual awareness and, ultimately, the Kingdom of God. Often preachers from all the evangelical denominations shared the preacher's stand and reaped the benefits in new members.

Camp meetings, however, were obviously restricted to the summer or early fall when the weather permitted outdoor activities. Increasingly as the province became more settled and urban centres grew, large permanent buildings were available for year-round protracted meetings. They performed a similar and equally important role in more conventional surroundings.[20] As its name implies, the protracted meeting involved an extended series of afternoon and evening gatherings lasting from a few days to several months.[21] This daily communion created a significantly pious and fervent climate. It retained many of the qualities of the camp meeting in an urban setting and offered several particular advantages as well. It was not drastically affected by the weather and, since the gatherings were necessarily smaller due to the limitations of the buildings, a warm sense of fellowship and shared experience was possible. It was also much easier to control rowdyism and to discipline and direct those in attendance. As well, participants could return home after the service to carry out necessary chores or to sleep. Although this broke the sense of isolation, the preachers would normally visit the penitent during the day to continue their spiritual nurturing.[22] Moreover, since the work was centred on one congregation, a degree of continuity and fellowship was provided to assist the new convert. This offered an opportunity to make the conversions more conscientious and permanent.

Until about 1840 in Old Ontario, the picture of revivals remained basically the same. Although there were peaks and valleys, the procedures rarely changed. In an important sense, mass evangelism blended into the rhythm of provincial life and merged into the social conventions of the times. Like barn raisings or fall fairs, revivals permitted a social and recreational outlet as well as spiritual renewal. Community projects, political changes or questions of moral reform often owed their first public expression to the informal associations begun at revival services.[23] On a different level, they also permitted young people to meet in an appropriately controlled setting.[24] Such opportunities were scarce and necessarily prized by those involved.

Even with this basic institutionalization of revivals, the churches were constantly obliged to meet two criticisms. First, it was claimed that the results were transitory and wildly distorted; second, both rampant enthusiasm and rowdyism added an inherent impropriety and unrespectability to the proceedings. In response, nearly every report about revivals by the church made it clear that the new converts were carefully examined and, as much as possible, their change of heart was authenticated.[25] The leaders kept careful statistics and attempted to measure the long-term increases in the surrounding congregations. Nevertheless, because of backsliding and the transitory nature of "enthusiasm," the reliability of their statistics must be seriously questioned.[26]

As for the second criticism, this was more difficult to answer. Although emotional conduct was not considered excessive when it reflected the presence of the Holy Spirit, the leaders of revivals did try to direct enthusiasm to its proper ends and at appointed times—a goal that became especially important as revivals centred their operations in the larger towns and cities. Rowdyism, however, was something different. This kind of conduct could never be totally removed, and indeed all public gatherings—from picnics to barn raisings—had a rowdy nature quite normal by the standards of the times. Yet, that said, rowdyism did pose a problem for the church. While church reports normally discounted such disruptions, often maintaining that no rowdyism was present,[27] the stockades and guards remained as stark testimony to the threat. In their defence, however, it must be remembered that revivals were not originally designed for the ardent churchgoer; rather they were to transform the sinner. It was the drunken troublemaker who represented the most prized catch at a revival.[28] To keep him or her out would undermine a central purpose of the services. Revivals were not designed to be exclusive; they aimed at reshaping the entire community.

In more general terms, revivals did much more than convert individuals. The anti-Calvinism, antidenominationalism and ethical concerns within revivalism, and its tendency to enlarge the role and power of the laity in relation to the functions and professional leadership of the ordained clergy, effectively challenged the pre-established conception of the church and thereby redirected evangelical Christianity.[29] In effect, revivals reasserted the early church's assumption that all the people were called as ministers to enlarge and defend God's kingdom. Since preaching and exhorting were the principal means of imparting spiritual knowledge, a laity called to preach clearly undercut the Calvinist view that preaching was reserved for the ordained.[30]

Furthermore, the essence of revivalism stood in stark contrast to Calvinist notions of election and predestination, and drew Protestants to a Wesleyan position. While Baptists, Presbyterians, Anglicans, as well as Methodists were attracted to the potential of revival, it was Wesley's emphasis on prevenient grace—a kernel of goodness residing in man even after Adam's fall—which allowed mankind the freedom to receive God's ubiquitous grace.[31] This was not free will, but it did allow a more active participation in spiritual reformation and acted to stimulate even greater revivals. So profound was the impact of Wesley's revivalism in Ontario that by the close of the nineteenth century predestination was rarely preached and its theological implications were either abandoned or ignored.

Revivalism was also characterized in a broader sense by a new interdenominationalism, or more accurately, antidenominationalism, at least among evangelical churches. Traditional loyalties were shattered and new patterns of ecclesiastical organization took their place. Revival ministers often attacked institutional notions of the church. "Above all," as one scholar has noted, "they thought of themselves as instruments of the work of God, which was independent of all traditional forms of religious life. For that reason they insisted that the true church was invisible, except as it became visible in limited, tentative and purified form in the wake of their preaching."[32] The older denominations in Ontario held their own only when they came to terms with the revival message. Not only did revivalism attract support from all evangelical Christians, it diminished peculiar denominational doctrine and simplified theology so that all might share in "the great, central, saving truths" of Christianity. On another level, revivalism reinforced antidenominationalism since it emphasized social and ethical concerns as central elements in the progress to Heaven. After gaining a personal conversion, the individual had to strive for a continuing growth in grace through the appointed means of the church and also through "good works."[33] Such a thrust transcended denominational theology and dogma and placed Christian charity squarely in the mainstream of religious practice. Allies from all churches were welcome in the fight for a moral world.

While revivalism thus expanded the function of the laity, undermined denominational exclusiveness and Calvinist theology and stressed ethical conduct,[34] it most critically attacked formality and demanded commitment from the entire religious community in the battle to save souls. Any missed opportunity created incredible anxiety; the eternal damnation of the lost soul was the source of terrible emotional pain. As a consequence, this awful responsibility unleashed a determination which conquered personal hardship in the quest to evangelize the world. The great call of the age was to raise Christ's standard throughout all nations.

However, revivalism also released a myriad of countervailing forces as the century advanced. It spun off literally hundreds of splinter churches with their own particular perception of revivalism. Most believed that the mainline denominations had themselves abandoned individual salvation to present-world concerns and later to liberal theology. With the breakdown of denominational loyalties and with a conception of *church* that abandoned ecclesiastical bonds and exalted voluntary association, there was little to restrain this movement.

Paradoxically, revivalism also gave a higher profile to what William Westfall has called "the shadow of progress."[35] A variety of apocalyptic groups emerged to condemn the entire notion of real progress and to look for the immediate end of the world and the personal rule of Christ. While these groups built on the same theological and experiential ideologies as the evangelical revival, and drew their support from the same clientele, they took their beliefs to a conclusion which the older denominations could only condemn. The mainline churches never subscribed to Adventist notions of an early return of Christ.[36]

Perhaps the greatest impact of the eighteenth-century Wesleyan movement and its early nineteenth-century manifestations was the demands it made on its adherents. Methodism created a sense of fellowship[37] which assaulted the familiar relations of class, occupation, race, church and even family. In their stead, it offered the intimacy and discipline of the class meeting, the prayer meeting, and the love feast, as well as the fraternity of the shared quest for salvation.[38] A profound sense of oneness was born among believers which permitted and even demanded that the individual sever former social and economic ties.

While all religious movements offer a sense of community, the attractiveness of Methodism lay in its openness, not its exclusiveness. All were free to enter. Although it demanded separation from the corrupt world, it never became isolated from the society at large. It was under too heavy an obligation to evangelize to shut itself off in utopian experimentation. This receptiveness also permitted the crossing of linguistic and national boundaries. Methodism was not the church of the English or Scottish or German; in Old Ontario, therefore, it acted to break down ethnic boundaries and ease assimilation of immigrants into an Upper-Canadian society. Equally, the success of Methodism lay in its missionary organization. Without the necessity of a settled parish organization, its itinerancy could reach out and touch the lives of Upper Canadians more quickly than other ecclesiastical bodies. It was also more adept at addressing the personal and practical needs of the pioneer settler.[39]

Through the mass evangelism of camp and protracted meetings, the intimacy and fellowship of the love feast and class meeting went public. These institutions expanded the communal nature of Wesley's original revival and permitted a significant fulfilment of his mission.[40] They also became major instruments in the evangelization of the English-speaking world and were originally so successful in Upper Canada because of the weak church authority and the limited presence of normal church services.

Nevertheless, Old Ontario was not a static, isolated community. It was linked to the international, cosmopolitan centres and shared in the new ideologies and priorities affecting Anglo-American society. Through its own maturing urban centres and social institutions with their burgeoning wealth and intellectual sophistication, these values were distilled during the nineteenth century into more appropriate patterns of religious fellowship and social order. Under this new order, class, race and kinship would also re-emerge to bind the community. The new broader values helped to impose three important changes on traditional mass evangelism. First, the new agency of professional evangelists appeared and reflected the initial challenge to old-style revivals by urbanization. While these evangelists at first increased the popularity of revivals, they later shared and even accelerated their wider transformation. Second, although remaining popular, the normal revival institutions declined in relative importance and were significantly altered to meet the perceived needs of urban-industrial society. And third, a major rift developed between the emphasis on revivalism and mainline Protestantism.

By the late 1830s and early 1840s, mass evangelism was in decline. Perhaps its novelty was gone; perhaps there were sufficient regular church services to take its place. Certainly, mass gatherings were frowned upon in the post-rebellion period, especially when arousing emotional fervour was the avowed purpose. However, the new phenomenon of professional, travelling evangelists gave revivals a new lease on life and indeed dramatically expanded their appeal.

Evangelists such as Lorenzo Dow and Charles Finney[41] had earlier made their mark on American and British evangelical Protestantism, but none had ever sustained a mission in British North America. The first such revivalist in Canada was James Caughey. Born in Ireland about 1810, Caughey was raised in the United States and entered the regular Methodist ministry. In 1840, after receiving what to him was a special call from God to evangelize Great Britain,[42] he set out from upstate New York via Lower Canada and the Maritimes. In the early winter of 1840, he was delayed in Quebec City by the urge to preach and joined William Harvard in a revival in that city. Harvard himself became an able spokesman for mass evangelism.[43] After three successful months at protracted meetings and temperance gatherings, Caughey repeated the work throughout the spring of 1841 at St. James Street Methodist Church in Montreal, one of the largest Protestant churches in the Province.[44]

Years later, after Caughey had earned an international reputation, this early endeavour was perhaps given greater signficance than at the time. Nonetheless, considering that Caughey and Harvard were ministering to British Wesleyans, with their deep-seated hostility to revivalistic techniques,[45] and that they were operating in the cautious political and religious setting of Lower Canada shortly after the Rebellions of 1837–38, their work must be considered eminently successful. According to some sources, over 500 were converted and over 120 were placed on trial in Methodist congregations in Montreal alone.[46] Of equal significance, the achievement was attributed to Caughey the professional evangelist. Harvard reported:

> ...while the works of conversion and entire sanctification were both encouragingly going on among us previously to the coming of our beloved brother [Caughey]; yet...the rapid and extended spread of that grace is mainly to be attributed to the blessing of God which has accompanied the impressive and evangelical ministry, and fervent and persevering toils in the prayer-meetings, of that beloved servant of God.[47]

Subsequently, Caughey visited Canada on several occasions. From Christmas 1852 until March 1853 he was in Kingston where "1028 registered some special Blessing" and "183 afterwards professed to be sanctified."[48] From the 24th of March until the 5th of July, he laboured in Hamilton and had great success among both the clerical and lay leaders in the city. There, under Caughey's guidance, 630 were converted "from the world," by which was meant from among persons with no prior religious commitment, 103 were converted from among other (non-Methodist) denominations and over 400 continued to meet in Methodist classes after his departure. In describing this revival, John Carroll wrote:

> ...we must also say, that the original, searching and deeply spiritual preaching of our friend [Caughey,] clothed as it was by so rich an unction of the Spirit; and the influence of his name, joined to what I may be allowed to call his admirable revival tactics, by which the official and praying members, and indeed the whole church, were enlisted, and their efforts directed in the work of saving souls, were the principal immediate means, under God, of this revival.[49]

In 1856 Caughey evangelized Belleville and Brockville and was still "a burning and shining light"[50] in the interest of earnest revivalism. He powerfully influenced young men such as William Parker, Henry Tew and Nicholas Willoughby to enter the Methodist ministry and indirectly had a similar effect on Albert Carman, later head of the Methodist Church, and Nathanael Burwash, who trained succeeding generations of ministers at Victoria College.[51] The *Christian Guardian* and other Methodist publications cited the urban-centred, professionally led protracted meetings as model gatherings which should be imitated across the province. Since cities were transportation and communication centres, especially after the arrival of the railway and telegraph, mass evangelism could draw on a larger hinterland and, equally important, the revival techniques and message were broadcast by the newspapers to a national and international audience. The later 1850s, in fact, represented the peak of institutional revivals in Ontario.

After Caughey's success, Ontario became a fertile field for international revivalists. Each in turn reinforced the basic intellectual elements of revivalism: antidenominationalism, lay participation, ethical conduct and opposition to Calvinist exclusiveness. Their individual success was based as well on the key doctrines they preached, their organizational ability and, to a degree, the novelty they brought to the services. Dr. Walter and Mrs. Phoebe Palmer were notable personalities at Canadian camp meetings throughout the third quarter of the nineteenth century; Mrs. Palmer was especially effective in strengthening the active role of the laity in preaching. In fact, her talent, commitment and money were critical elements in the renewed revivalism throughout North America and she was particularly influential within the American Methodist church in fostering the holiness movement, which preached the necessity of achieving entire sanctification through individual conversion.[52] Samuel Jones, another American Methodist evangelist, based his success on his "quaint" style and antidenominationalism. Using folksy expressions and a Wesleyan theology reduced to a few simple principles, he preached spiritual renewal, temperance and social fellowship. His hope was to introduce rudimentary religion to a mass audience rather than to increase the strength of any particular denomination. In Toronto he preached: "A man who has got no religion at all, he is not sectarian. If he's got a great deal, he is not sectarian; but if he's got enough religion to make him sectarian, he is the most despicable I ever saw on earth."[53] Other less well-known evangelists also had significant, although more circumscribed, success. A young Henry Bland, for instance, recorded in 1858 that "I felt greatly quickened and blessed by the service" led by William French,[54] and Nathanael Burwash later recalled the important work of "California" Taylor in revival services in 1862.[55] In the 1880s Edward Payson Hammond visited the major centres in Ontario and combined "brilliant literary attainments and deep biblical research" with the simple, popular attributes of a "great actor."[56] By way of novelty, he directed his message at children and drew in his larger audience from this base. As well, he preached in Baptist and Prebyterian churches and thus gained support from across a broad Protestant spectrum.

Among native Canadian preachers, the most popular and effective were Ralph C. Horner and the team of John Hunter and Thomas Crossley. Horner was an evangelist within the Montreal Conference of the Methodist Church and preached in the Ottawa Valley and Eastern Ontario in the 1880s and 1890s. Later he would form his own church, the Holiness Movement Church of Canada (Hornerites). Crossley and Hunter preached throughout English Canada from the mid 1880s until well into the twentieth century. Modelling themselves on the team of Dwight L. Moody and Ira Sankey, they represented the summit of professional evangelism in Canada and their influence is still remembered.

The early achievements of most of these evangelists were based on the clear and constant preaching of conversion and entire sanctification.[57] Entire sanctification, complete holiness, Christian perfection—the terms were synonymous—was a Wesleyan doctrine[58] demanding a further growth in grace after conversion. Gradually, through prayer, maturing experience and good works, the convert might ascend this second peak of faith and achieve a perfect, earthly love of God. Although backsliding to damnation remained an ever-present possibility, it was the quest for holiness that became the consuming passion of revivalism in the last half of the nineteenth century. As Canadians increasingly grew up in a sound religious environment, the search for a state of grace higher than that of the commonality of the Protestant community became the rallying cry of the evangelist.[59]

The evangelists' success was also founded on what Carroll called "admirable revival tactics." Revivalists knew from experience and training how to draw in their audience and bring it to the critical moment of decision. Despite their autonomy from congregational or denominational links, they were also deeply indebted to the active co-operation of both and especially to the assistance of the local clergy and laity. Long before they arrived on the scene, preparations were under way. Often beginning with special prayer meetings, the revival gradually led to a widening of the circle of people promoting it until a large proportion of the community was working on its behalf. The organization was worked out, the press was mustered and, through the clergy's active participation, the necessary "authority" and respectability were achieved. As the revival proceeded, the victories were monitored and the converts were nurtured in their faith by the evangelist and the itinerant brethren.

As the success of the evangelists expanded, their message and techniques were broadcast throughout the continent and beyond. Articles, tracts and books brought their work into every household. For instance, Charles G. Finney's early study, *Lectures on Revivals of Religion*, James Caughey's *Earnest Christianity Illustrated* and James Watson's *Helps to the Promotion of Revivals* went through numerous editions. Collections of sermons and biographies of revivalists were also extremely popular in Ontario.[60] These books inspired their readers by the stories of vast conversions and individuals brought to God and spread both the fame of the evangelists and the flame of revival.

Equally important, both the religious and secular press constantly recorded the work of revival in Ontario and abroad. For years, the exploits of Moody and Sankey and their compatriots and the sermons of T. DeWitt Talmage were reported to an avid Ontario audience.[61] The leadership provided by these and other evangelists and the press coverage they generated helped sustain revivals in the villages and rural areas of the province,[62] while at the same time transforming revival services from isolated, largely rural phenomena organized by local individuals to city-centred, professionally managed events. Indeed few understood better than the independent professional evangelist how vital the mass media had become to this process of transformation and, more generally, to the consolidation of community values.

As the century progressed, wave after wave of enthusiasm swept over the province, generated both locally and from the United States and Great Britain. However, mass evangelism reached its peak in the late 1850s, with subsequent high points in the 1870s and 1880s.[63] Paradoxically, despite their continued popularity, the importance of traditional revival services significantly waned over the last half of the century. They became isolated from mainline Protestantism and remained important only on the fringes of Ontario or, ecclesiastically, in splinter churches. For the remainder, mass evangelism was transformed to suit the perceived needs of an increasingly *urbane* population and the earnest message was seriously circumscribed.[64] Hence, by the close of the century, the Ontario religious landscape was vastly different from that of a half-century earlier.

While mass evangelism was considered by many as critical for the viability of church institutions and Christian discipline, it was seen as a mixed blessing for institutionalized denominations. As Methodism entrenched itself in the province it became fearful of internal dissension and defections, even in the interest of preserving an evangelical purity. British Methodism had been torn apart by lay revolts and the revivalism of Lorenzo Dow in the first decade of the nineteenth century. The New Connexion and Primitive Methodists were only the first of literally hundreds of groups which separated in order to fulfill their revival mandate. Their arguments were always the same: the church had abandoned true revivalism and forsaken God's vision for the world's salvation. Under revival enthusiasm, they could justify separation, especially since their allegiance was not to any denomination but to an ideological movement.

Consequently, while the nineteenth century in Ontario was marked by a breaking down of denominational differences,[65] there was a countervailing spinning off of millennial and special-interest groups. One need only mention the Millerite, Davidite, Mormon, Catholic Apostolic (Irvingite), Free Methodist, Salvation Army and Hornerite churches, all of which made heavy intrusions in Protestant Ontario, to illustrate the point. It was with considerable fear, therefore, that even staunch revival supporters could ask, "May we not hope that the great revival of the nineteenth century will be free from polemical strife, and will not result in raising up another distinguishing name among Christians?"[66] Among many mainline Protestants, revivals had to be restrained to avoid the strife of secession; this, in itself, drove many avid revival supporters out of the denominations.

Furthermore, the reliance on revival converts for increases in membership could be dangerous for the long-term well-being of the Methodist
church. Many joined the preacher James Richardson when he cautioned that
they "were like the morning cloud and early dew. Though some stood firm
and worked out their salvation, yet many turned back, even to perdition."[67]
The convert who lived only for revival was not a sure foundation for the
institutionalized, urban church. The *Christian Guardian* warned:

> There are some people whose religious life depends alto-
> gether on revivals. So long as they can feed on the high
> religious feeling and excitement of a special time of awak-
> ening they are happy, earnest and progressive Christians;
> but when the tide of special influence is gone, they relapse
> into a condition of indifference from which they are only
> aroused by the next revival.[68]

The Bible Christian church shared this position, noting that revivalism

> ...has led in numerous instances, we fear, to undue trust in
> occasional efforts and to laxity in that constant attention to
> Christian duty so essential to a healthy state of piety....It is
> with painful feelings we state our conviction that an undue
> reliance on occasional efforts has, among other things, tended
> very extensively to lower the standard of piety in this privi-
> leged Province.[69]

The Methodist churches came to believe that quiet, reverential, intelligent
and abiding worship provided a truer spiritual awakening and a more
secure foundation for Christian progress.[70]

As important, revival converts had to be nurtured to a higher religious
life by the church's regular operations. Too often such converts were not
prepared to maintain an intimate, disciplined relationship with the church.
As a result, many church members joined the skeptical public in challenging
the validity of the revival-based conversion experience. By the 1860s,
Methodism was no longer the fervent body of converts the evangelistic
gatherings had implied; orderly, rational development appeared more effective and more legitimate under the altered conditions of Victorian Ontario. This was certainly more in harmony with the general goals of the
denomination and the larger society. In sum, regular worship and tradi-
tional-style revivals were diverging on fundamental issues and becoming
antagonistic movements in the churches. At the same time, it was quite
natural for revival services to decline since regular church buildings were
increasingly available for worship. In fact, emotional enthusiasm seemed
doubly inappropriate in church buildings which themselves reflected part
of the transformation to a respectable presence in the local community. Even
the church's architecture came to reflect stability, order and a respectful

quest for God.[71] Much of the original rationale and appeal of revivalism had disappeared.

Revivals tended to interfere with the continuous religious supervision of the congregation and the local community. During periods of mass evangelism, the itinerant and lay leaders were obliged to be absent from the broader pastoral responsibilities demanded by the urbanizing church and to neglect the vital auxiliary institutions such as Sunday schools and missionary societies. As well, special services placed an inordinate strain on the preachers and their co-workers.[72] The Methodist church was becoming a complex social organization which required constant vigilance and which could ill afford such distractions.

Furthermore, it became increasingly difficult to refute the criticisms of emotional excess levelled at the camp and protracted meetings. Even loyal Methodists began to describe this kind of behaviour as a form of paganism.[73] There was a fine line between ardent zeal and ignorant enthusiasm and it was too easily trespassed to suit a large proportion of Methodists. Respectability became a major priority as institutionalized Methodism sought a credible role as a moral leader in Victorian Ontario. The denomination, therefore, consciously de-emphasized or remoulded evangelistic services to make them more socially acceptable.

The clearest indication of this change was an expanding trust in a gradual growth to grace as opposed to a dramatic conversion experience.[74] Slow, even progress seemed more in keeping with the contemporary secular concepts of human development. Faith was evolutionary, advancing quietly to the vital moment of decision, and conversion came like the emergence from a long tunnel, not like a flash of lightning. Education and methodical study, originally so important to Wesley's perception of true spiritual renewal,[75] were re-emphasized since they fitted more clearly into the pattern of late nineteenth-century development in Canada, Great Britain and the United States. Ontario society placed a deep trust in education as the surest foundation for economic and social progress and it was only a small step to the belief that education could remake fallen humanity and create heaven on earth. In these circumstances, old-fashioned revivals seemed out of touch with the major intellectual trends affecting Victorian Ontario.

As part of the transition to more acceptable forms, there was even a questioning of the techniques and long-term effectiveness of independent evangelists. Although a faction in the church was anxious to expand this type of specialized ministry, others saw destructive elements in its work. The Methodist Episcopal Church as early as 1866, for example, condemned the lack of control over those lecturing and preaching in its pulpits. Independent evangelists, it was thought, tended to disrupt the regular operations of the church and upset the harmony of the entire church body.[76] The Methodist Church of Canada added that the use of such speakers undermined the regular itinerancy.

> While these so-called evangelists may be both zealous and
> sincere...yet their teaching is often dangerously unscriptu-
> ral. Ministers to our church cannot be too careful in giving
> countenance to men who are responsible to no church au-
> thority, and whose chief claim to recognition seems to be
> their ability to disparage and slander all who will not adopt
> their views.[77]

Such professional evangelists were subject to no disciplinary, theological or
administrative restraint and held strongly antidenominational views. Dwight
L. Moody, the most popular evangelist of the 1870s, was considered too
millenarian for Ontario Methodism and others were even less theologically
sound, relying on meaningless cant.[78] Of course, this opposition to revivalists was also part of a larger struggle between those wishing to create a
mature, institutionalized denomination that could meet the challenge of
immorality and skepticism and those striving to maintain Methodism as
part of a grand evangelical movement, without narrow denominational
loyalties, that could revitalize the nation and the world.

The mistrust of uneducated preachers and their lack of reasoned preaching turned many away from professional revivalists, especially among the
wealthy and urbane lay leaders.[79] In order to control evangelists without
losing the benefits of their work, it was decided to relieve "suitably en-
dowed" itinerants of their circuit responsibilities and to employ them as full-
time evangelists.[80] This move, in itself, reflected the decline of fervour and
the increasingly specialized work of the regular clergy.[81] Yet, the example of
Ralph Horner illustrated that even conference evangelists could not always
be controlled; he refused to be restrained by the church's doctrines or
discipline and was expelled from the Methodist ministry. Such cases strengthened the argument that the long-term interests of the church lay in the
regular means of worship.[82]

Under these pressures revival institutions severely declined by the end of
the century. However, Methodism was always hesitant to abandon completely any of its means of grace; adaptation was the more common approach. Thus the peculiar revival agencies were transformed to suit better
the requirements of Protestant Ontario. Camp meetings and protracted
meetings and even the role of professional evangelists, while condemned as
excessively emotional and irrational by large segments of Methodism, were
also attacked by the more evangelical wing of the connexion because they
had apparently lost their reliance on the unrestrained presence of the Holy
Ghost. Revival was demanded for revival services.[83] This perception was
probably valid as early as the 1860s. Although still more fervent than other
church worship, mass evangelism shared in the general decline in emotional
pietism. Rousing exhortation, fervent prayer and confession diminished in
importance.

The Campground at Grimsby ca. 1876

The preaching that came to dominate the services was also aimed less at arousing emotional enthusiasm.[84] Rather than dwelling constantly on man's fallen state and the road to salvation, sermons were directed at the whole range of skepticism and immorality abounding in Victorian Ontario. Even professional evangelists responded to the preferences of their large, middle-class clientele and preached morality and ethical conduct.[85] They also spoke more frequently of a positive, orderly, advancing society and of the institutional means for its fulfilment. The essentially optimistic and progressive urban Protestant community did not require the constant threat of damnation and thus, with the partial exception of the Holiness Movement preaching, the emphasis on earnest individual salvation was significantly reduced.[86]

These changing orientations, in turn, limited mass participation and weakened the role of the laity in the conduct of revivals.[87] This contributed to a further decline in the significance of revivals by removing much of their original rationale and energy. Camp meetings tended to become formal, annual gatherings for general religious fellowship. Social refreshment, which came with a vacation from the routine of daily life, continued to keep them popular, but they bore little resemblance to the old-time revivals. By the 1870s, the various larger Methodist connexions had instituted permanent campgrounds which stressed the healthy as well as the moral atmosphere of a park.[88] At Grimsby, for instance, there were summer cottages, boat services and all the social amenities to attract an urban, middle-class clientele. Special services were offered for two or three weeks during the summer but recreation and relaxation in a moral, suburban setting became the central function.[89]

Similarly, Thousand Island Park became a popular site for camp meetings. In 1882 the *Christian Guardian* advertised it as follows:

> There is no more healthy and pleasant summer resort than Thousand Island Park, on the St. Lawrence. The scenery is picturesque and beautiful. The water is cool and clear. The air is pure and bracing. Good order and interesting services are maintained. Fishing, boating and bathing are available to any extent. The first of the series of services of the season was begun last Friday, under the direction of the Rev. Dr. Hibbard, and is now in full blast.[90]

The Methodist Episcopal Church described it as a "coveted summer retreat from the extreme heat of city life and a favourite resort for amusement."[91] Not only was it considered a "powerful impulse to all the vital activities of the church," it also gave "promise of early yielding a handsome revenue to other connexional interests."[92]

While these vital interests no longer stressed emotional piety, the new camp meetings were being used to address the needs of the contemporary church and to link the denomination to, rather than segregate it from, the newly urbane Ontario community. Revival services served as excellent forums for temperance meetings and for Sunday school and missionary conventions,[93] and their educative value was expanded as sermons dealt with Methodist history, the pastoral work of the church, science and higher criticism and the modern Sunday school.[94] Despite the decline in the revival's function as an agency of conversion, the Methodist Church recognized that the new purposes of revivals were equally valuable and more central to the church's modern mission.[95] Even though expectations remained high that the unchurched urban poor would be attracted to city-centred revivals, this class found little appeal in the services.[96] The new camp and protracted meetings were in fact aimed especially at second and third generation church members who, having never strayed far from institutional religion, found little consolation in traditional revivalism.

Revival enthusiasm did not disappear completely from late-Victorian Ontario. There were still groups that attempted either to maintain old-style revivalism or to capture and redirect its energy and commitment to solve the perceived problems of contemporary industrial society. These two groups represented the right and left wings of Canadian Protestantism.

On the right were a number of groups and individuals who fell within the general designation of the Holiness Movement. As indicated earlier, its major concern was the achievement of entire sanctification through individual conversion. This ideology influenced not only Ralph Horner's church but also the Free Methodists, the Salvation Army and the host of pentecostal churches in Ontario.[97] While desertions occurred, this movement did not seriously wound mainline Methodism during the nineteenth century. In fact, after the passing of the first-generation leadership, many members drifted back into their old ecclesiastical homes. As well, traditional evangelism found a receptive home among fundamentalists. In emphasizing the literal veracity of the Bible and rejecting higher criticism, they also withstood the main progressive ideologies influencing Ontario. Old-style revivalism and especially its stress on emotional, personal conversion, maintained a fellowship which provided a comfortable bulwark against modernism, liberal theology and the atomizing pressures of urban society.

On the left, the social gospel offered a collectivist, institutional approach to the evils of urban society. In its most radical form, it advocated a fundamental realignment in Ontario's social and economic relations. It merged revivalism's energy and ethical priorities with secular socialist ideology and demanded a new partnership of church and state to meet the challenge of the twentieth century. With the power and authority of this alliance and with an education system harnessed to assist, it believed that evil could be truly driven from the world and Christ would reign in a post-millennial community of saints. The success of the social gospel movement hinged on its ability to attract skeptical or even reluctant followers who supported the vision if not the means of its achievement. While many abandoned the mainline Protestant churches, others remained to reinforce the churches' social commitment and mission to modern society.

Despite their evident polarities on the Protestant ideological scale, the right and left wings had much in common. Although they chose different responses, both were shaped by the same forces, shared the same intellectual milieu, felt the same urgency and reacted against the same conditions. They were equally frustrated by the seeming inability of the mainline churches to respond to the "real" needs of society. Furthermore, both represented the Canadian arm of large international movements, both reacted against legislated doctrine and theology and attempted to tackle the challenges of the period pragmatically, and both stressed the moral and ethical obligations of Christianity.

In these regards, they fulfilled the original elements of revival. Because both believed in an essentially democratic organization, the laity was able to play a large role in their operations. The conservative churches trusted in a called rather than a trained ministry and the exhortation and testimony of the laity remained central elements of their worship. The social gospel also downplayed the theological differences in what it meant to be a minister and, with an essential trust in the goodness of mankind, found a strong and active role for the laity in the field of social justice.

Moreover, both assumed that all mankind was capable of salvation. Calvinist notions of predestination had long since departed from Ontario Protestantism and this was particularly true among groups committed to the regeneration of either the individual or the general society. In both cases, the revivalist conviction that man was progressing was re-expressed. Similarly, both the right and left were characterized by a lack of denominational discipline and loyalty. The result was a proliferation of fundamentalist, pentecostal, and evangelical churches and a nearly constant reshuffling of affiliations among "revived" individuals on the right. Paradoxically, while the development of these right-wing churches apparently exacerbated denominational differences, it in fact worked to establish a pattern of loyalty to ideological tenets shared by several denominations rather than, as in the nineteenth-century concept of church, to any one ecclesiastical polity. On the left, close and easy co-operation across denominational lines and in secular organizations was common. The left wing was particularly successful in popularizing its social and ethical mission in industrial, urban settings.

In the centre, where the majority of churchgoers continued to support mainline Protestantism, there often developed a clash between the priorities of evangelism and social services. Most profoundly, however, these elements have blended rather than contended in Protestant leaders in Canada during the twentieth century. Nevertheless, this tension has been extremely healthy in clarifying the Protestant mission for this century, especially as it faced the twin assaults of mass non-Protestant, non-Anglo-Saxon immigration and the emergence of a complex industrialized society. Both the general revival experience and the particular revival institutions, which were transformed to suit the nineteenth-century urban ethos, acquired forms that continue to serve the modern denominations. Revival remains, therefore, a major, albeit transformed impulse defining the Ontario religious community.

1   See Charles G. Finney, *Lectures on Revivals of Religion* ([Boston, 1835], Halifax, 1848), 3. Revivalism denotes in this study both a general spiritual renewal among individuals and the specific techniques and institutions of mass evangelism.

2   See the definition of urbanization used by Dale Postgate and Ken McRoberts, *Quebec, Social Change and Political Crisis* (Toronto, 1980), 47.

3   Any consideration of urbanization naturally raises questions about the definition used. Urbanization has traditionally been perceived as the process of expansion and development of the physical city, a statistically measurable unit, or as concentrations of population involved in economic specialization and a complex division of labour. Such definitions satisfy historians of the industrial city and are especially appropriate in identifying internal spatial structures associated with occupation or other quantifiable activities. They also provide valuable starting points for sociological analyses of the city.

    However, on a different level, urbanization involves creating an identifiable environment with its own "set of practices, of common habits, sentiments and traditions." Through various processes at work in the urban area, new groupings and behaviour are produced which distinguish that area from its rural periphery. The city then defines its own sense of social order which is often expressed in terms of respectability, sophistication (urbanity) or cosmopolitanism, and which is built on an openness to new ideas and a general trust in change.

    These traits are never universally adopted in any urban centre, but they reflect the perceived qualities of urban life especially among the community leaders. And it is these values which the city transmits through its metropolitan system of controls to the smaller centres and rural hinterland. In this paper, urbanization is used to reflect the development of these values and their transmission across the Ontario hinterland. Through this process, the goals and aspirations of the city gradually come to predominate throughout the region. Hence the attributes of urbanity are not limited to the city as artifact or physical site. In this way, for instance, revival values adapted to suit the perceived needs of the urban centres gained predominance across the province.

4   *Minutes of the Annual Conferences of the Wesleyan Methodist Church in Canada from 1824 to 1845* (Toronto, 1846), i.

5   Methodist Episcopal Church, *Minutes of Niagara Conference* (1845), 10; John Wesley, *The Appeals to Men of Reason and Religion*, ed. Gerald R. Cragg, vol. XI in Frank Baker, ed.-in-chief, *The Works of John Wesley* (Oxford, 1975), intro., 25.

6   Cragg, intro., 10.

7   Albert Outler, ed., *John Wesley* (New York, 1964), intro., 29.

8   Lovett H. Weems, *The Gospel According to Wesley* (Nashville, 1982), 5. Scripture, tradition, reason and experience are commonly known as Wesley's quadrilateral.

9   Arthur Kewley, "Mass Evangelism in Upper Canada before 1830" (Th.D. diss., Victoria University, 1960), 2.

10 John W. Grant, ed., *Salvation! Oh the Joyful Sound* (Toronto, 1967), intro., 15; Wesleyan Methodist Church, *Minutes of Annual Conference* (1846), 12–16; *Earnest Christianity* 2 (1874), 364.

11 *Christian Guardian* (Toronto) [hereafter *CG*], 4 Sep. 1830, 330.

12 J. Wesley Johnston, "Tongues of Fire", in his *The Baptism of Fire and other Sermons* (Toronto, 1888), 28.

13 Kewley, 4; Charles Hawkins, "The Law of Revivals", in his *Sermons on the Christian Life* (Toronto, 1880), 64; *CG*, 4 Dec. 1830, 9; 5 Aug. 1840, 162.

14 *CG*, 18 Oct. 1843, 206.

15 Whitney Cross. *The Burned-Over District, 1800–1850* (New York, 1950).

16 United Church Archives [hereafter UCA], Portraits and Letters of Ministers at St. James Street Methodist Church, Samuel Coate to Joseph Benson, 13 Sep. 1805.

17 John Carroll, *Past and Present...*(Toronto, 1860), 62–63.

18 Kewley, 83; see also *CG*, 31 May 1854, 133.

19 Carroll, 64–65.

20 Wesleyan Methodist Church, *Minutes of Annual Conference* (1846), 20.

21 *CG*, 13 Jan. 1841, 46; 2 Apr. 1856, 103; 13 Jan. 1875, 13; George Douglas, *Discourses and Addresses* (Toronto, 1894), 13.

22 *CG*, 23 Feb. 1841, 58.

23 Kewley, 5.

24 Gerald Craig, *Upper Canada: The Formative Years, 1784–1841* (Toronto, 1963), 166.

25 *CG*, 18 Jan. 1843, 50; *The Wesleyan* (Montreal) [hereafter *TW*], 4 Feb. 1841, 113.

26 Although individual charges report significant increases in membership during and immediately after a revival, there are almost always reports of severe declines in membership over subsequent months or years. Nonetheless, the enthusiasm engendered by revivals often lasted long enough for a new church to be built or an itinerant minister to be assigned to the charge. These institutional developments stabilized growth and made it more permanent.

27 See *CG*, 4 Dec. 1830, 9; 11 July 1838, 142.

28 *CG*, 3 July 1833, 135.

29 Timothy L. Smith, *Revivalism and Social Reform* (Gloucester, 1976), 8.

30 Victor Shepherd, "Calvin's Doctrine of Church, Ministry and Sacrament", United Church of Canada, Committee on Archives, *The Bulletin*, no. 29 (1983), 75.

31 John Wesley, "On Working Out Our Salvation", in *The Works of John Wesley*, X (London, 1811), 79; see also Ole Borgen, "John Wesley and the Sacraments", Canadian Methodist Historical Society, *Papers* 2 (1980), 2.

32 James W. May, "From Revival Movement to Denomination: A Re-examination of the Beginnings of American Methodism" (Ph.D. diss., Columbia University, 1962), 4.

33 The regular means of grace included preaching, prayer, the sacraments and confession, among others. One of John Wesley's major contributions to Protestant theology was to reintroduce "good works" as a means of advancement to spiritual safety. Charity, if it proceeded from a fallen individual, meant nothing. But charity done by a converted person could legitimately promote the attainment of heaven.

34 Smith, 8; Melvin Dieter, *The Holiness Revival of the Nineteenth Century* (Meteuchin, N.J., 1980), 14, 19; *CG*, 21 Oct. 1840, 206; 2 Dec. 1857, 33.

35   William Westfall, "The End of the World: An Aspect of Time and Culture in Nineteenth-Century Protestant Ontario", in Association for Canadian Studies, *Religion/Culture: Comparative Canadian Studies* [proceedings of the 1984 annual conference], vol. 7 in the series *Canadian Issues* (1985), 78–79.

36   See "Advent", *The Encyclopedia of World Methodism*, I (Nashville, 1974), 52–55.

37   May, 15.

38   The class meeting was a compulsory, weekly gathering of a small group of penitent Methodists seeking salvation. It met under the spiritual and disciplinary guidance of a class leader who represented, especially in pioneer Methodism, a sub-pastor of the Society. Prayer, hymn singing, personal testimony and mutual support made it an intimate and effective basis for Methodist church membership. After 1850, however, its effectiveness, like that of the revival, declined.

The love feast was also an important devotional service for Methodists and a valuable source of spiritual fellowship. Modelled on the early Christian church's *agape*, it was used in place of communion in the absence of an ordained minister and at special gatherings of church members. Non-members were generally excluded. Prayer and hymns usually preceded and followed the communal eating of a small meal, usually bread and water.

39   Neil Semple, "The Impact of Urbanization on the Methodist Church in Central Canada, 1854–1884" (Ph.D. diss., University of Toronto, 1979), 128–31.

40   Russell E. Richey, "Community, Fraternity and Order in Methodism", Canadian Methodist Historical Society, *Papers* 4 (1984), 4–5; W. Reginald Ward, "Class, Denomination and the Development of the Connexional Frame of Mind in the Age of Bunting", ibid., 3–4.

41   Lorenzo Dow (1777–1834) was a Methodist preacher who was born in Connecticut and began to preach in 1794. He travelled to Britain in 1799, 1805 and 1818 and introduced camp meetings there. He greatly influenced Hugh Bourne, the founder of the Primitive Methodist Connexion. Charles Grandison Finney (1792–1875), a Congregationalist minister and educator, was raised in western New York State and was a powerful evangelist in the eastern cities of the United States. He attacked Calvinist notions and accepted "free grace." His influence carried over to Congregational and Baptist congregations and he taught a generation of evangelical ministers as president of Oberlin College.

42   Daniel Wise, "A Brief Sketch of Mr. Caughey's Life", in James Caughey, *Earnest Christianity Illustrated*, 3rd ed. (Toronto, 1857), 16.

43   See William Harvard, *Defence of Protracted Meetings* (London, 1841).

44   *TW*, 4 Feb. 1841, 128.

45   Harvard, 15.

46   Caughey, *Earnest Christianity Illustrated*, 16; *TW*, 1 Apr. 1841, 144.

47   *TW*, 4 Feb. 1841, 113.

48   *CG*, 20 July 1853, 162.

49   Ibid.

50   *CG*, 30 Apr. 1856, 119.

51   UCA, Nathanael Burwash Papers, box 28, draft autobiography, ch. 1, 10.

52   Dieter, 38–44; *CG*, 22 July 1857, 166.

53   Samuel Jones, *Sam Jones and Sam Small in Toronto* (Toronto, 1886), 29.

54.   UCA, Henry Flesher Bland Papers, diary 7a, 1858, 37.

55   Burwash autobiography, ch. 1, 58.

56   R. Durham, *The Revival in St. Catharines* (St. Catharines, [1880?]), 20.

57   *TW*, 4 Feb. 1841, 113; *CG*, 25 Mar. 1857, 98.

58   UCA, John Wesley Papers, John Wesley to George Gibbon, 9 Apr. 1785.

59   A debate, which is not explored in this study, soon emerged over the preconditions for achieving, and the timing of, the second blessing. This issue introduced seeds of disunity into Protestant revivalism which ultimately led to a redrawing of the entire portrait of Protestantism in Ontario and, indeed, throughout North America.

60   See Robert Boyd, *The Lives and Labours of Moody and Sankey* (Toronto, 1876); Isaac B. Aylesworth, ed., *Sermons by the Rev. T. DeWitt Talmage…*(Ottawa, 1878).

61   See *Canadian Methodist Magazine* [hereafter *CMM*] 4 (1876), 251; *CG*, 19 Jan. 1881, 20.

62   *CG*, 27 May 1885, 322.

63 Dieter, 59; Stephen Bond, *Notes on 1. Methodism*...(n.p., n.d.), 38; UCA, Alexander Sutherland Letterbooks, Alexander Sutherland to Richard W. Woodsworth, 19 Feb. 1885. As revivals were not reported in a systematic way, it is impossible to generate statistics on their frequency, or on the numbers converted or subsequently backsliding, sufficiently precise to support a quantitative analysis of the scope of revival activity in our period.

64 Semple, 116–17.

65 In 1884 the Methodist Church of Canada, the Primitive Methodist Church, the Bible Christian Church and the Methodist Episcopal Church united to form the Methodist Church. In 1875, the Canada Presbyterian Church (a union of the Free Church and the United Presbyterian Church) joined the Presbyterian Church of Canada in Connexion with the Church of Scotland to form the Presbyterian Church in Canada. The united Methodist and Presbyterian churches held discussions concerning co-operation and possible union with the Church of England and other Protestant denominations throughout the 1880s.

66 William Arthur, *May We Hope for a Great Revival* (Toronto, 1867), 67.

67 UCA, Egerton Ryerson Papers, James Richardson to Egerton Ryerson, 8 Apr. 1832.

68 *CG*, 23 Apr. 1883, 132.

69 Bible Christian Church, *Minutes of Annual Conference* (1861), 8; see also Wesleyan Methodist Church, *Minutes of Annual Conference* (1870), 102.

70 *CG*, 23 Apr. 1883, 132.

71 See William Westfall, "The Sacred and the Secular: Studies in the Cultural History of Protestant Ontario in the Victorian Period" (Ph.D. diss., University of Toronto, 1976), ch. 4.

72 *CG*, 9 May 1849, 117; Bible Christian Church, *Minutes of Annual Conference* (1866), 12–13.

73 *CG*, 7 Feb. 1885, 70; Kewley, 11.

74 H. R. Niebuhr, *The Social Sources of Denominationalism* (New York, 1957), 63.

75 Cragg, intro., 14.

76 Methodist Episcopal Church, *Minutes of Bay of Quinte Conference* (1866), 57.

77 Methodist Church of Canada, *Minutes of Toronto Conference* (1877), 68.

78 UCA, Henry Flesher Bland Papers, diary, 17 Aug. 1876, 282–83; *CG*, 31 Jan. 1877, 36; 14 Mar. 1877, 86.

79 Methodist Church of Canada, *Minutes of Toronto Conference* (1877), 67; John Davison, *An Address Delivered at the Ordination of Seven Ministers* (Toronto, n.d.), 20–23.

80 Methodist Church of Canada, *Minutes of Montreal Conference* (1875), 53; ibid. (1883), 72.

81 Methodist Episcopal Church, *Minutes of Ontario Conference* (1882), 20; *CG*, 20 Feb. 1878, 57.

82 Wesleyan Methodist Church, *Minutes of Annual Conference* (1870), 102; *CG*, 26 Sep. 1866, 154; Hawkins, 57.

83 UCA, Albert Carman Papers, W. Barnett to Albert Carman, 3 Oct. 1881.

84 See Aylesworth, *Talmage*. Sermons of the period were also heavily influenced by the scholarly examples of William Morley Punshon, president of the Wesleyan Methodist Church in Canada from 1867 to 1872. He directed his sermons at the intellect; see *CG*, 29 Apr. 1874, 132.

85 See Jones, *Sam Jones*; Aylesworth, *Talmage*; *CG*, 12 Jan. 1870, 6.

86 *CG*, 29 November 1876, 382.

87 *CG*, 2 Feb. 1872, 18; 22 Apr. 1874, 124.

88 *CMM* 8 (1878), 110–11; *CG*, 16 Sep. 1874, 293; Harriet P. Youmans, *Grimsby Park, Historical and Descriptive* (Toronto, 1900), 10.

89 *CMM* 8 (1878), 111–13; Dorothy Turcotte, *Greetings from Grimsby Park* (Grimsby, 1985).

90 *CG*, 19 July 1882, 258.

91 Aylesworth, *Talmage*, i-ii.

92 Methodist Episcopal Church, *Minutes of Bay of Quinte Conference* (1878), 91.

93 *CMM* 4 (1877), 373–74; 22 (1885), 127.

94 Ibid. 12 (1880), 277; Aylesworth, *Talmage*.

95 *CG*, 29 Aug. 1883, 276; see also Methodist Episcopal Church, *Minutes of Ontario Conference* (1879), 84–85.

96 *CG*, 29 July 1874, 233; 5 May 1875, 141.

97 Ralph Horner, *Pentecost* (Toronto, 1891); Ralph Horner, *Ralph Horner, Evangelist* (Brockville, 192[?]).

Church Architecture and Urban Space: The Development of Ecclesiastical Forms in Nineteenth-Century Ontario

WILLIAM WESTFALL and MALCOLM THURLBY

During the mid-Victorian period the religious architecture of Ontario changed dramatically as the revived medieval style overwhelmed the traditional manner of building churches. Before 1840 classical vernacular and neoclassical styles had enjoyed the greatest popularity among religious groups, and good examples are still to be seen in the Methodist Meeting House at Hay Bay of 1791 and St. Andrew's Presbyterian, Niagara-on-the-Lake, built in 1831.[1] In this period examples of medievalism are rare and very tentative in nature—a few superficial Gothic details added on to a James Gibbs-inspired preaching-box, as exemplified by John G. Howard's Holy Trinity, Chippawa, of 1840.[2] After this date, however, references to medieval models became more precise, masonry construction increased, and buttresses, window tracery and arch mouldings became more convincing in a medieval sense. The change is again clearly seen in the work of Howard, whose Christ Church, Tyendinaga, was constructed between 1840 and 1842. Here there is a far more serious attempt to recreate the essence of medieval architectural detailing than in his earlier effort at Chippawa.[3] Now the new medievalism seemed to carry all before it, and by the 1870s the revived style, which encompassed both the pointed Gothic and the round arched Romanesque,[4] had become the norm for church building in Ontario. Not only the Anglicans and the Roman Catholics but also Presbyterians, Methodists and Baptists participated in this stylistic revolution, giving a visual unity to the religious architecture of the province. Indeed the transformation was so extensive that by the end of the century few classical structures even remained,[5] and in the minds of many the revived medieval style had come to shape the very image of how a church should appear.

This transformation in the religious architecture of Ontario reveals many important features of the new culture that was emerging in the province in the mid-nineteenth century. While one might be tempted to attribute stylistic change to the vagaries of international taste, to the people who built these churches style was not a matter of serendipity; the manner of building churches changed and developed for important social and cultural reasons. For example, in 1853 when one of the province's most talented architects, William Hay, analyzed "the present revival of Christian architecture," he explained the process of stylistic change in terms of a rich social and cultural aesthetic. He integrated style with social values and tied the advent of the revived style to the birth of new attitudes about religion and society. "Christian architecture," he wrote,

> is the name given to that peculiar style of building, commonly called Gothic, which predominated in western Europe in the Middle Ages. It derived its origin from the efforts of Christians...to embody the principles and characteristics of their faith in the structures which they reared for the services of their religion. The name is used to distinguish it from Pagan Architecture (which continues to be) the favourite style for civil and monumental architecture and until the late revival of Christian Art, most of our ecclesiastical edifices came under this category.[6]

For Hay, the style of a building expressed certain social and cultural values; consequently, the distinction between the neoclassical and the Gothic was also a distinction between paganism and Christianity. To take up the revived style was to take up the Christian values that this style embodied, and in this way architectural change assumed a reformist and even messianic character: it was part of an aesthetic that set out to change the social and religious values of the nineteenth century.

The integration of style, aesthetics and social values underlines the importance of analyzing architecture not only in terms of the history of style but also in relation to the society and culture in which architecture exists. In these terms, some of the reasons why the medieval revival gained such strength in Ontario become readily apparent. For example, medievalism began to flourish in the province as the religious structure of Ontario was undergoing a series of important changes. The old division of the colony into establishmentarians and dissenters was breaking down as the provincial state secularized the clergy reserves and removed the United Church of England and Ireland from its privileged position in the provincial university. These changes at once broke the age-old alliance of church and state and allowed the dissenters to emerge from the shadow of the official establishment. The revived medieval style met the needs of both sides of the old battle-lines. It provided the Anglicans and Presbyterians with a religious vocabulary that stressed a sense of historical continuity rather than the old utilitarian arguments of social benefit, while it provided the former sects with a tangible symbol of their arrival at the centre of Canadian religious life.[7]

The popularity of the new style was also aided by the attempt to articulate a sense of identity for the new Canadian nation-state and by the developing character of the architectural profession in Ontario. The Gothic revival enjoyed strong British associations; in the eyes of many, the style emphasized the strong historical links between the new nation and the political, social and cultural values of the mother country. For this reason the style was able to grow and mature within the strong nourishing currents of late-nineteenth-century imperial nationalism.[8] Furthermore, the articulation of the Victorian Gothic and Romanesque variations of the revived style took place at almost the same time that architects in Ontario were working hard to create an effective professional organization. In this case, style came to the aid of the profession since the ability to work effectively within a medieval vocabulary became one of the badges that set an architect apart from a mere contractor or builder.[9]

These social and intellectual developments help to explain why the medieval form became the dominant religious metaphor in Victorian Ontario. But they leave unanswered a number of other important questions about the architectural and cultural history of the medieval revival in Ontario. While we can begin to account for the popularity of the medieval revival we still must explain why the revival followed a certain path in Ontario, one that was different from the ones followed elsewhere. If the Gothic or Romanesque church became a cultural symbol, why did this symbol assume a specific form in Ontario? To consider these questions one must again examine the revival not only as an architectural movement but also in relation to the society in which it developed.

The relation between architecture and the environment is especially important in this case because it defined a series of very specific tensions that architects had to address. On the one hand, medievalism was a *revived* style that tried to reproduce old buildings in the hope that they could perform certain social and religious purposes—in Hay's words "to embody the principles and characteristics of [the] faith." On the other hand, these new churches had to meet the needs of nineteenth-century worshippers within a physical environment that was not necessarily conducive to the aesthetic principles of medieval design. For example, the medieval plan did not provide space for Sunday schools and church offices; nor did the plan, which had been created within a medieval rural setting, speak effectively to an environment in Ontario that was becoming increasingly urban in character.[10]

The way architects responded to the tensions between the aesthetic principles of the revival and the needs of congregations and the Ontario environment explains in large part the development of the medieval revival in Ontario's ecclesiastical architecture. New needs and the character of urban space altered the inherited forms of the medieval revival which in turn altered the character of urban space in Ontario. In this dialectic, one can trace what so many historians have tried so hard to find—the adaptation of European forms into what one might be so bold to call an Ontario religious style.

The aesthetics of the medieval revival were set out in a truly massive body of architectural, social and cultural commentary in which the proponents of the revived style attempted to explain not only the architectural principles of this manner of building but also the way in which this style should relate to its immediate environment. Augustus Welby Pugin, for example, gave the aesthetic and social qualities of the revival a powerful visual content when in 1836 he juxtaposed in his famous book *Contrasts* a medieval view and a contemporary view of the same town.[11] Pugin was both an architect and a theoretician and his two drawings illustrate effectively the way the revival brought together a way of building churches and a religious critique of contemporary social values. In the first drawing (Fig. 1) the medieval city is dominated by the spires of churches and the prominent placing of other religious structures; the modern town, in contrast, is dominated by factory chimneys and warehouses. The details of the two views expand upon the meaning and significance of this juxtaposition. In the modern town, for example, St. Marie's Abbey has fallen into ruin and the area to the south of the church, formerly occupied by monastic offices, is now the site of the ironworks. The tree-lined river bank is replaced by warehouses, and a former playing field is covered over by a prison built along Benthamite lines. The bridge across the river which used to be free is blocked by a toll gate, while the public fountain which once welcomed the thirsty traveller is chained and securely locked.

The contrast, in short, developed at two interrelated levels; the contrast in architectural style also expressed a contrast in the social and religious values of the medieval and modern eras. According to Gothic aesthetics, the architecture of the middle ages embodied the religious values of what had come to be seen as a distinctively Christian period. To build anew in the medieval manner provided a way of recreating this body of Christian values precisely when these values were being overwhelmed by the materialism of the present age. The revived medieval form, in sum, tried to make an important social and cultural statement. By recreating the values of the past it hoped to transform the values of the present.

When the aesthetics of the revival are introduced in this way it is clear that Gothic architecture was one part of a larger romantic movement that deeply coloured not only architecture, but also literature, painting and music in Canada. Romanticism in architecture, for example, had its counterpart in the nature poetry of the Confederation poets, in the landscape paintings of Horatio Walker and Lucius O'Brien, and in the new melodic structure of popular songs and hymns.[12]

In all these examples one can find a common romantic form—a way of organizing the relationship between art, audience, and the process of social

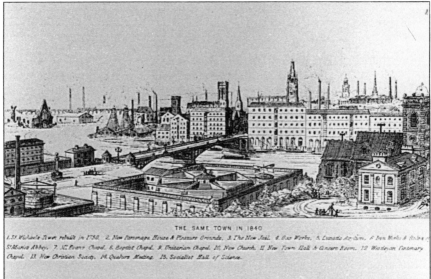

THE SAME TOWN IN 1840

1. St Michael's Tower, rebuilt in 1750. 2. New Parsonage House & Pleasure Grounds. 3. The New Jail. 4. Gas Works. 5. Lunatic Asylum. 6. Iron Works & Ruins of St Maries Abbey. 7. M. Evans Chapel. 8. Baptist Chapel. 9. Unitarian Chapel. 10. New Church. 11. New Town Hall & Concert Room. 12. Wesleyan Centenary Chapel. 13. New Christian Society. 14. Quakers Meeting. 15. Socialist Hall of Science.

Catholic town in 1440.

1. St Michaels on the Hill. 2. Queens Cross. 3. St Thomas's Chapel. 4. St Maries Abbey. 5. All Saints. 6. St Johns. 7. St Peters. 8. St Alkmunds. 9. St Maries. 10. St Edmunds. 11. Grey Friars. 12. St Cuthberts. 13. Guild hall. 14. Trinity. 15. St Olaves. 16. St Botolphs.

Figure 1: *Contrasted towns, 1440 and 1840, from A. W. N. Pugin,* **Contrasts**...,
2nd ed. (London, 1841)

and cultural change. Art was *re*-creation: it sought to recreate what were in effect icons of another age. In addition, romantics believed that the values embedded in these icons could be presented in such a way that they could inspire observers to alter their way of life. Moved by the immediate emotional power of art, the audience would undergo a spiritual transformation.

Inspired by the ideals embedded in the great building or noble ruin, inspired by the power of the great story or sermon, the individual would be transformed into a hero and set out on a quest to change the world.

This romantic relationship between building and beholder was clearly summarized in an article in *The Canadian Architect and Builder,* the leading architectural journal in Canada, and after 1890 the official voice of the Ontario Society of Architects. Using the occasion of a visit to the American mid-West in 1888, a contributor to the journal criticized the quality of church architecture in the United States by explaining to it readers the true character of a church and the impact that this character should produce on the observer:

> The form of every part of a church should speak to mortal man of God and immortality. Where is the man who can be impressed or led to give one single thought to eternity, when everything about him, even to the decoration, speaks in the coarse and vulgar tongue of his weekly surroundings? A man who enters a church decorated after the manner of a theatre or a saloon, will be more likely to have his thoughts go back to the last play he saw, or of the companions with whom he had very probably his last drink than to a retrospection of his actions, and of the obedience and reverence which he owes to his Maker....Of one thing we may be certain, and that is that nothing is too good for the house of God....A church should speak through every stone in its walls of refinement and culture, meekness and courage, and obedience and reverence to the Almighty.[13]

The aesthetics of romanticism, in short, assume a certain pattern: form embodies values which in turn were meant to play directly upon the feelings and emotions of an audience. The revived forms of medieval architecture were an inspirational device; the church a romantic metaphor of salvation.

The romantic principles of re-creation and inspiration, however, were not only abstract doctrines. The church was not a mere monument to the values of the past, it was a living institution. The symbolic character of its architecture had to be tied to the day-to-day roles that the building had to perform. A church not only had to address the principles of romantic aesthetics, at the same time it had to satisfy the needs of the people who inhabited this architectural space. Furthermore, the living church was part of a living world and had to achieve a romantic effect in relation to an environment that could assume a wide variety of spatial dimensions. As this romantic preoccupation with re-creation and inspiration are analyzed in relation to these environmental considerations the specific tensions that confronted the medieval revival in Ontario become readily apparent. Architects who worked within the romantic framework had to resolve a number of problems as the medieval form came into conflict with the realities of the Ontario environment.

Figure 2: St. Michael's, Long Stanton, Cambridgeshire, from the northwest

In the first instance, the touchstones of the Gothic revival were for the most part rural in origin. For example, one of the most famous models, advocated for colonial churches by the Cambridge Camden Society, the leading authority on the Gothic revival, was St. Michael's, Long Stanton (Fig. 2), a church that displayed all the proper elements of Gothic design—chancel, nave, porch—but one that was nonetheless a small parish church in a small village just north of Cambridge. And even when larger models were proposed the original is almost invariably from a rural context, a point exemplified in Frank Wills's use of Snettisham (Norfolk) parish church as the basic model for Christ Church Cathedral, Fredericton, New Brunswick (1845).[14] How could one adapt these rural models to the needs of the urban environments of Ontario?

Secondly, the models of the Gothic revival did not address a number of the liturgical and institutional needs of the Ontario denominations that used this style. While writers like John Ruskin had succeeded at an intellectual level in Protestantizing what had begun as a Catholic and high church movement, the shape of the Gothic church—with porch, nave and chancel—still reflected the liturgical traditions of medieval worship rather than the common practice of Presbyterians, Methodists and Baptists in Ontario. To meet their needs one had to alter the shape of the interior space, but changing this shape might alter the general form of the church which in turn might undermine the power of the church to act as an inspirational device.

Thirdly, the Gothic had to confront the problems posed by the character of urban space itself. According to romantic aesthetics, the ability of a church to inspire and elevate grew out of the sense of monumentality and presence that a church could achieve in relation to its immediate surroundings. In a visual sense the revived medieval church should dominate and control its environment. This goal, however, proved singularly difficult to achieve and sustain because the shape of urban space in Ontario was motivated by other considerations. By the time the revival began in earnest, the Georgian town plan, which reflected neither medieval nor romantic sensibilities, was firmly in place. In addition, as towns expanded beyond the boundaries of these plans it became clear that the shape of new growth reflected the pace of land speculation rather than moral authority of religious institutions. In Ontario the institution of private property and the habit of rectangular building lots would assure the continuation of a seemingly infinite progression of right angles. In Europe, urban growth seldom obliterated the irregular core; consequently the town continued to be keyed to the medieval church or cathedral; in Ontario, medievalism had to adapt itself to a symmetry that seemed to be beyond its control.[15]

Furthermore, urban space was not static. It was undergoing a continual process of adaptation, reorganization and change. The process of social and economic development organized and reorganized the urban structure of the province. Some urban centres grew, others stagnated after mid-century, while in larger urban centres new types of cities grew up on top of older ones.[16] This process presented more problems for Gothic architecture. The message that a church proclaimed was tied to a particular setting, but the power of this romantic statement could easily be lost as the changing urban context altered the relationship between the building and its environment. A church was a sermon in stone, but what happens when urban change alters the context of this sermon or removes the audience that was meant to read its story?

The *Ecclesiologist*, published by the influential Cambridge Camden Society, argued in 1842, "Instead of new designs,…real ancient designs, of acknowledged symmetry of proportions or beauty of detail should be selected for exact imitation in all their parts, arrangements and decorations."[17] This instruction to reproduce the ancient in an era which seemed intent upon destroying the very fabric of an older social order was not simply an expression of nostalgia for a golden age in the past. The recreation of medieval churches was closely tied to the way romantic revivalists understood the nature of a church itself. The leaders of the revival defended "ancient designs" in practical, indeed almost utilitarian, terms. The excellence of "acknowledged symmetry of proportions" and "beauty of detail" rested upon their "purposefulness" and "truthfulness." In laymen's terms, these designs were truthful because the architectural articulation expressed the religious purpose it was meant to perform. The church building was like a tight-fitting skin drawn around a series of sacred components; consequently, the external contours of the building—porch, nave and chancel—

marked clearly the different religious purposes associated with each of these spaces.[18]

The decoration of the church followed the same principles. It should avoid anything that could be seen as sham and pretention; it should be integrated into the very structure of the building (one should decorate construction rather than construct decoration); and it should achieve its romantic effect by expressing truthfully its own nature (brick should be seen to be brick, stone to be stone). When all these elements were brought together the re-created medieval design could make a bold romantic statement—it could proclaim the presence and power of the sacred to a secular world.[19]

In both Britain and Canada, however, it was not always possible to adhere to "real ancient designs...in all their parts, arrangements, and decorations." A number of problems quickly arose which would lead to a general opening-up of the revived medieval style. For example, one of the most celebrated churches of the Gothic revival, All Saints, Margaret Street, London (Fig. 3), had to adapt the principles of the revival to a small site in the West End that was in effect boxed-in by older buildings on three sides. Here the architect, William Butterfield, set the chancel and three-bay nave of the church along the backline of the site with the porch part way along the south side of the nave and the tall tower at the southwest. The clergy house at the southeast corner of the site and choir school at the southwest completed the arrangement, creating a small forecourt between the entrance arch at the street and the south wall of the nave.[20] One would be hard pressed to find an ancient model for this arrangement, and yet the details of the church—which were copied from precise medieval antecedents—the decoration, and the picturesque variation of volume (varying the length, width and particularly the height of sections of the structure to differentiate them) all conform to the romantic principles of the revival. The church had the power "to domineer by its elevation over the haughty and Protestantized shopocracy" that surrounded it.[21]

In Ontario architects also faced the need to alter and develop the strictly archaeological use of the Gothic style, but the problems that initiated this process were of a different type. While a small rural congregation might be able to worship within one of the models set out by the Cambridge Camden Society, a larger town or city congregation was constrained by the limitations imposed upon the medieval form by its own needs and the financial implications of urban building sites. In the first instance, the remarkable statistics of denominational growth, especially in urban centres, led congregations to try "to build for the future" by increasing the seating capacity of their new churches.[22] One set of solutions to this problem, given the models of Gothic design, would entail extending the length of the nave of a smaller medieval model, or moving towards a more cathedral-like scale.[23] But both ideas would necessitate a larger urban site and increased construction costs. The future might benefit, but unfortunately the central administrations of these denominations were anxious not to rely too heavily upon future generations to pay for the present construction costs.

Figure 3: All Saints', Margaret Street, London (1849–50), by William Butterfield, from **The Builder** *11 (1853)*

Consequently, architects and builders in Ontario were pushed towards a different solution—the inclusion of galleries within a medieval framework as in William Thomas's St. Andrew's (now St. Paul's) Presbyterian, Hamilton, begun in 1854.[24] But galleries, in turn, presented their own architectural problems. One distinguishing feature of the rural Gothic form was its low walls and high, steeply pitched roof. Galleries, however, raised the height of the side walls, which resulted in a less acutely angled gable and a shallower pitch to the roof. At the same time, galleries tended to push out the sides of the nave in order to accommodate either a larger gallery at the west end or a horseshoe-shaped gallery that occupied all but the east end of the sanctuary (Fig. 4).[25]

The introduction of amphitheatrical seating arrangements in a number of Protestant churches beginning in the 1870s led to a similar result.[26] The revived Gothic form, with its desire to present visually the three principal elements of a church (porch, nave and chancel) reflected a medieval liturgical tradition of worship that met the new needs of high churchmen and Roman Catholics. But the form was not as well suited to the religious practice of Methodists, Presbyterians and Baptists. For them, the central focus of worship was the pulpit and the central ritual of their worship was tied to the sermon. Consequently, they began to abandon the medieval rectangular seating plan in favour of an arced arrangement of seats facing a raised pulpit platform. Where this new pattern was set down within the traditional medieval plan the long length and narrow width of the nave restricted the circumference of each row of seats, thereby defeating the very purpose of this innovation—Beverley Street Baptist Church, Toronto, pro-

Figure 4: St. Andrew's (now St. Paul's) Presbyterian, Hamilton (1854), by William Thomas

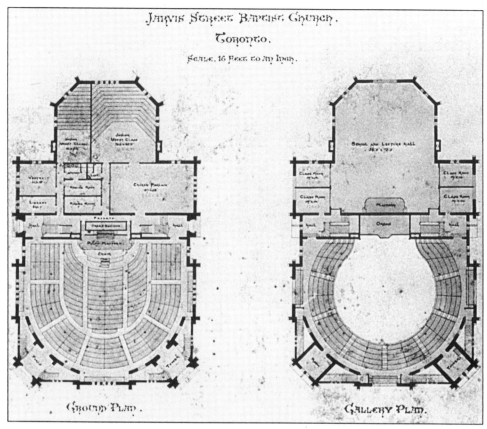

Figure 5: Plan of Jarvis St. Baptist, Toronto (1874–75), by Langley, Langley & Burke

vides a good example. Once again architects were forced to widen the nave and create a squarer space in which a fuller arc of seats could be placed before the pulpit (Figs. 5 and 6).[27]

A third internal tension arose out of the new administrative and institutional needs of Victorian religious life. By the mid-nineteenth century the Sunday school was fast becoming an integral feature of congregational life;[28] in addition, many congregations needed administrative offices, libraries and kitchens to service the growing list of church-related activities. A single room might meet most of these needs for a small congregation, but only a sizeable facility with several rooms could satisfy the requirements of large urban congregations. Once again the demands for new types of space put pressure on the medieval model.

Anglicans often met these new demands through an expanded parish hall, clearly differentiated from the church building although joined at times by a short extension running out from a door at the chancel end of the nave. A parish hall of this type, when added to a rectory and the church, gave the

Figure 6: Knox Presbyterian, Galt, now Cambridge (1869), by James Smith, facing pulpit platform

architect the opportunity of organizing a cluster of interrelated religious buildings that might reproduce, as at St. John's, Port Hope, a rural monastic ethos within an urban setting.[29]

Methodists, Presbyterians and Baptists approached the same problem in two different ways. On the one hand, they could use the basement of the church as a schoolroom, or on the other hand they could place the Sunday school and offices in what had been the chancel or the transept in the medieval design. The first solution could work well if the site were on a small elevation so that both the front door of the church and the door to the basement at the east end would be at grade level (Fig.7). But where this "hillside" arrangement was not possible, the basement solution meant raising once again the height of the entire church and sending the congregation up a long flight of stairs to reach the sanctuary of a church that seemed to be set on stilts; Knox Presbyterian, Elora, suggests the nature of the problem.[30] For this reason, a large number of Protestant congregations preferred to adapt either the transept or the chancel of the medieval form in order to accommodate the new spatial requirements (Figs. 5, 8 and 9).[31]

All these attempts to address the problems of internal space help to explain the changing form of Protestant church architecture in Ontario. Quite clearly, architects had to develop and modify the "real and ancient designs" that had been set down for their guidance. But while this Protestantized Gothic might have strained the limits of Anglican ecclesiological orthodoxy, it nonetheless maintained the basic aesthetic principles of the medieval revival. The new internal arrangement might have dispensed with the chancel—which after all was not especially truthful or purposeful in Protestant forms of worship—but the galleries and curved seats still focussed upon what was most fundamental to Protestant religious practice: the centrally placed pulpit platform clearly emphasized the words of the Bible and the preacher. The platform was often raised up a few steps and accommodated a reading desk, pulpit and communion table. The power of this focus was further enhanced by the growing popularity of including seats for a gowned choir and setting the whole platform against a background of organ pipes (Figs. 6 and 10).[32] The architectural handling of the new schoolrooms and offices also maintained the spirit of revived medievalism. Even though the size of the modified chancel or transept might alter the exact proportions of medieval design, these parts of the church were still clearly differentiated from the sanctuary, usually by a lowered roofline and a different manner of fenestration. In this way the church could maintain a sense of functional differentiation as well as achieve a general picturesque effect (Fig. 11).

Similar considerations also help to explain the increasing popularity of the Romanesque variation of the medieval style in late-nineteenth-century

Figure 7: Design for a new Baptist Church, Port Hope (1867), by Henry Langley

Figure 8: Knox Presbyterian, Woodstock (1897)

Ontario Protestant church architecture.[33] The increased centralization in the internal arrangement of these churches led to the abandonment of a clear differentiation of the main facade and the aisle walls that was characteristic of the medieval basilican form (Fig. 12).[34] As the church plan became more square, the north, south and west walls were given similar gabled facades. The inclusion of large pointed traceried Gothic windows in these facades did not always meet with happy results; the soaring quality of the window could well be blunted by the squat proportions of the wall. In addition, if the walls were of brick or smooth ashlar, the overall appearance might lack a convincing impression of solidity. But if the solidity were achieved through the use of large hammer-dressed stonework, the delicate Gothic window tracery would be in danger of being overwhelmed. The heavy round-arched Romanesque met these problems by making a bold monumental statement and yet allowing for a considerable amount of light to penetrate all three of the external walls of the sanctuary (Fig. 13).

In sum, the demands that congregations and urban space placed upon medieval archetypes of the revival helped to expand the rural Gothic church into a more substantial structure. The religious architecture of Ontario, however, did not develop solely in relation to internal spatial requirements. The principles of the medieval revival demanded that the church building as a whole should make an important social and cultural statement. The external appearance of the church should be able to stand out from and dominate its surroundings so that those who beheld the church might be inspired by the presence and power of the sacred.

To a certain extent the ways in which architects responded to internal problems helped the church to make such a bold statement. As galleries, new seating arrangements and schoolrooms increased the mass of the building, the church as a whole became more monumental in appearance. But the question of presence and inspiration did not end at this point. The ability to inspire turned upon the spatial relationship between the church and its external environment. For this reason, architects had to consider questions of location, siting and external architectural features in order to marry this aspect of romantic aesthetics to the environment of Ontario.

Here, too, the British medieval antecedents presented more problems than they resolved, in that they were tied to ancient sites that were often

Figure 9: Central Methodist, Woodstock (1875), by Langley, Langley & Burke

Figure 10: Knox Presbyterian, Woodstock (1897), facing pulpit platform

rural or village-like in character. In this context, the visual impact of a small church was increased by the fact that it was often set apart by a churchyard and could stand out above the low height of the surrounding structures. On occasion, such a small-scale environment might recur in Ontario, lending the small ecclesiologically correct parish church, such as St. John the Baptist, Lyn, the same aesthetic impact one might associate with its British antecedents.[35] But even in small towns this model had difficulties in realizing its proper visual effect. As cemeteries were removed from churchyards, the village church lost one of its romantic associations and came to occupy simply another town lot. In addition, the two- or three-storied height of Ontario main streets threatened to overwhelm the small church if it were placed at the centre of the town.

Larger urban settings increased the external pressures upon the small medieval form. In Toronto, for example, many denominations used this small scale of design to build a church for a new congregation usually in a recently developed part of the city. The architectural drawings of some of these churches are very revealing. The design for St. Peter's, Carlton Street (Fig. 14), for instance, not only reproduces the architectural elements of St. Michael's, Long Stanton, it also attempts to reproduce the rural ethos, with certain Canadian additions, that was associated with this Gothic model. But even if such settings at first enjoyed a semi-rural character, the process of urban growth quickly surrounded many of these small churches with groups of urban structures that often overwhelmed the church visually—reducing the power of the romantic statement and leaving the church as little more than a religious dot in a commercial and residential streetscape.[36]

The symmetrical dimensions of urban space in Ontario created another set of problems for the architects who tried to follow the aesthetic principles of romantic architecture. A number of older towns in the province conformed, at least in their initial stages of development, to Georgian assumptions of town planning. Here building lots, squares and markets were set down within a pattern of straight streets that often gave particular prominence to major public buildings such as town halls and courthouses. The symmetry of these designs stressed the aesthetic values of harmony, order and balance. The classical proportions of the first Anglican and Presbyterian churches reinforced this aesthetic, and the close architectural relationship between courthouse, jail and church served as a visual reminder of the close relationship between church and state during the early decades of the nineteenth century.[37]

Figure 11: Wesleyan Methodist, Port Hope (1874–75), by Smith and Gemmell

Figure 12: First Presbyterian, Brockville (1878–79), by James P. Johnston

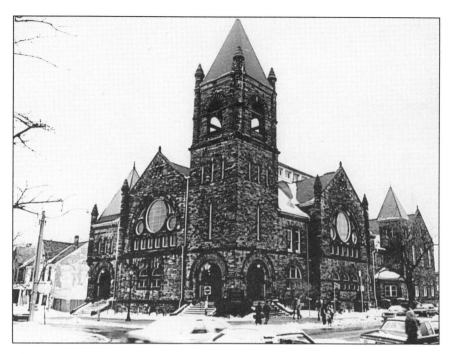

Figure 13: Trinity Methodist, Toronto (1889), by Langley, Langley & Burke

The revived medieval style, however, had a different visual agenda. It rejected both the aesthetics of classical design and the old alliance with the secular institutions of the state. The Gothic church sought to stand out from and dominate its immediate urban environment. On occasion, the older Georgian character of urban space might help the aesthetic goals of the new church. If, for example, a medieval church could be placed at a prominent point in the old design, and the scale of the surrounding urban buildings remained at a height of two-and-a-half or three stories, then the classical proportions of the town could serve as an effective backdrop for the romantic interplay between the church and its environment. In terms of both style and scale the large Gothic church could make a clear break with its surroundings. The court house square in Brockville provides an open vista for no less than four churches, imparting to them a clear sense of monumentality and presence (Fig. 12). In Toronto, this relationship reached an incredible height when, in 1872, the congregation at the Adelaide Street Methodist Church left their old plain chapel for a truly massive medieval edifice that was in fact built upon what had been an open town square. The new Metropolitan Church, the cathedral of Methodism, soared above its setting, realizing the precise romantic impact that was so central to romantic aesthetics (Fig. 15).[38]

Urban development in Ontario, however, did not maintain the principles of Georgian design. As towns grew they moved beyond the limits of

Figure 14: St. Peter's Anglican, Carlton St., Toronto (1865), by Gundry and Langley

the old town plans and incorporated new areas that had grown up in a seemingly haphazard fashion, monitored only by the interests of land developers and the habit of building within a rectangular pattern of intersecting streets. New churches in these areas had to achieve their romantic effect within a setting formed by a single line of buildings, or by the right-angled corner at the intersection of two streets. Faced with such an environment, architects developed another set of variations on the medieval theme in order to realize a romantic effect. For example, they opened the principal facade to the main street, often setting the building a short distance back from the line formed by other buildings. They also, where possible, tried to leave enough space along the sides of the building to expose the romantic presentation of building materials, windows and volumes; and ideally placed the church on a hill or a raised site, as at St. Thomas, Belleville.

It was the use of spires and towers, however, that allowed architects to emphasize the presence of the church and realize the romantic goals of the revived medieval design. Once more, medieval models were adapted for Ontario use. From a cathedral model one might incorporate a twin-towered facade, possibly with spires, as well as a tower or flèche at the crossing.[39] In the medieval parish church, single towers are usually located at the west end of the nave or over the crossing, although exceptions are found in which a tower may be placed either at the northwest or southwest angle, or even transeptally towards the east end.[40] Such asymmetrical tower placement appealed to the romantic sensibilities of the Victorian revivalists, and indeed Pugin went so far as to advocate asymmetrically placed towers, an idea frequently taken up by other British architects. In Ontario the specific character of the urban environment led architects to place towers and spires much more freely, quite literally moving them all around the church building in order to mark a change in function and to enhance the romantic presentation of the church itself. For example, the placing of these vertical elements responded almost invariably to the visual lines of the street—the tallest tower growing up at the principal corner of the site so that it would be clearly visible along the main street or along both streets if the church were built on a corner site. Indeed one can trace the movement of towers and spires as an architect would adapt the same basic church designs to the character of different urban sites.[41]

Such placement of towers and spires could achieve an even more striking effect when the site offered special possibilities. For example, in Guelph, where the short but prestigious Douglas Street ends at the site of the Anglican church, the architect, Henry Langley (a real master of this technique), moved the tower and spire to the precise point where it terminated the vista. The effect continues to be singularly striking (Fig. 16). In sum, the placing of the tower and spire allowed the architect to give the church a strong visual presence, and even when the adjacent streets filled up with residential and commercial buildings, the church continued to make a powerful cultural statement.

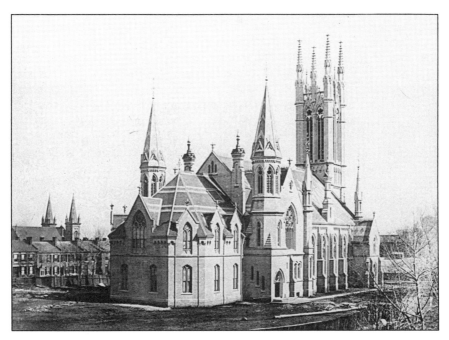

Figure 15: Metropolitan Methodist, Toronto (1870–72), by Henry Langley

The religious architecture of Ontario, then, developed in relation to a specific set of problems. During the last half of the nineteenth century the shape of the church changed as the spatial needs of worship and the demands of an urban environment altered the revived medieval form. The recurrence of these problems and the consistency of the architectural response created a set of church forms that at once met the requirements of Ontario's religious groups and the spatial qualities of the Ontario environment.

The development of this Ontario architectural form in the late nineteenth century also makes an important statement about the way religion in general tried to address the process of social change. The church building tried to control its urban context by reminding a developing world of the reality and moral authority of the sacred. In this way, architecture reflected the same moral and ethical concerns that characterized a whole group of religious and social movements such as missions, sabbath observance and temperance. All sought to create a strong moral atmosphere that might guide the Christian through the hazards of a materialistic age. The spires that tried to rise above the towns of Ontario were moral beacons to a secular world.

But the same forces that had initiated this process of change continued to shape and reshape Ontario society. Medievalism tried to establish a presence in the face of a new urban environment but it could not stop urban development itself. People continued to move from the countryside to the small town, and from towns to cities. As this process continued, urban development altered once again the relationship between religious forms and their immediate context, undercutting the equipoise between secular and sacred forces that the Victorians had tried so hard to establish and maintain. Over time, this led to the breakdown of both the revived medieval style and the romantic cultural assumptions upon which it had been built.

Perhaps the mid-sized town would continue to provide an urban context in which the aesthetics of romantic architecture might flourish well into the twentieth century. Centres like Galt, Guelph and Brockville might grow, but their large Victorian churches continued to retain a strong visual presence in what remained a reasonably low-scale urban environment. In an interesting way, this might add a visual confirmation to the common association of old-style religious values and small-town life in Ontario.

The church in the village or large urban centre was not as fortunate. The process of rural depopulation robbed any number of small centres of the wealth and population that sustained the traditional forms of religious life. Here the old environment might be reduced to only a small Gothic structure at a rural crossroads, now given over to domestic or other secular functions—a ghostly reminder of what once had been. Large urban environments presented another set of problems. In these centres, the process of functional segregation and suburbanization put severe strains upon many urban congregations. As the core was given over to exclusively commercial use, and as older neighbourhoods changed their ethnic, religious and class composition, the old Victorian church with its emptying Sunday school and loyal, aged and dwindling congregation could no longer sustain the religious life to which it was once accustomed. Hard-pressed congregations began to amalgamate, or abandon their buildings for new ones in the suburbs. At the same time, the physical scale of the urban setting was reducing the aesthetic power of these structures. In the early twentieth century, tall commercial buildings and large factories were coming to rival the church spire as the dominant feature of the urban landscape.[42] What was once a skyline of spires was becoming crowded with series of office blocks and innumerable chimneys.

Figure 16: St. George's Anglican, Guelph (1873), by Langley, Langley & Burke

Church builders followed their clients to the suburbs and here they continued to build some important examples of revived medieval architecture that maintained the principles of romantic design in their internal arrangements, external appearance and siting. Indeed, in a suburb that was exclusively residential in character these churches achieved a sense of presence and dominated their surroundings. But in the migration to the suburbs something that had been central to the revival was lost.

Pugin, the Cambridge Camden Society, John Ruskin and their romantic brethren in Canada held a vision of a common humanity. People might be deeply scarred by their fallen nature and endangered by the materialistic forces of their own times, but their very imperfections drew them together and underlined their common need for religious and social redemption. The medieval revival tried to present an architecture that proclaimed this message to all people; the Gothic church that soared above the Victorian town aspired to the same universal quality.

The church that found its way to the wealthy suburb, however, spoke to a more limited audience. Like the rival churches of St. Asaph's and St. Osoph's in Stephen Leacock's *Arcadian Adventures with the Idle Rich*, many of these churches looked down with majesty upon the residences of the well-to-do, their more humble past buried safely away in another part of the city. To the rector of St. Asaph's, the tall spire of his church seemed "to point, as it were, a warning against the sins of a commercial age."[43] But after indulging in this ecclesiological association, Leacock goes on to tell us that this architectural warning had little impact upon the minds of the wealthy congregation or upon the financial practices of the businessmen who dined within the shadows of the Mausoleum Club. Perhaps Leacock's sense of irony suggests a conclusion to this interesting architectural evolution. Religion and art had tried to temper the social problems that accompanied the breakdown of the older alliance of church and state. They had tried to inspire society with a moral system. Over time, however, they came to reflect the very social divisions within an urban industrial order that they had tried so hard to monitor and control.

---

1   For Hay Bay Methodist Meeting House see Marion MacRae and Anthony Adamson, *Hallowed Walls: Church Architecture of Upper Canada* (Toronto, 1975), 28–30, ills. II–12/13. For St. Andrew's, Niagara-on-the-Lake, see ibid., 199–204, ills. VIII–2/5, and Eric Arthur, *St. Andrew's Church Niagara-on-the-Lake*, School of Engineering, University of Toronto, research bulletin 153 (Toronto, 1938). For other neoclassical designs see St. George's Anglican Cathedral, Kingston (1825) [MacRae and Adamson, 208, ill. VIII–10, which shows the building before the 1891 addition, and Leslie Maitland, *Neoclassical Architecture in Canada* (Ottawa, 1984), 114] and St. Raphael's, Glengarry (1821) [MacRae and Adamson, 532–56, ills. III–3/5]. The popularity of classicism for churches in Toronto down to 1850 is demonstrated by the following buildings: St. James' Anglican Cathedral (1831) by Thomas Rogers [MacRae and Adamson, VIII–6/7]; St. Andrew's Presbyterian Church, Church and Adelaide streets (1830), by John Ewart (tower added in 1841 by John G. Howard) [Eric Arthur, *Toronto: No Mean City*, 2nd ed. (Toronto, 1974), 65, pl. 84; Maitland, 108, pl. 96]; Wesleyan Methodist Chapel, Richmond Street (1844), by Richard

      Woodsworth [Maitland, 113, pl. 10]; Zion Congregational Church, Bay and Adelaide streets (1837–40), by William Thomas [Maitland, 116, pl. 104; Arthur, 67, pl. 89]; St. Paul's Roman Catholic Church, Lot (now Queen) Street (1823) [MacRae and Adamson, 82, ill. IV–2]; Bond Street Baptist Church (1848) [MacRae and Adamson, 209–10, ills. VIII–12/13].

2   James Gibbs (d. 1754) designed, among other London churches, St. Martin-in-the-field and St. Mary-le-Strand. His *A Book of Architecture* (London, 1728) remained a standard reference on Georgian design for more than a century. For Holy Trinity, Chippawa, see MacRae and Adamson, 94–97, ills. IV–6/8. Other examples of superficial Gothicisms include Christ Church, Moulinette (1837), now relocated at Upper Canada Village [MacRae and Adamson, ills. V–18/19]; Old St. Paul's, Woodstock (1834); the Baptist Church, Haldimand (1824) [MacRae and Adamson, ill. X–42]; St. Andrew's Free Church, Kirkhill (1845) [MacRae and Adamson, ill. X–49]; St. Vincent-de-Paul, Niagara-on-the-Lake (1834) [Peter John Stokes, *Old Niagara-on-the-Lake* (Toronto, 1971), 100–101]; Trinity Anglican, Port Burwell (1836).

3   MacRae and Adamson, 99–104, ills. IV–13/14. Other examples of this trend include St. John's, York Mills (1843), by John G. Howard [Arthur, 77, pl. 106]; St. George the Martyr, John Street, Toronto (1844), by Henry Bower Lane [Arthur, 76, pl. 105], of which only the west tower survived the 1955 fire (the arch mouldings, capitals, bases and detached shafts of the west doorway, although executed in wood, represent very good copies of Early English originals); St. John's, Peterborough [MacRae and Adamson, 91, ill. IV–5]; Christ Church, Holland Landing [MacRae and Adamson, 99–100, ill. IV–11]; St. Paul's, Kingston (1846), by Henry Bower Lane, which, although having a lath and plaster barrel vault in the nave, does have good Early English mouldings and stiff leaf capitals to the main arcade [City of Kingston, Ontario, *Buildings of Architectural and Historical Significance*, III (Kingston, 1973), 131–35]; St. Michael's Roman Catholic Cathedral, Toronto (1845), by William Thomas (tower in 1865 by Henry Langley, dormers in 1890–91 by Joseph Connolly) [Arthur, 86–90, pls. 126–29]; St. James' Anglican Cathedral, Toronto (1850), by Cumberland and Ridout [Arthur, 127–32, pls. 206–9].

4   The Romanesque aspect of the Gothic revival has been little-studied, but it must be emphasized that the Gothic revival was not solely concerned with the pointed arch. The round-arched Romanesque was very popular for churches in England in the 1830s and 1840s and continued to be used in the second half of the century, during which time it became an important element of the Gothic revival in Ontario. See Thomas Cocke, "The Rediscovery of Romanesque", in *English Romanesque Art 1066–1200* [exhibition catalogue] (London, 1984), 360–91, and review by Malcolm Thurlby, *Gesta* 24 (1985), 85. See also Henry-Russell Hitchcock, *Early Victorian Architecture in Britain* (New Haven, 1954), 99, where reference is made to A. W. Pugin's St. Michael's, Gorey, Co. Wexford (1839), which stands at the beginning of a tradition in Ireland of the so-called Hiberno-Romanesque and is reflected in Ontario in Joseph Connolly's Roman Catholic churches of Holy Cross, Kemptville (1887) and St. John the Evangelist, Gananoque (1891) [Louis J. Flynn, *Built on a Rock: The Story of the Roman Catholic Church in Kingston 1826-1976* (Kingston, 1976), 254–68; Malcolm Thurlby, "The Irish-Canadian Pugin: Joseph Connolly", *Irish Arts Review* 3 (1986), 16–21, especially 20–21]. Hitchcock, 104–5, discusses St. Mary's, Wilton (1840), by Wyatt and Brandon which is labelled "Lombardic" to distinguish it from English Romanesque, and has been called the "most important Anglican church erected about this time." See Charles L. Eastlake, *A History of the Gothic Revival* (1872 ed. rep. New York, 1970), 218. For Romanesque revival churches in Britain in the 1840s see Hitchcock, 139–42. An interesting early example of Romanesque revival in Ontario is St. Thomas' Anglican Church, Shanty Bay (1838–39) [Alan Gowans, *Building Canada: An Architectural History of Canadian Life* (Toronto, 1966), 83, 93–94, pl. 113]. For a general discussion of Romanesque churches in Ontario see MacRae and Adamson, 219–39. For the development in the United States see Carroll L. V. Meeks, "Romanesque before Richardson in the United States", *The Art Bulletin* 35 (1953), 17–23, and the interesting remarks by Marcus Whiffen and Frederick Keeper, *American Architecture 1607–1976* (London, 1981), 197, suggesting that the use of round-arched

Romanesque rather than the pointed Gothic was favoured by Protestants in being "Free from the taint of popery."

5   The most important examples still extant are St. Andrew's, Niagara-on-the-Lake [see note 1]; St. Andrew's, Williamstown [MacRae and Adamson, ill. II–22]; Christ Church, Amherstburg [ibid., ill. III–8]; Christ Church, Vittoria [ibid., ill. III–16]; St. George's Anglican Cathedral, Kingston (begun 1825, remodeled 1846 and extended 1891; the extension conforms to the classicism of the original design following the models of Christopher Wren's St. Paul's Cathedral, London, and St. Stephen's, Walbrook) [City of Kingston, Ontario, *Buildings of Historical and Architectural Significance,* I (Kingston, 1971), 10–16].

6   William Hay, "The Late Mr. Pugin and the Revival of Christian Architecture", *Anglo-American Magazine* 2 (1853), 70. In equating paganism with classicism and Gothic with Christianity, Hay is following Pugin who referred to churches built in the classical style as a "bastard imitation of pagan edifices, unworthy and unsuited to so sacred a purpose." See Augustus Welby Pugin, *Contrasts: or, A Parallel Between the Noble Edifices of the Fourteenth and Fifteenth Centuries, and Similar Buildings of the Present Day: shewing the Present Decay of Taste: Accompanied by appropriate Text* (Salisbury, 1836; 2nd rev. ed. London, 1841, rep. Leicester, 1973), 19.

7   For a good example of Methodist ecclesiology see "God's Presence in God's Rest", in *Sermons by Rev. W. Morley Punshon,* II (London, 1883), 98–111. For a general description of religious architecture and social change see William de Villiers-Westfall, "The Dominion of the Lord: An Introduction to the Cultural History of Protestant Ontario in the Victorian Period", *Queen's Quarterly* 83 (1976), 47–70, and William Westfall, *Two Worlds: The Protestant Culture of Nineteenth-Century Ontario* (Montreal, 1989).

8   Compare, for example, John Ruskin's description of the Gothic with Carl Berger's analysis of the "northern" theme in Canadian national thought; see John Ruskin, *The Stones of Venice,* 3 vols. (London, 1851–53) and Carl Berger, "The True North Strong and Free", in Peter Russell, ed., *Nationalism in Canada* (Toronto, 1966), 3–26.

9   For a contemporary account of the formation of the Ontario Society of Architects, see *The Canadian Architect and Builder* [hereafter *CAB*] 3 (1890), especially 40–41. Two interesting articles on the professionalization of architecture are G. F. Stalker, "The Relation of an Architect Towards His Client" and "The Relation of an Architect Towards Contractors", *CAB* 2 (1889), 124. See also Kelly Crossman, *Architecture in Transition: From Art to Practice 1885–1906* (Montreal, 1987). As early as the 1830s and 1840s, with the beginnings of the architectural profession in Ontario, several architects distinguished themselves by mastering medieval and classicizing styles. For example, William Thomas, who designed Toronto's neoclassical St. Lawrence Hall (1850) and Don Jail (1858) [Arthur, pls. 187–92, 226–27], used pointed Gothic for St. Michael's Roman Catholic Cathedral, Toronto (1845) [see note 3], St. Paul's Anglican church (now Cathedral), London (1846), and St. Andrew's (now St. Paul's), Hamilton (1853) [MacRae and Adamson, 145–53], and the round-arched "Lombard" Romanesque style for St. George's, Guelph (1851) [ibid., pl. IX–4)], and Zion Chapel, Toronto (1856) [ibid., pl. IX–5].

10   See, among others, J. M. S. Careless, "Metropolis and Region: The Interplay between City and Region in Canadian History before 1914", *Urban History Review,* no. 3–78 (1979), 99–118. For a more recent overview of the literature on the process of metropolitan development, see Gilbert A. Stelter, "A Regional Framework for Urban History", ibid. 13 (1985), 193–206, and Alan F. J. Artibise and Paul-Andre Linteau, *The Evolution of Urban Canada: An Analysis of Approaches and Interpretations,* Institute of Urban Studies, report no. 4 (Winnipeg, 1984).

11   See note 6.

12   For an interesting study of hymns see Margaret A. Filshie, "Sacred Harmonies: The Congregational Voice in Canadian Protestant Worship", in Association for Canadian Studies, *Religion/Culture: Comparative Canadian Studies* [proceedings of the 1984 annual conference], vol. 7 in the series *Canadian Issues* (1985), 287–309.

13 Abacus, "Notes on a Trip to the West", *CAB* 1 (1888), 5.

14 On the Cambridge Camden Society see James F. White, *The Cambridge Movement: The Ecclesiologists and the Gothic Revival* (Cambridge, 1962). For Christ Church, Fredericton, see Douglas Scott Richardson, "Christ Church Cathedral, Fredericton, N.B." (M.A. diss., Yale University, 1966); Phoebe Stanton, *The Gothic Revival and American Church Architecture: An Episode in Taste, 1840–1856* (Baltimore, 1968), 127–58; Robert L. Watson, *Christ Church Cathedral, Fredericton: A History* (Fredericton, 1984). See also Douglas Richardson, "Hyperborean Gothic: Or Wilderness Ecclessiology and the Wood Churches of Edward Medley", *Architectura* 2 (1972), 48–82.

15 See Gilbert A. Stelter, "The Classical Ideal: Cultural and Urban Form in Eighteenth-Century Britain and America", *Journal of Urban History* 10 (1984), 351–82, and his "The City Building Process in Canada", in Gilbert A. Stelter and Alan F. J. Artibise, eds., *Shaping the Urban Landscape: Aspects of the Canadian City Building Process* (Ottawa, 1982), 1–29; and Michael Doucet, "Speculation and the Physical Expansion of Mid-Nineteenth Century Hamilton", ibid., 173–99. In Britain the tension between the use and inherited form led to an important debate over the development of the Gothic style. In general this debate pitted those who argued for the maintenance of an archaeologically correct style against those who asserted that the style should be developed to meet the needs of contemporary usage. On this question see David B. Brownlee, "The First High Victorians: British Architectural Theory in the 1840s", *Architectura* 15 (1985), 33–46.

16 See Isobel K. Ganton, "Land Subdivision in Toronto, 1851–1883", in Stelter and Artibise, 200–213; Peter Goheen, *Victorian Toronto, 1850 to 1900; Pattern and Process of Growth* (Chicago, 1970); Michael Katz, *The People of Hamilton, Canada West: Family and Class in a Mid-Nineteenth Century City* (Cambridge, Mass., 1975); and Jacob Spelt, *The Urban Development in South-Central Ontario* (Toronto, 1972).

17 "A Hint on Modern Church Architecture", *The Ecclesiologist* 1 (1842), 133. Pugin spoke in a similar manner: "We seek *authority*, not originality...; for the establishment of *a principle, not individual celebrity*," A. Welby Pugin, *The Present State of Ecclesiastical Architecture in England* (London, 1843), 113; and, writing in the third person: "Mr. Pugin, we believe, never claimed the least merit on the score of originality: nor does he profess to invent new combinations, but simply to revive, as far as circumstances and means will admit, the glorious but till lately despised works of the Middle Ages," ibid., 13.

18 In this connection Pugin refers to "propriety": "*that the external and internal appearance of our edifice should be illustrative of, and in accordance with, the purpose for which it is destined,*" A. Welby Pugin, *The True Principles of Pointed or Christian Architecture* (London, 1841; rep. London, 1973), 50.

19 On design Pugin states: "*The two great rules for design are these: 1st, that there should be no features about a building which are not necessary for convenience, construction, or propriety: 2nd, that all ornament should consist of enrichment of the essential construction of the building,*" Pugin, *True Principles*, 1; "All plaster, cast-iron, and composition ornaments, painted like stone or oak, are mere impositions, and although very suitable to a tea-garden, are utterly unworthy of a sacred edifice. Let every man build to God according to his means, but not practise showy deceptions; better is to do a little substantially and consistently with truth, than to produce a great but fictitious effect. Hence the rubble wall and oaken rafter of antiquity yet impress the mind with feelings of reverent awe, which never could be produced by the cement and plaster imitations of elaborate tracery and florid designs which in these times are stuck about mimic churches in disgusting profusion," ibid., 53.

20 On William Butterfield and All Saints, see especially Paul Thompson, *William Butterfield* (London, 1971), and his "All Saints' Church, Margaret Street, Reconsidered", *Architectural History* 8 (1965), 73–87; Hitchcock, 580–94.

21 A. J. Beresford-Hope, *The English Cathedral of the Nineteenth Century* (London, 1861), 235. See also George L. Hersey, *High Victorian Gothic: A Study in Associationism* (Baltimore, 1972), 104–19.

22   For statistical information on church construction, denominational growth and general
      population increase, see William Edward de Villiers-Westfall, "The Sacred and the
      Secular: Studies in the Cultural History of Protestant Ontario in the Victorian Period"
      (Ph.D. diss., University of Toronto, 1976), app. 2, 324–35.

23   For an extension of the nave, see St. Paul's Anglican, Bloor Street, Toronto (1860)
      [Arthur, 146–47, pl. 237]. The best examples of cathedral-like scale are the Church of Our
      Lady of the Immaculate Conception, Guelph (1876), by Joseph Connolly [MacRae and
      Adamson, 167, ill. VI–26] and Metropolitan Methodist, Toronto (1870–72), by Henry
      Langley. The former was not designed in 1863, as stated by MacRae and Adamson, for
      Connolly did not arrive in Canada until 1873; see Malcolm Thurlby, "The Irish-
      Canadian Pugin", *Irish Arts Review* 3 (1986), 18–20.

24   Malcolm Thurlby, "Nineteenth-Century Churches in Ontario: A Study in the Meaning
      of Style", *Historic Kingston* 35 (1987), 96–110, fig. 9.

25   The Roman Catholics of Ontario remain, almost invariably, true to Puginian practice in
      restricting galleries to the west end of their churches. The one notable exception to this
      rule is Notre-Dame Basilica, Ottawa [MacRae and Adamson, ill. X–10; Malcolm Thurlby,
      "Ottawa Gothic", *Rotunda* 21 (1988), 24–27]. The Anglicans were also, in the main, more
      faithful to medieval models in omitting galleries, although an important exception was
      St. James' Cathedral, Toronto [Arthur, pl. 209].

26   It is difficult to date with authority the introduction to Ontario of this new arrangement
      of seats. John Ross Robertson claims that Jarvis Street Baptist (1874–75), by Langley,
      Langley & Burke, was the first to use it in Toronto; see his *Landmarks of Toronto:...*, 4th
      ser. (Toronto, 1904), 42–43. Excellent examples of amphitheatrical seating plans are
      Central Methodist, Woodstock (1875), by Langley, Langley & Burke [MacRae and
      Adamson, 295 for plan], Wesleyan Methodist, Port Hope (1874–75), by Smith and
      Gemmell [plans are held in the sanctuary); First Presbyterian and First Baptist,
      Brockville (both 1878–79), both by James P. Johnston; Central Presbyterian, Galt (now
      Cambridge) (1880); Dundas Street Central Methodist, London (1895); St. Andrew's
      Presbyterian, Prescott (1892), by James P. Johnston; Spring Street Methodist, Westport
      (1889). Architects and builders of Nonconformist churches in Victorian England
      occasionally flirted with the idea of amphitheatrical seating. It was strongly advocated
      by Philip Sambell, architect of Truro, who wrote on the subject to the *Baptist Magazine* 33
      (1841), 355, but the number of examples actually built is very small. See Christopher G.
      Wakeling, "The Architecture of the Nonconformist Churches during the Victorian and
      Edwardian Years" (Ph.D. diss., University of East Anglia, 1983), 46–48, 58. It is therefore
      unlikely that our Ontario examples owe anything directly to English models, although
      at a more general level it is interesting to note that in the 1870s there is an increased
      emphasis on centralization in Nonconformist church planning; see James Cubitt, *Church
      Design for Congregations: Its Development and Possibilities* (London, 1870).

27   A number of Anglicans also applauded this internal rearrangement, although Anglican
      churches continued to adhere to the older long nave and chancel plan; see Sir Daniel
      Wilson, "Church Builders", *Evangelical Churchman*, reprinted in *CAB* 2 (1889), 42–43. The
      somewhat awkward equation of the arced arrangement of seats within the essentially
      basilican plan may be seen, for example, in Knox Presbyterian, Galt (1869), by James
      Smith; Beverley Street Baptist, Toronto (1886), by Langley and Burke; and especially
      James Street Baptist, Hamilton (1879), in which Joseph Connolly adheres to his Irish
      Catholic sources in dividing the church into nave and aisles with columnar arcades.

28   For an excellent study of the institutional development of Methodism with special
      reference to Sunday schools, see Neil Semple, "The Impact of Urbanization on the
      Methodist Church in Central Canada, 1854–1884" (Ph.D. diss., University of Toronto,
      1979).

29   Other good Ontario examples of the grouping of Anglican buildings are St. Paul's,
      Kingston (1846), and St. Paul's Cathedral, London (1844).

30   Further good examples of the sanctuary raised above a basement are Mount Carmel
      Methodist Episcopal, Troy (1873), and First Baptist, Beamsville [MacRae and Adamson,
      ills. IX–20, X–31].

31 For the adaptation of the transept, see Wesleyan Methodist, Port Hope; for the modified chancel, see Central Methodist, Woodstock.

32 For the raised pulpit platform against a background of organ pipes, see Wesleyan Methodist, Port Hope; Central Methodist, Woodstock; First Presbyterian and First Baptist, Brockville.

33 The influence of the work of Henry Hobson Richardson and the so-called Richardsonian Romanesque style are particularly important in this connection; see Jeffrey Karl Ochsner, *H. H. Richardson: Complete Architectural Works* (Cambridge, Mass., 1982). Some examples of the Richardsonian style in Ontario Protestant churches are Trinity Methodist, Toronto (1889), by Langley and Burke; St. Andrew's Presbyterian, Prescott (1892); Knox Presbyterian, Woodstock (1897); First Presbyterian, Chatham (1892), by T. J. Rutley; and the Presbyterian church, Paris (1893), also by Rutley.

34 For example, First Presbyterian and First Baptist, Brockville; First Presbyterian, Galt; First Presbyterian, Chatham; Paris Presbyterian, Paris; St. Andrew's Presbyterian, Prescott; and St. Andrew's Presbyterian, Kingston.

35 Thurlby, "Meaning of Style", fig. 1, and MacRae and Adamson, 161, ill. VI–19. Two other examples are St. James-the-Less, Toronto (1858) [MacRae and Adamson, 156, ill. VI–15]; and St. Paul's, Almonte (1863).

36 St. Stephen's-in-the-Fields, Toronto (1858), by Thomas Fuller, is a good example.

37 See Thomas Young's "View in King Street [Toronto] Looking Eastward", drawn in 1835 [Arthur, pl. 33].

38 For a contemporary description of this church see *Christian Guardian* (Toronto), 10 Apr. 1872, 116–17.

39 For example, St. Peter's Basilica, London (1880), by Joseph Connolly. Although not of cathedral status the church of Our Lady of the Immaculate Conception, Guelph, takes on cathedral appearance with an apse-ambulatory plan with radiating chapels, transept, a flèche at the crossing, and twin western towers which were originally intended, like St. Peter's, London, to receive spires; see Thurlby, "Irish-Canadian Pugin", 17–19.

40 Transeptally placed towers are most common in southwest England, where they follow the model of the Romanesque Cathedral at Exeter; see Malcolm Thurlby, "The Romanesque Cathedral of St. Mary and St. Peter at Exeter", in British Archaeological Association, Conference Transactions, *Medieval Art and Architecture at Exeter Cathedral* (forthcoming).

41 In the work of Henry Langley for example.

42 Professor Stelter describes these changes in the following way: "A kind of giantism prevailed, from the size of the new suburbs and the height of the buildings in the central core to the organization of new business enterprises and the building of enormous factories," Gilbert A. Stelter, "City-Building Process", in Stelter and Artibise, 28. Gunter Gad and Deryck Holdsworth make the same point in relation to office development in Toronto. They illustrate the change in scale and style of office building that occurred in the first decades of the twentieth century. "From now on," they argue, "the temples of commerce rose higher than the temples of God," Gunter Gad and Deryck Holdsworth, "Building for City, Region, and Nation: Office Development in Toronto 1834–1934", in Victor Russell, ed., *Forging a Consensus: Historical Essays on Toronto* (Toronto, 1984), 273–319.

43 Stephen Leacock, *Arcadian Adventures with the Idle Rich* (London, 1914; rep. ed. Toronto, 1969), 101.

Native Limited Identities and Newcomer Metropolitanism in Upper Canada, 1814–1867

TONY HALL

The most deeply rooted and all-embracing ethnic distinctions among Ontario's Aboriginal population are founded in the contrasting nature of the two major geographic features marking the provincial landscape: to the north, the Precambrian Shield, dominated by huge outcroppings of granite as well as by numerous lakes and streams; to the south, loamy undulating terrain, generally well drained and highly fertile. These are each the ances-

Veterans of the War of 1812 ca. 1886: (left to right) Jacob Warner age 92, John Tutlee age 91, John 'Smoke' Johnson age 93

tral homelands of two great cultural complexes of Native society known respectively as Algonkians and Iroquoians.[1] With the arrival of European colonists a host of new influences came to bear upon the outlines of this old ethnic configuration. Increasingly, Native communities were shaped according to the contingencies brought by the effect of new diseases,[2] the dynamics of the fur trade and the militarism associated with the imperialistic contest for commercial and political hegemony over North American territory.[3]

As enormous as were the adaptations already made, in 1814 Native people in Upper Canada—in this study the term encompasses present-day Ontario as far north as the watershed delineating the Great Lakes basin from the Hudson Bay and James Bay basin—were poised at the beginning of an era that would see them have to accommodate even greater Newcomer-imposed changes. In the developing atmosphere of relative peace and stability along the international border between the United States and the crown lands north of the Great Lakes, the fighting prowess of Native groups was no longer a major factor in the strategic calculations of military authorities in either London or Washington. Indian prestige and power were diminished correspondingly, just as wave after wave of Euro-American immigration pressured Native people towards the social, economic and even physical margins of the new settler society taking form in the fledgling frontier colony of Upper Canada. In this atmosphere, one where Native people often fell subject to the ravages of poverty, alcoholism and many other manifestations of social dislocation, there was little consolation in the apparently dimming galaxy of old Native spirit helpers and guides. And so Christian missionaries, who now tended to supplant military authorities as agents of colonialism *vis-à-vis* the Native population, found their messages falling on relatively fertile ground.

This missionary drive more and more became a major determining force of colonial Indian policy, aimed officially after 1830 at making reserves the site of self-sufficient Native communities with Christianity and agriculture as their basis.[4] With the progress of such initiatives, Aboriginal groups found themselves increasingly isolated from each other on those remaining islands of Indian land separated by growing seas of acquisitive Newcomers. Moreover, the adoption by many Native people of Christianity introduced into their societies new sources of religious differentiation, separating converts from traditionalists, Catholics from Protestants and Methodists from Anglicans.[5]

By mid-century Native people began experiencing yet more intense pressures to abandon their own claims to land and political autonomy. The new element in this process was the withdrawal of the imperial government from a directing role in the field of Indian affairs. The corresponding development was the assumption of authority by Indian Department officials responsible to the local legislative assembly. An increasingly acrimonious atmosphere of relations between the colonial administration and Aboriginal communities was the result, especially in matters involving land and Indian government. For Native people, the new political context created all sorts of possibilities for both alliances and disputes. Accordingly, the changing dynamics of Newcomer metropolitanism in Upper Canada played an increasingly influential role in the shaping of Native identities.

As late as the seventeenth century, the most sharply visible ethnic distinction among the Native people of the Upper Canada area still conformed fairly closely to the land's major geographic division. In the Precambrian Shield lived many small bands of people who moved seasonally over wide areas in their pursuit of fish, fowl and game. Some bands engaged also in small-scale gardening. A major bond between these groups was their ability to communicate in languages that were by and large mutually intelligible, even if differentiated by a number of dialects. Their speaking relationships helped maintain a Native linguistic family which was and is the most numerically powerful and geographically widespread of any in North America. Scholars have come to name this language family Algonkian, just as those Native groups united in this linguistic inheritance are known as Algonkians.[6]

In the more arable territories south of the Precambrian Shield coalesced societies which together are known as Iroquoians. As with the Algonkians, a shared heritage of related languages and dialects primarily distinguishes this ethnic grouping. Generally their community lives were centred in villages, moved only short distances from time to time when surrounding fields became agriculturally exhausted. The principal staples of survival in such societies were corn, beans and squash, always cultivated by women. There were other forms of associations, however, which marked Iroquoians as related peoples.

One of these was the Five, and later Six Nations Confederacy, whose original homelands at the time of contact with Europeans were situated in present-day upper New York state. Members of this association described themselves as the *Houdenosaunee*, the people of the extended lodge.[7] After the American revolution, the larger part of the Six Nations League chose to seek new homes rather than allow themselves to fall under the jurisdiction of the new United States government. British military authorities came to the assistance of their Indian allies, making two tracts available for League members in the Bay of Quinté and Grand River areas.[8] In the latter, the new arrivals also included a small number of Delaware from New York and Pennsylvania, Nanticoke from Maryland, Tutelo from the Carolinas and a few Creek and Cherokee families from the Alabama-Georgia-Carolinas area whose absorption within the Six Nations was not yet complete.

Essential to Six Nations ethnicity was the League's balance between group autonomy and the demands of wider federation. The basis of this polity was a shared belief in the principles taught by generations of Houdenosaunee faithkeepers—rules that had been divinely conveyed through the intervention of the prophet Deganawida.[9] Although in truth the League, consisting of the Mohawk, Oneida, Onondaga, Cayuga, Seneca and later the Tuscaroras (who joined in the 1720s),[10] was never a stranger to bitter internal dissension, it nevertheless had sufficient cohesion and resilience to make the Confederacy formidable throughout the colonial period.

The Houdenosaunee settlers at the Grand River were numerically powerful enough, and sufficiently representative of the Confederacy's major constituent parts, that they were able to design their new community along lines reasonably consistent with the League's original internal structures. Each of the Six Nations asserted control over separate sections of the reserve. As had been the tradition in their former lands, the League's "firekeepers," the Onondagas, became the host nation of the Grand River people's central seat of government. And in the workings of the Onondaga Council House, effort was made to maintain as much continuity as reasonably possible with the patterns of decision making practised before the migration into Upper Canada.[11] This distinctive and characteristic feature of Six Nations ethnicity—one which helped sustain the diversity within the League as well as its coherence *vis-à-vis* the outside world—remained operative throughout the nineteenth century.

There were several other Iroquoian groups with settlements in Upper Canada. As noted, the Six Nations community at the Grand River was established simultaneously with the Iroquois reserve in the Bay of Quinté. The latter became known as Tyendinaga. The settlement's Loyalist founders were almost exclusively Mohawks who had followed Captain John Deseronto during the American revolution.[12] Further east, at the point on the St. Lawrence where present-day Ontario, Quebec and New York state meet, is the St. Regis Reserve or Akwesasne as it is sometimes called. The community was founded in the final years of the French régime in Canada primarily by Mohawks who had allied themselves with the Roman Catholic Church and the government of New France. Accordingly, these people share the same Houdenosaunee origins as the Native settlers of the Grand Valley and Tyendinaga. Because of their background and their proximity to Montreal, many St. Regis men found employment in that city's far-flung fur trading enterprises.[13] When Montreal's importance in the fur trade weakened after 1821, it became common for St. Regis Indians to work in the lumbering industry in the Ottawa Valley.[14]

Upper Canada became the home to yet another Iroquoian community in 1840. The new settlers were Oneidas from New York state, part of the Six Nations group who had stayed in their original territory after 1783. The intense pressures on their lands in New York, along with the recognition that the Grand River community had become the most influential centre of gravity of the old League, led them to Canada. With their own money the Oneidas purchased 5,400 acres of good rich soil on the Thames River near Caradoc, southwest of London. In making the adjustment to their new setting, the Oneidas identified themselves closely with the Six Nations people at the Grand River.[15]

The Hurons were the remaining Iroquoian group resident in Upper Canada during the period under consideration. The name *Wendat* or *Wyandot*, a term of self-description originating in their own language, is used also to identify these people. The larger number of the Hurons or Wyandots were actually descendants of the Petun, an Iroquoian-speaking group whose home territory in the early seventeenth century was situated around the southeastern shores of Georgian Bay. By the late eighteenth century this group had settled on a reserve which included the area of present-day Anderdon township near Windsor. In spite of their linguistic orientation the Huron of the nineteenth century, like their seventeenth-century ancestors, were identified politically more with Algonkian peoples than with Iroquoians. In planting themselves astride both sides of the strategic Detroit River after 1701, the Hurons and Petuns, although small in number, remained a significant military, political and commercial presence in the area until the end of the War of 1812. In the decades that followed, a series of fights over real estate became a major preoccupation of the Hurons who remained on the Canadian side of the river. The resulting fragmentation of the community was part of a process by which the Canadian Hurons were soon virtually absorbed into the surrounding population. Near the end of the nineteenth century, when what remained of the Huron reserve was apportioned between 41 family heads, their ethnic extinction was in the final stages.[16]

In sum, a broad spectrum of ethnic diversity existed among the several Iroquoian groups settled in Upper Canada. A few common attributes were also shared by them. Except for the Wyandots, for instance, all had their origins in the League of the Houdenosaunee. And all groups favoured a way of life centred in fixed settlements. The preference of most Iroquoians for permanent community sites remained a characteristic which distinguished them from the largest number of their Algonkian neighbours until the early decades of the nineteenth century.

For the most part, Algonkian groups did not establish long-term, continuously inhabited settlements on specific plots of land until forced to do so by the mounting pressure of Euro-American immigration. Consequently, the identities of Great Lakes Algonkian peoples tend to be elusive. As they were usually on the move, contemporary seventeenth- and eighteenth-century observers were less likely to employ a common nomenclature in describing the various Algonkian groups they met in their travels.[17] With all their imperfectly understood diversity, however, the Great Lakes Algonkians were aware of their common linguistic inheritance. All, for instance, used the term *Anishinabe(k)* to identify themselves. Many of them still do. The word is thought to derive from an expression which could be translated as "spontaneous man" or "original man."[18]

One Anishinabek grouping of considerable importance to the Indian history of Upper Canada is the Three Fires Confederacy. A polity whose inner workings are only vaguely understood, the Confederacy was composed of the Ojibway, Ottawa and Potawatomi.[19] Analysis of the tribal names of the latter two groups gives some indication of how these people were ethnically differentiated. *Ode* in Algonkian is a verb describing the exchanging of goods. So as their name suggests, the Ottawa or *Odawa* were to assume major responsibility within the Confederacy for trading with other groups. The name Potawatomi is said to derive from the Algonkian term *Boodwenini*, meaning the one who keeps or tends the fire. Having the job of firekeeper implied that the Potawatomi assumed broader responsibilities for maintaining the traditional teachings and, through these teachings, the spiritual well-being of Three Fires members. There is more uncertainty about the origins of the term Ojibway. In any case, the name does not seem to offer any substantial clues about the role of this, the largest, group within the Three Fires Confederacy.[20]

Throughout the eighteenth century Three Fires people moved widely throughout the Great Lakes area. The Potawatomi[21] and the Ottawa[22] situated their mobile communities most often in territories south of the lakes— in the area of present-day Ohio, Indiana, Michigan, Illinois and Wisconsin. The Ojibway peopled the lands around Lake Superior and the Shield region to the north and east of Lake Huron. Around the end of the seventeenth century, one Ojibway group, who became known as the Mississauga, had pushed south from the Precambrian Shield, overcoming some resistance from Five Nations warriors.[23] The firm establishment of an Ojibway presence throughout Upper Canada proved of great importance for the other Three Fires people in the decades following the War of 1812. During this period the position of the Ottawas and Potawatomis was increasingly undermined by the actions of the United States government, just as their lands were being overwhelmed by a huge influx of Euro-American settlers. When the American government attempted to move all Indians east of the Mississippi to new homes on the other side of the great river,[24] many Ottawas and Potawatomis refused to leave the Great Lakes region. In the late 1830s and through the 1840s they chose instead to join the Ojibways of Upper Canada.[25]

In 1837 at Manitowaning on Manitoulin Island, British officials invited those Anishinabek resident in the United States to move northward into crown-controlled territories. Native people from throughout the Great Lakes area had gathered at this newly established Indian Department station[26] in order to receive the crown's annual tribute of "presents": guns, ammunition, kettles, fish hooks, blankets and the like. The giving of presents had grown into an annual tradition marking the formal continuation of the alliance between Indian peoples and the British military.[27] At Manitowaning the visiting groups were told by Samuel Peters Jarvis, chief superintendent of Indian affairs in Upper Canada: "Children, you must come and live under the protection of your Great Father or lose the advantage of annually receiving valuable presents from him."[28] The visitors were then given three years to move northward if they wished to continue receiving the crown's tribute. This development in British policy helped persuade a number of Ottawas and Potawatomis to migrate to Upper Canada.

Most of the Ottawas coming into British North America ended up in one of two locations. A group of Roman Catholics from the Arbre Croche mission in the Michigan area moved to the eastern end of Manitoulin Island, becoming the core of a new settlement named Wikwemikong.[29] The residents of this community, which grew rapidly from several waves of migration in the 1830s and 1840s, were the only Native group in Upper Canada to describe themselves henceforth as Ottawas, although many Indian settlers at Walpole Island were of the same background.[30] Walpole Island also welcomed a large number of Potawatomis, as many as 3,000 of whom entered Upper Canada from the United States.[31] Many of these people crossed into the colony at Sarnia, where a few settled permanently on the Indian reserve there.[32] Most, however, soon moved on from their camps in the Sarnia area, at times worrying local whites. In 1840, for instance, a farmer in the Raleightown area of the Thames Valley complained that some 200 Potawatomis were living on his land, "destroying," he wrote, "my peas, potatoes and apples and have one hundred horses on my pasture."[33]

The Potawatomis gravitated towards the many small Ojibway bands in Upper Canada, many of which at that time were, under the Christian churches' and the government's encouragement, just beginning to confine themselves to permanent settlements on fixed plots of land. Especially inviting to several hundred of the incoming Potawatomis was territory to the west of Owen Sound, where they soon outnumbered the Ojibway residents of the Saugeen Peninsula.[34] And many more of the migrating Potawatomis pushed into the more northerly reaches of the Great Lakes area. As they travelled among the thousands of islands in Georgian Bay, some Potawatomis were gradually absorbed among the Native inhabitants of this Indian domain.[35] Intermarriage was the most common means by which familial ties were added[36] to the strong links of relationships which already connected these ethnically kindred peoples.

The gathering together of many Three Fires people in Upper Canada increased the complexity and intensity of local factionalism of many Algonkian communities in the province. Peter S. Schmalz has documented this phenomenon with respect to the Saugeen Indians.[37] Generally, however, what is most remarkable about the Three Fires reunion in Upper Canada is the ease with which the peoples blended together. With the notable exception of the Wikwemikong Ottawas, or Odawas as they often describe themselves, the identity of the incoming Indians tended over the succeeding decades to become submerged beneath that of the resident Native people. Accordingly, while many families in the province maintained memories of their Potawatomi ancestry, they usually described themselves to outsiders as Ojibways.[38] And they were by and large thus considered by crown agents for official purposes.[39]

These, then, are the major contours of Algonkian ethnicity as they had developed in Upper Canada (known from 1841 as Canada West for administrative purposes) by the mid-nineteenth century. Regional variations among the Ojibway themselves, however, require more comment. As noted, the

Ojibways who pushed their way into southern Ontario were often described as Mississaugas, a term which may be derived from their expression for "many river mouths." In the early nineteenth century, the name Mississauga was most often associated with those Ojibways living north of Lake Ontario, around the mouth of the Credit River, at Lake Scugog, and further east in the Kawartha Lakes region.[40] In southwestern Upper Canada, in the vicinity of Sarnia and London, the expression "Chippewa" was often applied to the Ojibway people there. In fact, this term signifies simply another pronunciation of the word Ojibway. Since the designation Chippewa was officially adopted by the United States government, it has tended to prevail also in those parts of Upper Canada most subject to influences from south of the border.

While the Three Fires group was numerically the largest Indian collectivity in the colony, further diversity yet characterized the Upper Canadian Algonkian population. The Ottawa valley was the home of other Anishinabek peoples, the Algonquin[41] and the Nipissing.[42] Throughout the period under consideration, most of them continued to move widely over hunting territories on both sides of the Ottawa River. On the banks of the Thames near the Oneida settlement lived about 300 Moravian Indians, who were mostly of Lenni Lenape (Delaware) and Mahican ancestry. Shortly after the American revolution they had moved northward into the colony, where, as followers of Moravian missionary David Zeisberger, they established the Christian community of Fairfield.[43] Also entering Upper Canada at about the same time was a group of non-Christian Lenni Lenape known as Munsees.[44]

The range of limited identities among Native people in Upper Canada was contained within a remarkably small population base. In 1857 a group of special commissioners counted approximately 12,000 Indians throughout the region.[45] Their estimate suggests the profound effects of Euro-American colonization on the numerical strength of Native people in Upper Canada. Only a little more than two centuries earlier an estimated 21,000 Hurons had lived in an area of roughly 340 square miles.[46] Diseases like smallpox and measles, unknown before the arrival of Europeans, had taken an incredible toll.[47]

Since the American revolution, a third to a half of Upper Canada's Indian population was derived from Native groups who had migrated from south of the Great Lakes. The most populous Indian community in 1857 was the Grand River Reserve, with 2,550 residents. The other Six Nations settlements at Oneida, Tyendinaga and St. Regis had populations of 436, 520 and 685 respectively. The Algonkian speakers in Upper Canada were almost twice as numerous as the Iroquoians. In the southwestern region were approximately 2,500 Algonkians including the Muncees, Moravians and the Three Fires people at Walpole Island and Sarnia reserves. Farther to the north was a comparable population spread out between a number of communities. Three of these were on the Saugeen Peninsula. Other Anishinabek were settled on reserves at Rama on Lake Couchiching, on Snake Island in

Lake Simcoe, on Beausoleil Island in Georgian Bay, at Lake Scugog, and at Rice Lake, Mud Lake and Alnwick, all in the Kawartha region. The commissioners referred to earlier also reported that 1,226 Native people lived on Manitoulin Island. And they made reference in their report to 1,240 "scattered bands on the north shore of Lake Huron and Lake Superior." Theirs, however, was only a poor estimate.[48] At the time no government official had a very clear notion of the extent of the Indian population throughout the vast expanse of territory now known as Northern Ontario.

Clearly, then, diversity and reasonably rapid change characterized the ethnic makeup of Native societies in Upper Canada. During the decades following the War of 1812, the spread of Christian religion was among those forces influential in determining the evolving nature of group associations among the Indian population.[49] At the Six Nations reserve on the Grand River, growing tension developed between those professing the Newcomers' faith and Long House traditionalists whose conservatism had lately drawn renewed zeal from the teachings of the Seneca prophet Handsome Lake.[50] Among the Anishinabek, Walpole Island remained during the first half of the nineteenth century a centre of considerable Indian resistance against the evangelical inroads of missionary enterprise.[51] While there were such exceptions, however, most Native groups in Upper Canada embraced one form or another of Christian religion during this period. In allying themselves with church organizations, Indian communities tended to lose some of their cultural uniqueness and group autonomy, while at the same time gaining an association with potentially powerful intermediaries who could sometimes defend Native interests against the more acquisitive elements of colonial society. Moreover, besides teaching Christian theology, missionaries generally also provided instruction in English, literacy and farming, thereby further enhancing their utility in the eyes of those Indian groups with whom they became associated.[52]

South of the Precambrian Shield, where the rate of Newcomer-imposed change was the most rapid, a wave of Methodist enthusiasm spread very quickly among the Ojibways during the late 1820s and early 1830s. This religious movement drew considerable energy from a number of dedicated Indian evangelists who regularly conducted the missionary work of their church in the Ojibway tongue.[53] An intense rivalry between the Methodists and the Church of England during this period resulted in the latter's effort to initiate its own missionary enterprise among the Indians. While the Church of England had an old association with some segments of the population at Grand River and Tyendinaga,[54] however, the Anglicans experienced great difficulty in winning converts among the Anishinabek.[55] Their major breakthrough occurred around Sault Ste. Marie after 1833, when the Reverend William McMurray married into one of the leading Ojibway families in the area. Thereafter Chief Shinguacouse and many of his followers allied themselves with the Anglican Church.[56]

The final significant missionary drive directed at the Indians of Upper Canada during the first half of the nineteenth century was that of the Roman Catholic Church. This effort was led by members of the Society of Jesus, who after 1842 set out to labour among Native people often descended from ancestors that Jesuit priests first evangelized during the French régime in Canada. The Jesuits' return was roughly concurrent with the influx from the United States of Indian refugees, many of whom were already practising Roman Catholics. Among one such group the Jesuits found a particularly warm welcome. They therefore headquartered their evangelical campaign in the Odawa community of Wikwemikong, where they created the Holy Cross mission in 1844. From this base the Catholic missionaries expanded their enterprise, achieving greatest success among the Anishinabek of the Precambrian Shield.[57] Given the Jesuits' preference for incorporating many aspects of Native culture within the broader framework of Christian evangelization, their kind of religion was probably best suited to the circumstances of Indians ranging over a part of the country still rich in wildlife. Farther to the south it was Methodism that probably best served Native needs, since its demands for almost total transformation of Indian ways of life were more in accord with the all-encompassing adaptations required of the Aboriginal inhabitants of good agricultural territories.

These three churches competed quite intensely for Indian adherents. As more and more Native people accepted Christianity, their societies tended also to incorporate some of the factionalism separating Catholicism from Protestantism, and Methodism from Anglicanism.[58] In siding most consistently with the missionary efforts of the Church of England, the colonial government's Indian Department officials added heat to the atmosphere of religious controversy that increasingly permeated the lives of Native people in Upper Canada.[59]

While the British Indian Department had long since become an important institution in the lives of most Indian people living north of the Great Lakes, the colonial government began asserting new forms of coercive authority over Native communities in the mid-nineteenth century. This development, one closely associated with the transfer of responsibility for Indian affairs from the imperial government to the provincial government, brought a variety of new factors to the shaping of Native identities.

The colonial legislature enforced its newly acquired metropolitan dominance over Native people by imposing a uniform legal régime on all Aboriginal communities throughout the recently united Canadas. In taking this action, the colonial legislature paid little attention to the many ethnic distinctions that differentiated the various Indian groups throughout the province. To some extent, Indian communities responded in kind. Several Aboriginal groups moved tentatively towards the achievement of common Indian positions as a means to consolidate their rapidly deteriorating power base. The goal was to find common purpose in a shared sense of Indianness.

Yet the new political context also created new pressures for certain kinds of political division within and among some Aboriginal communities. While unity was the ideal, inevitably there was disagreement among some Indian leaders about the strategies that should be followed in the face of the new threats and, in some instances, the new opportunities. Thus, while the assertion of local colonial control over Indian affairs set unifying forces in motion that tended to lessen limited Native identities, the trend was not entirely uniform. Political divisions in colonial society found various kinds of reflection in the alignment of political factions among Indians. Furthermore, the effort to impose a common régime of Indian registry on the Aboriginal population of Upper Canada, created a basis for future schisms between the inhabitants of Indian reserves and those Native individuals who for one reason or other found themselves outside the government's legal definition of Indian status. New dynamics began to appear in the unfolding of limited and shared Aboriginal identities in the region.

The roots of Indian registration lie in the British military's procedures in distributing presents to the Native people. With the negotiation of most of the Upper Canadian Indian treaties during the early decades of the nineteenth century,[60] there was added cause for the colonial government to develop a system for recording the identity of Native residents within the province. Generally, however, the question of who was eligible to receive benefits from the crown was left to the local Indian leadership. Such decisions were made, according to one of the colony's lieutenant governors, on the basis of "their own unwritten laws and customs."[61] When the crown's representatives signed a treaty in 1819 with the "Principal Men of the Chippewa Nation of Indians," for instance, the following terms were outlined: the chiefs agreed to cede 552,190 acres in the London area, while retaining two tracts for their own use—one described as 15,360 acres in extent and the other as two miles square. In return, the crown promised the "said Nation of Indians" 600 pounds annually, "for ever," half in currency and half in goods.[62] There was nothing in this agreement to stipulate the membership of the Chippewa Nation, or how the 600 pounds was to be apportioned among them. The implication is that these were to be internal decisions to be left to the national entity with which the crown was treating.

This was not the pattern in 1850 when William Benjamin Robinson, a brother of the famous Upper Canadian chief justice, negotiated with the Indian bands living around the northern shores of the Upper Great Lakes.[63] Two transactions resulted: the Robinson-Huron Treaty covering a 35,700 square mile area around Georgian Bay, and the Robinson-Superior Treaty covering 16,700 square miles north of the largest Great Lake. In the Robinson treaty documents, the Ojibway parties to the agreement were described as "subjects" of the Queen. Moreover, the crown promised to distribute a "perpetual annuity," payable to the "said Chiefs and their tribes," and to provide an added yearly payment of one pound to each "individual" covered by the treaties. Furthermore, a specific number count was given of what was then believed to be the entire Indian population in each treaty area.[64]

The differences between the treaties signed in 1819 and 1850 give clear indications of the pattern of change in the often loosely orchestrated development of colonial Indian policy. While in 1819 the Indian parties to the agreement were described as a "Nation," in 1850 they were referred to as "tribes" and as "Her Majesty's subjects." This shift in legal terminology was accompanied by a subtle but influential modification in the arrangements for paying annuities. Unlike the framers of the treaty signed in 1819, Robinson built into the 1850 documents a provision which would see money paid to Indian individuals as well as to groups. By establishing the legal basis for payments directly to individuals, the possibility was opened that colonial officials could circumvent the Native communities' own leadership in deciding who would receive the benefits called for by the treaties.

Lending added significance to the determination of how treaty annuity provisions were to be fulfilled was the fact that qualifications for receiving these payments also became the basis of the right to live on Indian reserves. And as Native people were inundated by wave after wave of immigrating Newcomers, bringing the total population of Upper Canada to almost a million by the mid-nineteenth century,[65] Indian reserves became the principal enclaves of Aboriginal ethnicities. Faced with a flood of new influences brought from other places, Indian people gravitated to these plots of land as almost the only remaining locales where they could continue to maintain cohesive Native communities in a rapidly changing environment. Accordingly, the reserves became a primary link enabling their residents to maintain a degree of continuity with their ethnic traditions. Moreover, by establishing 21 new Indian reserves, 3 in the Superior region and 18 in the lands surrounding Georgian Bay, the Robinson treaties were instrumental in firmly entrenching this type of community in the social, legal and institutional structures of Ontario.

The Robinson treaties are significant for yet another reason. Chiefs Shinguacouse and Nebennigoebing had asked that the treaties include provision for a number of half-breeds. The chiefs wanted them each to receive 100-acre land grants in freehold tenure. Although Robinson refused, he told the chiefs that they were free to include the Metis among those who could share in the benefits of the treaty.[66] Hence a new pressure was brought to bear for half-breed peoples either to identify themselves thoroughly with their Indian relatives or to break off from them, at least in a legal sense. As a result, the beginnings of an institutional structure were set in place which hampered the further development of a distinct form of Metis ethnicity in Upper Canada.[67] The Robinson treaties, then, foreshadowed an increasingly influential role for the emergent Canadian state in the manner Aboriginal identities would henceforth be shaped.

In the wake of the Robinson treaties, significant pockets of Aboriginal ethnicity persisted outside of the legal and physical barriers marking the outlines of the Indian reserves. The Temagami Indians, for instance, although resident in the Robinson-Huron area, were not party to the 1850 transactions. As a result, they were forced into a prolonged struggle to secure government recognition of their rights to reside on a plot of land. (It was not until 1943 that they were assigned a 600-acre site on Bear Island.[68] Even today, their status in Canadian law remains unresolved.[69])

Non-participation in treaties was not the sole reason some Native groups and individuals found themselves placed outside the developing government definitions of Indian status. Another factor was religious factionalism. This is well illustrated by the fate of one Potawatomi clan that had settled with an Ojibway group on Beausoleil Island in Georgian Bay. Because of the Potawatomis' resistance to Christianity, their names were not included in the Beausoleil band list compiled by special commissioners appointed in 1856 to investigate Indian affairs in the province of Canada. Essentially, the commissioners' task was to assess the condition of all Native communities throughout the colony in preparation for the transfer of direct responsibility for Indian affairs from the British Colonial Office to the local legislature.[70] With the British withdrawal, the old custom of distributing Indian presents was to come to an end. Because this activity was so thoroughly intertwined with the making of yearly treaty payments, the commissioners attempted to sort out the annuity system from the presents-distribution system. It was in the course of this task that they set about making a registry of Beausoleil Island band members. In outlining their reasons for excluding the pagan Potawatomi clan, the commissioners explained:

> [These Potawatomis], who came from Lake Michigan, remain heathens though every effort has been made to Christianize them. They have no money payments; but the Beausoleil Indians have offered to receive them into their Band and share the annuity with them if they will abandon their heathenish customs and embrace Christianity.[71]

The work of the commissioners was to prove influential in articulating the philosophies and procedures which were to be adopted first by the government of the province of Canada and later by the federal government. The following definition from their report, for instance, became the basis for the law governing Indian registry throughout the country until 1985:[72]

> The word "Indian" in <u>Western</u> <u>Canada</u> [Upper Canada] is held, more perhaps from usage than from any legal authority, to comprise not only all persons of pure Indian blood, but also those of mixed race, who are a recognizable member of any band or tribe resident in Canada, and who claim descent on the father's side. An Indian woman marrying a white loses her rights as a member of the tribe, and her children have no claim to the land or moneys belonging to their mother's nation.[73]

Although the commissioners did not report until 1858, the Canadian legislature moved to claim authority over Indian affairs in June 1857, three years before the official transfer of power took place.[74] The 1857 legislation was entitled "An Act to Encourage the Gradual Civilization of Indian Tribes in Canada, and to Amend Laws Respecting Indians."[75] Its most significant feature was its assertion of the local legislature's outright power to determine Indian status. While former actions undertaken within the authority of the imperial government were aimed in this direction, the new legislation signified the culmination of the process. The cutting edge of the bill's bite into the autonomy of Indian communities was its creation of a legal mechanism by which individuals could be led out of official Indianhood. After 1857 adult male Indians could apply to become enfranchised citizens of the province. If these individuals could prove themselves sufficiently "civilized" before a board established for the purpose, the law stated that they could leave their Indian band and assume private ownership of a portion of their former reserve's land. As well, they would be given their share of whatever moneys were being held for their band in trust by the government. The enfranchisement of an adult male family head carried with it the automatic result that his wife and any children would be crossed off their band's registry, thereby also gaining citizenship.

In an era when unfettered individualism was the prevailing economic orthodoxy, the act sought to induce Indians to leave behind what might be called the collectivist foundations of Native culture. As one government report had earlier anticipated, in some Indians

> the value of separate and personal rights might thus be taught, and the [Indians'] present quasi corporate mode of holding their lands and transacting their business, would be superseded as the people became more assimilated to the manner and habits of the white population.[76]

The 1857 initiative thus represents a modification in the strategy of the colonial government's Indian "civilizing" policy, first officially adopted in 1830.[77] Rather than attempting to integrate whole groups into the dominant mores of Christian colonial society, the enfranchisement legislation marked an increased emphasis on the remaking of a few Native individuals. "The example held out by the admission of [the] more enlightened [Indian] members to all the privileges of a Citizen," it was argued, "will be the highest incentive to exertion."[78]

Many of the key features of the 1857 act were implicit rather than explicit. The act formalized a legal duality between two major categories of residents in the province: Indians and citizens. The principle was codified that to be an Indian was not to be a citizen, and to be a citizen was not to be an Indian. In claiming the authority to make this distinction, the provincial government was removing from Indian groups the power to determine who properly belonged in their own communities. The full implications of the change, however, remained for future generations to discover. What was most distressing to Indian bands at the time was that the act set out a legal means of enfranchisement with no reference to the wishes of the affected communities. Provincial authorities were claiming the power to subdivide Indian land without the approval of the Indians' own local governing bodies. What followed was a widespread and bold reaction among Native groups to this legislative assault on their self-determination—an assault which inauspiciously marked the provincial legislature's first major move as the responsible agent of the crown's Indian policy. That the local authorities would move to assert their control over Indian affairs in such a menacing way confirmed the conviction of some Native leaders that their best interests could be served only by holding closely to the imperial tie.

By October 1858 the Indian protest against the legislation, and against the commissioners' newly published report, had become organized to the point that a major assembly took place of Native delegations from throughout the province. The site of the proceedings was the Onondaga Council House at the Six Nations' Reserve near Brantford. Representatives were present from all the Iroquois communities in the Canadas—Grand River, Tyendinaga, St. Regis, Oneida and Caughnawaga, the large Mohawk reserve just west of Montreal. Among the Anishinabek delegations in attendance were groups from Walpole Island, Alnwick and Rice Lake. The minutes of the meeting record speaker after speaker decrying the local legislature's initiative. "It blasts our dearest hopes as a race," said one. Another declared that "there is nothing in [the legislation] to be to their benefit; only to break them to pieces." There were references to how the government's actions had made the wampum appear black—or in other words, to how the government was breaking old promises. A spokesman of the Six Nations, John Smoke Johnson, summed it all up. In a message to the government Indian agent present, he conveyed his people's "unanimous vote" that "they pray for a Repeal of sections of the Civilization Act which would admit the Enfranchisement." And, he explained: "They do not wish to be given over from the care of the Imperial Government to the care of the Provincial one and therefore subject to the Commissioners' Report."[79]

During the first three years that the enfranchisement legislation was in place, only three Indians applied to become citizens. In all but these rare instances, the Aboriginal leaders who gathered at the Onondaga Council House succeeded in convincing their people not to co-operate with the government.[80] On the other hand, the Indian protest received virtually no formal recognition from Canadian officials. In his report on the Indian Department for 1858,[81] Richard Pennefather, superintendent general for Indian affairs, made only passing reference to the council. He tersely noted: "As the Council was not called with the Sanction of the Government, I did not attend it, and have abstained from noticing the representations thereat."

In spite of the superintendent general's zeal not to notice what took place, however, his report does offer a significant, if brief, elaboration about the meeting's seriousness and its content. He reported:

> Much uneasiness was manifested by the Indians with reference to the course likely to be pursued with regard to the

> management of their affairs in the future. A great council
> was held last autumn in which the tribes of Upper Canada
> almost unanimously refused to surrender any more land.

A subsequent major gathering for voicing Aboriginal grievances against the colonial government took place two years later. In September 1860 Indian leaders assembled at Sarnia to greet the Prince of Wales. They offered the royal visitor their formal expression of loyalty and friendship. After this ceremony, however, the Indian delegates, some of whom were veterans of the War of 1812, assembled together in grand council. The chiefs invited Indian Department officials to take part, but the latter declined. "The [regional] Superintendents should not be parties to or recognize in any way this grievance meeting," one official noted.[82]

Nevertheless, the Indian Department sent an interpreter, Francis Assikinack,[83] to record some of the meeting's proceedings. In his account of the grand council he observed that "nearly every Indian band in Upper Canada was represented."[84] In attendance were the Indian delegates who had met the Prince of Wales and 150 "warriors." According to Assikinack's account, there were two major factions who attempted to dominate the proceedings. One group of chiefs, apparently the largest, had as its spokesman David Wawanosh. At several junctures this group asserted through Wawanosh their desire that the council should focus on three subjects: Indian fisheries, the fate of unsurrendered Indian lands, and the theft by former Indian Department officials of Indian funds that were held in trust by the government.

The effort by the Wawanosh group to develop clearly stated resolutions on these subjects, however, was repeatedly frustrated by a delegation seeking sanction from the council for redress of the specific grievances of three Wesleyan Methodist Indians from the Owen Sound area, David Sawyer or Ke-zig-ko-e-ne-ne, Mrs. William Sutton or Nah-nee-ba-we-quay, and Abner Elliot. All three were among those Indians from the Saugeen Peninsula who had attempted to purchase lots carved out of territory ceded by members of their own Newash Band under dubious circumstances. In the case of David Sawyer and Mrs. Sutton, a Native woman originally from the Credit River Band who had married a white agricultural instructor employed by the Wesleyan Missionary Society, it was their own farms that they had attempted to purchase back. Although they had followed all the rules to purchase the lots in freehold tenure, they found themselves facing a dictate from the Indian Department that disqualified them from becoming landowners.[85]

The main body of chiefs at Sarnia dismissed the grievances of Mrs. Sutton and the others as "the concern of private individuals rather than of the Council as a whole." It seems, however, that Mrs. Sutton had in fact succeeded in elevating the matter beyond the personal to an issue of higher principles. By the time the chiefs assembled at Sarnia she had already brought her concerns to Quaker audiences in New York, to the Aborigines'

Protection Society in Britain and, ultimately, through the intervention of the Society, to Queen Victoria herself.[86] Mrs. Sutton's major complaint was that the laws of the province of Canada had reduced Indians who could not, or would not, be enfranchised to the status of minors. The only major legal authority recognized in Native individuals was that of a few delegated chiefs to cede Aboriginal land title.[87]

As was widely reported, she detailed for Queen Victoria the problems faced by Indian people in Canada. She declared:

> 1.   That their land is held by tribal tenure; by which arrangement it appears the members of the tribe have no individual rights; so that, if the chiefs of the tribe can be gained over, by whatever means, their holdings may be sold away from them at any time, without redress or compensation.
> 2.   That being in law minors...they have no legal powers of action—cannot vote for members of Parliament, or contract or enforce debts; are excluded from Government schools, and, in other respects, placed under disabilities, which are not known as regards any other class of persons in the colonies, whether fugitive slaves, or settlers, or refugees from any part of the world, and which do not exist as regards Indian settlers in the United States.[88]

Queen Victoria referred Mrs. Sutton to the Duke of Newcastle, secretary of state for the colonies, who was about to accompany the Prince of Wales on his trip to Canada. When the matter eventually came before them in their Canadian travels, however, it seems that Superintendent General Pennefather convinced the colonial secretary that any imperial intervention on behalf of Mrs. Sutton would amount to an unwarranted intervention in the responsible government of the local colonial legislature.[89]

Among those Indian delegates who met with the Prince of Wales at Sarnia were several chiefs from Manitoulin Island. This Manitoulin delegation included representatives of two competing Indian factions.[90] By the spring of 1861 these factions were engaged in a rapidly intensifying debate matching two very different visions of the future. One group sought to retain their Aboriginal independence in an exclusively Indian island domain. They saw themselves as allies of the British sovereign rather than as subjects. The other group believed it was inevitable that their communities must develop under colonial law. They saw little point in resisting the influx of non-Indian settlers into their homeland on Manitoulin Island.

There were powerful forces at work in the early 1860s which stimulated Manitoulin Natives to elaborate these different visions. Manitoulin together with the 23,000 other islands that make up the Georgian Bay archipelago had been designated by treaty in 1836 as a permanent Indian refuge.[91] Lieutenant Governor Sir Francis Bond Head reserved this region as an Aboriginal homeland in the expectation that many Indian refugees from the United

States would take up residence there.[92] To some extent this emigration had taken place but not on the scale originally envisaged. By the early 1860s there were influential commercial interests centred in Toronto pushing the government to help advance the city's metropolitan expansion into little-exploited hinterlands in the northwest.[93] The push to open Manitoulin for non-Indian settlement was part of this trend, one that would soon lead to the annexation by Canada of the vast Hudson's Bay Company territories. Seen in this way the turmoil surrounding treaty negotiations on Manitoulin Island in 1862 foreshadowed what was to take place several years later at Red River when crown officials employed similar heavy-handed tactics in efforts to force the full weight of Canadian jurisdiction on unwilling indigenous peoples. In both these incidents the figure of Clear Grit William McDougall loomed large.[94]

The bastion of Indian self-confidence and independence was the Odawa settlement of Wikwemikong at the eastern end of the island. No doubt the resolve of the Catholic Wikwemikongians to resist the jurisdictional intrusion of the colonial government was strengthened by their close collaboration with the Jesuit priests who lived and worked in their midst.[95] By 1861 the Jesuits had made certain that Indians throughout the island were aware of the mounting interest by outsiders in assuming control of Manitoulin lands. With this awareness most Manitoulin Natives developed a corresponding unwillingness to co-operate in any way with the government Indian agent on the island, George Ironside. In the spring of 1861, for instance, Ironside found it impossible to take a census of Manitoulin residents:

> The Indians have been made to believe most implicitly that there is a design on the part of the government to deprive them of their land—that I am working secretly to that end, and that the present census taking is merely a prelude to that end.[96]

The Indians were not wrong. In the autumn of 1861 a group of commissioners from Toronto met with the Manitoulin chiefs to inform them that the government was planning to open two townships on the island for non-Indian settlement. The Indian legal claim to the island, the commissioners continued, was tenuous at best. The chiefs, however, unanimously and vigorously rejected these assertions. They did so in such clear terms that the commissioners thought it best to withdraw their plan to begin a survey of the island.[97]

For a time it seemed that the islanders' united front would hold. Virtually no group or individual would publicly sanction the cession of Indian title to Manitoulin lands. Many general council meetings involving delegates from all the Indian communities throughout the island had been devoted to the painstaking development of this common position.[98] In the autumn of 1862, however, Commissioner of Crown Lands William McDougall used unexpected tactics to fracture the apparent unity of the Manitoulin

Indians and thereby advance the government's objectives. On 4 October, at a general council of Manitoulin chiefs, McDougall proposed new terms for a treaty. As expected, the principal Indian spokesmen rejected all his offers. The lands commissioner then disbanded the meeting, only to reconvene the assembly two days later. This time McDougall declared that the treaty would exclude the eastern end of the island, that is, Wikwemikong. Wikwemikong chiefs were thereby cut out of the proceedings. McDougall then moved quickly, apparently by prearranged signal, to obtain the signature of 16 Indian individuals willing to cede the largest portion of the island to the west of Wikwemikong.[99]

In the years that followed many Manitoulin Indians expressed tremendous bitterness about how the treaty—"that fraud"[100]—was obtained. At Wikwemikong the families of those few individuals believed to have collaborated with the government were expelled from the community.[101] There were charges that McDougall had bribed Indians during the period between the two meetings and made others drunk.[102] Legitimate questions were asked about the authority of those who signed the treaty to speak for all Indians on the western portion of the island. The controversy spilled over into virtually every aspect of island life. The fishing grounds around Manitoulin became an especially contentious battleground of competing claims. The result was dangerous confrontations between armed police, priests and Indians—confrontations that were probably a factor in the unsolved murder of a government fisheries official.[103]

Throughout the turmoil the Wikwemikong leadership repeated their assertion that the treaty was invalid and that the government must recognize the fraudulent nature of the bargain.[104] In many cases, Indians living in the ceded portion of the island joined the chorus of protest.[105] Try as they might, however, the Wikwemikongians could never reconstruct the Indian solidarity that seemed to exist before the treaty.[106] At a general council at Manitowaning in 1863 Wikwemikong Chief Wah-kai-keghik tried to convince those who signed the treaty to renounce their deed in the following fashion:

> We know what will be the result when the whites come and live among us. They will do the labour that is required on the Island, and will of course make money and to you, my friends, will be given the lowest meanest work to do as servants—such as, carrying water, cutting up wood, cleaning stables, making baskets and when the land you have ceded shall have been divided among yourselves and white settlers, what land will your children have? Our families are increasing. The Indians are increasing in number. How can all our descendants be provided for? We have no other reserve besides this. My friends we want to eat out of one dish as it were[;] we do not wish to break a part of it to give away. All of us who met together at Me-tche-wedig-nong, and held a grand council there, agreed that we should eat

out of one dish. We feel convinced that the Indians would be better off if they kept the Island for themselves than if they surrendered a part of it.[107]

To Wah-kai-keghik's arguments Chief Misheguong-pai, one of the treaty-signers, responded:

The future will tell what Indians will be better off. You who oppose to make a treaty or we who consent to make it. We have hitherto obeyed the Queen and Her officers, we mean to do so still. We place ourself in the good keeping of the Government. My friends, we are no longer independent people. We cannot live as our forefathers did. We are dependent on the white man for many things essential to our welfare. The Queen is our monarch[;] she has authority over us. My friends, I cannot agree with what you have said. I tell you plainly I shall not aid your projects....My friends, we cannot resist the tide of emigration. The whites are coming nearer and near to us. They will at last surround us, but they will not drive us away before them.[108]

Increasingly it was political decisions made in response to non-Indian pressures on their territories that determined the nature of relations among Aboriginal individuals and groups. The constant evolution of Native identities was therefore driven in part by the politics of colonial land development and land exploitation.

The frustration of the Indians at Wikwemikong only increased their resolve to operate their own band government independent of any interference on the part of the colonial government. By the spring of 1866, however, the Canadian government was no longer willing to accommodate such independence. A proclamation was issued declaring that the laws of the province of Canada applied to all of Manitoulin island. And the government enforced its jurisdiction in Wikwemikong by requiring the community to reinstate those Indians who had been exiled following the treaty negotiations of 1862.[109] When one of these exiled individuals, Kitchie Baptiste, returned to Wikwemikong in May of that year, there were aggressive protests opposing his re-entry. The five leaders of the protest, who also happened to be members of the Wikwemikong band council, were arrested as a result of their actions and jailed at Sault Ste. Marie.[110] The heavy weight of Canadian law was at last made to prevail, however uneasily, at Wikwemikong Unceded Reserve.

Thus, by the eve of Confederation, as a result of the concerted efforts of Indian Department officials, the autonomy of Indian communities in Upper Canada had been dramatically undermined and Native people had been cajoled and coerced to acquiesce in the authority of the local legislative assembly.[111] Living within the provincial boundaries but outside the legal framework of provincial citizenship, Native people were increasingly subject to what, for them, can truly be called an *irresponsible* government—They were deprived of effective Aboriginal governments answerable to Native people as a consequence of the very process by which non-Indian residents of the province acquired a significant increase in their capacity for self-government and for ensuring that the executive branch of the colonial government was *responsible* to them for its actions. An old imperial pattern was being renewed—one that would be re-enacted many times—as liberated colonials used their newly gained autonomy to increase the oppression of indigenous peoples.[112]

Given, then, the increasingly marginalized status of Native people during the decades leading up to Confederation, there were, of course, no Aboriginal delegates representing Indian interests at the conferences where the terms of the British North America Act were negotiated. Accordingly it is not surprising that the institutions of the new Dominion of Canada included no decision-making role for those deemed to be Indians. Instead, the fathers of Confederation placed "Indians and Lands reserved for the Indians" under the jurisdiction of the new federal Parliament.[113] Henceforth, the constitutional settlement of 1867 would become one of the major vehicles that enabled non-Indians to advance so effectively their metropolitan dominance over Aboriginal peoples and Aboriginal lands throughout the Dominion.

1   Mary A. Drake, "The Eastern Woodlands—A Regional Overview", in R. Bruce Morrison and C. Roderick Wilson, eds., *Native Peoples: The Canadian Experience* (Toronto, 1986), 297–301; Bruce G. Trigger, "Cultural Unity and Diversity", in his, ed., *Northeast*, vol. XV in William C. Sturtevant, gen. ed., *Handbook of North American Indians* (Washington, 1978), 798–804.

2   Alfred W. Crosby, "Virgin Soil Epidemics as a Factor in Aboriginal Depopulation in America", *William and Mary Quarterly*, 3rd ser., 33 (1976), 289–99; Henry F. Dobyns, "Native American Population Collapse and Recovery", in W. R. Swagerty, ed., *Scholars and the Indian Experience: Critical Reviews of Recent Writings in the Social Sciences* (Bloomington, 1984), 17–35.

3   Trigger, *Natives and Newcomers: Canada's "Heroic Age" Reconsidered* (Montreal, 1985); Francis Jennings, *The Ambiguous Iroquois Empire: The Covenant Chain Confederation of Indian Tribes with English Colonies from Its Beginnings to the Lancaster Treaty of 1744* (New York, 1984); A. L. Burt, *The United States, Great Britain and British North America from the Revolution to the Establishment of Peace after the War of 1812* (New Haven, 1940).

4   Donald Boyd Smith, "The Mississauga, Peter Jones and the White Man: The Algonkians' Adjustment to Europeans on the North Shore of Lake Ontario to 1860" (Ph.D. diss., University of Toronto, 1975); John Sheridan Milloy, "The Era of Civilization—British Policy for the Indians of Canada, 1830–1860" (Ph.D. diss., Oxford University, 1978); Anthony J. Hall, "The Red Man's Burden: Land, Law, and the Lord in the Indian Affairs of Upper Canada, 1791–1858" (Ph.D. diss., University of Toronto, 1984).

5 Elizabeth Graham, *Medicine Man to Missionary: Missionaries as Agents of Change Among the Indians of Southern Ontario, 1784–1867* (Toronto, 1975); John Webster Grant, *Moon of Wintertime: Missionaries and the Indians of Canada in Encounter since 1534* (Toronto, 1984), 71–95.

6 Regna Darnell, "A Linguistic Classification of Canadian Native Peoples: Issues, Problems and Theoretical Implications", in Morrison and Wilson, *Native Peoples*, 22–44; John Price, *Indians in Canada* (Scarborough, 1979), 21–54.

7 Elizabeth Tooker, "The League of the Iroquois: Its History, Politics and Ritual", in Trigger, *Northeast*, 418–41.

8 Robert J. Surtees, "The Iroquois in Canada", in Francis Jennings et al., eds., *The History and Culture of Iroquois Diplomacy* (Syracuse, 1985), 72–79.

9 Tooker, 418–22.

10 David Landy, "Tuscarora among the Iroquois", in Trigger, *Northeast*, 518–22.

11 Sally M. Weaver, "Six Nations of the Grand River, Ontario", ibid., 525.

12 Ernest A. Cruikshank, "The Coming of the Loyalist Mohawks to the Bay of Quinté", Ontario Historical Society, *Papers and Records* 26 (1930), 390–403; Charles H. Torok, "The Tyendinaga Mohawks: The Village as a Basic Factor in Mohawk Social Structure", *Ontario History* [hereafter *OH*] 57 (1965), 69–77; Surtees, "Iroquois", 75.

13 Surtees, "Iroquois", 69–72.

14 "Report of the Special Commissioners appointed on the 8th of September, 1856, to investigate Indian Affairs in Canada", in Canada (United Province), Legislative Assembly, *Journals* 16 (1858), app. 21, no pagination.

15 Jack Campisi, "Oneida", in Trigger, *Northeast*, 487–89; Surtees, "Iroquois", 79.

16 Elizabeth Tooker, "Wyandot", in Trigger, *Northeast*, 398–405; John Gilmary Shea, "An Historical Sketch of the Tionontates or Dionondadies, Now Called Wyandots", *The Historical Magazine* 5 (1861), 262–69; Hall, 131–33, 151, 186–92.

17 Donald B. Smith demonstrates some of the difficulties in Algonkian nomenclature in "Who are the Mississauga?", *OH* 67 (1975), 211–22.

18 For a discussion of the meaning of the word see William W. Warren, *History of the Ojibway Nation* (Minneapolis, 1974), 56–57. Warren was an Ojibway-speaking half-breed who wrote his history in 1852, based on the oral traditions of his mother's people. The work is an invaluable primary source of Indian history.

19 J. Joseph Bauxar, "History of the Illinois Area", in Trigger, *Northeast*, 600; Robert E. Ritzenthaler, "Southwestern Chippewa", ibid., 743.

20 Warren, 81–82. I have discussed these meanings with Kasper D. Solomon, an Ojibway-speaking elder from the Cape Croker Reserve. His interpretation corroborates Warren.

21 James A. Clifton, "Potawatomi", in Trigger, *Northeast*, 725–42.

22 Johanna E. Feest and Christian F. Feest, "Ottawa", ibid., 772–91.

23 Leroy V. Eid, "The Ojibway-Iroquois War: The War the Five Nations Did Not Win", *Ethnohistory* 26 (1979), 297–323; Peter S. Schmalz, "The Role of the Ojibwa in the Conquest of Southern Ontario, 1650–1751", *OH* 76 (1984), 326–52.

24 Ronald N. Satz, *American Indian Policy in the Jacksonian Era* (Lincoln, 1975); Francis Paul Frucha, *The Great Father: The United States Government and the American Indians*, I (Lincoln, 1984), 243–49.

25 Robert F. Bauman, "The Migration of the Ottawa Indians from the Maumee Valley to Walpole Island", *Northwest Ohio Quarterly* 21 (1949), 86–112, and his "Kansas, Canada or Starvation", *Michigan History* 36 (1952), 287–99; James A. Clifton, *A Place of Refuge for All Time: Migration of the American Potawatomi into Upper Canada, 1830–1850* (Ottawa, 1975).

26 Ruth Bleasdale, "Manitowaning: An Experiment in Indian Settlement", *OH* 66 (1974), 147–57.

27 Hall, 138–42, 228–30, 242–44.

28 Bauman, 99. Jarvis was chief superintendent of Indian affairs, Upper Canada, 1837–45.

29   Feest and Feest, 780; W. R. Wightman, *Forever on the Fringe: Six Studies in the Development of Manitoulin Island* (Toronto, 1982), 24–33; Le P. Edouard Lecompte, SJ, *Les jesuits du Canada au XIXe siècle* (Montreal, 1920), 195; Regis College Archives (Toronto), Father Julien Paquin, SJ, Papers, MS "Modern Jesuit Missions in Ontario".
30   Bauman, 86–112.
31   Clifton, 34. For a discussion of Clifton's estimate see Hall, 209.
32   Clifton, 67.
33   Ibid., 72.
34   Peter S. Schmalz, *The History of the Saugeen Indians* (Toronto, 1977), 22–56.
35   Clifton, 88.
36   Ibid., 96.
37   Schmalz, *Saugeen,* passim.
38   I make this observation on the basis of many conversations on the subject with Native people in the Georgian Bay area.
39   The Indian participants in, for instance, the Robinson-Huron Treaty, which was made in 1850, are described as "Ojibway Indians." Among them, however, were many of those Potawatomis and Ottawas recently arrived from south of the Great Lakes. Canada, Dept. of Indian Affairs, *Indian Treaties and Surrenders,* I (Ottawa, 1891), no. 61.
40   Smith, "Who are the Mississauga?", and his "The Dispossession of the Mississauga Indians: A Missing Chapter in the Early History of Upper Canada", *OH* 73 (1981), 67–87.
41   Gordon M. Day and Bruce Trigger, "Algonquin", in Trigger, *Northeast,* 792–97.
42   Day, "Nipissing", ibid., 787–91.
43   Leslie Robb Gray, "The Moravian Missionaries, Their Indians and the Canadian Government", in Canadian Historical Association, *Annual Report* (1955), 96–104; Elma E. Gray and Leslie Robb Gray, *Wilderness Christians: The Moravian Mission to the Delaware Indians* (Toronto, 1956).
44   Ives Goddard, "Delaware", in Trigger, *Northeast,* 224.
45   "Special Commissioners".
46   Conrad Heidenreich, *Huronia: A History and Geography of the Huron Indians, 1600–1650* (Toronto, 1971), 91–106.
47   See Crosby, 289–99.
48   In negotiating treaties at Sault Ste. Marie in 1850, William Robinson reported 1,422 Indians residing around the shore of Georgian Bay and 1,240 north of Lake Superior. Canada, *Treaties,* I, nos. 60–61.
49   See Grant, 71–95.
50   Anthony F. C. Wallace, *Death and Re-birth of the Seneca* (New York, 1972), 239–346.
51   Peter Jones, *Life and Journals of Kah-ke-wa-quo-na-by (Rev. Peter Jones)* (Toronto, 1860), 247–49; Paquin, "Modern Jesuit Missions", 39–47.
52   Hall, 230–31, 240–99.
53   The Methodists have produced a large literature describing their missionary work among the Indians in Upper Canada and later in Western Canada: for example, John Carroll, *Case and His Cotemporaries...,* 5 vols. (Toronto, 1867–77); John Maclean, *Vanguards of Canada* (Toronto, 1918); Mrs. Frederick C. Stephenson, *One Hundred Years of Canadian Methodist Missions, 1824–1924* (Toronto, 1924). See also Smith, "The Mississauga, Peter Jones and the White Man" and his *Sacred Feathers: The Reverend Peter Jones (Kah-kewaquonaby) and the Mississauga Indians* (Toronto, 1987).
54   Graham, 55.
55   See W. J. D. Waddilove, ed., *The Stewart Missions...* (London, 1838); James J. Talman, "Church of England Missionary Effort in Upper Canada", Ontario Historical Society, *Papers and Records* 25 (1929), 438–49; Bleasdale, 147–57.
56   Rev. Canon Colloton, "The Sault Ste. Marie Mission", in *Centennial Commemoration: One Hundred Years of the Church of England in Sault Ste. Marie Ontario, 1832–1932* (Sault Ste. Marie, 1932), 5–11.

57 Lorenzo Cadieux, SJ and Robert Toupin, SJ, *Les robes noires à l'isle du Manitou* ([Sudbury], 1982); Lecompte, *Les jesuits*; Paquin, "Modern Jesuit Missions"; Wightman, 24–33.

58 Hall, 242–44.

59 Ibid., 76–127.

60 See Robert J. Surtees, "Indian Land Cessions in Ontario, 1763–1862: The Evolution of a System" (Ph.D. diss., Carleton University, 1982); Ian Victor Basil Johnson, "The Early Mississauga Treaty Process, 1781–1819: An Historical Perspective" (Ph.D. diss., University of Toronto, 1986).

61 National Archives of Canada [hereafter NAC], RG 10–A–4, Dept. of Indian Affairs, Administrative Records of the Imperial Government, Chief Superintendent's Office, U.C., vol. 60, Lt. Gov. Sir Francis Bond Head to House of Assembly, [15–16?] Feb. 1836.

62 Canada, *Treaties*, I, no. 21.

63 Surtees, "Cessions", 240–53; Hall, 331–40.

64 Canada, *Treaties*, I, nos. 60–61. On the background of the Robinson treaties see Janet Elizabeth Chute, "A Century of Native Leadership: Shingwaukonse and His Heirs" (Ph.D. diss., McMaster University, 1986), ch. 6–7.

65 J. M. S. Careless, *The Union of the Canadas: The Growth of Canadian Institutions, 1841–1867* (Toronto, 1967), 150.

66 William Benjamin Robinson, special commissioner re. Indian claims, to Col. Robert Bruce, superintendent general of Indian affairs in Canada, 24 Sep. 1850, in Alexander Morris, *The Treaties of Canada with the Indians of Manitoba and the North-West Territories;...* (Toronto, 1880), 17–21.

67 On the earlier development of a Metis limited identity, see Jacqueline Peterson, "Ethnogenesis: The Settlement and Development of a New People in the Great Lakes Region, 1702–1815", *American Indian Culture and Research Journal* 6 (1982), 23–64.

68 Bruce W. Hodgins, "The Temagami Indians and Canadian Federalism: 1867–1943", *Laurentian University Review* 11 (1979), 71–100.

69 The Temagami Indians have mounted the most complex land claim ever brought before the Canadian courts. See *Attorney-General for Ontario v. Bear Island Foundation et al.* and *Potts et al. v. Attorney-General for Ontario*, in *Ontario Reports*, 2nd ser., 49, pt. 7, 17 May 1985, 353–490.

70 Milloy, 283–329.

71 "Special Commissioners".

72 Kathleen Jamieson, "Sex Discrimination and the Indian Act", in J. Rick Ponting, ed., *Arduous Journey: Canadian Indians and Decolonization* (Toronto, 1986), 112–36.

73 "Special Commissioners".

74 J. E. Hodgetts, *Pioneer Public Service: An Administrative History of the United Canadas, 1841–1867* (Toronto, 1956), 222–23.

75 Canada (United Province), 5th Parliament, 3rd Sess., *Statutes* (Toronto, 1857), c. 26.

76 Canada (United Province), Legislative Assembly, *Journals* 6 (1847), app. T "Report on the Affairs of the Indians of Canada", no pagination. This report is often referred to as the Bagot Commission Report after the governor general who appointed its members in 1842. See John Leslie, "The Bagot Commission: Developing a Corporate Memory for the Indian Department", in Canadian Historical Association, *Historical Papers* (1982), 31–52.

77 Milloy, ch. 2–3. See also James Douglas Leighton, "The Development of Federal Indian Policy, 1840–1890" (Ph.D. diss., University of Western Ontario, 1975).

78 "Special Commissioners".

79 NAC, RG 10–A–5, Dept. of Indian Affairs, Administrative Records of the Imperial Government, Civil Secretary's Office [hereafter Civ. Sec.], vol. 245, pt. 1, D. Thornburn to Richard T. Pennefather, 13 Oct. 1858. Pennefather was superintendent general of Indian affairs, Upper Canada, 1856–61.

80   NAC, RG 10–B–2, Dept. of Indian Affairs, Ministerial Administration Records, Deputy Superintendent General's Office [hereafter Dep. Sup. Gen.], vol. 287, J. Gilkinson to chief superintendent of Indian affairs, 4 Mar. 1863.

81   Civ. Sec., vol. 247 pt. 1, Pennefather, "Annual report of the Indian Department for 1858", 11 Jan. 1859.

82   Ibid., vol. 256, W. R. Bartlett to Pennefather, 25 Sep. 1860.

83   See Douglas Leighton, "Francis Assikinack", *Dictionary of Canadian Biography*, IX (Toronto, 1976), 10–11.

84   Civ. Sec., vol. 256, Francis Assikinack's account of the Grand Council, attached to Bartlett to Pennefather, 25 Sep. 1860.

85   The grievances are outlined at length in Enemikeese, *The Indian Chief: An Account of the Labours, Losses and Sufferings, and Oppression of Ke-zig-ko-e-ne-ne (David Sawyer) A Chief of the Ojibbeway Indians in Canada West* (London, 1867), 115–59.

86   Mrs. Sutton was authorized to speak in Great Britain on behalf of several chiefs assembled in general council. The chiefs included William Yellowhead of the Rama Reserve, John and James Aisance of Christian Island, and Peter Kegedonce. See Civ. Sec., vol. 243, Resolution of General Council, 9 July 1859.

87   Ibid., vol. 255 pt. 2, John Scoble to Philip M. M. VanKoughnet, July 1860. VanKoughnet was chief superintendent of Indian affairs, 1860–62.

88   *The Times* (London, U.K.), 4 July 1860; *Morning Star* (London, U.K.), 5 July 1860, cited in Schmalz, *Saugeen*, 111–12.

89   Schmalz, *Saugeen*, 113. See also *Christian Guardian* (Toronto), 5 Sep. 1860, 30 Jan. 1861.

90   Civ. Sec., vol. 258, George Ironside to Pennefather, 5 Mar. 1861.

91   Canada, *Treaties*, I, no. 45.

92   See Hall, ch. 3.

93   This theme, of course, has been developed at length by J. M. S. Careless in his work on George Brown and the other clear Grits who worked for and around the Toronto *Globe*.

94   William McDougall was principal negotiator of the Manitoulin Treaty of 1862. In 1869 he became the first lieutenant governor of Rupert's Land and the North West Territories. It was McDougall who thus embodied the assertion of Canadian sovereignty over the territories against the competing claims of the Red River Metis who followed Louis Riel. Again McDougall found himself in conflict with a powerful group of Native people with intimate connections to the Roman Catholic hierarchy.

95   Cadieux and Toupin, *passim*.

96   Civ. Sec., vol. 258, Ironside to Pennefather, 12 Mar. 1861.

97   Ibid., vol. 262 pt. 1, Proceedings of a Council Assembled at Manitowaning on the Great Manitoulin Island on 5 Oct. 1861.

98   Paquin, "Modern Jesuit Missions", 210–11; NAC, RG 10–CI–3, Dept. of Indian Affairs, Field Office Records—Superintendency Records, Northern (Manitowaning) Superintendency [hereafter Manit. Sup.], vol. 573, Ironside to Pennefather, 8 Mar. 1861.

99   Paquin, "Modern Jesuit Missions", 213–15; Frank A. Myers, "The Manitoulin Treaty", *The Manitoulin Recorder*, 1 Sep. 1960; McDougall's account is given in Morris, 22–24; see also Canada, *Treaties*, I, no. 94.

100 Manit. Sup., vol. 615, petition from the people of Wikwemikong to the governor general, 18 June 1866.

101 Ibid., vol. 573, Ironside to William Spragge, deputy superintendent of Indian affairs, 16 Jan. 1863. Spragge was one of the two crown signatories to the treaty of 6 Oct. 1862, McDougall being the other.

102 Dep. Sup. Gen., vol. 288, William Gibbard to Commissioner of Crown Lands [William McDougall], 9 Dec. 1862.

103 Douglas Leighton, "The Manitoulin Incident of 1863: An Indian-White Confrontation in the Province of Canada", *OH* 59 (1977), 113–23; Wightman, 48–52.

104 Manit. Sup., vol. 574, Charles Dupont to Spragge, 18 Jan. 1864.

105 Dep. Sup. Gen., vol. 292, Indians of Sheshegwaning to the governor general, 28 May 1863. See also Canada (United Province), Legislative Assembly, *Sessional Papers* (1863), no. 63 "Return...A Copy of the Treaty made at Manitoulin...by Sir Francis Bond Head...", no pagination.

106 Wightman, 52–56.

107 Dep. Sup. Gen., vol. 284, Speech of Wahkaikeghik, 19 Jan. 1863.

108 Ibid., Speech of Misheguong-pai.

109 Ibid., vol. 525, Spragge to Dupont, 14 Mar. 1866.

110 Manit. Sup., vol. 574, Dupont to [William Macdonell?] Dawson, 28 May 1866.

111 See John S. Milloy, "The Early Indian Acts: Developmental Strategy and Constitutional Change", in Ian A. L. Getty and Antoine S. Lussier, eds., *As Long as the Sun Shines and Water Flows: A Reader in Canadian Native Studies* (Vancouver, 1983), 56–64.

112 For an insightful commentary on how this process unfolded with the independence movement of the Thirteen Colonies, see Francis Jennings, *Empire of Fortune: Crowns, Colonies and Tribes in the Seven Years' War in America* (New York, 1988), 457–84.

113 This phrase, s. 91, item 24, in the British North America Act, is the sole mention of Native people in the founding document of the Canadian confederation.

Early Compact Groups in the Politics of York

GRAEME PATTERSON

Then none was for a party;
Then all were for the state;
Then the great man helped the poor,
And the poor man loved the great;
Then the lands were fairly portioned;
Then spoils were fairly sold.

Thomas Babington Macaulay,
Lays of Ancient Rome (1842)

Towards the end of his life William Warren Baldwin wrote a memorandum for "the use of an abler mind [than his own] at some future day to take up with effect" which he bound into his copy of Charles Buller's *Responsible Government for Colonies* (London, 1840).[1] It was his hope that "the brief notes of reference here offered may assist some future Historian of these regions and…form a useful introduction to the perusal of the little work…bound up in this volume." Baldwin began his account of the origin of the struggle for "responsible government" in 1822, the year a joint protest of Upper and Lower Canadians was made against a proposed union of the two colonies. In periods previous to this, he explained, "many were the public complaints," but "the official documents connected with such of them as were agitated in the assembly previous to the year 18[—] must be rare if not altogether lost to public reference as the Parliament House with all its papers was burned to the ground by the American Army…in the year 1813…and was burned again by accident in the year [date omitted, 1824] with its library and papers."[2]

Given this absence of documentation, it might be supposed that Dr. Baldwin would have sought to assist the future historian by recalling relevant events. Significantly, it seems, he did not do so. What follows below treats what he was content to leave forgotten.

In history generally, and in Upper Canadian history in particular, concepts of élitist government have frequently been juxtaposed as opposites to others of democratic government. In this way the Baldwinite achievement of "re-

William Warren Baldwin M.D., 1775–1844

sponsible government" has been viewed as a triumph of democracy over its opposite, "compact government." To nineteenth-century historians, like J. M. McMullen,[3] J. C. Dent[4] and William Kingsford,[5] this particular juxtaposition gave expression, albeit in quite different ways, to virtually the whole meaning of the pre-Confederation era.

It is, of course, a delusion to suppose that élite groups are ever absent from, or are not necessary to, the functioning of democracies. A simplistic, populist-like aversion to élites as élites *per se*, which derives in part from the rhetoric of parties of opposition such as that led by Baldwin, has had the effect, however, of masking significant structural change in political, social and ideological forms. It is well known, for example, that the achievement of "responsible government" was the inevitable result of the emergence of modern political parties in a parliamentary form of government. It is less well known that these parties were the product of complicated struggles between rival groups of several sorts—here termed *compacts*—which slowly transformed themselves into modern parties. The main focus of interest of this present study is the examination of an early phase of one such struggle within which Baldwin was caught up. Preliminary to that undertaking, however, we must be concerned with definitions.

An élite is by definition a minority group within some larger hierarchical structure. In this sense some, but not all, compacts may be thought of as élites. Small groups of appointed local officials, for example, like the early magistrates in the District of London, whose opponents time and again defeated them in elections to the House of Assembly, were certainly privileged minorities and therefore may be usefully regarded as belonging to an élite.[6] But there were other groups in the province, like one in the town of Kingston, represented in the assembly by Christopher Hagerman, which owed much of its strength to a democratic process of election.[7] Hagerman was certainly a Tory, a friend of the provincial executive and, from one point of view, an élitist. That viewpoint, however, is less than helpful in understanding, or even perceiving, the combination of interest groups within a larger interest group that made for the majorities Hagerman won at the polls. The idea of a compact, thought of as sometimes, but not always, containing non-élite interest groups would seem to be more useful in dealing with entities that were something more than simple factions and something less than modern parties.

Yet the word is not used here without misgivings. No concept in the tangled history of Upper Canada has so structured fundamental, mythopoeic misinterpretations of reality as have varying notions of "compacts." In treating the period 1791–1841, late-nineteenth-century writers generally supposed that the very processes of political and constitutional change had received their dynamic from the despotic activities of a single "family compact." Centred at York, but extended throughout the whole colony, it was thought to have given rise to early popular protest, to the emergence of a reform party in the 1820s, to rebellion in the 1830s, and to the final achievement of "responsible government" in the 1840s. It was, in short, a first mover of history.[8] No such use of the term is intended here.

Over the years few writers have agreed upon what "the family compact" actually was. In the eighteenth century the expression was simply an English translation of "Pacte de Famille," a name given to a series of treaties between the several branches of the House of Bourbon. It generally continued to mean "agreement," and not to refer to a collectivity of persons of any sort, until the early 1830s. William Lyon Mackenzie then applied it to a group of about 30 men who, he claimed, ruled the province and who, he established, were united by marriage.[9] But "family compact" was soon stripped of this meaning when Lord Durham, in seeking to apply it to the whole Tory party, not surprisingly discovered it to be "a name not much more appropriate than party designations usually are, inasmuch as there is, in truth, very little family connexion among the persons thus united."[10]

It is unnecessary to trace the term's further development in any detail here.[11] Suffice it to say that it has been used to designate both factions united by kinship and groups united only by varying sorts of common interest. It has also been used to refer to oligarchy, to quasi-aristocracy, to the administrative personnel of government, to the Tory party, to that party's leadership, to a social class, and to combinations of these and other elements. Assuming that it was created by the Constitutional Act, some writers have thought that it came into existence with that measure in 1791; others have believed that it really only took on form in the 1820s under the leadership of Archdeacon John Strachan. But more often than not the expression has been used so ambiguously as to be evocative of any meaning that might happen to reside in a particular reader's mind.

In recent years historians have been divided on the importance of family connections. G. M. Craig, applying the term "family compact" to a relatively small group of York officials, has noted that it had only a limited accuracy "since…its members were not all tied together by family connection, nor were they the ingrown, selfish and reactionary group the phrase was meant by its opponents to suggest."[12] And S. F. Wise, applying the term to the upper and upper middle classes, has likewise minimized the importance of family bonds.[13] Craig and Wise, like Durham, however, were thinking mostly of the party politics of the 1820s and 1830s when family ties signified little outside of the rhetoric of radicals like W. L. Mackenzie. But students of an earlier period, working mostly at a local level, have thought otherwise. Robert Burns, who identifies "the family compact" with an early Toronto upper class, has emphasized the importance of family ties,[14] as has Fred Armstrong in a study of an oligarchy of officials in the Western District. "The most important factor in appointment to local office," Armstrong concluded, "was probably family connection."[15] Quite different from the local groups examined by Burns and Armstrong was a powerful commercial compact, known to Baldwin as "the Scotch party," which grew up around John Askin of Detroit, Robert Hamilton of Queenston, Richard Cartwright of Kingston and their Montreal suppliers. But here, too, as a recent searching examination of Hamilton's connections by Bruce Wilson has shown, kinship was a factor of considerable importance.[16]

Although all of the above meanings of the word "compact" were completely unknown in the period under discussion, it will be used here to designate social and political interest groups which emerged prior to the formation of provincial political parties. These differed in type. In some, possession of power was almost exclusively dependent upon office holding and hence upon executive favour. Termed here *official compacts*, these groups tended to be relatively weak. In other groups, however, possession of office resulted from some other power basis, usually economic. Termed *commercial compacts*, these bodies were relatively strong and tended to be autonomous of executive control. Kinship was sometimes of importance in uniting groups of both sorts; but so too sometimes was ethnicity. More important than either of these factors, however, was common interest.

York's first compact, official in nature, originally took shape at Newark (Niagara-on-the-Lake), the temporary capital of the province before York was settled. It was headed by Peter Russell, a hitherto impecunious half-pay officer from Cork, Ireland, who, upon the recommendation of his old commanding officer, Lieutenant Governor John Graves Simcoe, was made receiver and auditor general in 1791. He was also given seats upon both the Executive and Legislative councils. By reason of these offices, particularly that of executive councillor, and more particularly by reason of Simcoe's continuing favour, Russell acquired great power and influence. Yet he reached the height of his power only between the summer of 1796 and that of 1799 when, again upon Simcoe's recommendation, he was made president of the Executive Council and administrator of the colony to act for the lieutenant governor during the latter's prolonged absence in England. Then in late 1799 his power began to erode when Simcoe, whom he had hoped to succeed, was replaced instead by Lieutenant General Peter Hunter.

During Hunter's own lengthy absences on military duty in Lower Canada, he appointed not an administrator to act for him but a committee of the Executive Council consisting usually of Russell, Æneas Shaw and Chief Justice John Elmsley, who was replaced in 1802 by Chief Justice Henry Allcock. The president of this committee, with whom Hunter corresponded, was not Russell but first Elmsley and then Allcock. Russell had quarrelled bitterly with both of these men, most notably with Elmsley whom he had forced to move from Newark to York in 1798.

Simcoe, who favoured decayed gentlefolk like Russell for appointment to high office, had been much prejudiced against "mercantile people [who] added to their precarious [financial] situation here have rose from obscurity so rapidly and apparently to their neighbours as would lessen rather than add to Government could they afford the necessary atttendance [sic] [at the capital]."[17] Nonetheless, of the five members appointed to the Executive Council in 1792—Jacques Duperon Baby, William Robertson, Alexander Grant, William Osgoode and Russell—two, Baby and Robertson, were merchants while a third, Commodore Grant, who controlled shipping on the lakes, had close mercantile connections. And of the nine original appointees to the Legislative Council, six—Baby, Robertson, Grant, Richard Duncan, Robert Hamilton and Richard Cartwright—had mercantile interests.

Russell, fully sharing Simcoe's prejudice against *arriviste* merchants, felt much threatened by them. "And when your Grace is informed," he wrote to a secretary of state,

> that there is now in this Province a great many individuals (particularly Merchants) who, having no official Duties to discharge, nor any official Rank to support, have devoted their whole time and attention to the improvement of their fortunes; & that in consequence many of them are...in possession of from 20 to 50,000 Acres of land in it, and, tho' neither from birth, education, nor habits of life entitled...to put themselves on a level with us [office holders], will eventually leave fortunes to their families considerably beyond what we can hope for our own...; We trust that your Grace will not refuse to lay at his Majesty's Feet our humble Prayer....[18]

Russell was praying for additional land for executive councillors. Involved here, however, was more than the politics of greed. He and his social class were caught up in a struggle for social and political dominance.

This perception was not shared, or was ignored, by the Scottish Peter Hunter who favoured merchants, especially Hamilton and Cartwright. He admired their practical good sense and expert knowledge, and supported their plans for economic development. Simcoe's old favourites, moreover, were not necessarily his. "The Executive Council are all good men," Hunter allowed, "but I could not help observing that your old Friend Mr. Russell is avaricious to the last degree and would certainly...have granted lands to the Devil and all his Family (as good Loyalists) provided they could pay the Fees."[19] Hunter not only would not let Russell continue to act as president-administrator but within the Executive Council he forced him to take a seat below those of Baby and Grant, whose names preceded his on Simcoe's commission. "The Consequence," wrote the humiliated Russell, "is that I have the mortification of being commanded by those to whom I was lately Superior, without having done anything to merit this degradation."[20]

The humiliation of Russell, to whom Hunter was at least always polite, was as nothing compared to that of the provincial secretary and registrar, William Jarvis. Rebuking him for lazy incompetence, Hunter on one occasion threatened to "unjarvis" Jarvis. "The Secretary has come home crying like a child from the treatment he has met with," wrote his wife, Hannah, after one particularly painful interview with the general, "and dare not open his lips; those who saw the manner he was treated advised him to command himself and be silent, as words were what was sought for that some hold might be had against him."[21] Feared and hated by some, Hunter died on 21

August 1805, unlamented by those he had alienated. "...I think the Ministry must have scraped all the Fishing Towns in Scotland to have met with so great a devil," declared Mrs. Jarvis, "—the wretch I am told half an hour before his Death, Damned every one around him in his usual manner....A Tyrant in all his Departments—hated by all—except a few Lying...mischief making sycophants and dependents."[22] Harsh and bitter language of this sort explains in part the view of Hunter later entertained by persons like Judge Robert Thorpe, who never knew the man but was well acquainted with his enemies. It also helps explain why the Hunter administration came to be viewed as an aberration from a norm—as to some degree perhaps it was—and why as a mistaken corollary it was thought possible to return to the *status quo ante* of the Simcoe and Russell administrations. This latter delusion accounts for a good deal of the more extravagant political behaviour of the Anglo-Irish—including that of Baldwin—during and after the Hunter régime.

Upon the death of Hunter, Russell, assuming he was again president and administrator, convened a meeting of the Executive Council attended by himself, Æneas Shaw and John McGill. There Shaw and McGill unexpectedly joined forces, inducing Russell to agree that, by reason of seniority of appointment, Alexander Grant and not he should be president and administrator. Again the rationale for this latter power play was that Grant's name preceded Russell's on the original commission of 1792.[23] Shaw, McGill and Grant, however, were all Scots, the latter having mercantile interests; and these factors, the friends of Russell came to believe, had governed the situation.

One of these friends was a fellow Irishman, Robert Thorpe, who had just arrived from Prince Edward Island as a newly appointed puisne judge of the Court of King's Bench. Thorpe, as Bruce Walton has demonstrated,[24] advised Russell that "the Leadership in Council does not in general depend upon the order in which Ministers [*sic*] happen to be placed in the instrument of their appointment (unless expressly so decided by the Sovereign) but <u>upon that and the Priority of Time when they are sworn into office</u> [emphasis Russell's]...."[25] Russell then asked Grant to convene a special meeting of the council to reconsider the issue. This he did; but to Russell's chagrin the council declined to pursue the matter any further. Thus began one of the more fundamental polarizations in Upper Canadian politics.

Meanwhile Russell had acquired a clientele of Anglo-Irish friends and relatives who, having like him faced bankruptcy and ruin in the old country, hoped for much from Upper Canada and Russell's influence in it. First among these was his close friend and cousin, William Willcocks, a failed merchant from Cork, who arrived on 24 November 1792.[26] Included, too, were Willcocks's son Charles and, for a time, his second cousin once removed, Joseph Willcocks. Having arrived on 20 March 1800, the latter served as Russell's private secretary and general factotum, living on the best of terms with his employer until 23 August 1802. Then, having presumed to court Russell's half-sister, Elizabeth, he was thrown out.[27] The most interesting client from our point of view, however, was the young physician William Baldwin who arrived with his ruined father, Robert, younger brother and four sisters in June 1799, just about four months before Russell was succeeded by Hunter. This close circle of friends was tightened by the bonds of marriage on 31 May 1803, when William Baldwin wed Margaret Phoebe, the daughter of William Willcocks. Binding further this group, and drawing to it persons like Judge Thorpe, was a strong sense of common Irish identity, common dismay at the Hunter succession of 1799, and that of Grant in 1805, as well as the perceived threat of a rival compact of Scots.

This rival compact, as perceived by the Russell circle, is described in the correspondence of Robert Thorpe. "I find that General Hunter...had a few Scotch instruments about him (Mr. McGill and Mr. Scott) that he made subservient to his purposes," wrote the judge, "and by every other individual he and his tools were execrated."[28] Executive Councillors McGill and Scott were connected with certain "scotch [sic] Pedlars" who had insinuated themselves into Hunter's favour. A chain of these merchants was "linked from Halifax to Quebec, Montreal, Kingston, York, Niagara & so on to Detroit." This "Shopkeeper Aristocracy" had "stunted the prosperity of this Province & goaded the people until they have turned from the greatest loyalty to the utmost disaffection."[29] The "extortion, partiality and negligence under General Hunter," Thorpe further observed, "which his weak and wicked tools have followed up with the President [Grant] whom they made (without any right) for their own purposes has been exposed and has set the people mad...."[30]

Behind these exaggerated and highly partisan charges lay a distorted truth. In 1806 there were seven members of the Executive Council; but, of these, Jacob Mountain, the English Bishop, never attended and Jacques Baby, a French Canadian, attended only a few weeks of the year. Apart from Russell, the remaining active members—Alexander Grant, Æneas Shaw, John McGill and Thomas Scott—had all been born in Scotland. Although only Grant seems to have had mercantile interests, and only Scott—the attorney general and later chief justice—had been appointed during the Hunter administration, these men, as we have seen, do seem to have joined forces against their Irish colleague.

But there is good reason to suppose that Russell's friends assigned a much greater importance to the factor of national origin than did either Hunter or his fellow Scots. Although by 1806 Elmsley and Allcock had both departed the province, Hunter had treated these two Englishmen, after all, as *primus inter pares* among the other executive councillors. The "Shopkeeper Aristocracy," moreover, was considerably less Scottish than Thorpe indicated. Insofar as this aristocracy existed, its leading, and founding, members would have been James McGill and Isaac Todd of Montreal, Richard Cartwright of Kingston, Robert Hamilton of Queenston and John Askin of Detroit. Of these only McGill and Hamilton were Scots; Todd and Askin were both Irish, while Cartwright was an American Loyalist. Certainly these men worked together and all appear to have been close friends; but, whatever united them, it was scarcely common national origin.

Interestingly and significantly, in assailing these merchants, the Irish, concentrating upon alleged national origin, paid little or no attention to family ties. This is in striking contrast to the attacks William Lyon Mackenzie was to make upon his "family compact" in the 1830s. The main focus in the Executive Council of this early Irish anger, of course, was John McGill, who was not related to the James McGill of Montreal, and Attorney General Scott, who not only had no mercantile interests but seems not even to have been married.[31] But if the Irish had felt inclined to assail a "family compact" in 1806, Alexander Grant would have made a very good target. For he was a brother-in-law of John Askin, who was the father-in-law of Robert Hamilton. Hamilton, in turn, had established four cousins—Robert, William, Thomas Dickson and Thomas Clark—as leading merchants in the Niagara peninsula. These latter were of course all Scots; but that would seem to have been entirely incidental to their being Hamilton's relatives.[32] And perhaps the same point may be made with respect to other Scottish merchants like William Robertson of Detroit, who was linked to Askin and Hamilton by marriage through his brother Samuel's widow, Catharine Hamilton, née Askin.

In contrast to W. L. Mackenzie, who was of relatively lowly origins and had no hope of receiving executive patronage, and in contrast also to later writers influenced by anachronistic concepts of "family compacts," Baldwin and his friends, although poor, were eighteenth-century Anglo-Irish gentry who owed what they had in life to family connections and patrons of one sort or another. So far from wishing to destroy this system they wanted to exploit it, to fashion effective "family compacts" of their own. Indeed, this was what their struggle with the merchants was all about. And this was what the profoundly conservative William Baldwin's own early politics were all about.

Even if the Scottish party had no existence outside of the Irish imagination, it would have had real historic importance. It lay behind Thorpe's early attempts at discrediting the surviving "Scotch instruments" of the Hunter régime. And these attempts most probably lay behind his later proposals for colonial ministerial responsibility, proposals which very closely resemble those to be made by Baldwin in 1828[33] but of which the latter seemed to remember nothing in 1840.

When the Baldwins arrived at York in 1799 they were welcomed warmly into the Russell-Willcocks circle. Russell, indeed, immediately undertook to secure 1,200 acres of well-situated land for William and another 1,200 for his father, Robert. But because Robert perversely, but characteristically, wanted to live near an old Irish friend, they first settled about 30 miles to the east of the capital in Clarke, a township in the sparsely populated Newcastle District. There it was possible for Russell to have Robert appointed county lieutenant for Durham; but there, too, it was impossible for William to establish a medical practice. Therefore he moved back to York in 1802 during the Hunter administration.

At York he lived in the home of William Willcocks, opened a school for boys to supplement his meagre income from medicine, and in 1803 wed Phoebe Willcocks. This marriage eventually became the foundation of the restored Baldwin family fortune. Along with her sister, Maria Willcocks, Phoebe inherited the bulk of her father's estate in 1813. Then the much larger estate of Peter Russell was willed to the two sisters when Russell's half-sister, Elizabeth, died in 1822. Finally Phoebe inherited the income from Maria's share of these estates in 1834. Said to amount to over 100,000 acres of prime land, much of it in or near the capital, these bequests made the Baldwins one of the richest families in the province.[34] Normally this growing wealth, along with William's proven ability, could have been expected to elevate him high in the councils of the executive. It did not. Instead it provided a most comfortable basis for the "independent" politics pursued by the doctor in the eighth parliament (1820–24) and the politics of opposition he pursued in the tenth (1828–30). But to understand fully what happened we must return to the politics of an earlier period.

In the year of his marriage Baldwin's financial circumstances were very different. Land then had so little value that Russell, himself, was almost entirely dependent upon his salary; as for old William Willcocks, he teetered on the verge of bankruptcy until the day of his death. As Russell was so bitterly aware, wealth derived primarily from commerce and only secondarily from government office. Government office, however, was certainly an attractive alternative to school teaching.

But in 1803 yet another alternative offered itself. Lawyers, who were much in demand, were in very short supply, so short, indeed, that the lieutenant governor was authorized to license for practice otherwise educated men who could satisfy the chief justice that they had mastered the essentials of English law. By 5 May of that year Baldwin—having learned the law, it is said, from a copy of Blackstone's *Commentaries on the Laws of England* borrowed from Peter Russell—was duly licenced.[35]

Within the legal profession the young doctor advanced rapidly. In 1807 he became a bencher of the Law Society of Upper Canada. In 1811–15, 1820–21 and 1832–36 he served as its treasurer, sometimes combining this office with that of secretary. Much in demand in the courts, Baldwin was probably even more active as a solicitor, his most important client being his friend Laurent Quetton St. George, a leading merchant but not a Scot. Thus, by the time Phoebe began to inherit her large estates, William was well established by way of his own efforts.

He was, however, a disappointed man, his prominence having resulted in relatively little recognition by the executive branch of government. It is true that in 1806 Grant had made him acting clerk of the Crown and Common Pleas when that office became vacant upon the death of David Burns; but this, it appears, was merely a matter of temporary convenience, Baldwin having already acted as Burns's deputy. He lasted in office only until 12 March, when John Small received the permanent appointment.[36] This same year he became master in chancery. This office, however, appears not to have been in the gift of the executive but in that of the Legislative Council.[37] Then, on 16 November 1808 Lieutenant Governor Francis Gore approved his appointment as registrar of the Court of Probate;[38] and on 22 July 1809 he was commissioned judge of the Home District Court.[39] Gore, who much mistrusted William by reason of his association with Thorpe, C. B. Wyatt and other undesirables, appears to have been trying to conciliate the doctor.[40] And, for reasons unknown, Baldwin succeeded his father as surrogate judge of the Home District. That, however, was the last piece of executive patronage he received until Sir Charles Metcalfe named him to the Legislative Council of the United Canadas in 1843, by which time his son Robert had become joint premier. Baldwin died, however, before he could take his seat.

The close connection between the compact group to which one belonged and access to executive patronage was revealed in January 1806, when it was rumoured that the office of clerk of the Legislative Council was about to become vacant by reason of the alcoholism and impending death of its incumbent, James Clark. This office, which paid £125 a year for about six weeks' work, was much sought after.[41] When the wife of William Willcocks approached Peter Russell to secure it for her son Charles, Elizabeth Russell recorded in her diary:

> Peter told her that he had already applied to the President [Alexander Grant] for a friend, (it was Dr. Baldwin but he did not tell her so.) and told him he had already alloted it to another. My brother did not tell her who, but it is the President's son-in-law; this he told Peter in confidence.[42]

In point of fact, the president's son-in-law seems not to have been appointed, probably because Grant changed his mind about sacking Clark.[43] Early in the administration of Francis Gore, however, the new lieutenant governor, deciding that Clark "should no longer hold a responsible position to which his vices render'd him inequal [*sic*],"[44] appointed John Powell.

Powell was the son of Gore's favourite executive councillor, William Dummer Powell, and was possibly already engaged to Isabella, the daughter of another executive councillor, Æneas Shaw. The elder Powell, it should be remarked, also persuaded Gore to appoint John Macdonell attorney general and, upon Macdonell's death at the Battle of Queenston Heights, he persuaded General Sheaffe to appoint John Beverley Robinson to the same position *pro tempore* even though the latter had not yet been called to the bar and, indeed, was not yet of age. Of Macdonell's appointment, Powell observed: "This gallant youth had been called to the High Station of Atty. General at my Special Intercession with a view to relief from doubtful Characters sent from England & a desire to encourage the youth of the country." To which a not otherwise unadmiring biographer felt obliged to add: "We may be reasonably certain that the fact that Macdonell was the fiancé of Mary Boyles Powell, Mr. Justice Powell's daughter, was no detriment to him."[45] As for Robinson, in 1812 he was thought to be a suitor of Anne, another daughter of Powell, who was obsessed by the young man to the point of madness.[46] As for Baldwin, who regarded both Macdonell and Robinson as rivals, the "doubtful characters sent from England" were his close friends.

Under circumstances such as these Baldwin's own patron was of little use to him. Indeed so helpless was Russell that on 9 February 1806 he appealed to the newly appointed Judge Thorpe to use his influence to have the doctor's temporary appointment as clerk of the Crown made permanent.[47] Thorpe duly wrote a glowing recommendation to Lord Castlereagh, who was secretary of state for war and the colonies as well as probably being Thorpe's own patron.[48] Nothing, however, came of it.

Then in 1812 Baldwin made a curious attempt of his own at reaching behind the Upper Canadian executive to the authorities in England. When the solicitor generalship became vacant he attempted to use the influence of Charles Wyatt, a "doubtful character" who, having been dismissed from office as surveyor general by Gore, had returned to England. Wyatt, in turn, wrote to the former attorney general, William Firth, another "doubtful character," who also had departed the province at odds with the executive. Firth replied in the most friendly terms; but, as he acutely observed, he did not think that they were "the likliest [sic] people to succeed in obtaining situations for their friends at home or abroad."[49] It is strange that Baldwin did not understand this without being told.

In 1812, however, the doctor's judgement may have been affected by frustrated ambition. For, with the appointment of his rival Macdonell, Baldwin's rage, bitterness, envy and disappointment overflowed. "Mr. McDonell [sic] the Attorney General," he wrote to Firth,

> —non fero tempori sed in amplo [sic]—according to his address by the Court and his signature to all public instruments is such a paragon of excellence he leaves no commendable qualifications for others to found pretentions on[;] he is made Col' of Militia and Provincial Aide de Camp to General Brock—the field[,] the cabinet and the Forum are all the scene of his renown—His honors rain upon him, they come in tempests—Lest you should charge me with envy I do assure you I feel none toward him. I can with the greatest indifference see him erect his crest and spread his spangled tail in the sunshine, and am only annoyed when I see him in his celestial adoration forget those around him and set foot upon them.[50]

This same year Baldwin, taking offence at some of Macdonell's remarks, challenged him to a duel. It ended bloodlessly when Baldwin sensibly fired wide after Macdonell declined to take aim at him.[51]

It has been suggested by two of Baldwin's biographers that Macdonell "was an ardent member and supporter of the so-called Family Compact."[52] As we have seen, he was indeed a client of Powell. But he was not perceived after this fashion by the doctor. Indeed Baldwin seems not to have connected his rival's rise with Powell, an American Loyalist. He appears rather to have thought of him as a member of the ubiquitous "Scotch Party." And he thought in the same fashion of another Scottish merchant and future provincial secretary, Duncan Cameron, a "bird of ill omen" who, upon the appointment of Isaac Brock as administrator, was "again flapping about Govt. House." Brock, Baldwin thought, wanted to avoid following in the steps of Gore but "the bird lime is still adhesive to the branches of the administration."[53]

The term "Scotch Party," and related theory, were current at least as late as 1817 when Samuel Smith became administrator. Baldwin's friend G. M. Detlor then observed that this change in the executive was inconsequential "as the Scotch Party are at the Head yet, and have it all among themselves."[54] The strange thing is that little or nothing is heard of it thereafter. It must have been particularly maddening to the Baldwin circle when yet another Scot, closely connected with the late Richard Cartwright and married to the widow of Andrew McGill of Montreal, became an executive councillor and chief advisor of Lieutenant Governor Peregrine Maitland, who administered the colony from 1818 to 1828. Yet one of the few charges John Strachan's enemies seem never to have made against him was that he favoured fellow Scots.

What then is to be made of Baldwin's curious memorandum of 1840 with which we began this essay? Read one way it suggests that the idea of "responsible government" *as first conceived of* is to be found embodied in, it seems, an unspecified handbill or newspaper report on the proceedings at a public meeting held at York on 15 August 1828 and in letters he addressed to Lord Goderich, the former Whig prime minister and secretary for war and the colonies, and Edward George Stanley (later Lord Stanley), Goderich's former parliamentary under-secretary for the colonies. These two letters, wrote the doctor, "contain the development of the nature of the responsibility required and of the means of effecting it after the example of the British Constitution. The suggestion in its distinct shape was made by Robert Baldwin [his son]...in private conversation with me on the occasion of penning those letters...." But this idea, the document suggests, was somehow foreshadowed in the petition against the union of 1822 even though it did not "touch on the point of Responsible Government." He had in mind that "it might be valuable as presenting evidence of the claims to constitutional rights entertained by the people, in contradistinction to the sentiments of the executive authorities...and of their dependents & partizans...."[55] What he meant here, one supposes, was that the 1822 petition was evidence that the people of the colony, as distinguished from the supporters of the executive, saw themselves as possessing the same rights as subjects in the mother country. Pushed further in 1828, this conviction implied that they were entitled to "responsible government."

All of which suggests that the idea of "responsible government" or, more properly, of colonial ministerial responsibility, did not come into existence until the 1820s, a notion which is patently untrue but which has been subscribed to by many Canadian historians. Thorpe advanced the idea in 1806-7. Pierre Bédard of the *Parti Canadien* did the same thing about the same time in Lower Canada. The concept had been contended for, moreover, by Baldwin's own father, Robert, in Ireland in the 1780s.[56] With the exception of what went on in Lower Canada, William Baldwin must have been aware of all this. Was he then deliberately attempting to mislead historians with his helpful memorandum?

Such may have been the case. On the other hand, like many others, he may simply have been confused by ideas which came to be associated with the slogan "responsible government" in the 1830s. Imbedded in the historiography of "responsible government" are two contradictory ideas: one, that the concept was old and easily understandable; and two, that it was new and difficult to grasp and, because of this, it was an act of inspired genius on the part of Baldwin to have first conceived of "responsible government" in 1828. That it was old and easily understood was asserted by Lord Durham when he wrote of its application: "It needs no change in the principles of government, no invention of new constitutional theory to supply the remedy which would...completely remove the existing political disorders. It needs but to follow out consistently the principles of the British constitution...."[57] That it was a new idea whose emergence was attended by all sorts of conceptual difficulties was to be asserted by a great many historians like Aileen Dunham, who treated it in a chapter significantly entitled "The Dawn of a New Conception."[58] Durham was right; Dunham and the rest were mistaken, and Baldwin may have shared their error in confounding "difficulty in applying a well understood idea" with "difficulty in grasping an idea."

In other words, Baldwin's memorandum may reflect his own difficulty in accepting the propriety of colonial ministerial responsibility. In 1806-7 the Russell circle sympathized with Mr. Justice Thorpe; but not all of its members need to have agreed with all of his ideas or to have deemed his political activities either prudent or practical. Russell, himself, so distanced himself from Thorpe that as late as July 1807 Gore seems to have been entirely ignorant of their earlier association. For he then wrote to the old councillor requesting that a highly confidential meeting of the Executive Council be held in Russell's home. "I have not communicated my intention to the Clerk of the Council," declared Gore, "as I wish the reference I intend making to be confidential."[59] The lieutenant governor would scarcely have done this had he suspected a connection between Russell and Thorpe. As for Baldwin, despite the suspicions of Gore, he seems never to have been directly involved in the judge's political activities—with which he may well then have disagreed.

To agree with Thorpe on colonial ministerial responsibility involved disagreeing with Blackstone, from whom Baldwin appears to have learned most of his law. In 1811, moreover, when the House of Assembly threatened to impeach the latter for having sought the arrest of a member—his enemy Macdonell—Baldwin declared "that this house was not entitled to privilege as being a House of Assembly and not a House of Parliament," a doctrine fundamentally at odds with those of Thorpe.[60] Nor is there any reason to think that Baldwin would then have found Thorpe's constitutional doctrine desirable even if he deemed it to be within the law. Indeed, as Edith Firth has remarked of the election of 1820: "one of the most eloquent candidates defending his government position and expressing his gratitude to a beneficent administration was Dr. W. W. Baldwin."[61]

The implication here is that the doctor was moderate because he still had hope for executive patronage. This may well have been the case even though in his address he also emphasized the importance of "independence" from the executive and special interest groups on the part of both the electorate and its representatives.

Certainly he then seemed well pleased with the constitution as it stood.[62] But a change in his position would appear to have been taking place by 1822, when with the petition against the union he contended that British subjects in colonies had all the rights of those in the mother country—a doctrine contrary to Blackstone but quite in line with the views of Thorpe. This idea, of course, was to be axiomatic to his contention of 1828 that colonials were entitled by common law to ministerial accountability to their own legislatures. By 1822, then, Baldwin would seem to have begun changing his mind.

As Baldwin also seems slowly to have understood, his new doctrine, which was viewed by many as essentially separatist, along with what was made of the persons with whom he associated, combined to completely damn him in the eyes of the Executive. "...Mr. [W. W.] Baldwin is an Attorney, Barrister, and Doctor of Medicine here, who long held two or three subordinate Offices, and who is allowed to hold the situation of a Judge of the Surrogate Court," wrote Maitland in 1828. "His assistance and friendship," he continued, "have not been wanting...to the promoters of discontent, and I believe I may state truly, that with the exception of his son, he is the only person throughout the Province, in the character of a gentleman, who has associated himself with the promoters of Mr [Joseph] Hume's projects."[63] Dr. Baldwin would have been more than slow of understanding if by the end of the Maitland administration in 1828 he had not well understood that he had no hope of attaining high office.

If surprising, it is perhaps also very significant, that it took Baldwin so long to reach this bitter conclusion. Here most probably lies the explanation of the memorandum he addressed to future historians. For if "responsible government" was an easily understood concept with which he, for one, had been perfectly familiar from at least the time of his early manhood, why had it taken him so long to advance the noble principle? This, it is suggested, was a question Baldwin preferred to avoid. Hence, while perhaps not lying when discussing the origins of "responsible government," he avoided embarrassing, if highly relevant, references to the early history of the colony.

Fundamental to understanding the politics of Baldwin and of many others in the 1820s are not only their interests but also an accurate understanding of the politics in which they were caught up in earlier times. Involved here is not just an understanding of the structure and function of those entities which have here been termed "compacts" but also the relationship of these bodies to the House of Assembly and more especially to the Executive Council. The latter has received surprisingly little critical attention from historians despite the fact that until 1820 shifts of power within it seem to have been as significant politically, if not more significant, as those which took place in the assembly. These changes, of course, were much less visible and were not completely understood even by those directly affected by them.

Much better understood and generally subscribed to, if scarcely ever acted upon, was the ideology which informs the lines of Macaulay with which this essay began. "Then none was for a party; Then all were for the state" was a political ideal of many who were themselves long entangled in factional conflict. In part this was because dominant factions, and more especially disciplined modern parties, were destructive of the idealized "balanced" constitution, of the "blessings" of which they all professed themselves to be entitled. This constitution was upset when one faction dominated the Executive Council. But when a single party came to dominate the assembly the balanced constitution was completely undone. For these reasons, in part, political addresses of the period are replete with denunciations of faction and praise of "independence": of the independence of electors from the influence of landlords and creditors and, above all, of the independence of representatives from the executive, from partisan interest and, indeed, from the electors themselves. Ideologically, this was almost the antithesis of ideas axiomatic to notions of "responsible government": control of the executive by a party within the legislature, and the accountability of the party, as distinguished from just the representatives, to the electorate. The former set of ideas, however, were those to which Baldwin gave eloquent expression in his electoral address of 1820. Nonetheless, within the next eight years he would shed these notions to become the theorist of colonial ministerial responsibility. The latter theory, as explained in Baldwin's memorandum of 1840, would structure the thought of the historians of Upper Canada up to the present day.

---

1 Metropolitan Toronto Central Library, Canadian History Dept., Baldwin Room [hereafter MTCL], William Warren Baldwin Papers, untitled memorandum, n.d. [1840?], enclosed in his copy of Charles Buller, *Responsible Government for Colonies* (London, 1840).

2 Ibid. In point of fact the library sustained very little damage in the second fire. See Edith Firth, ed., *The Town of York, 1815–1834* (Toronto, 1966), 17–18, Grant Powell to George Hillier, 30 Dec. 1824.

3 John M. McMullen, *The History of Canada* (Brockville, 1855; 2nd ed. 1862; rev. ed., 2 vols., 1891–92).

4 John C. Dent, *The Last Forty Years: Canada Since the Union of 1840* (Toronto, 1881). See also G. H. Patterson, "John Charles Dent", *Dictionary of Canadian Biography* [hereafter *DCB*], XI (Toronto, 1982), 246–49.

5 William Kingsford, *The History of Canada*, 10 vols. (Toronto, 1887–98). See also J. K. McConica, "Kingsford and Whiggery in Canadian History", *Canadian Historical Review* [hereafter *CHR*] 40 (1959), 108–20.

6 See G. H. Patterson, *Studies in Elections and Public Opinion in Upper Canada* (Ph.D. diss., University of Toronto, 1969), ch. 1.

7 See ibid.; also S. F. Wise, "Tory Factionalism: Kingston Elections and Upper Canadian Politics", *Ontario History* 57 (1965), 205–25, and "The Rise of Christopher Hagerman", *Historic Kingston* 14 (1966), 12–23.

8 An interesting and controversial argument for again emphasizing grievances and official abuses of power has recently been put forward by Paul Romney in his *Mr. Attorney: The Attorney General for Ontario in Court, Cabinet, and Legislature, 1791–1899* (Toronto, 1986), 62–65.

9 W. L. Mackenzie, *Sketches of Upper Canada* (London, 1833), 409.

10 C. P. Lucas, ed., *Lord Durham's Report on the Affairs of British North America*, II (Oxford, 1912), 107.

11 I have done so elsewhere. See G. H. Patterson, "An Enduring Canadian Myth: Responsible Government and the Family Compact", *Journal of Canadian Studies* 12 (1977), 3–16.

12 G. M. Craig, *Upper Canada: The Formative Years, 1784–1841* (Toronto, 1963), 107.

13 S. F. Wise, "The Origin of Anti-Americanism in Canada", in D. W. L. Earl, ed., *The Family Compact: Aristocracy or Oligarchy?* (Toronto, 1967), 143.

14 Robert Burns, "God's Chosen People: The Origins of Toronto Society, 1793–1818", Canadian Historical Association, *Historical Papers* [hereafter CHA, *HP*] (1973), 213–28; also his "The First Elite of Toronto: An Examination of the Genesis, Consolidation and Duration of Power in an Emerging Colonial Society" (Ph.D. diss., University of Western Ontario, 1974).

15 Frederick H. Armstrong, "The Oligarchy of the Western District of Upper Canada, 1788–1841", CHA, *HP* (1977), 96.

16 Bruce G. Wilson, *The Enterprises of Robert Hamilton: A Study of Wealth and Influence in Early Upper Canada, 1776–1812* (Ottawa, 1983).

17 E. A. Cruikshank, ed., *The Correspondence of Lieut. Governor John Graves Simcoe...*, I (Toronto, 1923), 263–65, Simcoe to Henry Dundas, 23 Nov. 1792.

18 E. A. Cruikshank, ed., *The Correspondence of the Honourable Peter Russell...*, I (Toronto, 1932), 163–64, Russell to the Duke of Portland, 18 Apr. 1797.

19 National Archives of Canada [hereafter NAC], MG 11–[CO 42], Great Britain, Public Record Office (London), Colonial Office Papers, original correspondence, mfm. [hereafter CO 42], vol. 324, pp. 349–50, Peter Hunter to John King [under-secretary of state for colonies], 27 Oct. 1799.

20 Ibid., vol. 339, pp. 169–70, Russell to King, 22 Sep. 1799.

21 A. H. Young, ed., "Letters of William Jarvis, Secretary of Upper Canada, and Mrs. Jarvis, to the Rev. Samuel Peters, D.D.", Women's Canadian Historical Society of Toronto, *Transactions* 23 (1922–23), 57–61, Hannah Jarvis to Peters, 6 Nov. 1801.

22 NAC, MG 23–HI–3, Jarvis Family Papers, Hannah Jarvis to Peters, 28 Sep. 1805.

23 CO 42, vol. 339, p. 165, Executive Council of Upper Canada, minutes, 7 Sep. 1805 (copy).

24 Bruce Walton, "An End to All Order" (M.A. diss., Queen's University, 1977), 169.

25 CO 42, vol. 340, Russell to Edward Cooke [under-secretary of state for war and the colonies], 18 Sep. 1805. Cooke was under-secretary in 1804–06 and 1807–09. In this connection, Russell's unusual usage of *Ministers* rather than *Councillors* is certainly in line with Thorpe's peculiar notions of the Executive Council. See G. H. Patterson, "Whiggery, Nationality and the Upper Canadian Reform Tradition", *CHR* 56 (1975), 25–44, and Milo Quaife, ed., *The John Askin Papers*, II (Detroit, 1930), 485–87, Alexander Grant to Askin, 24 Oct. 1805.

26 Edith Firth, "William Willcocks", *DCB*, V (Toronto, 1983), 854–60.

27 Elwood Jones, "Joseph Willcocks", ibid., 854–59.

28 Douglas Brymner, ed., *Report on Canadian Archives 1892* (Ottawa, 1893), 39, Robert Thorpe to Cooke, 24 Jan. 1806.

29   Ibid., 57–59, Thorpe to Sir George Shee [under-secretary of state for war and the colonies], 1 Dec. 1806.

30   Ibid., 46–47, Thorpe to Cooke, 1 Apr. 1806.

31   W. Stewart Wallace, "Thomas Scott", in his *Macmillan Dictionary of Canadian Biography*, 3rd ed. (Toronto, 1963), 675.

32   Carol Whitfield and collaborators, "Alexander Grant", *DCB*, V, 363–67; also Wilson, *Enterprises*.

33   Patterson, "Whiggery".

34   But just how rich it is impossible to determine.

35   W. P. Bull, *From Medicine Man to Medical Man...* (Toronto, 1934), 26.

36   Brymner, *Report* , 361, Alexander Grant to Lord Castlereagh, 12 Feb. 1806; Frederick H. Armstrong, *Handbook of Upper Canadian Chronology and Territorial Legislation* (London, 1967), 110.

37   This is unclear. In his election address of 1820 Baldwin suggests that it was in the gift of the crown but in 1812 he was both dismissed from and reappointed to this office by the Legislative Council. See Ontario Bureau of Archives, *Ninth Report* (1912), 17–29.

38   *Upper Canada Gazette* (York, U.C.), 19 May 1808.

39   Archives of Ontario, MS 88, Baldwin (William Warren and Robert) Papers [hereafter AO, Baldwin Papers (all references are to W. W. Baldwin)], Commission of Appointment, 22 July 1809.

40   Ibid., C. B. Wyatt to Baldwin, 6 Apr. 1809: "Few events I assure you could have given me more sincere pleasure than to learn of Mr. Gore's disposition to befriend you as mentioned in your letter of 17th of October last...."; also Baldwin to Quetton St. George, 28 Dec. 1809.

41   Richard A. Preston and collaborators, "James Clark (Clarke)", *DCB*, V, 188–89.

42   Quoted in A. S. Thompson, *Spadina: A Story of Old Toronto* (Toronto, 1975), 54.

43   Preston, "Clark".

44   Ibid.

45   W. R. Riddell, *The Life of William Dummer Powell* (Lansing, 1924), 225–26, fn. 9.

46   Ibid., 135–41.

47   AO, MS 75, Russell Family Papers, Peter Russell to Thorpe, 9 Feb. 1806.

48   Brymner, *Report* , 40–41, Thorpe to Lord Castlereagh, 4 Mar. 1806.

49   AO, Baldwin Papers, Wyatt to Baldwin, 2 Nov. 1812.

50   Ibid., Baldwin to William Firth, 22 Apr. 1812.

51   Thompson, *Spadina* , 66–68.

52   R. M. and J. Baldwin, *The Baldwins and the Great Experiment* (Toronto, 1969), 88.

53   AO, Baldwin Papers, Baldwin to Firth, 12 June 1812.

54   MTCL, Quetton St. George Papers, G. M. Detlor to St. George, 27 Feb. 1817.

55   All quotations in this para. are from Baldwin's memorandum.

56   Patterson, "Whiggery".

57   Lucas, *Durham's Report* , II, 278.

58   Aileen Dunham, *Political Unrest in Upper Canada, 1815–1836* (London, 1927; Toronto, 1969), ch. 10.

59   AO, Russell Papers, Francis Gore to Russell, 1 July 1807.

60   See Patterson, "Whiggery".

61   Firth, *York*, xxxxvii.

62   MTCL, W. W. Baldwin Papers, Election Address, undated.

63   Firth, *York*, 117, Sir Peregrine Maitland to Sir George Murray, 11 Sep. 1828.

On the Eve of the Rebellion: Nationality, Religion and Class in the Toronto Election of 1836

PAUL ROMNEY

The general election of June 1836 was a crisis in the history of Upper Canada. The new lieutenant governor, Sir Francis Bond Head, acting on instructions from the Colonial Office to conciliate the colony's Reformers, had appointed two of the most respectable, along with a politically neutral administrator, to his Executive Council. Three weeks later, not only these but their three senior colleagues had resigned in protest against Head's refusal to consult them in matters pertaining to the governance of the colony.

Underlying this quarrel was a controversy over the very nature of the polity. Under the existing authoritarian institutions, the provincial executive was unaccountable to the inhabitants. The Reformers, generally speaking, desired not only that the lieutenant governor should be guided by his executive councillors in his political acts but that the councillors themselves should hold office at the pleasure of the people as represented in the lower house of the provincial legislature, the House of Assembly. Two of the three newly appointed councillors, John Rolph and Robert Baldwin, had been leading advocates of this doctrine when it was first incorporated in the Reformers' political platform in 1828.

The provincial legislature was in its second session; a Reform-dominated House of Assembly had been elected in 1834. The speaker of the house, Marshall Bidwell, had formed with Rolph, Baldwin and Baldwin's father, William Warren Baldwin, the quadrumvirate responsible for placing "responsible government" on the Reformers' agenda in 1828. Under Bidwell's influence the Assembly supported the resigning councillors by withholding funds requested by the executive. Head retaliated by refusing to sign several bills authorizing expenditure on local improvements. In an unprecedented departure for the sovereign's representative in Upper Canada, he descended into the arena of electoral politics by personally initiating a campaign to convince the public that the issue lay not between authoritarian and liberal rule but between loyalty to the Empire and Yankee republican sedition. For several weeks, loyal addresses flooded into the government house from all

On the Elections of 1836.

————ooo————

TO THE UPPER-CANADIANS, LOVERS OF THE
BRITISH CONSTITUTION, AND SUPPORTERS
OF SIR FRANCIS HEAD.

Awake ye! awake ye! the call hath gone forth;
It hath echo'd along through the woods of the North.
Awake ye! free sons of the wide forest land!
Awake from your slumber! the struggle 's at hand!

Arouse ye! arouse ye! the foemen are nigh;
They dream they can triumph, their boastings are high;
Their watchword is treason, their faith but a name,
Their breathings but ruin, destruction their aim!

Awake ye! awake ye! come forth, one and all;
Could the sons of your sires e'er be deaf to that call?
Sworn friends to your country, remember your vow!
'Tis the hour that she needs you,—be true to her now!

Come forth from your homesteads, wherever they be,
By the dark-rolling stream—by the lonely prairie,
From the woods by the sweep of the Huron's broad tide,
To the dark pines that wave by the Ottawa's side!

Awake! be ye born mid the hills of the Gael,
Or the fair quiet homes in the rich English vale,
Or the bright flashing streams 'neath the soft changeful skies
Of the green "isle of beauty," we call ye, Arise!

Unite ye! unite in the patriot band,
As your sires did of yore for their loved father-land,
When the banner of England stream'd forth on the breeze,
From the cliffs of Kinsale to the wild Orcades!

Awake ye! awake! see that flag is on high,
The bright star of our hope—see it gleam in yon sky!
'Tis the same that for ages hath flown o'er the war,
O'er Cressy's dark plain, or thy waves, Trafalgar!

Long the Lion hath slept,—with his slumbers they've play'd;
Now he springs from his rest, and they shrink back dismay'd;
And the cheeks of the cravens grow livid and pale,
When the war-shout of Britain rings out on the gale!

In their treason they dream'd, in their phrenzy they spoke
Of the nations they'd call to bend ye to their yoke;
But their power or their threats ye may fling to the air,
For your Chieftain, for ye, bid them " come if they dare!"

Oh! rally around him! the dauntless, the true!
Whom dishonour ne'er tainted, whom falsehood ne'er knew;
Who hath waked up your slumbering spirits to life,
And the heart of each patriot nerved for the strife!

Awake ye! awake ye! arise to the call!
'Tis the crisis of fate, ye must struggle for all;
'Tis your country that calls, 'tis the hour of her doom!
Ye will shout o'er her triumph, or weep o'er her tomb.

Awake ye! awake ye! arise in your might!
For your homes, for your freedom, for honour, for right!
By your sons yet unborn! by your sires in their graves!
We conjure ye arise! and be freemen or slaves!

June 1836.

"*On the Elections of 1836.*" *Broadsheet, from a text in* **The Patriot**
(*Toronto*), *21 June 1836*

over the province. Then Head took another unprecedented step by exercising his constitutional prerogative to dissolve the legislature before it had reached its term of four years. In the ensuing election the Reformers were routed.[1]

The stunned losers blamed the debacle on the unconstitutional practices of their opponents. Undoubtedly, abuses of executive power and the violence and intimidation practised by the Orange Order each played a large part in the government victory. However, a major, and perhaps the decisive contribution was that of the large influx of British immigrants who had settled in the colony within the last decade, many of whom voted on this occasion for the first time.[2]

But whether it took the form of Orange violence or pro-government voting, the entire immigrant contribution to the election must have been perceived by many of the older residents as an act of violence against their community. The immigration that inundated Upper Canada from the late 1820s on was a manifestation of what Harold Innis termed "cyclonic" shifts in factors of production from areas of low to areas of high profitability. But this particular cyclone was one which, if not man-made, had been deliberately channelled with the intention of altering the political complexion of Upper Canada. During its first three decades, the colony had been settled mainly by land-hungry immigrants from over-settled New England. After the Anglo-American war of 1812–14, the colonial administration feared that the renewed influx of Americans would pose a threat to the province's connection with England and persuaded the imperial government to ban it. The other side of this strategy was the encouragement of immigration from Great Britain. From this point of view, the election of 1836 was the pay-off of a deliberate effort to change the political culture of Upper Canada by altering the province's demographic structure.[3]

In those days there was no secret ballot. Everyone who wished to vote had to struggle to the hustings through the surrounding throng, exhibit his qualification to the returning officer's satisfaction and announce his preference publicly, whereupon it was recorded in the poll book. The poll book of the Toronto election of 1836 was published soon afterwards in a newspaper. By linking it to other records (city directories, the municipal assessment roll and the provincial manuscript census of 1842) it is possible to measure the voting according to an assortment of variables.[4] By analyzing it according to the voters' ethnic identity and date of arrival in Upper Canada, we can measure the effects of this man-directed demographic cyclone in a particular constituency.

Toronto, however, was no typical Upper Canadian riding. Most were predominantly rural, but Toronto was the largest of the colony's seven small urban constituencies. It was, indeed, unique even among these. The others had all grown up mainly as commercial entrepôts. Toronto had been founded in the wilderness in 1793, as the town of York, to serve as the provincial seat of government, and until the 1820s government was almost its only trade. It was a good trade for those who enjoyed the monopoly of it—enough in itself to support a modest local commerce—and in the 1820s the town's mercantile component began to expand with the intensification of settlement in its back country. Stimulated by the surge of immigration in the late 1820s, the capital quickly outstripped Kingston to become the largest urban centre by far in Upper Canada. In 1836, its population swollen to ten thousand, Toronto boasted in addition to the paraphernalia of a seat of government many of the social and economic attributes of a mid-nineteenth-century commercial city: its own bank and insurance company, merchants specializing in wholesale, luxury manufacturers, hotels, trade unions, a poorhouse. Its leading citizens already dreamed of that ultimate instrument and symbol of metropolitan power, a railway link to its commercial hinterland.[5]

Toronto's economy, then, was a comparatively complex one, quite different in its contours from the typical, mainly agrarian Upper Canadian constituency. In analyzing the voting in such a city—one sustained partly by its governmental and partly by a variety of commercial functions—we must look out for influences cutting across the broad pattern of ethnic antipathy which the government assiduously cultivated in the province at large. To this end we rely chiefly on the voters' occupations, and on their wealth as deduced from the municipal tax roll.

What is envisaged is not an exhaustive analysis of the 1836 election.[6] The purpose of this exercise is to consider its leading features in the light of the city's early history, with the object of sketching a political contour map of Toronto society which reflects the influence both of Toronto's position on the periphery of the British Empire and of the earliest stages of the city's growth into an economic and political metropolis. The data we shall be using are not complete, especially those relating to religion and nationality; nor do these particular data reflect a random sample, derived as they are from the 1842 census and from non-numeric sources which tend to be weighted in favour of the rich and successful. This is not a serious difficulty, however; we are not doing science here, and our data are ample to sustain imaginative discussion of the dynamics of Toronto politics in 1836.

Toronto's electoral history was as distinctive as its socio-economic morphology. Taken together, the other Canadian urban ridings (Kingston, Niagara, Brockville, Hamilton, Cornwall and London) elected a Reformer only once out of a total of 15 polls. Toronto did so 3 times in 8 elections, though the successful Reformers represented the riding in only 3 of the 21 parliamentary sessions between the capital's enfranchisement in 1820 and the union of the Canadas in 1841. Its first MPP, victorious in three successive elections from 1820 to 1828, was the provincial attorney general, John Beverley Robinson. When Robinson was appointed chief justice of Upper Canada in 1829, the ensuing by-election was won for Reform by Robert Baldwin. A trivial procedural error voided the return, but a second by-election in January 1830 confirmed it. In the general election held later that year, however, the riding contributed to the conservative trend in the province as a whole by returning the district sheriff, William Botsford Jarvis, in preference to Baldwin. Four years later, Toronto again contributed to the provincial trend. In a six-day cliff-hanger, Jarvis was beaten by the Reformer James Edward Small, but only by 260 votes to 252. The voting was punctuated by scenes of violence which reflected the village capital's growth into a raw, turbulent colonial city.[7]

In 1836 the Reformers re-adopted Small as their candidate. He belonged, like Baldwin, to one of the city's leading families, for his father had been clerk of the Executive Council for nearly 40 years and had also enjoyed for a quarter-century the secondary but lucrative office of clerk of the Crown and Pleas. Small's younger brother had inherited the lesser office, but the candidate himself, passed over for more distinguished posts, held only a lowly and unfulfilling place as a commissioner of the Court of Requests, the local tribunal for the trial of petty debt cases. Prior to 1834 he had twice unsuccessfully opposed the radical tribune, William Lyon Mackenzie, in the surrounding county of York and had challenged even the patrician Baldwin from a conservative vantage in the Town of York by-election of 1829. With such credentials he was not to every Reformer's taste, but as an Anglican, a lawyer and a patrician himself he was evidently the type of Reformer the capital was willing to elect. In one respect at any rate he was especially suitable, given the nature of the campaign launched by Lieutenant Governor Head: a less likely spokesman for republican sedition could scarcely be imagined.[8]

The nomination of Small's opponent marked a minor departure for Toronto's Tories. William Henry Draper had not been born in Upper Canada, belonged to none of the leading official families and had not even lived long in the city. An Anglican of genteel English parentage, he had run away to sea at the age of 15 and settled in the colony in 1820. He spent most of the next decade in the Port Hope–Cobourg area, becoming a lawyer and serving in the office of the solicitor general's brother before moving to the capital to work for Attorney General Robinson. After Robinson's elevation to the bench Draper became a partner of the new solicitor general, Christopher Hagerman. Draper's career suggests that he was being groomed for stardom by the official élite; however, an amiable eloquence masked his ambition and helped earn him the nickname "Sweet William." The ideal candidate in a city swollen by British immigrants, the 35-year-old advocate was making his political debut.[9]

Both candidates had well-organized campaign committees, and the capital's lively press provided each with one or more propaganda vehicles. The Tories presented their cause as that of loyalty, of "good" and "constitutional" government, and of a civil tranquillity that would aid in the pursuit of prosperity. The Reformers disputed this ground with them and staked out as their own turf "responsible" government—their term for the subordination of the executive to the House of Assembly—and resistance to the hegemonic pretensions of the Church of England. The latter, a major plank in the Reform platform for a decade, had acquired renewed importance a few months previously when the retiring lieutenant governor, Sir John Colborne, had created 44 Anglican rectories out of the clergy reserves—lands set aside by the colony's founding charter, the Canada Act of 1791, for the support of "a Protestant Clergy." Under the act such rectories could be created only with the advice and consent of the executive council. Colborne's action, therefore, while it galled the sensibilities of Upper Canada's militant nonconformists, also provided a perfect illustration of the need to make the executive council responsible to the House of Assembly.

Small's electoral address was long, oddly shrill and ill-adapted to wooing the floating voter:

> Whether supported or deserted by you in this memorable struggle for the maintenance of our civil and religious liberties, my all shall still be consecrated to your service. Should it possibly be my fate to be discarded by you in such a cause, I shall at all events reserve to myself as an inheritance for my children, an imperishable record, that I was sacrificed in the fearless and patriotic discharge of a sacred constitutional duty.[10]

Most of the voters rejected Small's invitation to prove themselves worthy of him. Halfway through the six days allotted for polling, Draper was ahead by 287 votes to 202 and the Reformer resigned from the contest; martyrdom was his. The Reformers' newspaper condemned his withdrawal as premature. It asserted that he had had 147 pledged votes in reserve, "which would (it was believed) have secured his Election; but because they did not press forward *immediately*, amid scenes of violence and unparalleled ruffianism, a few of his friends advised him to retire." The pro-government *Patriot* declared that Draper had had 125 pledges left, a claim it would shortly back up by printing their names.[11] It is hard to credit the *Correspondent*'s claim that violence at the hustings played a critical part in the result. Violence there no doubt was, but it seems to have been less intense than when Small won in 1834. The Reform organ alleged that two Tory aldermen had secretly sworn in a posse of partisan special constables, who helped Tory voters to reach the hustings while impeding Reform supporters.[12] Since the city council was controlled by a Reform majority, and Small himself was an alderman, such tactics could have afforded the Tories a temporary advantage at most.

One expression of Toronto's idiosyncrasy was its heavily British electorate. Only 31 of the 276 voters whose nationality is known had been born in North America (Table 1.A). A large majority of the British-born voted for Draper, while those of North American birth favoured Small. Voters who had arrived within the last decade were proportionately stronger in Draper's support than earlier immigrants (Table 2.A). Of the British-born voters who can be linked to the 1842 census, more than half had arrived since 1827.

Table 1: Voting by Land of Birth and Religion

	T	R	Total		T	R	Total
A: Land of Birth[a]				**B: Religion**[b]			
Ireland	66	36	102	Ch. of England	115	15	130
England	70	26	96	Ch. of Scotland	13	12	25
Scotland	23	24	47	Ch. of Rome	9	10	19
Canada	10	13	23	Wes. Meth: Canadian	2	16	18
U.S.A.	3	5	8	British	14	1	15
				Other Nonconformist[c]	12	34	46
Total	172	104	276	Total	165	88	253

Sources: Statistics reported in this and subsequent tables are compiled from one or
more of the following: *Patriot and Farmer's Monitor* (Toronto), 1 July 1836; *York
Commercial Directory, Street Guide and Register...1833–4* (York U.C., [1833]);
City of Toronto Directory...for 1837 (Toronto, [1836]); City of Toronto Archives,
RG 5–F–1, Finance Department, Assessment Rolls; National Archives of Canada, RG 31, Statistics Canada, Census Records, Toronto City 1842, mfm.
C1344. For a discussion of my treatment of the data obtained from these
sources, see my "Voters Under the Microscope: A Quantitative Meditation on
the Toronto Parliamentary Poll Book of 1836", paper presented to the Canadian Historical Association, Vancouver, June 1983, copy on deposit at City of
Toronto Archives.

T   voted for Tory candidate
R   voted for Reform candidate
[a]   known voters comprise 60 percent of Tories, 52 percent of Reformers
[b]   known voters comprise 58 percent of Tories, 49 percent of Reformers
[c]   comprising:

	T	R	Total
Other Methodist	0	8	8
Secessionist Presby.	7	14	21
Congregationalist	1	8	9
Baptist	4	7	11
Other (Unspecified)	0	7	7

Table 2: Voting by Period of Arrival in Upper Canada, Land of Birth and Religion

	Pre–1815		1815–26		Post–1826		Total		
	T	R	T	R	T	R	T	R	All
A: Land of Birth[a]									
England	7	2	13	12	31	8	51	22	73
Ireland	4	2	18	16	31	11	53	29	82
Scotland	3	2	9	5	4	11	16	18	34
U.S.A.	1	2	2	0	0	0	3	2	5
Canada	7	12	0	0	0	0	7	12	19
Total	22	20	42	33	66	30	130	83	213
B: Religion[b]									
Ch. of England	19	6	30	5	46	3	95	14	109
Ch. of Scotland	3	1	3	2	5	7	11	10	21
Ch. of Rome	0	0	3	2	3	6	6	8	14
Wesleyan Methodist:									
Canadian	0	5	0	8	2	3	2	16	18
British	0	0	2	0	10	1	12	1	13
Other Nonconformist	0	7	4	16	7	11	11	34	45
Total	22	19	42	33	73	31	137	83	220

Note: voters linked to the 1842 census only

T   voted for Tory candidate

R   voted for Reform candidate

[a]   known voters comprise 45 percent of Tories, 41 percent of Reformers

[b]   known voters comprise 48 percent of Tories, 41 percent of Reformers

These favoured Draper by 66 to 30—a much higher ratio than the earlier arrivals, who voted for him by 54 to 39.

These data provide *prima facie* evidence for the effectiveness of Lieutenant Governor Head's ethnically slanted appeal, but if we define our ethnic groups more narrowly even more striking numbers are obtained. Of the British-born voters (Table 1.A), the Scots and the 18 Roman Catholics (all Irishmen) split almost evenly. The Protestant residue, all of them Irish or English, voted for Draper by 128 to 52. Applying this refinement to our census-linked sample (Table 2.A), we find a very lopsided preference for Draper among English and Protestant Irish voters who had arrived since 1827. The few Scots voted for Small by 11 to 4 and the Roman Catholic Irish (Table 2.B) by 6 to 3. The English and Protestant Irish majority, by contrast, favoured Draper by 59 to 13.

These figures hint at a pronounced ethnic pattern in the voting, but an equally strong pattern emerges from the denominational breakdown. Of the 253 voters whose religious affiliation is known, more than half belonged to the Church of England (Table 1.B). These voted for Draper by 115 to 15. Evidently Toronto was not the place to campaign against the hegemonic pretensions of the Church of England! The rest of our sample falls into two groups: those who split evenly and those who voted strongly for Small. The former group comprises the adherents of the Churches of Scotland and Rome. The latter consists of a cluster of small nonconformist Protestant sects: non-Wesleyan Methodists, secessionist Presbyterians, Baptists, Congregationalists, and a few adherents of unspecified, probably evangelical Protestant sects.

One denomination deserves special notice. The Wesleyan Methodists ostensibly emulated the Churches of Scotland and Rome in splitting evenly. This denomination was riven by faction, and in 1840 it separated into two churches, the "Canadian" and "British" Wesleyan Methodists. The former were voluntarists, hostile to any connection between church and state.[13] The rupture is reflected in our data, which are taken from the census of 1842. Those of our sample who in 1842 were to be British Wesleyans voted for Draper by 14 to 1, and those who were to be Canadian Wesleyans (most of them British-born) voted for Small by 16 to 2.

All the pro-Reform denominations were voluntarist; in fact, the correspondence between Reform voting and voluntarism is probably even more pronounced than the numbers suggest. The seven secessionist Presbyterians who voted Tory were all Irish, while all those who voted Reform were of Scottish or North American birth. The Irishmen may have been lured to the Reverend James Harris's church, without being voluntarists, by the fact that Harris was Irish and followed the Irish form of Presbyterian service. Likewise, some of the Scottish-born adherents of the Church of Scotland may have been voluntarists who preferred the Scottish form of Presbyterian worship.[14] It may well be that 90 percent or more of the voluntarist voters supported Small.

Upper Canadian politics in the 1830s, and attitudes towards the Rebellion of 1837, have generally been interpreted in terms of national identity and religious affiliation. Graeme Patterson stressed the antipathy between British-born and North American-born inhabitants in his survey of electoral politics in Middlesex County, the Johnstown District and the Bay of Quinte region. Colin Read and Ronald Stagg discovered a North American-born preponderance among the western and Toronto-area rebels respectively. Stagg found too that many of the rebels belonged to voluntarist sects whose teaching did not stress submission to the secular authority, while the neutrals tended to be voluntarists who were instructed to render unto Caesar that which was Caesar's.[15] Our figures may seem to confirm these findings so completely as to make further investigation redundant, but to stop here would be to presume that people's place in the provincial economy had no influence on their political views. Our data on this aspect of the Toronto voters' social identity allow us to test this proposition as well.

The franchise in urban constituencies was based on a low property qualification: ownership of realty worth £5 a year or rental of property worth £10 a year.[16] This was low enough to enfranchise the great majority of householders, but many adult males of the lower classes, especially if unmarried, were not householders but boarders, either in the parental household or with an unrelated family (perhaps their employer's), or even in an inn.[17] As a result, the electorate was an occupational cross-section of Toronto male society, but a biased one. The largest single occupational category among the voters of 1836 was *labourer*, but the 48 labourers who voted were probably less than 10 percent of all Toronto labourers. Only 14 out of at least 127 licensed carters voted. A larger number would no doubt have done so had the election continued, and we must allow for a number of qualified abstainers; still, on the most generous estimate no more than a quarter of the labourers and carters were qualified to vote. We may assume, by contrast, that few if any of the city's lawyers, physicians, merchants and tavernkeepers were not enfranchised. Such disparities must be borne in mind in interpreting the voting, but at any rate we have evidence of political affinities across the whole range of the city's adult male population.

In order to analyze the voting by occupation, the voters were sorted into functional categories according to the way they made their living. This is preferable to the status categories devised by Michael Katz in his study of the social structure of mid-nineteenth-century Hamilton, because the latter would introduce a deleterious subjective element into the analysis.[18] In any case, some occupations cannot be fitted into a single status category. *Tavernkeeper*, for instance, included both the landlord of the North American Hotel, the highest-assessed building in the city at £300 a year, and at the other extreme the likes of James Watson, tinsmith and landlord of the Rising Sun, assessed at £15, and John O'Keefe, labourer and landlord of the Harp and Crown, assessed at £20. Artisan voters present a similar problem, since in most cases we cannot be sure whether they were masters or journeymen.

The functional categories were defined to reflect Toronto's economy. In order, from Table 3: *Producers* includes everyone involved in manufacture.

Semi- and Unskilled Labour is composed mainly of labourers but includes the occupations (often cognate with "labourer") of carter, sailor, cowkeeper and limeburner. *Store- and Tavernkeepers* includes purveyors of drink, food and lodging. *Professional/Administrative* comprises members of the professions and a range of "white-collar" government officials, both senior and junior. *Mercantile/Financial* consists mainly of merchants but also includes the cashiers (chief executive officers) of two banks, a merchant's clerk and one of the commissioners of the Canada Company, a gigantic incorporated land speculation by British capitalists.

Four minor groupings are included for the sake of completeness, although they play no part in the analysis. *Private Means* encompasses a wide range of social circumstances, from the very rich to the distinctly impecunious, from the classically educated to the barely lettered. Voters from every part of this range bore the great catch-all designation "gentleman." *Agriculture* is mainly made up of market gardeners and yeomen, some of the latter residing outside Toronto. (Every possessor of sufficient property in a riding, including non-residents, could vote in it.) *Non-Administrative Governmental* covers a handful of public employees in sub-administrative jobs, people who might otherwise have been carters or labourers, storekeepers or tavernkeepers. A slightly larger handful of *Unclassifiable* occupations includes four ship captains, a wharfinger, a cattle jobber, three haircutters and one of Chief Justice Robinson's servants.

This occupational breakdown covers all but four of the voters; in fact, the number of occupations exceeds the number of voters. This is because some voters boasted different occupations in different data-sources. Most often these were described as "labourer" in one source, the alternative designation being sometimes artisanal (usually "carpenter," suggesting an ambiguity of occupational status among building workers), and sometimes "storekeeper" or "tavernkeeper," suggesting a livelihood derived from an assortment of seasonal, part-time or co-operative family enterprises.

The strong pro-government bias in the *Professional/Administrative* and *Mercantile/Financial* categories is not surprising (Table 3). Many of the first group were either senior officials themselves or members of the élite professions—law and medicine. Most of the rest were either junior officials or members of the lesser professions or quasi-professions, who were either government-employed (such as teachers) or dependent on the patronage of government or the wealthy (such as architects and land agents). Public voting was likely to make government employees and dependents opt for Draper even if their secret preference was different, but there is no reason to suppose that it was, especially in the case of government employees. One of the main complaints against the existing constitution was that it enabled a clique, the so-called Family Compact, to control appointments to public office. Under such circumstances, political orthodoxy tended to be a prerequisite of government employment.

The élite status of the *Professional/Administrative* grouping is confirmed by its inclusion of 35 of the 51 voters accorded the courtesy title "Esquire" by

Table 3: Voting by Occupational Group

	Tory	Reform	Total
Producers (in manufacturing)	94	114	208
All Other (Non-Producers)	198	104	302
Semi- and Unskilled Labour	30	34	64
Store- and Tavernkeepers	37	27	64
Professional/Administrative	47	7	54
Mercantile/Financial	39	13	52
Private Means	18	7	25
Agriculture	10	10	20
Non-Admin. Governmental	5	3	8
Unclassifiable	12	3	15
Total	292	218	510

one or more of our data-sources. By this measure the *Mercantile/Financial* grouping is ambiguous in status. It included only five Esquires, and two of these were among the four non-merchants. Still, while commerce had suffered its social ups and downs during Toronto's brief existence, by 1836 its leading practitioners at least can be counted as a subset of the city's élite. For this there were two main reasons.

Unlike the two main early centres of Upper Canada, Niagara and Kingston, York's commercial function had until recently been far outweighed by its administrative one. While two or three merchants, notably William Allan and Alexander Wood, had attained élite status in the early years, local merchants could not generally amass incomes to put them on a footing with the leading administrators. This began to change in the mid 1820s, as the capital became the centre of a flourishing agricultural hinterland. By the mid 1830s Toronto was the place to be, a fact reflected in the influx of young, well-capitalized entrepreneurs such as James Newbigging, Isaac Buchanan and Thomas Dennie Harris.[19]

The second reason was the anxiety of the administrative élite to establish the capital's economic pre-eminence in Upper Canada. When Kingston capitalists had tried to form the colony's first chartered bank in 1819, the official élite had used their predominance within the government to "kidnap" the charter by substituting the names of leading residents of York for the original Kingstonians in the act of incorporation; but subsequently they had to look beyond their own resources to keep their prize inflated with capital. In the early 1830s it was desirable to add an insurance company to the city's financial institutions, and by 1836 a railway too was thought necessary to its economic growth. These imperatives disposed the official élite to look kindly on any substantial capitalist, if his politics were at least half-decent.[20]

Two events symbolized the new partnership. In 1833 the town's growth required an enlargement of the magistracy, which administered both local government and petty criminal justice in the capital until its incorporation in 1834. Several leading merchants were appointed, including William Proudfoot (who was to succeed William Allan in 1835 as president of the Bank of Upper Canada) and Alexander Murray (the partner of James Newbigging, who was himself to become a magistrate in 1837).[21] The second event was to occur in 1837, when the Upper Canada Club was formed to accommodate a civic élite grown too large to gather round the largest dinner table. Here patricians and merchants would meet in equal numbers and on equal terms. One of its most ardent promoters was Newbigging, a director of Toronto's own British America Fire and Life Assurance Company and leading promoter of the Toronto and Lake Huron Railroad.[22]

Yet although by 1836 Toronto's leading merchants could claim membership in the civic élite, their lesser competitors could not. Reporting the magistral appointments of 1833, the Tory *Courier of Upper Canada* regretted the omission of the energetic and public-spirited Thomas Carfrae Jr. Carfrae himself, it is recorded, felt his exclusion as a slight. He had in fact been on the short-list, but he was a significantly different sort of merchant from those who got the nod. They were centrally located wholesalers, some of whom specialized in a particular commodity such as dry goods, hardware, or wines and spirits. Carfrae ran a relatively small general store on the fringe of the commercial district. Two years later he quit commerce to become collector of customs at Toronto—a lucrative post but probably not one that would have attracted Toronto's merchant princes in 1836, although William Allan had held it for many years into the 1820s. Still, in this capacity Carfrae in due course would become a member of the Upper Canada Club.[23]

While criticizing Carfrae's omission from the magistracy, the *Courier* also regretted the entire exclusion of the artisan class:

> It would have been at once just and judicious…to have placed the names of two or three respectable Mechanics upon the Commission. There has been a sort of proscription exercised towards this class of the Inhabitants of Canada which we have ever looked upon to be as senseless as it is unjust.

Such snobbishness was rampant in the sea of new faces called Toronto. Any man of wealth might pretend to consequence by parading in a carriage, and the impulse of yesterday's new wealth to mark itself off from today's must have been strong. When the *Patriot* scoffed at a reference to a Reform city councilman, who happened to be a builder, as Joseph Turton *Esquire*, its Reform rival asked:

> What higher claims to distinctions have the Coffin-makers, and musk-rat hunters, and servants, and sons of Tailors, and Stone masons, &c., who now fill high offices under the Crown, than Mr. TURTON?...The aristocracy in Great Britain and Ireland have some *artificial* claim to superiority over their fellow-men. Their long lineage gives them an acknowledged (we do not say a just) title to pre-eminence. But this country cannot boast of antient [sic] blood....[24]

A year later William Lyon Mackenzie chided an inconsistent *Courier* for deriding a recently defeated Reform MPP (who would be hanged for his part in the Rebellion of 1837) as "Blacksmith Lount":

> It is customary for an upstart aristocracy to endeavour to cast contumely on their more unassuming neighbours, by such names as "Lount the Blacksmith," "Ketchum the Tanner," "Mackenzie the Printer," "Hogg the Miller," &c. adding some stale witticism in order to create a laugh at honest labour....Is it a degrading thing for a man to have learnt a good trade? [25]

Toronto's artisans were aware of economic as well as social discrimination. In 1823 the saddlers and harnessmakers had protested ("with all respect and humility") against the import of allegedly inferior American goods. In 1827 "A British Mechanic" complained in the press about officials who sent "large sums of money out of the Province for the purchase of various articles of mechanism, such as carriages, saddlery, cabinet-ware, hats, boots, &c., while our own mechanics who pay the taxes for the support of these same officials, are left to struggle with difficulty and distress." The cabinetmakers petitioned in vain for higher duties on American furniture in 1830 and 1831. In 1836 the City of Toronto Mechanics' Association was formed to lobby for the "Protection of Mechanical Labour."[26]

By the mid 1830s a few artisans, especially in basic industrial trades such as building and tanning, had got very rich; but their wealth was usually the result of decades of labour, of profits salted away in realty which began to fetch a high price as immigration boomed. Even they might resent the quick fortunes earned by lawyers and officials, or the instant social prominence won by young merchants like Newbigging, Buchanan and Harris who flocked to the capital to exploit the bonanza. The only rich masters in their thirties were of the second generation: men such as William Ketchum, tanner, and John Harper, builder, both of whom belonged in 1836 (like Small, their candidate) to the Reform majority on the city council. Ketchum—handsome, well-educated, a railway fan—would be welcomed into the Upper Canada Club in 1837. A year later, tainted by rebellion, he would be a refugee in the United States.[27]

It is tempting to interpret the preponderance for Small among the *Producers* grouping as evidence of an artisan class consciousness; but first we must ask whether the split reflects class consciousness *within* the grouping. After all, a 55 percent preference for Reform is not exactly a bloc vote, and this is the one grouping which comprises a complete cross-section of the voters in terms of wealth, from very rich masters to propertyless journeymen. It has in fact been argued that the problem that enforces this fusion—the difficulty of distinguishing masters from journeymen—is itself evidence of social homogeneity within trades. J. R. Vincent cited the failure of the British census authorities in the nineteenth century to persuade artisans to reveal their status as evidence of "a feeling that people engaged in making the same kind of thing were the same kind of people....If in the nineteenth century the pattern of self-description implies that the social distance a shoemaker might move above or below the normal shoemaker was not important to them, then it probably was not objectively important either."[28] R. S. Neale challenged this proposition by citing the Bath election of 1847, in which the poorer shoemakers showed a pronounced bias towards the Radical candidate and the wealthier towards his Conservative opponent.[29]

The odds against Toronto artisans sharing an all-embracing "artisan" class consciousness are increased by the evidence of labour militancy in the booming city. Toronto's master-craftsmen may have felt themselves to be second-class citizens, but there was real friction in some trades between them and their journeymen. Both the Toronto Typographical Society (founded in 1832) and the city's tailors were to strike later in 1836. Three years previously there had been strife in the building industry, a booming business which offered scope for self-assertive journeymen. Both the carpenters' and joiners' society and that of the bricklayers, plasterers and masons had complained of failure to pay or delay in paying their members for work, arising from the system whereby journeymen received only part of their pay by the week and the rest in a lump when the master was paid for the contract.[30]

Yet in fact, the *Producers* grouping as a whole shows no split comparable to the Bath shoemakers of 1847, nor does any individual trade (Table 4). Every level of wealth within the grouping shows an unusual degree of support for Reform. True, there is a difference between the lowest, which probably comprised all the journeyman voters and the smallest masters, and those which included the middling and wealthy masters, but it is not of a sort which can be construed into a political expression of mutual economic antipathy between them. The grouping is more fruitfully dissected along lines suggested by J. R. Vincent in his survey of British poll books—that is, according to whether its members were involved in the manufacture of luxuries or common necessities. Vincent numbered coachbuilders, jewellers, saddlers, butchers, bookbinders and artists among occupations that "appear in the pollbooks as epiphenomena of a mainly Tory landed ruling class, as a sort of upper servants."[31] Adding to the list watchmakers, confectioners, cabinet-makers and upholsterers, as well as the single gunsmith, silver-

Table 4: Voting by Wealth and Occupational Group: Producers Compared to Non-Producers

Residential Assessment (£)	Producers Building Trades		Producers Shoe Makers		All Producers		Non-Producers		All Voters Producers and Non-Producers		
	T	R	T	R	T	R	T	R	T	R	Total
0–24	10	25	5	12	44	63	45	29	89	92	181
25–69	11	10	4	5	32	28	69	34	101	62	163
70 and Higher	1	2	0	0	4	7	52	7	56	14	70
Total Known	22	37	9	17	80	98	166	70	246	168	414
No Data	4	5	2	1	14	16	32	34	46	50	96
Total	26	42	11	18	94	114	198	104	292	218	510

T voted for Tory candidate
R voted for Reform candidate

smith, coachspring-maker and "looking-glass manufacturer, gilder and carver" in the Toronto poll book, we find a striking deviation between the voting of the two subgroups—a deviation probably expressive of the luxury producers' dependence on the patronage of the élite (Table 5).

But if dependence is to be linked to pro-government voting in this case, and also in that of the lesser members of the *Professional/Administrative* grouping, how can we be sure that the poorer journeyman voters were not intimidated by their employers? The answer probably lies in the relatively equal split at the higher levels of the *Producers* grouping. There were plenty of potential employers on either side and presumably little scope for the supporters of either candidate to apply monopoly pressure to their servants. No Toronto trade in 1836 resembled in structure the shoemaking trade in Bath, where even in 1831 most of the city's 529 journeymen worked for 10 or 12 masters who owned shops employing from 30 to 60 workers.

The one known exception to this generalization points to political solidarity rather than strife between masters and journeymen. In 1833 Sheldon and Dutcher's iron foundry was employing 80 men. Four years later, in October 1837, William Lyon Mackenzie proposed making a coup d'état with "Dutcher's foundry-men and Armstrong's axe-makers, all of whom could

Table 5: Voting by Wealth:
Luxury and Non-Luxury Producers

Residential Assessment (£)	Luxury		Non-Luxury	
	Tory	Reform	Tory	Reform
0–24	14	4	30	59
25–69	10	4	22	24
70 and Higher	2	1	2	6
Total Known	26	9	54	89
No Data	5	1	9	15
Total	31	10	63	104

be depended on."[32] Dutcher and Armstrong were both radicals. The latter had represented in 1835 the same artisan-dominated ward which in 1836 was served by John Harper and William Ketchum. Even if Dutcher and Armstrong could have forced their workers to vote for Reform, it is absurd to suppose that they could have coerced them into insurrection. The latter's "dependability" as tools of rebellion must have issued from a genuine sympathy with their masters' political views.

Economic coercion may still have had an effect on some voters. The publication of a Toronto poll book was usually meant to glorify the righteous and expose the wicked to chastisement. This was assuredly the *Patriot's* aim in 1836; and when Reformers published the poll book of the next (1841) contest they explained: "The necessity of this publication arises in part from the fact that the patronage of the Compact and its agents has long been employed, almost exclusively, to build up its own friends, and to crush every independent tradesman and mechanic who voted on the side of Civil and Religious Liberty." On this occasion, the Reformers intended to expose the enemies of civil and religious liberty to that "public disapprobation and abhorrence" which could "most effectively be given, by the judicious exercise of the monied patronage of an indignant people."[33]

It was certainly the Reformers who complained of economic intimidation in 1836. Even before the *Patriot* printed the poll book, it was reported that:

> ...the wives of Executive and Legislative Councillors were known to hold out threats of loss of custom, &c., to those tradesmen who did not vote for the Court Candidate; and

> several honest reformers had no sooner voted to uphold
> their principles, than they received orders to send in their
> bills, or to stay the execution of orders previously given![34]

This suggests that the level at which economic pressure most likely influenced artisan voting was that of the middling masters. The government controlled a lot of spending power in Toronto.

Susceptibility to economic coercion must likewise be borne in mind in discussing our other large non-élite occupational groupings. We know little of the employment pattern of the labourers who make up the bulk of the *Semi- and Unskilled Labour* grouping, but there is no obvious monopoly of employment which might have constrained them. The civil government and the army must each have been a major employer, but the municipal corporation, which had public works under way, was in Reform hands. The grouping shows a major split between the carters, who voted Tory by 11 to 3, and the rest, who voted Reform by 31 to 19; but there is no obvious bread-and-butter motive for the divergence, although the carters may have had some unrecorded grudge against the municipality as their licensing agency. In the case of the *Store- and Tavernkeepers* grouping, such a motive did exist in the City Council's recent resolution deploring "the present extraordinary number of licensed innkeepers and vendors of spirituous Liquors in this City." Small, a vice-president of the Upper Canada Bible and Tract Society as well as an alderman, had introduced the resolution, which also set up a select committee to study the matter. The Reformers were to act on it before they left office in January 1837 by drastically reducing the number of licences; yet in June 1836 the prospect did not send the licensed victuallers scurrying to mollify Small at the hustings. They voted against him by 30 to 14.[35]

Considering the ethnic, religious and occupational data discretely, it seems that the voters' denominational affiliation exhibits the strongest correlation with the voting, followed by nationality and occupation. In this sense, and assuming that the votes were generally speaking uncoerced, religion might be called the "most important" determinant of political preference, with nationality and occupation progressively less so. But this is a very crude conclusion. We need to reconcile the pronounced ethnic and denominational patterns with the socio-economic one in a way that recognizes that a man's religion, nationality and employment were all reciprocally interactive elements of his world-view.

In the case of the *Professional/Administrative* grouping, the striking datum is the preponderance of Anglicans, all but two of whom voted Tory (Table 6.A). This is no surprise, since the bulk of the grouping consists of members of the official élite and recipients of their patronage. Anglicanism was a badge of conformity and an important attribute of élite status. There were fewer Anglicans among the *Mercantile/Financial* grouping, but virtually all of its members commanded in larger or smaller amounts that other,

Table 6: Voting by Land of Birth and Religion: Major Occupational Groupings

	Prof-Adm		Mer-Fin		Producers Lux-ury		Non-Lux		Semi-Unsk		Store-Tavern	
	T	R	T	R	T	R	T	R	T	R	T	R
A: Religion												
Ch. of England	35	2	16	2	15	1	19	6	7	2	10	0
Ch. of Scotland	2	0	5	3	1	0	3	6	1	0	2	2
Ch. of Rome	1	1	2	1	0	0	2	1	1	6	0	2
Wes. Meth:												
Canadian	0	0	2	0	0	0	0	14	0	1	0	2
British	0	0	1	0	4	0	6	1	0	0	1	0
Other Non-conformist	1	4	2	7	0	5	6	26	2	0	0	2
Total	39	7	28	13	20	6	36	54	11	9	13	8
B: Land of Birth												
England	18	1	9	2	13	2	12	17	2	2	6	3
Ireland	9	2	7	3	4	1	22	18	9	7	6	2
Scotland	6	1	11	4	1	1	2	12	0	0	1	3
Canada and U.S.A.	7	3	3	1	1	3	1	7	0	1	1	2
Total	40	7	30	10	19	7	37	54	11	10	14	10

Note: occupational groupings from Table 3
T   voted for Tory candidate
R   voted for Reform candidate

increasingly sufficient mark of election, financial capital. It is noteworthy that almost all of the Reform minority in this grouping belonged to the lesser merchants, not the upper stratum. They were generally old residents and may have shared the same resentment of well-capitalized newcomers that we have attributed to the Reformers among the wealthy master mechanics.

It is when we get among the non-élite groupings, and above all when we confront the difference between the *Luxury* and *Non-Luxury Producers,* that the problem of the relationship between socio-economic and other influences becomes most intriguing. The Tory preponderance among the Luxury Producers is matched by the unusually high proportion of Anglicans and low proportion of "Other Nonconformists" among them (62 and 19 percent of the group respectively), while the Non-Luxury Producers exhibit the reverse phenomenon, although the imbalance is much less (Anglicans 28 percent, Other Nonconformists 36 percent). A substantial part of the Tory-voting Luxury Producers were Anglicans recently arrived from England. At first glance, therefore, it might seem that the different voting of the two subgroupings was merely epiphenomenal or "accidental," having nothing to do with their different places in Toronto's economy: we might be tempted, that is, to explain the difference by the fortuitous fact that Toronto's growth in the preceding decade had given a disproportionate boost to the luxury manufacturing sector, creating openings which were naturally filled by this heavily pro-government cohort. Such reasoning founders on the fact that our analytical distinction between Luxury and Non-Luxury Producers is drawn from English example.[36] Religious nonconformity was strong among artisans in England as well as in Toronto. If our Toronto sample is typical of the English pattern, and luxury craftsmen in England, too, formed an exception in their denominational adherence as well as their voting, the fact that many of our Toronto subgrouping happen to have arrived with the ultra-loyalist cohort becomes analytically irrelevant. It remains legitimate to assume that the distinctive political bias of each subgrouping was connected with its place in Toronto's economy.

It would be wrong to make any simple causal connection between the Luxury Producers' voting, religious affiliations and place in the economy. Not all of them voted Tory simply from economic intimidation. The coachspring-maker was only a specialized blacksmith and could have survived as a blacksmith, albeit as one among many; the three portrait painters were also housepainters; the saddlers could have done workaday trade as harnessmakers. While the distinction between the two subgroupings is real, it is best conceived of as a difference of mentality. Most Non-Luxury Producers felt no pressing impulse to religious conformity, and some at least must have nourished a strong antipathy to the social élite. The Luxury Producers may also have nursed a grudge against an élite that preferred American saddles and cabinet-ware to theirs, but they must have felt a stronger incentive to be seen at St. James' Church. This does not mean that they worshipped with the élite out of calculation any more than they voted Tory out of calculation (though some of them probably did). It means that the more a tradesman was economically dependent on the élite, and not merely subject to its political control, the more likely he was to develop a world-view that harmonized with his subservience.

Subservient the typical voluntarist palpably was not. Egerton Ryerson had endless trouble and indifferent success in his efforts from 1833 on to shepherd the Episcopal Methodists into union with the British Wesleyans.[37] Like the inhabitants of the well-settled rural parts where the recalcitrant Methodists predominated, Toronto's voluntarists were not insecure pioneers huddling for spiritual shelter in the wilderness; they were masters of skills which promised security and independence. A Presbyterian minister newly arrived from Scotland in 1832 was scandalized to find the town's newly formed Church of Scotland congregation troubled by a refractory Congregationalist element (soon to secede) and the Reverend James Harris's secessionist church dominated by overbearing elders who insisted that anyone wishing to take communion at their altar be allowed to do so, whether or not he formally professed the principles of the church. The five men named by the Reverend William Proudfoot were all large or middling masters in the non-luxury trades, and all five voted for Reform in 1836.[38] Such men seceded readily, either because they would worship God wherever it pleased them to do so, or else because the inevitable flaws made no human institution an ideal harbour. They were not disposed to truckle to human authority, and authority had nothing to offer that could buy their obedience.

Whatever the connection between Tory voting and economic dependence was in the case of the Luxury Producers, it by no means follows that the bulk of the newly arrived Irish and English Anglicans were docile footmen of the social hierarchy. Most of them were patriotic subjects of the Crown, rallying eagerly to a cause they were convinced was in danger. Otherwise they were an unruly retinue. They did not grant their allegiance unreservedly to the élite; they let it on terms, and part of the rental was respect. Theirs was the outlook that E. P. Thompson has called "picaresque": independent, even disorderly, but bounded by a sense of individual transience that precluded any strong attachment to provident conduct.[39] Most of their voluntarist artisan neighbours, by contrast, possessed a vision of futurity that encouraged thrift and forethought. Theirs was an ethos of self-help— partly Smilesian and individualistic, no doubt, but also mutualistic and class-oriented.[40] They reserved their allegiance entirely, requiring from their leaders *pro tem*. not merely a condescending respect but the deference due from equal to equal. In these early decades, before the melting-pot of shared social experience had had a chance to homogenize Toronto's workingmen, the contrast between the two mentalities was especially sharp.[41]

In making these broad distinctions of mentality, we must take care not to impose a false homogeneity on important differences of ethos. Within some of the trades we have called "Non-Luxury," there may have been a range of practice and outlook as wide as that between a short-order cook and a master of haute cuisine. In order to know that the nonconformist denominations embraced a variety of styles, we need only read the comment of James Lesslie, William Lyon Mackenzie's friend, on a Methodist four-day meeting he visited in 1832. "The noise & tumult was excessive," recorded the Baptist stationer and druggist. "To appearance the scenes there exhibited have a tendency to bring true Religion into ridicule—Zeal and earnestness are not inconsistent with order & decorum but when the latter do not accompany the former the exciting cause may be suspect."[42]

On this subject, Lesslie's outlook resembled that of his fellow-Scot John Strachan, Anglican archdeacon and spiritual leader of Upper Canadian Toryism, rather than that of the typical Reform-voting Methodist.[43] When it came to politics, however, the important thing was that Lesslie was, in 1832 as in 1841 (when he was to publish the poll book), a devotee of "civil and religious liberty." A founder of the Toronto Mechanics' Institute, recently set up to foster adult education, he had attended the Methodist meeting in company with several fellow-members of the Institute, some of them at least no doubt voluntarist Methodist artisans.[44]

Bearing this caveat in mind, we can loosely summarize the Toronto election of 1836 as a contest between two informal alliances. On the government side were the administrative and commercial élites, certain elements that can be construed as their dependants (minor officials, luxury tradesmen, etc.) and the non-élite Anglican voters as a whole (virtually all of them English or Irish). On the Reform side the adherents of a cluster of voluntarist sects, many of them non-luxury tradesmen, loom largest, but we should also notice the Roman Catholics. Table 1.B shows an even split among them, but it probably masks a strong Reform vote among Irish Catholic labourers. Katz noted in his study of Hamilton that the higher an individual was in wealth and social standing, the more likely he was to survive in the contemporary record.[45] This phenomenon accounts for the relative sparsity of our data on the religion and nationality of voters in the *Semi- and Unskilled Labour* grouping (Table 6). It is likely that the six Roman Catholic Reformers in this grouping stand for a good many more.[46]

Extrapolating from our Toronto data to the province at large, we find no evidence that Egerton Ryerson exerted an effective conservative influence on the Wesleyan Methodists in 1836 or Bishop Alexander McDonell on the Roman Catholics. Nearly every Wesleyan who was not part of the recent influx voted Reform; those who were voted Tory (Table 2.B). This makes Ryerson's abandonment of Reform in 1833 look less like leadership than an astute change of horses. The data that hint at McDonell's impotence are striking, though the numbers are small. Seven of the nine Tory Catholics in our sample had voted Tory in 1834 and were therefore not converts attributable to McDonell.[47] Neither was at least one other, a prominent physician and alderman. However, we must take care in translating our conclusions into provincial terms. In the metropolis, the entire social structure founded on political and economic inequality was in full view at every moment. This may have strengthened the influence of class and made "Canadian" Wesley-ans among the Non-Luxury Producers less susceptible to Ryerson's example than their country cousins. Likewise, lower-class Irish Catholics in what was becoming an Orange stronghold may have been less disposed to kiss the sash at their bishop's behest than those living in relatively homogeneous and self-contained rural communities. The influence of William O'Grady, Irish ex-priest and editor of the *Correspondent and Advocate*, may also have made Toronto a special case.[48]

Our analysis confirms that recent immigrants were the bulwark of conservatism in 1836, although the few Scots and Catholic Irish among them seem to have been less enchanted with English Protestant imperialism than the majority. It is among the smaller ethnic groups—not only the Scots and the Catholic Irish but the North American-born as well—that the strongest correlation between voting and class appears (Table 6), though such small numbers are no more than suggestive. In Toronto, North American-born voters were a negligible electoral factor. The original American settlers, Loyalist and post-Loyalist alike, had been predominantly agrarian, and as long as land was abundant there had been nothing to force their descendants into the towns. As the capital, York had always been a British bastion, and that character had been reinforced by its recent growth under the stimulus of British immigration.

It is easy to see how the Home District's mushrooming metropolis might have become a focus of enmity for the North American-born denizens of the hinterland, even if it had not been the seat of oligarchy. Yet the flood of immigration that reinforced Toronto's Britishness had also inundated its back country and swept into the troubled townships of the London District. What fears of cultural engulfment and physical dispossession must have stirred in the old North American settlers as they saw the vacant lands that might have accommodated future generations occupied by aliens! In Toronto, the Reform vote of 1836 was partly reaction: the reaction of voluntarists to Anglican pretensions, of independent-minded manufacturers to patrician pretensions, of master-craftsmen and some of the pokier merchants to an inrush of well-capitalized rivals. In the countryside, the predominantly North American risings of 1837 were probably also reaction: the same reaction to looming dispossession that goaded the francophone rebels of Lower Canada. In Upper Canada it was the Yankees who, too late, attacked the wagon train.

In its larval form, this essay was a research paper for Professor Careless's graduate seminar in the history of Ontario. It pupated as a paper presented to the Canadian Historical Association, Vancouver, 1983. It takes wing with the aid of an independent scholar research grant from the Social Sciences and Humanities Research Council of Canada.

1   G. M. Craig, *Upper Canada: The Formative Years, 1784–1841* (Toronto, 1963), 232–36; Craig, "John Rolph", *Dictionary of Canadian Biography* [hereafter *DCB*], IX (Toronto, 1976), 683–90; Craig, "Marshall Spring Bidwell", *DCB*, X (Toronto, 1972), 60–64; J. M. S.

Careless, "Robert Baldwin", in Careless, ed., *The Pre-Confederation Premiers: Ontario Government Leaders, 1841–1867* (Toronto, 1980), 89–147.

2   Craig, *Upper Canada*, 237–39.

3   Ibid., 85–89, 124–31, 227–32.

4   *Patriot and Farmer's Monitor* (Toronto), 1 July 1836; *York Commercial Directory, Street Guide and Register...1833–4* (York U.C., [1833]); *City of Toronto Directory...for 1837* (Toronto, [1836]); City of Toronto Archives [hereafter CTA], RG 5–F–1, Finance Department, Assessment Rolls; National Archives of Canada [hereafter NAC], RG 31, Statistics Canada, Census Division, Manuscript Census Records, Toronto City 1842, mfm. C1344. I discuss my treatment of these data in "Voters Under the Microscope: A Quantitative Meditation on the Toronto Parliamentary Poll Book of 1836", paper presented to the Canadian Historical Association, Vancouver, June 1983, copy on deposit at CTA.

5   Edith G. Firth, ed., *The Town of York, 1793–1815* (Toronto, 1962) and *The Town of York, 1815–1834* (Toronto, 1966); F. H. Armstrong, "Metropolitanism and Toronto Re-examined, 1825–1850", in Gilbert A. Stelter and Alan F. J. Artibise, eds., *The Canadian City: Essays in Urban History* (Toronto, 1977), 37–50; Armstrong, "Toronto's First Railway Venture, 1834–1838", *Ontario History* [hereafter *OH*] 58 (1966), 21–41; G. P. de T. Glazebrook, *The Story of Toronto* (Toronto, 1971); Paul Romney, "A Struggle for Authority: Toronto Society and Politics in 1834", in Victor L. Russell, ed., *Forging a Consensus: Historical Essays on Toronto* (Toronto, 1984), 9–40.

6   The author is undertaking such analysis, incorporating geographical factors and a comparison of the voting pattern in 1836 with that in other Toronto elections, as part of a broader study of electoral politics in mid-nineteenth-century Toronto.

7   F. H. Armstrong, *Handbook of Upper Canadian Chronology*, rev. ed. (Toronto, 1985), 93–113 passim; Firth, *York, 1815–1834* , xxxvi-xlv, 90–138; Paul Romney, "The Ordeal of William Higgins", *OH* 67 (1975), 69–90; Romney, "Struggle", 29–30.

8   F. H. Armstrong, "James Edward Small", *DCB*, IX, 724–25.

9   George Metcalf, "William Henry Draper", in Careless, ed., *Pre-Confederation Premiers*, 32–88.

10 *Patriot*, 10 June 1836. See also *Patriot*, June 1836, *passim*, and *Correspondent and Advocate* (Toronto), June 1836, *passim*.

11 *Correspondent*, 29 June 1836; *Patriot*, 25 June, 1 July 1836.

12 *Correspondent*, 22 and 29 June 1836; see also *Patriot*, 21 June 1836.

13 John S. Moir, *Church and State in Canada West: Three Studies in the Relation of Denominationalism and Nationalism, 1841–1867* (Toronto, 1959), 8–9.

14 Ronald John Stagg, "The Yonge Street Rebellion of 1837: An Examination of the Social Background and a Re-assessment of the Events" (Ph.D. diss., University of Toronto, 1976), 214–15, 228–29, 300.

15 Graeme H. Patterson, "Studies in Elections and Public Opinion in Upper Canada" (Ph.D. diss., University of Toronto, 1969); C. Read, *The Rising in Western Upper Canada: The Duncombe Revolt and After* (Toronto, 1982); Stagg, "Yonge Street Rebellion".

16 John Garner, *The Franchise and Politics in British North America, 1755–1867* (Toronto, 1969), 83.

17 This is clear from the manuscript census of 1842.

18 Michael B. Katz, "Occupational Classification in History", *Journal of Interdisciplinary History* 3 (1972–73), 63–88; Katz, *The People of Hamilton, Canada West: Family and Class in a Mid-Nineteenth-Century City* (Cambridge, Mass., 1975). Note Katz's difficulty with *innkeeper*, which is placed in a different category in each work.

19 T. W. Acheson, "The Nature and Structure of York Commerce in the 1820's", *Canadian Historical Review* 50 (1969), 406–28; Firth, *York, 1815–1834*, xxiii-xxviii, 36, 70; M. L. Magill, "William Allan: A Pioneer Business Executive", in F. H. Armstrong et al. , eds., *Aspects of Nineteenth-Century Ontario* (Toronto, 1974), 101–13; Douglas McCalla, *The Upper Canada Trade, 1834–1872: A Study of the Buchanans' Business* (Toronto, 1979); Barrie Dyster, "Thomas Dennie Harris", *DCB*, X, 335–36.

20 Carol Laurie Vaughan, "The Bank of Upper Canada in Politics, 1817–1840", *OH* 60 (1968), 185–87; Peter A. Baskerville, "Entrepreneurship and the Family Compact: York-Toronto, 1822–1855", *Urban History Review* 9 (1981), 15–34; Armstrong, "Railway Venture"; Firth, *York, 1815–1834* , xxix-xxxi, 77.

21 Firth, *York, 1815–1834* , 288–89; *Patriot*, 26 Sep. 1837.

22 J. K. Johnson, "The U.C. Club and the Upper Canadian Elite, 1837–1840", *OH* 69 (1977), 151–68.

23 *Courier of Upper Canada* (Toronto), 10 Apr. 1833, reprinted in Firth, *York, 1815–1834*, 288–89; F. H. Armstrong, "The Carfrae Family: A Study in Early Toronto Toryism", *OH* 54 (1962), 171–72; NAC, RG 5–A–1, Civil and Provincial Secretaries' Offices, Secretaries' Correspondence, Upper Canada Sundries, vol. 121, pp. 6777472–78, vol. 136, p. 74747.

24 *Correspondent*, 1 Jan. 1835.

25 *Constitution* (Toronto), 27 July 1836.

26 Firth, *York, 1815–1834*, 49-50, 53–56, 328fn; *Toronto Directory...1837*, pt. 1, 47.

27 E. J. Hathaway, *Jesse Ketchum and His Times* (Toronto, 1929); Johnson, "U.C. Club", 165. For Harper see *History of Toronto and County of York, Ontario*, II (Toronto, 1885), 60.

28 J. R. Vincent, *Pollbooks: How Victorians Voted* (Cambridge, Eng., 1967), 52–53. Geoffrey Crossick, *An Artisan Elite in Victorian Society: Kentish London, 1840–1880* (London, 1978), notes (p. 114) the propensity of small masters to keep up their trade-union membership.

29 R. S. Neale, *Class and Ideology in the Nineteenth Century* (London, 1972), 67–80; Neale, *Bath 1650–1980: A Social History* (London, 1981), 356–58.

30 F. H. Armstrong, "Reformer as Capitalist: William Lyon Mackenzie and the Printers' Strike of 1836", *OH* 59 (1967), 187–96; Armstrong, "Metropolitanism", 48; Firth, *York, 1815–1834*, xxxii-xxxiv, 77–79, 87–88. For other manifestations see Charles Lipton, *The Trade Union Movement of Canada, 1827–1959* (Montreal, 1966), 6–7.

31 Vincent, *Pollbooks*, 15.

32 Charles Lindsey, *William Lyon Mackenzie*, rev. by G. G. S. Lindsey (Toronto, 1908), 349; Armstrong, "Metropolitanism", 45.

33 *The City of Toronto Poll Book* (Toronto, 1841), 3. The poll book was published by William Lyon Mackenzie's friend James Lesslie.

34 *Correspondent*, 29 June 1836.

35 CTA, RG 1–A, Journal of the Common Council, 2 and 8 Feb. 1836; CTA, RG 7–E, Proceedings of the Mayor's Court, 5 Jan. 1837; *Correspondent*, 11 Jan. 1837.

36 See p. 206.

37 Goldwin French, *Parsons and Politics: The Role of the Wesleyan Methodists in the Maritimes and Upper Canada from 1780 to 1855* (Toronto, 1962), 144–58; C. B. Sissons, *Egerton Ryerson: His Life and Letters*, I (Toronto, 1937), 206–35.

38 The five were Jacob Latham, builder, Peter Freeland, soapmaker, Andrew McGlashan, tanner, Edward Henderson, tailor, and Malcolm McLellan, tailor. See Firth, *York, 1815–1834*, 211–17.

39 E. P. Thompson, "Eighteenth-Century English Society: Class Struggle Without Class?", *Social History* [GB] 3 (1978), 133–65.

40 Crossick, *Artisan Elite*, 134–64.

41 See also Barrie Dyster, "Captain Bob and the Noble Ward: Neighbourhood and Provincial Politics in Nineteenth-Century Toronto", and Gregory S. Kealey, "Orangemen and the Corporation: The Politics of Class during the Union of the Canadas", in Russell, *Forging a Consensus*.

42 Dundas, Ont., Museum, Diary of James Lesslie, 24 Apr. 1832.

43. William Westfall, "Order and Experience: Patterns of Religious Metaphor in Early Nineteenth Century Upper Canada", *Journal of Canadian Studies* 20 (1985), 5–24.

44 J. M. S. Careless, "James Lesslie", *DCB*, XI (Toronto, 1982), 516–19.

45 Katz, *People of Hamilton*, 21, 121–32.

46 I discuss reform-oriented, lower-class Irish Catholics in Toronto at this time in "William Higgins"; see also my "Struggle" and "Daniel Sullivan", *DCB*, XI, 863–64. A calculation allowing for the different rate of "survival" in each grouping suggests that the Catholic vote may have been about 22-to-11 for Reform.

47 The Tory voters in the Toronto election of 1834 are listed in *Correspondent*, 29 Jan. 1835.

48 Edith G. Firth, ed., *Early Toronto Newspapers, 1793–1867* (Toronto, 1961), 8.

Land Policy and the Upper Canadian Elite Reconsidered: The Canada Emigration Association, 1840–1841

J. K. JOHNSON

The Canada Emigration Association came into existence on 15 October 1840 at a meeting held in the Grand Jury room of the district court house in Toronto, at which Sheriff William Botsford Jarvis presided over the creation of "an association of land proprietors," whose object was to establish "a system of emigration and colonization" for the benefit of immigrants to the province.[1] Societies set up to provide aid to immigrants were scarcely a new phenomenon in Upper, or Lower, Canada by 1840,[2] but the methods and the personnel of the Canada Emigration Association were sufficiently different from those of most immigrant societies to merit special study. The association was not a charitable organization but an innovative attempt by land-owners to centralize the process of private land sales and settlement and to prime the pump of immigration through the use of what might be called "bait"—by holding out to immigrants the possibility of free 50-acre parcels of land.

The concepts upon which the Canada Emigration Association was based did not spring suddenly into the collective minds of its founding members on 15 October 1840. They had their origin in a scheme devised in 1839 by Sheriff Jarvis himself. On 21 June 1839 he wrote to John Macaulay, secretary to Lieutenant Governor Sir George Arthur, to ask if Macaulay thought that the government would "countenance and assist a company or association" which was identical in structure and purpose to the one which was later organized, and which Jarvis had already discussed with a number of other prominent Upper Canadians, among them "Messrs. Hagerman, Boulton, Baldwin, Kirkpatrick, S. P. Jarvis, Billings and several others who approve of the plan I propose." Jarvis was therefore the founder of the association but not, as it turned out, its chief promoter. That role was filled by Dr. Thomas Rolph, who had himself emigrated from England in 1833 to practise medicine at Ancaster, and who for some time had been a well-known public crusader and publicist for the encouragement of British emigration to Upper Canada. He had published in 1836 a travel account which contained a

William Botsford Jarvis

section on the advantages of Upper Canada.[3] In 1839 he went back to England in company with Bishop Alexander McDonell. Rolph took with him a number of claims and petitions which he had agreed to advocate at the Colonial Office but his main purpose was much broader. With the "sanction" of former Lieutenant Governor Sir John Colborne, the "approval" of Lieutenant Governor Sir George Arthur and at the request of "the British population in Canada,"[4] he was to use his "energy and eloquence"[5] in the cause of emigration to Canada. Rolph made a tour of the British Isles, speaking extensively in public and private on the subject of emigration.

His greatest success was with large landholders, especially Highland Scottish landlords. The most notable result of his work was the formation in the spring of 1840 of the British North American Colonial Committee, a body whose membership included a long list of noblemen and landlords, among them the Earl of Mountcashell and the Duke of Argyll, as well as some British M.P.s and representatives of the Canada Company, the British American Land Company and the North American Colonial Association of Ireland, all of whom were to join together in promoting and financing emigration to Canada. Rolph was made secretary of this distinguished body.[6] At a meeting in June 1840 he told the members that "highland Proprietors" had promised to subscribe £5,000 to support emigration and a single "noble lord" had promised £1,000. But the burden of emigration was not to be born by "noble lords" alone. At the same meeting Rolph assured the audience that there were Upper Canadian landowners who were prepared to give away "considerable quantities" of land to immigrants sent out by the committee.[7] Not to be outdone, the committee chairman, Arthur John Robertson of Inshes House, Inverness, who owned some 30,000 acres in the Western and London districts of Upper Canada,[8] offered to donate alternate lots of his holdings to new settlers.[9] At a later meeting of the committee Rolph proposed the creation in Upper Canada of a parallel co-operating body which would receive immigrants sponsored by the committee and he outlined a scheme under which he thought the Upper Canadian organization should operate. Fifty acres donated by landowners would be given free on actual settlement, with the result that a desirable British settler would be acquired and the remaining 150 acres of a 200-acre lot would eventually improve in value. The Upper Canadian organization would open offices in each district where lists of available land would be consulted by prospective settlers.[10]

It is not clear who at that point were the proprietors who had already volunteered to donate some of their land, though it is likely that they included Sheriff Jarvis and some of the others whom he had originally consulted. What is clear is that Rolph's activities, when they became known in Upper Canada through newspaper reports, received widespread approval and support. He returned to Upper Canada in the summer of 1840 to what can genuinely be called a hero's welcome. A public banquet was organized in his honour in Toronto at the invitation of "all the judges, executive councillors, the mayor, high sheriff and...the chief respectability and political strength of the city."[11] The banquet was by all accounts a lavish affair at which both food and wines were "abundant," which may explain why chairman and Vice-Chancellor Robert S. Jameson, "in consequence of indisposition was obliged to retire," his place being taken by Sheriff Jarvis, evidently a man of sterner stuff.[12] From Rolph's point of view the occasion was a great success. It gave him a platform in Upper Canada from which to propose publicly a provincial "committee on emigration."

The banquet in Toronto sparked further activity in the way of both business and pleasure. Rolph went on a triumphal tour of Upper Canada during which he was again banqueted and praised for his efforts on behalf of immigration at Hamilton, Woodstock, Goderich and Brantford.[13] More significantly, the "committee on emigration" which Rolph had proposed quickly became a reality. On 25 September 1840 Sheriff Jarvis received a "requisition" to convene a meeting "to form a central committee on emigration" to act in concert with the British North American Colonial Committee in London.[14] The founding meeting, as already noted, was duly held on 15 October.

Why this sudden upsurge of enthusiasm for immigration? A number of factors were involved. Most Upper Canadians, certainly most prominent Upper Canadians, firmly believed, at least until the arrival of the famine Irish in 1847, that immigration *per se* was good for the province, though there might be some disagreement about the kind of immigrant who was most suitable. The number of prospective settlers coming to the province from Great Britain had dropped off suddenly and drastically after the Rebellion of December 1837. In 1838 the immigrant stream dried up almost completely; in 1839 there was some increase but the level was still very modest compared to that of the pre-Rebellion years.[15] Accordingly, any plausible means of increasing immigration was likely to find general acceptance and a scheme which had the moral and financial backing of so many high-born and influential members of British society clearly made a powerful impression on colonial minds. There was also a degree of public concern that some number of recent arrivals in the province were quickly moving on to the United States.[16] A plan which would make Upper Canada more attractive as a permanent home for immigrants was thus additionally welcome. Finally, as will become clearer shortly, a lot of important people in Upper Canada had a great deal of land which they wanted to sell. In the still recent period of unrest and recession they had felt the general economic pinch. They wanted to turn some of their unoccupied land into cash. For that, more people in the province were a necessity.

When Sheriff Jarvis, in accordance with the "requisition" he had received, convened the first meeting of the new association, a good deal of careful planning had evidently already been done. A series of eight resolutions were briskly moved, seconded and approved, which gave the association its name, its objectives and its rules of operation. Membership was set at £1 per year. The association's affairs were to be conducted by a somewhat unwieldy body consisting of a president, a treasurer, a solicitor, 2 secretaries, 3 trustees, 4 vice-presidents and 27 directors. In addition local branch associations were to be formed in each of the 20 districts of Upper Canada, the presidents and vice-presidents of which were also to be *ex officio* directors. It is indicative of the amount of preparation which had already been done that the names of prospective officers of the local branches for twelve of the districts were immediately submitted to the meeting.[17]

The officers of the association wasted no time. Two days later they met, with Vice-Chancellor Jameson once more presiding, to appoint a smaller committee composed of Jameson, Sheriff Jarvis, Dr. Rolph, John Henry Dunn, Henry Sherwood, J. W. Gwynne and Benjamin Thorne, to prepare a "prospectus" for public distribution.[18] The committee took over a month to complete this task but meanwhile the association continued to meet; the latter chose officers for the following year and heard reports on the state of the organization of district branches, which was proceeding at a satisfactory rate. The association also received messages from Governor General Sydenham, Lieutenant Governor Arthur and the commissioners of the Canada Company expressing their willingness to cooperate in the important work of the association.[19]

The prospectus, when finally presented to the directors for their approval at a meeting on 19 November, was an extended statement of the aims and intentions of the "landed proprietors" who made up the association's membership. "Chiefly intended for circulation in Britain," it began by soothing some possible fears of likely emigrants. The "political excitement" which had existed was "completely allayed" and economic conditions were good. The cost of a passage from Quebec or Montreal to Upper Canada was "moderate." The crops of 1840 had been "abundant" and provisions were consequently very cheap. This, however, was merely preliminary puffery leading to the real inducement, free land.

> To such emigrants with families as shall come out under the auspices or with the special recommendation of the societies at home, it is proposed to give fifty acres each, upon condition of actual settlement and clearing a space of ten acres of the front of their locations, erecting a dwelling

house, etc., for themselves, and clearing one-half of that portion of the road lying in front of the lot of which their grant forms a part. The use and possession of this land will be secured to them immediately, and after three years' actual residence, and the performance of the conditions above specified, a deed in fee simple, without charge, will be given to them.[20]

How would the system work in practice? The association's "Registry Office" in Toronto was to be a central data bank of "all lands possessed by private individuals" which were available for sale, lease or "free settlement under the direction of the association," with "every information connected therewith" including location, distance to roads, mills and markets, the nature of existing nearby settlements and "local peculiarities." It was not even necessary for the intending emigrant to come all the way to Toronto in order to examine the lists of available lands. Copies of the lists were to be sent to emigration societies "at home" permitting shopping for land on a mail order basis.

The association felt it necessary to explain why private enterprise rather than government was obliged to provide these services. There was only so much that government, "great as is its power, and wise and benevolent as they may be who wield it," could accomplish. The government of Upper Canada was "actively at work" especially in road building but there was "a vast amount of good" which "circumstances" (presumably financial) had made it impossible for the government to do. Hence the landed proprietors must make up the "deficiency." The members of the association were careful to make it clear nevertheless that they were men of business and not philanthropists. It was widely said that all the best land in Upper Canada had "passed into the hands of private individuals," in other words of land speculators. The association, in a burst of candour, agreed: "The great proportion of the land, especially in the older surveyed townships, comprehending the choicest locations in the neighbourhood of roads and navigable waters, now belongs to private individuals." But this, in fact, was the point. The lands were "at present unproductive to the owner...if retained in their wild state." The owners of such land were the association's "most zealous members" who, rather than have their property continue in "profitless fertility," were prepared to give a part of their lands away to persuade their "fellow countrymen" to turn them into "productive cornfields and animated pastures." This was not charity, it was not even generosity, for "they are well aware that, by the settlement and cultivation of a portion of their lands, the adjoining part will become better worth the purchasing by future emigrants, or by the settler himself, when he shall have become prosperous."

The prospectus explained that the association was not looking only for "such persons as have no money to pay" but was just as interested in "the comparatively affluent settler." They were quite prepared to take the money sooner rather than later. But all were welcome. The central registry system would provide the means to satisfy the needs of settlers of all sorts. The association offered "accurate information, statistical and otherwise," and an "endless choice of locality."

The system was soon in place. An office was opened in the court house in Toronto under the superintendence of Sheriff Jarvis, moonlighting as a kind of executive director of the association. Cash flow needs had not been neglected. Besides the £1 fee paid by ordinary members, directors, who as has been seen were numerous, were required to pay a fee of £12.10.0, and the association, like other real estate firms, charged a commission on sales made through its office. To save further on costs, no officer of the association was to be paid a salary during the first year of operation.

The Canada Emigration Association had been successfully launched. It was arranged that Dr. Rolph should go back to England as the association's "deputy" to continue the work of publicity and liaison there. The Toronto *Patriot* revealed that two of the association's prominent members, Jarvis and Dunn, had started the land registry process by placing "large acreages" at the disposal of the association. Jarvis had listed 1,600 acres and Dunn 2,000, of which he was prepared to give away one quarter.[21] William Morris wrote from Perth to say that he would "cheerfully" donate 50-acre parcels of land in order to attract people to "certain of my lots of land upon which I have not placed settlers."[22] Other members were urged to send in their lists of lands as soon as possible so that they could be sent to England with Rolph, who left early in 1841 with "official instructions" from the association to work with the British North American Colonial Committee or any other similar organizations.[23]

In May 1841 something of the scale of the association's operation to that point through the central registry system was made public with the advertisement in Toronto newspapers of lands which the association was offering for sale "upon easy terms of payment." Sheriff Jarvis, as secretary, listed 48,748 acres in 59 townships stretching across the province from the Ottawa to the Western districts.[24] In fact Jarvis understated the amount of land involved for as a result of incorrect addition his advertisement showed a total of only 46,267 acres. (So much for the benefits of a John Strachan education.) While a few of the properties were identified as "farms" or "improved farms," the vast majority were evidently "unimproved." Yet, as the association's prospectus had suggested, much of the land was in areas which had been settled for some time. Twenty-four of the advertised locations were in townships which fronted on the St. Lawrence or one of the Great Lakes. Geographically the largest concentration of land was in the Home District (17,155 acres), followed by the Newcastle District (8,200 acres), the Western District (7,600 acres), the London District (5,400 acres), plus smaller packages elsewhere. Very little of the land was in marginal areas so far as agricultural potential was concerned. A modern assessment suggests that only about 1,300 acres of the total were in areas unsuitable for long-term farming success—100 acres in Harvey Township in the Kawartha Lakes area, 200 acres in Hinchinbrooke Township in Frontenac County and

1,000 acres in Madoc Township in Hastings County. Some of the land could be said to have been on or near the agricultural frontier of the time, for instance some lots in present day Simcoe and Grey counties, but probably more than 90 percent could have been, sooner or later, turned into "productive cornfields."

How much of this land was bought "upon easy terms" or, if any, given away by the association is, unfortunately, unknown. The fact that the advertisement continued to appear in the papers for the next six months suggests that sales were not as brisk as the association might have wished. Slow sales, if slow they were, were not in any case the association's only cause for concern. For some time, despite the association's best-laid plans, there had been growing financial problems. Early in December 1840, a directors' meeting was told that the association was short of funds. The association had agreed to underwrite Rolph's return to England but the first annual subscriptions had failed to come in quickly enough to cover the expected cost. The directors resolved to personally subscribe additional funds over and above their original commitments and to put pressure on the branch associations to make immediate contributions to the central treasury. To pay for Rolph's expenses and to establish a pool of "general funds," a table of minimum fees for each district was set, ranging in amount from £50 for the Gore, Johnstown, Newcastle and Midland districts down to £20 for the Ottawa District, one quarter of which was to be collected immediately by the treasurer and the rest to be due by May 1841.[25] The provincial government was also appealed to for financial help. The response was sympathetic but disappointing: The association was doing good work and the governor general agreed to become the association's patron, but the government had no uncommitted funds at its disposal to devote to immigration.[26]

The association's money problems were never solved. The directors and friendly newspaper editors continued to urge "the friends of emigration" in Upper Canada to exert themselves in paying the dues "to which they stand pledged." The secretary was instructed once again to call on the local branches for funds. The "influential gentlemen" who had come together to form the association were criticized in the press for not doing their duty.[27] It was all to no avail. The money simply did not come in. By the autumn of 1841, when Dr. Rolph returned to Upper Canada, it was clear that the association was in bad shape. It had begun well but had not received enough "countenance, encouragement and support throughout the province."[28] Although Sheriff Jarvis still hoped that the association "would not be abandoned,"[29] abandoned it was. Whether or not the affairs of the association were ever formally wound up is uncertain. More likely it simply faded away. It disappeared from public view, at least so far as newspaper comment was concerned, sometime later in 1841.

What went wrong? There was, of course, nothing unusual for the time about an organization begun with high hopes and ambitious plans rapidly losing momentum and ending in failure. Two other groups formed around the same time may be cited as examples. The Upper Canada Club, the first exclusive social club in the province, was founded in 1837 but had failed by 1840.[30] A British Constitutional Society (one of many societies by somewhat the same name) was begun in Toronto in November 1842 as an extraparliamentary "loyal" movement opposed to the current Baldwin-Lafontaine ministry. Like the Canada Emigration Association, the British Constitutional Society set up branches throughout the province. And like the Canada Emigration Association, it had a brief existence, becoming moribund within a year.[31] In all three cases the pattern was much the same: initial enthusiasm which did not last and failure to provide adequate support, especially financial support, to the organization.

The Canada Emigration Association had some other problems which it did not share with other contemporary organizations. There was a certain amount of tension between the central association and its district branches. In May 1841 the editor of the *Patriot* deplored attempts by some branches to act "independently" of the provincial association. Kingstonians in particular were said to strongly resent being "auxiliary" to Toronto.[32] Besides internal divisions there may also have been a failure of leadership. The association was run on a voluntary basis with no full-time staff. Sheriff Jarvis as secretary was active and energetic but he had official duties and many other interests and involvements.[33] The only person who devoted all his time to the cause of immigration was Dr. Rolph but most of his work was in the United Kingdom. It is possible also that the association depended too much on Rolph's contacts with British proprietors and counted too much on his ability to coordinate both ends of an emigration system. Rolph himself was probably somewhat over optimistic and naive in his faith in the willingness of landowners on both sides of the water to follow through on their commitments. In Sir George Arthur's words, Rolph had "more enterprise than discretion."[34]

It was perhaps lack of discretion that got him mixed up in a situation in England which also had a good deal to do with the failure of the emigration scheme as a whole. There had been some doubts expressed in Francis Hincks's Toronto *Examiner* as early as December 1840 about the willingness of the British proprietors to spend money assisting emigrants to reach Upper Canada.[35] Hincks was right; the landlords, as it turned out, were more interested in making money than spending it. When Rolph went back to England in 1841 he became involved, not in a continuing voluntary and charitable movement, but with the formation of a commercial company, the British American Association for Emigration and Colonization. This company, which was to have had a capitalization of £500,000, planned to buy hundreds of thousands of acres of land in British North America, hoped to sell (via its chief Canadian commissioner, Sir Allan MacNab) 10,000 shares in Canada, and whose membership list included "thirty-nine baronets, four earls, four marquesses, the lords provost of Glasgow and Edinburgh, one duke, and various other personages and institutions,"[36] also came to a swift and inglorious end. In 1842 the company was found to be completely insolvent, only Rolph and one other shareholder having actually paid their

£25 for the association's stock.[37] Landowners, both British and Upper Canadian, were all for emigration but their enthusiasm had strict financial limits. In any case, it may have occurred to them that pump-priming methods were not after all really necessary. The number of immigrants, which had fallen so low in 1838 and 1839, jumped dramatically in 1840, increased again in 1841 and made another leap upward in 1842, when the second largest number to that date was recorded.[38]

The attempt by the founders of the Canada Emigration Association to systematize and "privatize" immigration into Upper Canada had failed, but the experiment is worth some further examination with a couple of general questions in mind. What kind of people were involved and what were their motives? The membership of the association may not have been quite so adorned with noble names as its British counterparts—the best it could do was a younger son of an Irish Baron, Hon. P. B. De Blaquière, and a hereditary Highland chief, the Laird of MacNab—but many of the names of the members of the association have a distinctly familiar ring. In short, as a group they were one more manifestation of the Upper Canadian political, social and economic "establishment."

The names are known of 39 people who attended meetings of the Canada Emigration Association in Toronto during 1840-41. The 39 can be broken down into subgroups in a number of ways. There were senior officers of government: R. S. Jameson, vice-chancellor of the Court of Chancery; J. H. Dunn, receiver general and member of the Legislative Council; W. H. Draper, attorney general and member of the Executive Council; John Elmsley Jr., member of the Legislative Council and S. P. Jarvis, chief superintendent of Indian affairs for Upper Canada. There were also some lesser officeholders: W. B. Jarvis, sheriff of the Home District; J. G. Spragge, master in chancery; James FitzGibbon, clerk of the Legislative Assembly and registrar of the Court of Probate; George Gurnett, clerk of the peace for the Home District; Andrew Mercer, marriage licence agent, and Charles Berczy, Toronto's postmaster. There were a number of prominent businessmen of Toronto and elsewhere in the Home District: Isaac Buchanan, George Munro (Toronto's mayor in 1841), John Ewart, business partners Benjamin Thorne and John Barwick of Thornhill and Holland Landing, William Laughton and Charles Thompson of Holland Landing, William Atkinson, William Stennett, William Proudfoot and J. W. Gamble. There were also professional men: the lawyers included W. H. Draper, A. N. MacNab, Henry Sherwood, Clarke Gamble, J. M. Strachan, G. S. Boulton, J. E. Small and Robert Dickson (member of the Legislative Council, 1842), and there was one doctor, W. C. Gwynne. Another sub-group, which might be labelled "half-pay officers and gentlemen farmers," included Captain Hugh Stewart, R.N., of Richmond Hill; Francis Boyd, also of Richmond Hill; Captain Ogden Creighton, late of the 81st Regiment, of "Clifton," Niagara Falls; Francis Hewson of Barrie; Lieutenant Edward G. O'Brien, late of the 68th Regiment, of Shanty Bay; and Captain Elmes Steele, R.N., of Medonte Township.

In addition to such "occupational" groupings it is not surprising to find a great deal of overlapping of offices and activities among members of the association. Six of those already mentioned were members of the House of Assembly of Upper Canada in the 13th Parliament of 1836–41: W. H. Draper, J. W. Gamble, A. N. MacNab, Henry Sherwood, J. E. Small and G. S. Boulton, as was W. B. Robinson. Four more, J. M. Strachan, Elmes Steele, J. H. Dunn and Isaac Buchanan, were to be elected in 1841.[39] There was overlap as well into other spheres—social, military and officeholding. The Home District Agricultural Society, for example, numbered among its members W. B. Jarvis, John Elmsley, Benjamin Thorne, E. G. O'Brien, J. W. Gamble, W. B. Robinson, Charles Thompson and William Atkinson.[40] There were 22 militia officers (13 at the rank of colonel or lieutenant colonel) and 21 magistrates.[41] And 20 of the 39 had also been among the original members of the aforementioned Upper Canada Club,[42] a Toronto institution which has been shown to have contained most of the members of Upper Canada's most influential, and also very overlapping, élite.[43]

The membership of the district branches was of a very similar cast. Familiar names turn up, such as Colonel John Prince in the Western District, Admiral Vansittart in the Brock District, Absalom Shade in the Wellington District, Adam Fergusson in Gore, sheriffs Ruttan of Newcastle, McMahon of Prince Edward and Moodie of Victoria, George Crawford of the Johnstown District and William Morris of the Bathurst District. For three districts, somewhat expanded lists of local members have survived and are worth brief notice. In the Victoria District the Canada Emigration Association branch had as some of its members: Edmund Murney, member of the House of Assembly for Hastings; Captain Henry Baldwin, steamboat operator; Sheriff Moodie; Henry Corby, distiller; Billa Flint, merchant; George Benjamin, newspaper owner and George Ridley, physician.[44] On the London District list were: militia colonels Mahlon Burwell and John Bostwick; John Harris, district treasurer; John B. Askin, clerk of the peace; John Wilson, first district warden (1841); Sheriff James Hamilton; James Givens, lawyer; Edward Ermatinger, retired fur trader; G. J. Goodhue, "millionaire" merchant and land developer and W. W. Street, banker.[45] If anything, the members of the Midland District branch were an even more striking group: three members of the Assembly, J. S. Cartwright (also president of the Commercial Bank), J. B. Marks and Anthony Manahan; five lawyers, F. M. Hill, John A. Macdonald, Charles Stuart, Thomas Kirkpatrick (also collector of customs) and J. R. Forsyth; ship owner and builder John Counter; banker F. A. Harper; merchant John Mowat; and doctors George Baker and James Sampson.[46] The general point to be made is that the Canada Emigration Association was one more version of the Upper Canadian central élite in connection with the district "oligarchies."

Does this account of the Canada Emigration Association add anything new to the numerous élite studies which have already examined the nature of the central and local élites of Upper Canada?[47] Perhaps a little. It suggests that among their many other overlapping interests these leading Upper Canadians had a strong collective concern with land and land sales. The association's prospectus stated that a great deal of the land in the province had "passed into the hands of private individuals" who had kept it undeveloped "with the view to their owner's obtaining higher prices." It is reasonable to suppose that many of the names just mentioned were also some of these "private individuals" who were among the "most zealous members" of the association. It might be possible, if almost fatally tedious, to establish by searching all surviving land registry or assessment records just how much land, and in what locations, was owned by known members of the association, but such an exercise is really unnecessary. A good number of the members of the association have already been identified in a variety of sources as having been involved at some point in land speculation or development on a sizeable scale. Among the Toronto-centred group the best known examples are Dunn,[48] Elmsley, Proudfoot,[49] Jameson,[50] S. P. and W. B. Jarvis,[51] Mercer,[52] J. M. Strachan[53] and W. B. Robinson.[54] Outside the Home District, other known speculator-developers include A. N. MacNab,[55] Malcolm Cameron,[56] Adam Fergusson,[57] G. J. Goodhue,[58] W. W. Street,[59] G. S. Boulton[60] and Wiliam Morris.[61] In the Kingston area alone, a study of the business élite at a somewhat later date has identified six of the association's branch members as having been much involved in land development schemes.[62] Perhaps some members of the association supported its objectives simply as an institution which might contribute to the general growth and prosperity of the province and not from motives of personal gain, but it would be stretching credulity too far to suppose that in an "association of landed proprietors" such disinterestedness was the general rule. The motives of most of the members were undoubtedly much more straightforward. They had land to sell which they had not yet been able to sell at a satisfactory profit and which they hoped to dispose of through the association at "higher prices."

The group of Upper Canadians involved in the Canada Emigration Association fits readily into an officeholding, professional-business-social *and landholding* establishment at the end of its period of greatest influence. (The group also included parts of a newer, emerging establishment of a later era.)[63] Politically they were, as might be expected, heavily conservative; of them all only Malcolm Cameron, who was a member of the Western District Branch, could be described as a dyed-in-the-wool Reformer.[64] What, then, does the experiment of the Canada Emigration Association tell us about the predominantly conservative, "establishment" view of immigration, and of the kind of people these prominent Upper Canadians wished to see become part of the population of Upper Canada? This question has, in fact, already engaged the attention of a number of Canadian historians, and their answers to it, though arrived at in some cases from different perspectives, have been quite similar. The consensus has been that the Upper Canadian establishment wished to create, through immigration, a landless, wage-earning class, whose presence would overcome the perceived problems of the high cost and scarcity of labour in the colony. By advocating such a policy they had accepted "Wakefieldian" theories of immigration which held that immigrants should be denied easy, or all, access to land so that they would be forced to form a necessary pool of labourers.

This version of the prevailing immigration theories of leading Upper Canadians was first advanced by H. C. Pentland in his 1961 Ph.D. dissertation, "Labour and the Development of Industrial Capitalism in Canada." As evidence of the ideas of "the privileged in Canada," Pentland quoted at length from a report written in 1840 by "a spokesman for privilege" in Upper Canada, William Allan.

> The greatest drawback to the employment of Capital in this country at present consists in the *high price of wages*, and the *extreme difficulty of procuring the labour* requisite for its profitable employment in *any* pursuit; and more especially in *agricultural* ones. Everything, therefore, that tends to lessen the *quantity of labour* in the Market, will also tend to exclude *capital from it*. But the main cause of the scarcity of hired labour in a new Country is the *Cheapness of Land*, and it seems to follow, as an irresistible conclusion, that the *Free gift of lands*, must increase that scarcity an hundredfold...

"The right course then," Pentland concluded, "was to make land costly, so as to keep men in the position of labourers and force down wages. This would avoid a community [here he again quoted Allan] 'composed exclusively of the occupiers of Free Grants—and we can hardly picture to our imagination anything more deplorable than the condition of a community so constituted.'"[65]

Lillian Gates, covering some of the same ground in her book *Land Policies of Upper Canada* in 1968, also cited Allan's opinions and identified him as a spokesman "for the large landholders" of Upper Canada.[66] Three years later, in his article "Land Policy, Population Growth and Social Structure in the Home District, 1793–1851," Leo A. Johnson quoted exactly the same statement by Allan used by Pentland. (It also appeared in the same form in three of Johnson's subsequent publications.)[67] He used Allan's ideas to help to show that "in influential circles both in Upper Canada and England," Wakefieldian principles had "taken hold."[68] According to Johnson, Allan spoke for "those who supported Simcoe's dream of creating an Aristocratic society of land-owning gentry."[69] Finally, in "Land, Labour, and Capital in pre-Confederation Canada," Gary Teeple, while not referring directly to Allan's statement, argued that "the land policies and practices of the ruling class from the Conquest to Confederation" had been Wakefieldian all along, in order "to create in the colony a working class."[70]

It must be said that the authors referred to were not claiming that Wakefieldian views of immigration and land policy were *universally* held in

Upper Canada. Pentland believed that most Upper Canadians disagreed with such views and that the Wakefield system was made unnecessary in any case by the arrival of large numbers of impoverished Irish immigrants in the late 1840s.[71] Teeple's argument was similar but he believed that a landless working class had appeared in Upper Canada even earlier, by the 1820s.[72] Gates also made it clear that Allan's views were not the prevailing ideas of the time, at least in government.[73] Nonetheless, all four historians were in agreement that the position taken by Allan in 1840 was representative of the ideas of the Upper Canadian élite—of "the large landholders," of "privilege," of the "ruling class," of the "aristocrats."

In 1840 William Allan was an executive councillor, a legislative councillor and governor of the British American Fire and Life Assurance Company. Obviously he was an important member of the political-economic élite. But how "representative" was he of his time and his contemporaries? Professor Peter Baskerville, who has examined Allan's business practices in a number of studies, has found him to be in some ways atypical of other leading Upper Canadian figures because of business attitudes that were old-fashioned, "increasingly...out of touch"[74] with the entrepreneurial style of the time. Although he had been the first president of the Bank of Upper Canada, he resigned in 1835 because he could not agree with what he saw as an unduly liberal lending policy.[75] In another article on Allan, Max Magill found his ideas of society and government "intensely narrow."[76] He was an old-fashioned businessman. He was also evidently a very private man. He was certainly not a "clubbable" man—unlike almost all of his fellow members of the Upper Canadian élite he was not a member of the Upper Canada Club[77]—and he was not a public man. When he agreed, reluctantly, in 1842 to be president of the British Constitutional Society, he announced that it was the first time he had ever taken a public political position.[78] Was he a typical large landholder? He has been said to have owned quite a lot of land[79] but he did not pursue large government grants nearly as assiduously as did many other prominent Upper Canadians, nor does he seem to have dealt in that very common commodity, loyalist "rights" to land.[80] The fact that he, unlike so many other large landholders, was *not* involved in the Canada Emigration Association also suggests that he was somewhat out of step with other large proprietors.

In the end the question of Allan's "representativeness" is perhaps somewhat beside the point. The fact is that neither the Upper Canadian élite in general, nor the government of the province in general, agreed with Allan. Even among his fellow executive councillors, his fellow landowners and his fellow businessmen, his was not the predominant view. There was no conspiracy on the part of "the ruling class" to create a landless wage earning proletariat in Upper Canada.

The few sentences written by Allan which have been so often quoted appeared in a report submitted to Lieutenant Governor Arthur in early June 1840.[81] It was one of three reports prepared at the time by members of the Executive Council on the subject of immigration and land policy. Allan's arguments were not accepted either by Arthur or by Governor General Sydenham. The policy statement which *was* acceptable to Arthur and Sydenham and which was eventually approved by the entire Executive Council was prepared by executive councillors A. W. Baldwin and R. B. Sullivan (who was also commissioner of crown lands). They were opposed to dividing Upper Canada into a society of "masters and servants." They did not want to see settlers "driven from the land." Upper Canada still had large amounts of crown land available, especially in the area recently ceded by the Saugeen Indians. They recommended free grants of 50 acres to settlers on the Owen Sound road, then just being opened.[82] This free-grant plan was approved by the council in September 1840[83] and some 150 families began settling on 50-acre lots along the Owen Sound road in November.[84] The scheme was put into effect even though it was technically illegal since free grants were forbidden by existing land legislation, the Land Act of 1837 (provision of free grants *was* written into a new Land Act in 1841), and was at variance with imperial "Wakefieldian" policies.[85] The government and the "landed proprietors" of Upper Canada were of one mind in favouring a system which would provide immigrants with land, in some cases free land, whether it came from the crown or from private sources.

It is not clear whether the idea of a revived program of free land grants in Upper Canada originated within the public or the private sector. The Baldwin-Sullivan report to Arthur was dated 5 June 1840. It was on 10 June that Thomas Rolph, in England, told a meeting of the British North American Colonial Committee that he knew that many Upper Canadian proprietors were prepared to donate land to settlers. Rolph later referred to the government's Owen-Sound-road scheme in a speech in Hamilton in October 1840.[86] Sullivan used the Canada Emigration Association's 50-acre plan as support for the government's scheme in another report written in December of that year.[87] Here again the question of provenance is not very important. The government and the association acted, in effect, together, which is not surprising considering that the association operated "under the patronage of His Excellency the Governor-General" and that the president and three vice-presidents of the Canada Emigration Association were senior government officeholders. It has been argued that the government's readoption of a free-grant policy stemmed mainly from a fear of losing "loyal" British settlers to the United States.[88] This may well have been a government concern—certainly it was a pet belief of the chief emigrant agent, A. B. Hawke[89]—and it may conceivably have also affected the thinking of private landholders to some degree, but it is probable that for them more mundane considerations, the kinds of considerations which have already been suggested, were paramount. They had land to sell and they wanted to create a demand for it. The Canada Emigration Association with its British connections was seen, for a time, as a means of fostering and channeling that demand.

In its assessment of the attitudes of the Upper Canadian élite toward land policy and immigration, this study of the Canada Emigration Association does not necessarily demonstrate that their motives were any more admirable than the motives which have been attributed to them. It does, however, make their motives and their activities more believable and more understandable.

1   *Colonist* (Toronto), 14 Oct. 1840.
2   See Rainer Baehre, "Pauper Emigration to Upper Canada in the 1830s", *Histoire sociale/Social History* [hereafter *Hs/SH*] 28 (1981), 329–67.
3   Thomas Rolph, *A Brief Account, together with Observations made during a visit in the West Indies, and a tour through the United States of America in parts of the years 1832–3; together with a Statistical Account of Upper Canada* (Dundas, 1836). A sketch of Rolph's career appears in William Canniff, *The Medical Profession in Upper Canada* (Toronto, 1894), 603–9. National Archives of Canada [hereafter NAC], RG 5–C–1, Civil and Provincial Secretaries' Offices, Upper Canada, Provincial Secretary's Correspondence, vol. 18, no. 2198, W. B. Jarvis to John Macaulay, 21 June 1839.
4   NAC, MG 11–[CO 42], Great Britain, Public Record Office (London), Colonial Office Papers, original correspondence, mfm. vol. 468, pp. 168–69, 204–5, 221–22; vol. 479, pp. 354–56.
5   C. R. Sanderson, ed., *The Arthur Papers...*, 3 vols. (Toronto, 1957–59), II, 143.
6   NAC, RG 5–A–1, Civil and Provincial Secretaries' Offices, Upper Canada and Canada West, Secretaries' Correspondence, Upper Canada Sundries [hereafter Sundries], vol. 247, pp. 134728, 134735; see also H. I. Cowan, *British Emigration to British North America* (Toronto, 1961), 123–24.
7   Sundries, vol. 247, p. 134728.
8   NAC, MG 19–A–3, Askin Family Papers, vol. 31, pp. 10394–96.
9   Sundries, vol. 247, p. 134728. Robertson was not the only British landlord whose motives for supporting emigration were not entirely philanthropic. The Earl of Mountcashell, an Irish nobleman, also owned a lot of Upper Canadian land, having previously bought most of Amherst Island from the family of Sir John Johnson, plus "land across the province." See J. O. Blackwell, "The Radcliffs of Amherst Island: The Vicissitudes of an Anglo-Irish Gentry Family during the 1840s", *Historic Kingston* 32 (1984), 20, 26.
10 *Patriot* (Toronto), 11 Aug. 1840.
11 T. Rolph, *Emigration and Colonization, Embodying the Results of a Mission to Great Britain and Ireland During the years 1839, 1840, 1841 and 1842* (London [U.K.], 1844), 50.
12 Ibid., 59.
13 Ibid., 74.
14 *Colonist*, 14 Oct. 1840.
15 Cowan, 288.
16 L. F. Gates, *Land Policies of Upper Canada* (Toronto, 1968), 257–58.
17 *Colonist*, 21 Oct. 1840. See also Metropolitan Toronto Central Library, Canadian History Dept., Baldwin Room, Robert Baldwin papers, "Suggestions for the Canada Emigration Society", [broadsheet postmarked 13 Oct. 1840]. This document lists proposed rules and regulations.
18 *Colonist*, 28 Oct. 1840.
19 Ibid., 25 Nov. 1840.
20 No copy of the prospectus seems to have survived. It is quoted at length in *Chambers' Information for the People* (Edinburgh, 1841), 266–67. All quotations from the prospectus are from this source.
21 *Patriot*, 27 Nov. 1840.
22 Ibid., 11 Dec. 1840.
23 Ibid., 26 Jan. 1841; Rolph, *Emigration*, 91.
24 *Patriot*, 18 May 1841.

25 Ibid., 11 Dec. 1840.

26 Ibid.

27 Ibid., 16 Mar., 4 May 1841.

28 Rolph, *Emigration*, 119.

29 Ibid., 135.

30 J. K. Johnson, "The U.C. Club and the Upper Canadian Elite, 1837–1840", *Ontario History* [hereafter *OH*] 69 (1977), 151–68.

31 *Patriot*, 8 Nov., 13 Dec. 1842; 3, 10, 24 Jan., 24 Feb. 1843.

32 Ibid., 4 May 1841.

33 See R. J. Burns, "William Botsford Jarvis", *Dictionary of Canadian Biography* [hereafter *DCB*], IX (Toronto, 1976), 411–12.

34 Sanderson, III, 276.

35 *Examiner* (Toronto), 26 Dec.1840.

36 Cowan, 125.

37 Ibid., 126.

38 Ibid., 288.

39 Sources used to identify the 39 men include: NAC, RG 1–L–3, Executive Council, Upper Canada 1764–1867, Land Records, Petitions for Land Grants and Leases [hereafter U.C. Land Petitions], vol. 101, C12/58, vol. 110, C16/165, vol. 297, L3/18, vol. 299, L5/32; F. H. Armstrong, *Handbook of Upper Canadian Chronology and Territorial Legislation* (London, 1967); J. R. R. Robertson, *Landmarks of Toronto*, III (Toronto, 1898); Simcoe County Pioneer and Historical Society, *Pioneer Papers* (Barrie, 1908); A. S. Miller, ed., *The Journals of Mary O'Brien* (Toronto, 1968); M. L. Smith, ed., *Young Mr. Smith of Upper Canada* (Toronto, 1980); F. R. Berchem, *The Yonge Street Story* (Toronto, 1977); J. O. Coté, *Political Appointments and Elections in the Province of Canada from 1841 to 1865* (Ottawa, 1866).

40 Robertson, *Landmarks*, III, 210; Berchem, *Yonge Street*, 126, 156.

41 NAC, RG 9–I–B–5, Dept. of Militia and Defence, Pre-Confederation Records, Adjutant General's Office, Upper Canada, Registers of Officers, vols. 6–7; RG 68, Registrar General, General Index to Commissions, 1651–1841, pt. II, pp. 348–512.

42 Sundries, vol. 183.

43 Johnson, "U.C. Club", 159–168.

44 G. E. Boyce, *Historic Hastings* (Belleville, 1967), 48, 86, 88, 96, 182; Canniff, 578–81.

45 Armstrong, *Handbook*; L. G. Thomas, "Edward Ermatinger", *DCB*, X (Toronto, 1972), 273–74; F. H. Armstrong, "George Jervis Goodhue, Pioneer Merchant of London, Upper Canada", *OH* 63 (1971), 217–32; J. K. Johnson, "The Businessman as Hero: The Case of William Warren Street", *OH* 65 (1973), 125–32; C. F. Read, "The London District Oligarchy in the Rebellion Era", *OH* 72 (1980), 195–209.

46 Armstrong, *Handbook* ; J. K. Johnson, "John A. Macdonald and the Kingston Business Community", in G. Tulchinsky, ed., *To Preserve & Defend: Essays on Kingston in the Nineteenth Century* (Montreal, 1976), 141–55.

47 See for example: Read; F. H. Armstrong, "The Oligarchy of the Western District of Upper Canada, 1788–1841", Canadian Historical Association, *Historical Papers* [hereafter CHA, *HP*] (1977), 87–102; M. S. Cross, "The Age of Gentility: The Formation of an Aristocracy in the Ottawa Valley", ibid. (1967), 105–17; E. M. Richards, "The Joneses of Brockville and the Family Compact", *OH* 60 (1968), 169–84; H. V. Nelles, "Loyalism and Local Power: The District of Niagara, 1792–1837", *OH* 58 (1966), 99–114; R. E. Saunders, "What Was the Family Compact?" *OH* 49 (1957), 165–78; Johnson, "The U.C. Club".

48 Saunders, 177.

49 Henri Pilon, "John Elmsley", *DCB*, IX (Toronto, 1976), 240–41; Barry Dyster, "William Proudfoot", ibid., 147.

50 Clara Thomas, *Love and Work Enough: The Life of Anna Jameson* (Toronto, 1967), 195.

51 Burns, 411.

52 F. H. Armstrong, "Andrew Mercer", *DCB*, X (Toronto, 1972), 509.

53 R. D. Hall, "James McGill Strachan", *DCB*, IX (Toronto, 1976), 751.

54 J. K. Johnson, "John A. Macdonald, the Young Non-Politician", CHA, *HP* (1971), 142.

55 D. R. Beer, *Sir Allan MacNab* (Hamilton, 1984), 17.
56 Johnson, "Young Non-Politician", 143.
57 E. H. Jones, "Adam Fergusson", *DCB*, IX (Toronto, 1976), 252.
58 Armstrong, "Goodhue", 226–27.
59 Johnson, "Businessman as Hero", 130.
60 R. W. Widdis, "Speculation and the Surveyor: An Analysis of the Role played by the Surveyors in the Settlement of Upper Canada" *Hs/SH* 15 (1982), 450.
61 Gates, 334.
62 Johnson, "Kingston Business Community", 147–50.
63 Ibid., 151.
64 J. H. Dunn, John Elmsley Jr., Isaac Buchanan and J. E. Small have usually been classified as moderate Reformers.
65 H. C. Pentland, *Labour and Capital in Canada, 1650–1860* (Toronto, 1981), 110. This book, based on Pentland's thesis, was published after his death.
66 Gates, 259.
67 "Land Policy, Population Growth and Social Structure in the Home District, 1793–1851", *OH* 63 (1971), 57; *History of the County of Ontario* (Whitby, 1973), 66; "The Political Economy of Ontario Women in the Nineteenth Century", in J. Acton et. al., eds., *Women at Work, Ontario, 1850–1930* (Toronto, 1974), 23; "Independent Commodity Production: Model of Production or Capitalist Class Formation?", *Studies in Political Economy* 6 (1981), 105.
68 L. A. Johnson, "Land Policy", 56–57.
69 L. A. Johnson, *Ontario County*, 66.
70 Gary Teeple, "Land, Labour and Capital in Pre-Confederation Canada", in his, ed., *Capitalism and the National Question in Canada* (Toronto, 1972), 45.
71 Pentland, 111–12.
72 Teeple, 52.
73 Gates, 259–61.
74 P. A. Baskerville, "Entrepreneurship and the Family Compact: York-Toronto, 1822–1855", *Urban History Review* 9 (1981), 23.
75 P. A. Baskerville, "Donald Bethune's Steamboat Business: A Study of Upper Canadian Commercial and Financial Practice", *OH* 67 (1975), 139.
76 M. Magill, "William Allan, A Pioneer Business Executive", in F. H. Armstrong et al., eds., *Aspects of Nineteenth Century Ontario:...* (Toronto, 1974), 111.
77 Johnson, "U.C. Club", 164.
78 *Patriot* , 8 Nov. 1842.
79 Magill, 112.
80 Allan's land petitions are in U.C. Land Petitions, vol. 3, A2/22, A3/38, A4/40, A8/1, A11/18, A13/14.
81 NAC, RG 1–E–3, Executive Council, Upper Canada 1764–1867, State Records, Submissions to the Executive Council, vol. 24. The report was signed jointly by Allan and R. A. Tucker, but since Tucker was a relative newcomer to Upper Canada it is probably correct to attribute the report primarily to Allan.
82. Ibid.
83. Gates, 261.
84. Upper Canada, Legislative Assembly, *Journals* (1841), app. MM.
85. Gates, 259–61.
86. *Patriot*, 9 Oct. 1840.
87. Sundries, vol. 250, p. 136037.
88. H. M. Morrison, "The Principle of Free Grants in the Land Act of 1841", *Canadian Historical Review* 14 (1933), 404.
89. Gates, 260.

Imperial Agendas and "Disloyal" Collaborators: Decolonization and the John Sandfield Macdonald Ministries, 1862–1864

PETER BASKERVILLE

The John Sandfield Macdonald ministries do not bulk large in Canadian historiography. Most writers on the Confederation period have either ignored them entirely or have concluded that they represent a failed but, in the kindest of interpretations, noble attempt to create a political structure which could encompass people of different languages and different religions.[1] This narrow perspective needs to be supplemented by a wider view. In the context of imperial-colonial relations, these governments threatened to undermine a delicate collaborative structure which had evolved over the previous decade and within which the interests of a powerful local élite, of British colonial administrators and of imperial investors intersected.[2] While no single group totally dominated the others, all depended on interaction, however uneven, for the attainment of sometimes common and sometimes disparate ends. During their brief and troubled two-year tenure, the John Sandfield Macdonald ministries managed to challenge central components of that structure and in the process probed the limits of human agency at the periphery of empire. By so doing they contributed to the basis and framework of subsequent Confederation negotiations.

A reassessment of those ministries sheds light on the tensions and complexities inherent in the general process of decolonization. Robin Winks has suggested that the role of the collaborator "was critically important within the formal empire."[3] Yet from the imperial perspective the movement from formal to informal empire depended no less upon the successful cultivation of a group of loyal colonial collaborators. In the Canadas this group was a loosely knit coalition of politicians, businessmen and financiers who to a greater or lesser degree required assistance from imperial interests (governmental, or financial, or both) for the realization of their personal, party and colonial goals. Various imperial interests also came to rely on

John Sandfield Macdonald

colonial leaders and institutions for the attainment of their particular ends. Not surprisingly, even before J. S. Macdonald's tenure as government leader, tensions and cross-purposes characterized the collaborative process. In this sense, the process under investigation in this paper—the interplay between imperial agendas (political and financial) and colonial leaders (political and financial)—was far from static. Thus the term structure is used in a dynamic sense "to refer to conditions shaping actions which persist over a certain period of time." As certain of those conditions were challenged, internal realignments occurred and the structure itself was modified.[4]

To appreciate the nature of this change a discussion of the collaborative structure as it existed prior to the Macdonald ministries is essential. After the context is set, the nature of the Macdonald ministries' challenge will be examined, imperial reaction noted and the general consequences sketched. In the concluding section some comments on the general significance of this approach to imperial-colonial relations will be offered.

Prior to 1847, imperial financial guarantees and direct political involvement through the governor general's office combined to coerce and conciliate colonial acquiescence to general imperial ends. While never perfect—the French refused to be coerced—these tactics ultimately proved insufficient to meet the pressures occasioned by an economic downturn, the repeal of the Corn Laws and the granting of responsible government in the late 1840s.[5] New mechanisms for the cultivation of loyalty had to be found. While many in the colony and some in the British colonial administration argued for direct imperial loans or subsidies for the construction of colonial railways to maintain imperial loyalty, in the end, and after much protracted negotiation, such formal measures were deemed unnecessary.[6] An increasingly buoyant economy coupled with colonial government guarantees began to attract significant private investment from London financiers.

Important merchant banks situated in the city of London had been involved in Upper Canadian governmental finance since the mid 1830s. Two of them, Glyn, Mills and Co. and the Baring Brothers, began to extend their official relationship as the government's London financial agents to include increasingly large investments in Canadian railway development.[7] Their efforts were facilitated by the local colonial government via a process of financial guarantees. Local financial institutions, especially the colony's official resident bank, the Bank of Upper Canada, also played important roles. Imperial investors looked to these financial institutions for support in the carrying out of their colonial investment programs. When the London financial market became tight, those institutions were expected to provide interim financing. By the mid 1850s, the Canadian government, Canadian railways, Canadian banks and London financiers were bound together in a web of interrelated investment activity.[8]

Under this structure, the imperial government exercised an indirect role. The movement towards informal empire, of course, made this inevi-

The Bank of Upper Canada, Toronto, ca. 1851

table. Ever cost-conscious, imperial administrators happily stepped back both from direct involvement in colonial politics and from the financing of railways and other colonial entrepreneurial activity. At the same time the Colonial Office continued to guard zealously its remaining prerogatives, the main one being the setting of the timing for the ensuing stages of devolution.[9] Control of the agenda, however, depended on the acquiescence of loyal colonial collaborators. And since the cultivation of such support could be achieved only indirectly via the suasion of the governor general, the assistance of private financiers in the city of London, or a combination of the two, the maintenance of imperial prerogatives became a difficult and tension-filled endeavour. Ironically, the process of decolonization, if it was to occur according to the dictates of the imperial agenda, required heightened rather than casual administrative attention.

Colonial initiatives in constitutional, financial and economic affairs impressed this fact upon imperial administrators. Sir Edward Bulwer-Lytton, the colonial secretary, felt that an unsolicited but official Canadian proposal for federation in 1858 was clearly too precipitous a move for present consideration. The "power...to regulate and guide negotiation" had to remain in imperial hands. The measure was quietly, but effectively, shelved.[10] When the Francis Hincks–A.-N. Morin government pushed for the institution of a decimal currency in the early 1850s, the Treasury Board saw this plan as an unwarranted intrusion on a central symbol of imperial rule and capitulated only in the late 1850s.[11]

The Cayley-Galt tariffs of 1858–59 shed the clearest light on the intricate nature of the collaborative process as it existed on the eve of John Sandfield

Macdonald's accession to power. The tariffs emerged from and struck at the economic and financial heart of the imperial-colonial relationship. Most historians have argued that these measures were either essentially protective or primarily revenue-producing in intent. In fact, the context from which they emerged strongly suggests that the tariffs were meant to achieve both ends. Work by D. F. Barnett and Andy Den Otter have persuasively demonstrated the protective characteristics of those tariffs. By raising duties against British and American manufactured goods and by lowering duties on inputs required for the home manufacture of those products, the Cayley-Galt tariffs issued a ringing challenge to the imperial perception of the proper trading position of its colonies.[12] As such, the tariffs reflected a growing desire on the part of colonial leaders to encourage local economic diversification, assist local capital formation and decrease commercial dependence upon Great Britain.

But if from one perspective the tariffs can be seen as a movement to economic independence and in that sense a nationalist measure,[13] they were at the same time designed to strengthen the financial and economic relations which underlay the existing collaborative structure. The system of private London investment facilitated by colonial government guarantees and aided by timely assistance from local colonial financial institutions was on the verge of total collapse. The end of the Crimean War had led to decreased foreign demand for Canadian wheat and had coincided with a series of poor harvests in Upper Canada. British and American economic difficulties placed further pressure on the province. The Grand Trunk, Great Western and Northern Railways, major recipients of British capital, all defaulted on their interest payments, thus forcing the local government to honour its guarantees. So, too, did many Upper Canadian municipalities. At the same time, with the decline in capital construction and trade, revenues fell. Overextended in their normal business, the Bank of Upper Canada and other local banks could no longer provide sufficient interim aid.[14] In this context the provincial government had to find ways to increase its revenue or it, too, would be in danger of defaulting on its increased debt payments.[15]

Imperial reaction to the tariffs reflected the complexity of the imperial-colonial relationship. The value of Canadian securities in the city of London fell. The new colonial secretary, the Duke of Newcastle, at first roundly condemned the tariffs. Large landed proprietors and private financiers like Edward Ellice, who claimed to have "greater interests in Canada than any other person in the Country," demanded their repeal.[16] But others, including prominent financiers in London, accepted with silence the tariff changes of the late 1850s. Glyn, Mills and Co. and the Baring Brothers, heavily involved in the Grand Trunk Railway, in loans to the Canadian government, and, for Glyn, in loans to and investments in the tottering Bank of Upper Canada, probably hoped that the tariff would provide some support and protection for British creditors.[17] The financial ties which had emerged during the movement from formal to informal empire and which underlay the delicate collaborative structure of the late 1850s made the prospect of maintaining traditional economic relations complicated indeed. Merchant bankers in London did not necessarily share the same interests as industrialists in Sheffield,[18] or retired gentlemen living comfortably on their country estates, or colonial theorists resident at the Treasury Board and Colonial Office. Thus, as the decade of the 1860s began, the problem for the imperial administrators was not simply in maintaining control of an agenda; rather, they had first to determine of what that agenda would consist and for whose interests, both in England and in the colony, it would be formulated.

On the eve of John Sandfield Macdonald's accession to power in May 1862, the elements of such an agenda seemed close to being finalized. Under Newcastle's aegis, the Colonial Office began to work with those London financiers who were most involved in underwriting Canadian affairs. Finding some means for dealing with the Grand Trunk Railway's escalating debts proved to be the key problem. Despite pressure from Glyn and Baring, and despite his best efforts, Alexander Galt, the Canadian finance minister, had exhausted all means of colonial support for this venture.[19] A two-tiered solution gradually emerged. The first concerned the tapping of imperial assistance for the construction of an intercolonial railway. As Donald Roman has demonstrated, such assistance was viewed as essential indirect relief for the ailing Grand Trunk.[20] By linking Halifax to the Grand Trunk's main line, the Intercolonial would ostensibly open up new trading territory to the railway. The infusion of massive new capital into British North America would, by itself, stimulate general trade and development.

All this required great sums of money. Newcastle knew that the high Canadian tariff had immeasurably increased the already difficult task of convincing the cabinet to view favourably any large grants to the Canadian colonies. By mid-April 1862 his worst fears were realized. Cabinet turned down the requests made by a colonial deputation early in the year for direct aid and instead offered a 2 to 2.5 percent reduction in general interest charges courtesy of an imperial guarantee. Newcastle suspected that this would be insufficient to attract colonial participation and noted sharply that better terms required strong evidence of proper conduct on the part of the colonial leaders.[21]

From Newcastle's perspective, such conduct could best be demonstrated by the passage of two pieces of legislation. The first had to effect a significant lowering of tariffs and the introduction of some other more locally based revenue-raising measures. To continue the tariff at the present rate presented an "inescapable obstacle" to the funding of the Intercolonial.[22] Emerging from the *Trent* Affair of December 1861 and the consequent fears of future American aggression against British North America, the second measure concerned the passage of a bill which would reorganize and upgrade the colony's militia. As the civil war to the south escalated, the fate of the militia came increasingly to be seen as the touchstone for imperial-colonial relations.[23]

In part, because of these complicating factors, Newcastle realized that he would have to go beyond the government in his search for capital. Reflecting the changing nature of imperial-colonial financial relations occasioned by the process of decolonization, the colonial secretary actively sought assistance from private financiers in London. He arranged meetings with the Barings, Glyn, Mills and other wealthy financiers on the subject of the Intercolonial, a transcontinental telegraph and the purchase of the Hudson's Bay Company. While by May 1862 nothing had been firmly decided, prospects for some degree of assistance seemed possible in all three areas.[24]

In these matters, Edward Watkin,[25] appointed by the Grand Trunk as its supervising manager in the summer of 1861, became Newcastle's chief intermediary between the city of London and the Colonial Office.[26] An indefatigable promoter and an experienced railway manager, Watkin believed that Intercolonial construction and westward expansion were absolutely necessary to resuscitate the Grand Trunk.[27] In addition to lobbying in London to effect the ends shared by Newcastle and himself, Watkin also attempted to create a favourable structure in British North America. While this, the second component for the resolution of the Grand Trunk's financial troubles, required intense arm-twisting in the Maritime provinces, Watkin's main activity focussed on Upper Canada. He initiated negotiations for the fusion of the Grand Trunk with the Great Western and the Buffalo and Lake Huron railways in order to cut competitive costs, rationalize administration and create a unified road to join with the projected Intercolonial in the east. After hiring the Great Western's general manager and following tense discussions with the Great Western's London board, he approached the John A. Macdonald–G.-E. Cartier government with an omnibus bill for the refinancing and reorganizing of Upper Canada's railway system.[28]

Imperial interests pressured the Macdonald-Cartier government throughout the spring 1862 parliamentary session. As Watkin informed Baring: "Keep poking every one up. It is absolutely necessary." And so they did. Baring and Glyn wrote individual letters to Cartier and Galt urging them to see to the passage of the railway measure. Newcastle, through the governor general, Lord Monck, stressed the importance of lowering tariffs and passing a satisfactory militia bill if Canada desired any future substantial imperial aid. Imperial hopes rested on the effective co-operation of loyal colonial collaborators. "But, after all," Watkin wrote, "all depends upon the Ministry. If they will stand true—really true—to what they have promised we shall, I hope, succeed...."[29]

The government did permit the Grand Trunk fusion bill to be introduced—albeit by a private member little schooled in the complexities of the issue—and narrowly missed being defeated on second reading. Galt did bring down a budget which promised some movement in the direction of lower customs and the introduction of an alternative revenue-raising method, the stamp tax. But the House never voted on it. Before it could, the government was defeated on its Militia Bill, introduced by the co-leader, John A. Macdonald, and defended by him despite his, according to Lord Monck, continual state of "drunkenness."[30]

The Macdonald-Cartier government fell in May 1862 for a number of reasons. From the perspective of this paper, however, the most fascinating factor concerns that government's too close public relationship to certain imperial interests. Even the Bank of Upper Canada waged a strong campaign against the fusion bill because it provided imperial financiers with guarantees for Grand Trunk payments ranking ahead of those granted the beleaguered bank.[31] As spokesmen and apologists for the Grand Trunk, and by extension for private British capitalists led by the government's official London financial agents, Glyn and Baring, the Macdonald-Cartier ministry had in the eyes of many Canadian politicians and government critics lost all ability to act independently. "The unpopularity and prejudice [towards the Grand Trunk] I wrote to you about before, have in no way abated," Rose privately informed Baring. "The old men [of the defeated government] were both powerless, and suspected by reason of their antecedents."[32] The government's half-hearted attempts to push the railway, militia and budget legislation suggests that it was only too well aware of this difficulty and, in an ineffectual manner, was attempting to back away from too close a public association with imperial interests. While its temerity in this respect succeeded in angering imperial spokesmen, it did little to convince wavering colonial politicians.

Initial reaction by imperial authorities to this crisis in the collaborative process set the context for the two-year rule by John Sandfield Macdonald and his supporters. Three points characterized the imperial perspective. In the first place, the imperial-colonial agenda was set in stone. This meant that any tampering, adjustments or new advice were neither desired nor happily heeded. The imperial centre expected the new ministry to complete existing plans concerning the Grand Trunk, the Intercolonial, the militia and the tariff. Anything less would be disloyal. Sandfield's government seemed to have little room to manoeuvre at this level.[33]

Secondly—and this, when put in the context of the general literature on imperial-colonial collaboration, seems an almost classic perspective—imperial representatives argued that the previous mediators had suffered defeat due to inefficient, sloppy and corrupt administration. The advent of fresh faces provided an opportunity for systematic administrative reform. Such reform, of course, could be carried out only under the aegis of an experienced British bureaucrat appointed by the Colonial Office. The modernization of especially the fiscal system would, it was thought, preclude future disruption to the collaborative structure.[34]

Finally, in what again appears to have been a classic manoeuvre, the imperial centre did not put all of its eggs in the new government's basket. Albeit piqued at the old government's inefficiency and trade policy, imperial representatives nevertheless continued to listen to and cultivate the political opposition throughout Sandfield's tenure as colonial leader. This tactic, made even more appealing due to the precarious balance of power that existed between the various political parties, was nicely compatible with the push for administrative reform. Modernization, by preventing the recurrence of the past and lamentable "system of abuse," would make the re-emergence of the old and known collaborators a welcome possibility.[35]

For their part the old ministerialists and their supporters quickly assured the Colonial Office and the London financiers that this was only a temporary setback, and that they, the new opposition, would ensure that the current government carried out imperial desires. In order to temper any possible enthusiasm on the part of imperial authorities for change, these colonial confidantes presented collective character assassinations of the incoming ministry. Not only were they drawn from "the extreme liberal ranks," John Rose, one of the more influential of the confidantes, wrote, but they were on the average "very inferior—scarcely respectable." On the basis of such information the Duke of Newcastle, Thomas Baring and G. C. Glyn wrote despondently about the future of their various interrelated projects.[36] The J. S. Macdonald ministries were damned and nearly discounted before they had had time to warm the seats of power.

Despite being constrained by a slim margin of support in the local assembly, by a distinctly *a priori* unfriendliness on the part of imperial authorities and London financiers, and by enormous financial problems bequeathed by their predecessors, Macdonald and a number of his key ministers gradually initiated a program of fiscal and administrative reform. This program not only directly challenged control of the imperial agenda but, had it been allowed to run its intended course, would have undermined the central basis of imperial plans. By focussing on five interrelated key issues—the militia, general economic and financial policy, the Grand Trunk, the Intercolonial and administrative reform—we can elucidate the nature of that challenge, examine the imperial reaction to it, and more clearly define the role of collaborators within the process of decolonization.

Reform of the militia bulked large in imperial calculations.[37] Gladstone's government did not wish to incur heavy liabilities for the defence of British North America. At the same time, from reasons of pride as well as from a reluctance to permit the United States to aggrandize itself at the expense of Great Britain, the British government was determined that the colonies should have adequate protection. From the outset, Newcastle and to a lesser extent Monck believed that J. S. Macdonald could not be trusted in this matter. Angered by the colony's continued commitment to the "delusion" of a voluntary militia and dismissing as insignificant the increase in appropriation from $84,000 to $250,000 for its maintenance, Newcastle issued a sharply written despatch highly critical of the new ministry's defence policy.[38]

Macdonald's reply struck at the nub of the collaborative process. As Ronald Robinson has pointed out, "two interlocking sets of linkages...made up the collaborative mechanism." One related to imperial desires, the second to local needs and attitudes. The nature of the latter determined to a great extent the degree of success possible in realizing imperial ends. It was the collaborator's job to bring the two sectors together. If, for whatever reasons, the mediating group failed to accomplish this, the imperial government was left stranded.[39] For two reasons Macdonald felt that it was impossible to marry imperial ends and local attitudes on the militia matter. First, he pointed out, "military tastes and aspirations have not been cherished by our people"—a fact reconfirmed by the recent elections. Secondly, the public demanded a program of strict economy in government expenditure. The elected representatives, he argued, were the only proper judges as to the content of that program. The electorate would not stand for the imposition of direct taxes and especially not for the purpose of military spending. Therefore, Macdonald concluded, our hands are tied. "Popular liberties are only safe when the actions [sic] of the people restrains and guides the policies of those who are invested with the power of directing the affairs of the Country."[40] Reports from Monck and other confidantes asserting that the public, contrary to Macdonald's perception, was "in advance" of the government in military matters only intensified imperial frustration.[41] Far from acting as loyal mediators, the Sandfield Macdonald government seemed to be obstinately blocking the possibility of genuine rapprochement.

The government's economic and fiscal policy seemed to further confirm imperial preconceptions. William Howland, the new finance minister, ignored Galt's promises of lower tariffs and instead maintained high duties, arguing that revenue requirements dictated such a policy.[42] Of more importance, he launched an initiative, which his successor Luther Holton would follow up, aimed at the heart of the old collaborative system. He explored, albeit tentatively, the possibility of restructuring the management of the provincial account in England. This "person of very small calibre," John Rose caustically warned Baring, is indulging in the "Utopian notion" of being "independent" of London financiers. In the end Howland did not break away from Glyn and Baring but he did succeed in forcing the London agents to lower their transaction costs for certain sectors of provincial business.[43]

The desire to dismantle parts of the existing collaborative mechanism underlay the ministry's actions concerning railway development. The new government refused to reintroduce the fusion bill on which Watkin had worked for the past eight months, and it very nearly delayed taking any action on the financial reorganization desired by the Grand Trunk. Only a letter presented by Thomas Galt, Alexander Galt's brother and a lawyer for the Grand Trunk's London investors, stating that in the absence of such a measure the London financiers would immediately foreclose on their loans and then close the road, convinced a reluctant cabinet to proceed.[44] The final straw proved to be the government's decision in July to revoke an arbitration process set up by its predecessor for determining the amount owed by the government to the Grand Trunk for postal deliveries. Watkin's angry plea that the whole financial reorganization was predicated on receiving swift and adequate payment for these deliveries fell on deaf ears.[45] No longer did the Grand Trunk and, through it, the London financiers, enjoy a close and cozy relationship with the colonial government. The collaborative structure built up over the past decade was under attack.

The intensification of Grand Trunk difficulties made a resolution of the Intercolonial railway matter all the more acute. Although in September 1862 Canadian delegates agreed with Maritime representatives on a plan for financing the road, the plan, when made public, elicited strong adverse comment both from within J. S. Macdonald's party and from the general Canadian electorate.[46] This internal pressure, coupled with information received from England to the effect that Newcastle and much of his government were strongly supportive of the Intercolonial idea, stiffened the Canadian government's resolve to bargain "for the best possible Canadian terms." Before sending Louis V. Sicotte and Howland to London for further discussions on the Intercolonial, Macdonald, through Watkin, made the Canadian bargaining position known to the imperial authorities. Unless some plan for westward expansion was set in motion, the Canadian delegates would not be able to support the Intercolonial scheme.[47]

Both Newcastle and his predecessor as colonial secretary, Edward Bulwer-Lytton, strongly favoured westward expansion. In fact, the Duke had already been attempting to convince the Hudson's Bay Company to free up a right of way for a road and telegraph line to British Columbia and to attract funding from London to carry out this project.[48] When news of Canada's demands reached Newcastle, he redoubled his pressure on London financiers for support. While Glyn and several others of lesser stature were willing, Thomas Baring, increasingly wary of investing large sums into Canadian developmental projects, refused.[49]

Under the pressure of Canadian demands, the informal alliance forged during decolonization between London financiers and the Colonial Office began to break down. Newcastle had few options left open to him. The recent debate on the militia matter convinced him that the sending of an official publishable despatch to Canada would be counter-productive. Since the Canadian delegates made it clear that they would not assent to any projects which required an increase in local taxes, Newcastle was left with the prospect of convincing Gladstone to grant an imperial guarantee for the western telegraph project in order to effect a resolution of the Intercolonial scheme.[50] This he despaired of achieving, and in late December 1862 he informed Howland and Sicotte, the Canadian representatives, that such aid would not be forthcoming. The Canadians withdrew from the discussions and after issuing a clumsy public statement criticizing Gladstone's sinking fund requirements—thus making this the pretext for their withdrawal—they returned home, leaving the Intercolonial project in disarray.[51]

As imperial frustrations intensified, Newcastle and Monck looked more and more to the panacea of administrative and fiscal reform as the means for achieving their several objectives. "I am sure," Monck wrote Newcastle, "that this [the lack of such reform] lies at the very root of our difficulties."[52] He believed that proper restructuring would result in a fiscal surplus even without the introduction of new taxes.[53] Newcastle agreed and merely awaited an official colonial request to send over a properly qualified Englishman to conduct the review.[54] He waited in vain. The Macdonald government, in this as in other matters, had its own agenda. Under Macdonald's skillful management, the process of administrative reform cut more deeply than Newcastle ever intended.

In late November Macdonald set up a commission to investigate the financial and departmental workings of past governments and, despite Monck's belief that it would be worse than useless if no Englishman sat on it, three resident Canadians conducted the investigation. Much to the discomfort of imperial interests and the "loyal" opposition, the commission conducted an exhaustive series of public hearings between December 1862 and April 1863. The collected evidence implicated the J. A. Macdonald-Cartier government, the Bank of Upper Canada, the Grand Trunk Railway and the Barings and Glyn, Mills in the spending of public money without proper public authorization.[55] For five months, Sandfield Macdonald's government shrewdly kept the sometimes shady and questionable activities of these central elements of the old collaborative alliance before the Canadian public.[56] It had the desired effect. In the end, this extended display of dirty linen saved Macdonald's political skin.

By January 1863 Newcastle was nothing short of furious at what he perceived to be the obstructionist activities of the Canadian ministry. Frantically, he looked for some means of applying effective pressure. Disregarding his previous strictures to Monck to stay clear of involvement in the colonial legislative process, he advised the governor general to stop Macdonald from introducing any negative Intercolonial bill in the forthcoming legislative session. Feeling that the Canadians had dealt with imperial interests in a "shabby" and even "treasonous" manner, he openly hoped for their swift defeat.[57] Doubtless aware of Newcastle's displeasure, the "loyal" opposition exerted unremitting pressure on the ministry and carried a vote of non-confidence in early May.

Clearly, Newcastle wanted Monck to invite the old collaborationists to form a new government.[58] Instead, the governor general gave Macdonald the opportunity to form a new government and, when he succeeded, granted him an immediate dissolution. This angered both the Duke of Newcastle and the old collaborationists, who argued that favouring a defeated premier over a "loyal" opposition was neither fair nor constitutional.[59] Monck's action in this regard can be understood only in the context of the strong feeling directed against the old collaborationists by the general public on account of the commission's persistent revelations. The governor general continued to hope for administrative and fiscal reform and believed that this could be accomplished only by a government which had not been associated with the past "abuses."[60] In this instance, Monck's definition of imperial priorities differed from that of his immediate supervisor, the Duke of Newcastle, and led to the continuance in power of what Newcastle had already labelled as a "treasonous"—and would soon term a "corruptly pro-American"—administration.[61]

In fact the new coalition engineered by Sandfield Macdonald gave Newcastle little reason for hope. Only with reference to militia matters did that government enact legislation consistent with Newcastle's desires.[62] The premier of New Brunswick correctly reported that the new group was even more opposed to the Intercolonial than the old.[63] Believing that his best chance was to play on Upper Canada's desire for westward expansion, Newcastle strove to bring the Hudson's Bay Company and London financiers together to work out a practicable plan for a telegraph and road to British Columbia. With Watkin's assistance, such an arrangement seemed to be in place by late June.[64] The colonial secretary then used it as a carrot, warning the Canadian leaders that imperial support for westward expansion was directly dependent on their honouring their eastern, that is their Intercolonial, obligations.[65] On the matter of westward development the Canadians, however, demanded more imperial support than Newcastle could provide. And on the matter of eastward linkage, the best the Canadians offered was the underwriting of a survey for the Intercolonial.[66]

Despite its fragile balance of power in the local legislature, Macdonald's second ministry deepened its assault on central components of the old collaborative structure. Luther Holton, the new finance minister, took the lead in this campaign.[67] As early as 1860 he had expressed disgust at the machinations carried out between the Macdonald-Cartier Government, the Grand Trunk, the Bank of Upper Canada and the province's London financial agents. The findings of the recent commission only strengthened his resolve to sever old relationships and enter "upon a new Era."[68] An analysis of his attempts to do so sheds light on both the desired and possible extent of human agency at the periphery during the movement from formal to informal empire.

Holton, suspicious of the extent of the demand, resisted pressure from the Grand Trunk for an immediate settlement of the postal payments.[69] Incensed, Watkin accused Holton and the government of the "wrongful detention of the Company's property." Holton responded by denying Watkin, the Grand Trunk's chief Canadian administrator, the right of direct communications with the government, pending receipt of a written apology.[70] The gloves were off. Local imperial confidantes labelled this a "wanton and cruel exercise of official despotism."[71] The Grand Trunk responded by publicly pressuring local politicians to unseat Macdonald's ministry. In London, Grand Trunk sympathizers circulated rumours concerning the government's avowed anti-railway policy, thus helping to precipitate a fall in the value of Canadian securities.[72]

Working within this environment, Holton conceived and began to implement a comprehensive policy concerning imperial-colonial financial and economic relations. In a carefully prepared pre-budget statement, he promised to move directly towards the balancing of expenditures and incomes by cutting the former and increasing the latter through stamp taxes, transferring some provincial expenditures to local accounts and increasing canal tolls. At the same time, he promised a reduction in overall import duties. It was a budget seemingly consistent with the demands of London financiers and imperial spokesmen. Even the Grand Trunk railway stood to benefit from increased traffic due to the imposition of duties on canal trade. It helped give the Macdonald government credibility in at least some imperial circles and to that extent tended to offset the hostility of the old collaborationist elements in London, the Colonial Office and the colony.

In one revealing respect, however, Holton's pre-budget statements promised imperial interests more than he was prepared to deliver. As he confided to George Brown, "I think any very <u>violent changes</u> in our Customs tariff should be avoided." His reluctance did not stem from his desire to raise revenue—in fact he believed that most of the required additional income would come from proposed stamp duties. Rather he feared that lowering the tariff would "raise a storm of enraged special interests about our heads." This fear reflected the precarious legislative advantage held by the Macdonald government. It also suggests that the high duties commanded significant support from an important local sector determined to maintain the tariff's protective characteristics. From the imperial perspective, these structural factors alone made the possibilities for effective collaboration extremely difficult. To offset them would require not simply a change of government but also, as imperial strategists gradually came to understand, the implementation of an incentive package designed to neutralize local vested interests.[73]

The fact that Holton's policy was not simply shaped by these constraining influences added urgency to imperial calculations. From Holton's vantage point, the budget was also and most importantly designed to move the colonial government the first step along the path of disentangling itself from unequal economic and financial relations with British capitalists. The more self-sufficient in a financial sense the Canadas could become, the easier it would be to realize this objective.

The removal of the government's main account from the Bank of Upper Canada to the Bank of Montreal represented the second step. An institution which had helped prop up governments in the 1850s, the Bank of Upper Canada was itself in need of government assistance in the 1860s. It depended on government advances in order to conduct its normal business. Holton saw this situation as untenable. The locking up of government capital in the bank made him all the more dependent on Glyn and Baring for advances to meet interest payments. His removal of the account, therefore, signified more than political revenge on the ailing fiscal ally of the old collaborationists. By transferring the account to the larger and solvent Bank of Montreal, Holton freed up government capital and provided the colony with a reliable local, as opposed to imperial, source for official borrowings. This point stood at the centre of the rationale for transfer. As Holton informed Brown, "I have a great horror of going to Glyn and Barings in [the guise of?] paupers again." The strengthening of local financial arrangements enabled him to float a needed loan locally, cancel a planned trip to negotiate with the agents in England and, Holton believed, put the colony in a stronger position to "dictate" future terms.[74]

Buoyed by these arrangements, Holton addressed a candid letter to the financial agents regarding the Grand Trunk's political activity. After outlining the extent of colonial aid to that enterprise, he came directly to the point: as "politicians...and as patriots we deprecate the introduction of such an element [political meddling] into our political contests." As for the anti-government attacks in London, Holton averred that it was incumbent on the financial agents and "other friends of Canada in England...to counteract these sinister efforts by all available and legitimate means." It was a nice turning of the screw. Glyn and Baring were being asked to defend publicly a government which, according to their local agents, was actively undermining their substantial colonial investments.[75]

More than rhetoric was at stake. The "diplomatic drapery" of Holton's official correspondence with the London agents only imperfectly masked a new system in the making.[76] Budget reform and the transferal of the government account provided the foundation for that system. A new Audit Act, worked out with the expert assistance of the government's auditor, John Langton, was drafted to deal with the problems revealed by the commission of inquiry.[77] No more would it be possible, Holton informed the London agents, to make unauthorized advances to privileged institutions.[78] Holton fervently believed that, taken together, fiscal prudence, tight audit control and sound local financial arrangements would enable the colony to enter into "ulterior arrangements in England" and to be, fiscally, in "a position of independence of Glyns."[79]

For Holton, this fiscal disengagement represented the *sine qua non* of decolonization. It logically preceded all other forms of independence. Matters of political devolution and territorial expansion as sanctioned by the imperial agenda were of secondary importance to him. In fact, to the extent that those programs threatened to increase local costs, they were incompatible with his primary objective. It is insufficient, therefore, to see Holton and the ministry he represented as simple nay-sayers, characterized by "no policies, no ideas, no principles of action" and by "abject failures."[80] Even during the first administration, it will be recalled, Howland and Sandfield Macdonald had argued for and attempted to attain fiscal independence. In this respect Holton was simply more comprehensive and aggressive. The push for fiscal autonomy struck at the heart of the collaborationist system put in place by the official imperial proponents of decolonization. As such, the initiative, advanced during a period of great internal stress and international crisis, stands as an early example of Canadian fiscal and economic nationalism.

Somewhat ironically, the Macdonald government's central objective also led them to pursue a course of reform parallel to that desired by the imperial centre. Thus their attempts to "modernize" the accounting and administrative system of the provincial government undermined the old collaborative structure while, at the same time, helped put into place a more efficient and stable system capable of dealing with the imperial goals of territorial expansion and political devolution. These initiatives also, and from the imperial perspective perhaps most importantly, laid the foundations for an administrative system capable of dealing safely and efficiently with continued British capital investments.

For these reasons it is insufficient to claim that following Macdonald's resignation in March 1864—due to his ministry's final inability to command assembly support—events swept "away such negative politicians."[81] Even though J. A. Macdonald, Cartier and Galt returned to power, they could no longer simply return to the old ways. The fact that the comprehensive Audit Act was one of the first bills introduced into the new assembly symbolizes the nature of the change. Not only were Galt's relations with the financial agents more subject to "Parliamentary sanctions," but he was also on occasion able to use the powerful Bank of Montreal as a bargaining tool in negotiations with the government's London agents.[82] While this was far from all that Holton desired, it at least represented a step in the direction of fiscal autonomy and professional administrative practice.

The ultimate significance of the John Sandfield Macdonald ministries, however, can be best appreciated within the context of literature which argues that the process of collaboration is the key to understanding core-periphery or imperial-colonial relations. Most such studies of collaboration focus on the interaction between white Europeans and natives in Africa, Asia or Latin America.[83] This study of the significance of collaboration within the context of the transition from formal to informal empire in a white settlement colony helps to provide some balance to that emphasis. It is also a useful corrective to those world-system analysts such as Emmanuel Wallerstein who tend to discount the possibilities for local autonomy at the periphery.[84] Rather than assuming the dominance of external forces, a focus on the process of collaboration permits the depiction of complex interaction between discrete colonial and imperial sectors. It also permits the investigation of local rivalries and the assessment of local policies and motivations. Finally, it allows one to assess the possibilities for human agency at the periphery.

Certainly this particular study suggests that the phrase "imperial-colonial relations" needs refinement in order for it to have any historical utility. Interest groups abounded at the periphery and at the centre. While it might be argued that these interests were simply fragments of a similar socio-economic class, the divisions between them in terms of policy and action were nevertheless significant. To assume homogeneity at either the centre or periphery or, indeed, across the two, is to mask a much more complex historical context. Until one attempts to chart that reality, one can have no means of knowing the point at which some larger category such as class or, somewhat more problematically, core and periphery have any analytical validity.

In terms of class background and interest, for example, the personnel of the J. S. Macdonald ministries did not differ appreciably from that of the old collaborationists. Yet through political exigencies these men had more often than not found themselves on the outside of colonial politics looking in. This freedom from past entanglements allowed them to push for greater local autonomy than could their predecessors. While Galt stood up to and defied certain powerful sectors at the imperial center by raising tariffs, he did so at least in part in order to protect other equally powerful imperial interests. Similarly, when he refused to provide any further local aid to Glyn and Baring, he declined only because he had exhausted all possible legal and, as the commission of inquiry revealed, some not so legal alternatives. It is not surprising that the interlocking economic and political structure which, with the aid of imperial concerns, Galt, Cartier and J. A. Macdonald had fashioned became an object of attack. To carve out a position of local power and independence for themselves, the new ministers believed that the structure had to be at the very least remodelled, if not completely dismantled. The pursuit of local political control led them, somewhat naturally, to adopt a more independent or even nationalist stance *vis-à-vis* imperial dictates.[85] This did not mean completely ignoring London politicians and financiers. Holton and J. S. Macdonald were, after all, good bourgeois politicians. Rather it meant seeking different arrangements with those imperial politicians and new agreements with, if possible, different financiers. Greater local fiscal autonomy facilitated a stronger bargaining position from which to attain these ends. The dynamic of local political conflict within a common socio-economic class went far towards setting the extent of human agency at the periphery.

All of this might have limited historical interest except for the fact that competition for local political control had a profound impact on imperial calculations. Despite a fragile legislative base, the Sandfield Macdonald ministries stood up to and threatened the realization of imperial ends. It is true that after two brief years of troubled tenure that government was forever defeated. But the imperial agenda did not emerge unscathed. The interaction recounted here forced imperial authorities and London financiers to meet head-on the problems of interacting with independently minded local élites. Faced with this challenge, prominent London financiers like Baring and Glyn backed off from large direct investment in Canada. This put added pressure on the imperial government to make up the difference.

As Robinson has commented, "the transition from one phase of imperialism to the next was governed by the need to reconstruct and uphold a collaborative system that was breaking down." This, he pointed out, referring to Afro-Asian peripheries, often required greater intervention on the part of the imperial centre, sometimes even leading to takeover.[86] The movement from formal to informal empire in white settlement colonies was, however, a somewhat more nuanced process. The activities of the J. S. Macdonald governments certainly led to a breakdown of the existing collaborative structure. This in turn led to a change in the conditions which had been shaping actions in imperial-colonial relations for the past decade. These changed conditions forced the imperial center to intervene more directly than it had been willing to do in the recent past. In this case, however, the intervention was of a fiscal, not a military or political, sort. To prevent the re-emergence of a non-collaborative group, Britain replaced colonial financial guarantees for infrastructural development with formal imperial guarantees. The John Sandfield Macdonald ministries forced the imperial government to intervene and up the ante in order to ensure that political control would devolve into the hands of loyal Canadian leaders.

Even in white settlement colonies the cost of ensuring loyal collaboration was considerable: by 1873 the guarantees totalled £8 million.[87] If the costs were high, so, for some, were the rewards. The colonial élite obtained access to a greater capital pool. The imperial government had at least forestalled the United States from taking over part of British North America. And the loyal collaborationists, in power for much of the quarter century following Confederation, ensured that Glyn and Baring continued to enjoy the lucrative position of Canada's London fiscal agent. Not until after John A. Macdonald's death in 1891 did the Bank of Montreal, despite repeated attempts, finally assume that role.[88]

1 The best published accounts are by Bruce Hodgins; see his *John Sandfield Macdonald* (Toronto, 1971), 56–74; "John Sandfield Macdonald and the Crisis of 1863", in Canadian Historical Association, *Historical Papers* (1965), 30–45; "John Sandfield Macdonald", in J. M. S. Careless, ed., *The Pre-Confederation Premiers* (Toronto, 1980), 246–314. For typical negative treatments see D. G. Creighton, *The Road to Confederation: The Emergence of Canada, 1863–1867* (Toronto, 1964); W. L. Morton, *The Critical Years: The Union of British North America, 1857–1873* (Toronto, 1964). The best unpublished analysis can be found in Donald Roman, "The Contribution of Imperial Guarantees for Colonial Railroad Loans to the Consolidation of British North America, 1847–65" (Ph.D. diss., Oxford University, 1978).

2 On the general nature of collaboration see Ronald Robinson, "Non-European Foundations of European Imperialism: Sketch for a Theory of Collaboration", in R. Owen and B. Sutcliffe, eds., *Studies in the Theory of Imperialism* (London, 1972), 117–42; Robin W. Winks, "On Decolonization and Informal Empire", *American Historical Review* 81 (1976), 540–56.

3 Winks, 552.

4 Bruce Andrews, "The Political Economy of World Capitalism: Theory and Practice", *International Organization* 36 (1982), 159, fn. 41.

5 Philip Goldring, "Province and Nation: Problems of Imperial Rule in Lower Canada, 1820–1841", *Journal of Imperial and Commonwealth History* 9 (1980), 38–56; W. G. Ormsby, *The Emergence of the Federal Concept in Canada, 1839–1845* (Toronto, 1969); J. M. S. Careless, *The Union of the Canadas: The Growth of Canadian Institutions, 1841–57* (Toronto, 1967); G. N. Tucker, *The Canadian Commercial Revolution, 1845–51* (New Haven, 1936).

6 Roman, ch. 1–2.

7 On the investment process see A. L. H. Jenks, *The Migration of British Capital to 1875*, 2nd ed. (London, 1963); Stanley Chapman, *The Rise of Merchant Banking* (London, 1984); D. McCalla, "Peter Buchanan, London Agent for the Great Western Railway of Canada", in D. MacMillan, ed., *Canadian Business History* (Toronto, 1972), 197–216; Peter Baskerville, "Americans in Britain's Backyard: The Railway Era in Upper Canada, 1850–1880", *Business History Review* 55 (1981), 314–36.

8 M. L. Magill, "J. H. Dunn and the Bankers", in J. K. Johnson, ed., *Historical Essays on Upper Canada* (Toronto, 1975), 194–216; Michael Piva, "The Canadian Public Debt, 1848–1856", paper presented to the Canadian Historical Association, Montreal, June 1980; Peter Baskerville, "The Pet Bank, the Local State and the Imperial Centre, 1850–1864", *Journal of Canadian Studies* 20 (1985), 22–45.

9 Ged Martin, "Launching Canadian Confederation: Means to Ends, 1836–1864", *Historical Journal* 27 (1984), 575–602; Bruce A. Knox, "Conservative Imperialism 1858–1874: Bulwer-Lytton, Lord Carnarvon, and Canadian Confederation", *International History Review* 6 (1984), 333–56.

10 Martin, 593; Knox, 341.

11 A. Shortt, "The Introduction of the Decimal System", *Journal of the Canadian Bankers' Association* 11 (1903–04), 13–30.

12 Andy Den Otter, "Alexander Galt, the 1859 Tariff and Canadian Economic Nationalism", *Canadian Historical Review* [hereafter *CHR*] 63 (1982), 151–52, fn. 3, provides a useful introduction to the relevant literature. D. F. Barnett, "The Galt Tariff: Incidental or Effective Protection", *Canadian Journal of Economics* 9 (1976), 389–407.

13 See O. D. Skelton, *Life and Times of Sir Alexander Tilloch Galt*, ed. by G. MacLean (Toronto, 1966), 139.

14 For the financial problems of the railways, municipalities and banks and their impact on the government, see A. W. Currie, *The Grand Trunk Railway* (Toronto, 1957); J. A. Faucher, *Histoire économique et unité canadienne* (Montreal, 1970) and his "Some Aspects of the Financial Difficulties of the Province of Canada", *Canadian Journal of Economics and Political Science* 26 (1960), 617–24; Baskerville, "The Pet Bank".

15 Fifty-six percent of incoming revenue went towards interest payments in 1857. By 1859 the proportion had dropped to 47 percent, which was still considerably higher than that of any year prior to 1857. Calculated from data in Canada [United Province], Legislative Assembly, *Sessional Papers 1860*, no. 3; …*1863*, nos. 6, 10. For figures prior to 1857, see Piva, tab. 1.

16 For Newcastle's reaction see National Archives of Canada [hereafter NAC], MG 24–D–21, Baring Bros. and Co. (London, Eng.), House Correspondence 1850–98 [hereafter Baring Papers], mfm. A834, A. T. Galt to Thomas Baring, 12 Nov. 1859 (private); NAC, MG 24–A–2, Ellice Family, Ellice-Rose Correspondence 1857–77 [hereafter Ellice Papers], mfm. C4645, Edward Ellice to Sir George Grey, 25 Nov. 1861.

17 For the nature of their investments see Baskerville, "The Pet Bank". Faucher, "Some Aspects", 620, claims that Glyn, Mills supported the tariff but offers no direct evidence for this. Neither George Carr Glyn nor Baring referred to it in their surviving correspondence to Galt and other Canadians. They did, however, complain when Galt took the tolls off the St. Lawrence canals in 1860, claiming that this would interfere "injuriously" with Grand Trunk traffic: Baring Papers, mfm. A834, Galt to Baring, 18 May 1860 (private); NAC, MG 24–D–36, Glyn Mills and Co. (London, Eng.) [hereafter Glyn Mills Papers], Letterbooks 1848–66 [hereafter LB], mfm. A540, Glyn to Galt, 2 June 1860.

18 Sheffield industrialists had presented a memorial against the tariff to the Colonial Secretary who had forwarded it to Canada; Den Otter, 175.

19 By mid 1860 the railway owed the Barings and Glyn, Mills some $2.5 million. In addition the railway owed considerable sums to both the Canadian government and the Bank of Upper Canada. See Peter Baskerville, ed. and comp., *The Bank of Upper Canada, A Collection of Documents* (Toronto, 1987), cv–cxxvii.

20 Roman, ch. 4.

21 NAC, MG 24–A–34, Henry Clinton, 5th Duke of Newcastle, Secretary of State for the Colonies [hereafter Newcastle Papers], Letterbooks 1859–64 [hereafter LB], mfm. A307, Newcastle to Lieutenant Governor [New Brunswick] Arthur Gordon, 5 Apr. 1862 (private); Newcastle to Governor General [Canada] Charles Monck, 12 Apr. 1862.

22 Ibid., Newcastle to Monck, 12 Apr. 1862 (private); Newcastle Papers, Correspondence 1849–64 [hereafter Corr.], mfm. A308, Monck to Newcastle, 16 May 1862 (private).

23 C. P. Stacey, *Canada and the British Army, 1846–1871* (Toronto, 1963), 117–79.

24 Baring Papers, mfm. C1369, J. Nelson to Baring, 22 June 1861; Newcastle Papers, LB, mfm. A307, Newcastle to Lord Palmerston, 11 Nov. 1861; [Great Britain, Parliament,] *British Parliamentary Papers: Colonies, Canada* [hereafter *BPP*], XXV, *Correspondence and Other Papers Relating to the Affairs of Canada, 1864–1866* (Shannon, Eire, 1969), 193–95.

25 Edward Watkin was experienced in British railway administration and British policies.

26 For an indication of Watkin's and Newcastle's joint activities see NAC, MG 24–E–17, Sir
    Edward William Watkin, Correspondence 1856–96 [hereafter Watkin Papers], vol. 1,
    passim; NAC, RG 30, Canadian National Railways [hereafter CNR Papers], vol. 10190,
    item 80, Under-Secretary Rogers [Newcastle's] to Baring, 13 Sep. 1862; Baring Papers,
    mfm. C1369, Watkin to Baring, [late in] Oct. 1862 (private); NAC, RG 1–E–7, Canada,
    Executive Council, State Records, Submissions to Council 1841–67 [hereafter Canada,
    Submissions], vol. 62, Watkin to Newcastle, 17 Dec. 1862 enclosed in 18 Feb. 1864;
    Newcastle Papers, LB, mfm. A307, Newcastle to Watkin, 15 June 1863; Newcastle to
    Monck, 20 June 1863; Ellice Papers, mfm. C4646, Ellice to John Rose, 24 June 1863
    (private).
27 Baring Papers, mfm. C1369, Watkin to Baring, [late in] Oct. 1862 (private).
28 The fusion negotiations can be traced in Hamilton (Ont.) Public Library, Central Branch,
    Archives and Special Collections, John Young 1860–62 [hereafter Young Papers],
    Thomas Reynolds to Young, 18 Sep. 1861; Richard Juson to Young, 7 Oct. 1861; 4, 23 Jan.
    1862; 22 Feb. 1862; Baring Papers, vol. 3, F. Head [President, G.W.R.] to Baring, 30 Jan.
    1862; mfm. C1369, Watkin to Baring, 5 Apr. 1862; CNR Papers, vol. 7, file 1660; NAC,
    MG 26–A, Sir John Alexander Macdonald, Political Papers, Correspondence Received
    [hereafter J. A. Macdonald Papers], vol. 297, C. J. Brydges to Macdonald, 2 May 1862
    (private).
29 Baring Papers, mfm. C1369, Watkin to Baring, 28 March 1862 (private) [quotation from
    here]; Newcastle Papers, LB, mfm. A307, Newcastle to Monck, 12 Apr. 1862 (private);
    Corr., mfm. A308, Monck to Newcastle, 16 May 1862 (private).
30 Glyn Mills Paper, Corr., mfm. A545, T. Galt to Glyn, 23 May, 21 June 1862; Newcastle
    Papers, Corr., mfm. A308, Monck to Newcastle, 16 May 1862 (private).
31 Baring Papers, vol. 3, Rose to Baring, 23 May 1862 (private); "Provincial Parliament" and
    "Affairs at Quebec", *Globe* (Toronto), 2 June 1862, 1, 2.
32 Baring Papers, vol. 3, Rose to Baring, 23 May 1862 (private); see also Glyn Mills Papers,
    Corr., mfm. A545, T. Galt to Glyn, 23 May, 21 June 1862.
33 Newcastle Papers, LB, mfm. A307, Newcastle to Monck, 26 July 1862.
34 Baring Papers, mfm. C1369, Rose to Baring, 23 May 1862 (private); Ellice Papers, mfm.
    C4645, Rose to Ellice, 23 May 1862 (private); Newcastle Papers, Corr., mfm. A308,
    Monck to Newcastle, 29, 30 May 1862 (private).
35 Newcastle Papers, Corr., mfm. A308, Monck to Newcastle, 30 May 1862 (private).
36 Baring Papers, mfm. C1369, Rose to Baring, 23 May 1862 (private); C1438, Baring to
    Watkin, 5 June 1862; Ellice Papers, mfm. C4645, Rose to Ellice, 23 May 1862; NAC, MG
    24–B–30–I, John Sandfield Macdonald, Personal and Political Correspondence [hereafter
    Sandfield Macdonald Papers], Watkin to J. S. Macdonald, 28 June 1862 (private); Glyn
    Mills Papers, LB, mfm. A540, Glyn to T. Galt, 4 June 1862.
37 Stacey, 136–46.
38 Newcastle Papers, LB, mfm. A307, Newcastle to Monck, 14 June [quotation from here],
    26 July, 22 Aug. 1862 (private); Corr., mfm. A308, Monck to Newcastle, 11 Aug. 1862
    (private); Baring Papers, mfm. A835, Brydges to Baring, 25 Aug. 1862; Canada, House of
    Commons, *Sessional Papers 1867–68*, no. 63, Newcastle to Monck, 21 Aug. 1862.
39 Robinson, 122.
40 NAC, RG 1–E–8, Canada, Executive Council, State Records, Orders-in-Council 1841–67
    [hereafter Canada, Orders], vol. 79, report of the committee of Council on Newcastle's
    dispatch of 21 Aug. 1862 (30 Oct. 1862), 16, 18, 22.
41 Newcastle Papers, Corr., mfm. A308, Monck to Newcastle, 11 Aug. 1862 (private); Ellice
    Papers, mfm C4646, Rose to Ellice, 3 Mar. 1863.
42 Canada [United Province], Legislative Assembly, *Sessional Papers 1863*, app. 1.
43 Baring Papers, mfm. C1369, Rose to Baring, 25 Oct. 1862 (confidential) [quotation from
    here]; NAC, RG 19–A–1–E, Canada, Department of Finance, Minister's Correspondence,
    Letterbooks 1859–86 [hereafter Finance], vol. 3375, W. Howland to Baring and Glyn, 19
    Sep., 20 Dec. 1862. The government also gave some thought to establishing "a sort of
    Ambassador" in England. Newcastle told Monck to "discourage so great a folly";
    Newcastle Papers, LB, mfm. A307, Newcastle to Monck, 23 Jan. 1863.

44 Glyn Mills Papers, Corr., mfm. A545, T. Galt to Glyn, 21 June, 2 Sep. 1862. Given the emphasis put on sectional differences in existing interpretations of the Sandfield Macdonald governments (see note 1 for references), it might be useful to point out that the ministry's reluctance to proceed with the fusion bill was not in essence the result of any deep-seated sectional antagonism between its Upper and Lower Canadian supporters. Politicians like Dorion and Holton from Lower Canada were at one with Upper Canadian Grand Trunk "doubters."

45 Canada, Orders, vol. 78, 14 July 1862; CNR Papers, vol. 20300, item 329, Grand Trunk Railway to Newcastle, [n.d.] Aug. 1862; Glyn Mills Papers, LB, mfm. A540, Glyn to John Ross, 31 July 1862; Glyn to Monck, 14 Aug. 1862 (private).

46 Newcastle Papers, Corr., mfm. A308, Monck to Newcastle, 12 Sep. 1862 (private). As with the Grand Trunk measure, opposition within the government to the Intercolonial measure crossed sectional lines. Dorion, a cabinet member from Lower Canada, resigned on this issue.

47 Sandfield Macdonald Papers, p. 10078, Thomas D'Arcy McGee to Macdonald, 2 Oct. 1862 [quotation from here]; Baring Papers, mfm. C1369, Watkin to Baring, [late in] Oct. 1862 (private). A lawyer, Sicotte was a moderate Reform leader from Lower Canada.

48 See Martin and Knox for Lytton's views. For Newcastle's activities see note 33, above, and *BPP*, XXV, 193ff.

49 Baring Papers, mfm. C1369, Watkin to Baring, [late in] Oct., 4 Nov. 1862 (private); Glyn to Baring, 4, 5 Nov. 1862; Glyn Mills Papers, Corr., mfm. A545, Baring to Glyn, 20 Sep. 1862.

50 Newcastle Papers, LB, mfm. A307, Newcastle to Monck, 29 Nov. 1862 (private); Canada, Orders, vol. 78, 22 Oct. 1862.

51 For the timing of the rejection of a subsidy for westward expansion, see Roman. It would have been difficult to cite westward expansion as the reason, since that had not formed part of the bargaining program outlined at the colonial conference in September. The sinking fund was a new wrinkle introduced by the imperial government, and so it became the best available, albeit weak, pretext. See Canada, Submissions, vol. 62, 28 Dec. 1863, for a reaffirmation of this pretext.

52 Newcastle Papers, Corr., mfm. A308, Monck to Newcastle, 24 May [quotation from here], 30 May, 27 June 1862 (private); LB, mfm. A307, Newcastle to Monck, 14 June 1862 (private).

53 Ibid., Corr., mfm. A308, Monck and Newcastle, 23 June 1862 (private).

54 Ibid., Monck to Newcastle, 11 Aug., 1 Sep. 1862 (private); LB, mfm. A307, Newcastle to Monck, 22 Aug. 1862.

55 Canada, Orders, vol. 79, 21 Nov. 1862; *First Report of the Financial and Departmental Commission* (Quebec, 1863).

56 NAC, RG 58, Canada, Auditor General, Memoranda and Letterbooks 1855–82 [hereafter Auditor Gen.], vol. 7, John Langton to Howland, 1 Apr. 1863.

57 Newcastle Papers, LB, mfm. A307, Newcastle to Monck, 6 June 1862; 8 Jan., 21 Feb., 20 June 1863; Newcastle to Gordon, 24 Feb. 1863 (private).

58 Ibid., Newcastle to Monck, 29 May, 20 June, 14 Aug. 1863 (private); Ellice Papers, mfm. C4646, Ellice to Rose, 9 June 1863.

59 Watkin Papers, vol. 1, A. T. Galt to Watkin, 24 May 1863 (private); Newcastle Papers, LB, mfm. A307, Newcastle to Monck, 14 Aug. 1863 (private).

60 Ellice Papers, mfm. C4646, Rose to Ellice, 3 Mar. 1863.

61 Newcastle Papers, LB, mfm. A307, Newcastle to Monck, 20 June 1863 (private). In this letter Newcastle urged Monck to "be prepared to maintain Imperial interests against them [the Sandfield Macdonald government] or we shall have serious results."

62 Stacey, 147–52; NAC, MG 11, Great Britain, Colonial Office 42, Canada, Original Correspondence [hereafter CO42], vol. 638, Monck to Newcastle, 16 Oct. 1863.

63 Watkin Papers, vol. 1, Samuel Tilly to Watkin, 7 June 1863. Newcastle's plan to use the colonies as a dumping ground for unemployed labourers was also blocked by the government; see Canada, Orders, vol. 80, 9 May 1863.

64 Newcastle Papers, LB, mfm. A307, Newcastle to Watkin, 15 June 1863; Canada, Submissions, vol. 62, 18 Feb. 1864.

65 Newcastle Papers, LB, mfm. A307, Newcastle to Monck, 20 June 1863 (private); Ellice Papers, mfm. C4646, Ellice to Rose, 24 June 1863 (private).

66 Canada, Submissions, vol. 62, 18 Feb. 1864; Canada, Orders, vol. 81, 18 Dec. 1863.

67 For Holton, see H. Klassen, "Luther Holton", *Dictionary of Canadian Biography*, X (Toronto, 1972) and "Luther Holton: Mid-Century Montreal Railway Man", *Revue de l'université d'Ottawa/University of Ottawa Quarterly* 52 (1981), 316–39.

68 NAC, MG 24–B–40–I, George Brown, Correspondence 1848–80 [hereafter Brown Papers], vol. 3, Holton to Brown, 30 Oct. 1860; 6, 13 Nov. 1860; 4, 22 Oct. 1863; 1, 21 Nov. 1863 (all confidential).

69 Finance, vol. 3376, telegram, Holton to Watkin, 22 July 1863.

70 Ibid., Holton to Watkin, 29, 31 July 1863. Watkin did not apologize until Jan. 1864; see ibid., Holton to Watkin, 21 Jan. 1864.

71 Baring Papers, mfm. C1369, Rose to Baring, 10 Oct. 1863 (private).

72 Finance, vol. 3376, Holton to Baring and Glyn, 25 Sep. 1863; University of Western Ontario (London, Ont.), D. B. Weldon Library, Regional Collection, Thomas Swinyard Papers, Private Letterbook 1862–64, Swinyard to C. Trowbridge, 25 Aug. 1863; Letters, vol. 1., Holton to E. Mackie, 3 Sep. 1863 (private) [filed under Jan. 1864]. In this letter (a copy) Holton referred to "the present atrocious conspiracy to gain possession of the Government for the purposes of the Grand Trunk...."

73 Baring Papers, mfm. C1549, Holton to Glyn and Baring, 16, 23 Oct. 1863; C042, vol. 638, Monck to Newcastle, 21 Oct. 1863; Ellice Papers, mfm. C4646, Ellice to Rose, 9 June 1863; Brown Papers, vol. 4, Holton to Brown, 21 Nov. 1863 [quotation from here].

74 For a comprehensive discussion of the bank's position see Baskerville, "The Pet Bank". Quotation from Brown Papers, vol. 4, Holton to Brown, 22 Oct. 1863. See also ibid., Holton to Brown, 1, 11, 21 Nov. 1863; 6, 17 Dec. 1863 (all confidential).

75 Baring Papers, mfm. C1549, Holton to Glyn and Baring, 31 Oct. 1863 [quotation from here]; mfm. A835, Watkin to Baring, [n.d.] Jan. 1864; Glyn Mills Papers, Corr., mfm. A543, Robert Cassels to Glyn, 29 June 1863 (private).

76 The phrase is Holton's in reference to Glyn's and Baring's correspondence to him. Brown Papers, vol. 4, Holton to Brown, 21 Nov. 1863 (confidential).

77 Auditor Gen., vol. 7, Langton to Howland, 1 Apr. 1863; Hodgins, *John Sandfield Macdonald*, 173; J. E. Hodgetts, *Pioneer Public Service: An Administrative History of the United Canadas, 1841–1867* (Toronto, 1955); H. R. Balls, "John Langton and the Canadian Audit Office", *CHR*, 21 (1940), 150–76.

78 Baring Papers, mfm. C1549, Holton to Glyn and Baring, 7 Dec. 1863.

79 Brown Papers, vol. 4, Brown to Holton, 1 Nov. 1863 (confidential). Holton also attempted to turn Glyn and Baring against the Grand Trunk. He did not succeed. See Baring Papers, mfm. C1549, Holton to Glyn and Baring, 7, 26 Dec. 1863; mfm. C1369, Rose to Baring, 11 Feb. 1864.

80 Morton, 132; Creighton, 491; Roman, 332, 336.

81 Morton, 132.

82 NAC, MG 27–I–D–8, Sir Alexander Tilloch Galt, Correspondence 1858–91, vol. 10, Galt to Glyn, 27 Dec. 1865.

83 See the review of the literature in Winks.

84 For literature on collaboration and the general issue of autonomy at the periphery, see Robinson; Winks; Daniel Glenday, "The 'dependencia' School in Canada: An Examination and Evaluation", *Canadian Review of Sociology and Anthropology* 20 (1983), 346–58. For a good review of Wallerstein see Andrews, 135–63.

85 The argument that the different economic policies of J. S. Macdonald's governments and those of Galt, Cartier and J. A. Macdonald reflected different sectional interests, the former representing Canada West and the latter Canada East, especially Montreal and the Grand Trunk, seems to break down in the face of Holton's (a Montreal politician) actions concerning the Bank of Upper Canada and Dorion's, McGee's and Holton's (all

Montreal politicians) stance against the Grand Trunk and the Intercolonial. Sectionalism, therefore, cannot be seen as the independent variable which explains the different governmental policies.

86   Robinson, 139.

87   These included £4 million in guaranteed loans for the Intercolonial Railway, a £0.3 million loan guarantee for the purchase of the Hudson's Bay Company and some £3.6 million in guaranteed loans for the construction of the Canadian Pacific Railway. See Roman, ch. 5, 6 and conclusion; D. M. L. Farr, *The Colonial Office and Canada, 1867–1887* (Toronto, 1955), ch. 3.

88   The role played by the old collaborationists in maintaining the government account at Glyn and Baring can be traced in Baring Papers, vol. 4, Rose to Baring, 29 July 1867 (private); J. A. Macdonald Papers, vol. 216, Galt to Macdonald, 6 Feb. 1870 (confidential); vol. 267, G. Stephen to Macdonald, 13 Jan. 1882 (private); vol. 259, Rose to Macdonald, 6 Feb. 1882 (private); Baring Papers, mfm. A838, Galt to T. C. Baring, 11, 21 Sep. 1883 (confidential); mfm A839, A. W. Currie to T. C. Baring, 14 Oct. 1892. M. Denison, *Canada's First Bank: A History of the Bank of Montreal*, II (New York, 1967), 172, 183–84.

Hidden Among the Smokestacks: Toronto's Clothing Industry, 1871–1901

GERALD TULCHINSKY

By the 1890s Toronto had become a prominent manufacturing city. Factories produced a wide variety of products, from heavy machinery and industrial items such as engines, forgings, brass fittings and engine oils, to consumer goods for both the well-off and the working classes, ranging from furnaces, pianos and silver plate, to biscuits, beer and whiskey.[1] Located in the industrial sectors of the city, on King, Queen or Adelaide streets, in the Swansea and Junction areas, or throughout central Toronto and along the Esplanade, these and other establishments had grown during the city's remarkable expansion of the 1880s. Many of them were substantial—in some cases very large—enterprises requiring considerable space for machinery, storage of raw materials and fuel, loading docks, stables and offices.[2] Three- to five-storey industrial buildings with tall smokestacks, marshalling yards and railway sidings were scattered across the city, pinpointing the location of Toronto's major nodes of industrial activity.[3] But, however important these large-scale enterprises were in Toronto's rise to industrial maturity, the fact that small workshops were much more numerous indicates great unevenness in the development of industrial capitalism during the late nineteenth century.[4] The most significant of these industries with small workshops were those which produced clothing by needlework from textiles, leather or furs. In fact, the apparel industry emerged during these three decades as the city's most important manufacturing sector.[5] As early as 1871 it was the leading employer in Toronto, and by 1900 it enjoyed the highest output by value and the largest value-added of any industry in the city. During the three decades following 1871, due to the enormous expansion experienced locally in this industry, Toronto emerged as a leading centre for custom and ready-made clothing in Canada with fully 25 percent of the national output and more than half of Ontario's.[6] And while clothing rose from eighth to third place by value of output in the Canadian industrial hierarchy,[7] Toronto became a national clothing centre where goods were manufactured and distributed across the entire country.

Dispersed widely about the city in tailoring and millinery establishments, in contractors' workshops and in numerous homes—hidden among the smokestacks of Toronto's burgeoning steam and iron industries—clothing has attracted only passing notice from business historians.[8] And the fact that it did not become transformed completely, or even mostly, to mechanized factory production and was largely seasonal in nature has probably tended to deepen its obscurity relative to industries with large factories, tall smokestacks and major business figures. Moreover, the absence of any company records, which is perhaps to be expected for such a volatile industry, makes it difficult to reconstruct its history in Canada. While its importance has been appreciated, little has been written specifically about the Toronto apparel trades in the second half of the nineteenth century,[9] except for the useful statistical evidence in Gregory Kealey's study of the Toronto working class, Guy Steed's examination of its historical geography in Canada and Alan Wilson's biography of womenswear manufacturer and retailer John Northway.[10]

Thus, many of the questions which naturally arise about the characteristics of the apparel industry and its evolution during the late nineteenth century have remained unanswered. What products were manufactured, how did production processes change in this period, how were entrepreneurs and workers recruited, and what effects did technological changes have on the capital structure and organization of the industry? How was it affected by changes in Toronto's wholesaling and retailing networks and what was its impact on the textile trade, both the import sector and the nascent domestic textile industry? How well does this sector fit into any of the general trends which seemed to be emerging in some late-nineteenth-century Canadian manufacturing industries of increasing spatial concentration, large-scale factories, technological change, organizational complexity and professional management?[11]

More specifically relevant to those students of Canadian business history who are influenced by Alfred Chandler's model of the growth of modern business enterprise, how closely does clothing manufacturing fit his proposition that "modern business enterprise appeared, grew and continued to flourish in those sectors and industries characterized by new and advancing technology and expanding markets."[12] In other words, did this industry experience the transition through which "the visible hand of management replaced the invisible hand of market mechanisms"?[13] How well did Toronto's clothing manufacturers fit into the ideology of the late-nineteenth-century Canadian businessmen who sought to control competition?[14] And how closely does the Toronto experience conform to the pattern existing in the American menswear industry which was recently described as being characterized by the concentration of workers, capital and technology in large factories in the 1870s and 1880s and by subdivision into two sectors thereafter?[15] What seems to have been the relationship between this industry's growth and tariff protection? And, finally, how well does apparel manufacturing fit the pattern of Canadian industrial development between 1870 and

1890 described by Gordon Bertram, who demonstrated that the industries registering the highest growth rates were either staples-based or tariff-protected?[16]

By studying this industry in Toronto between 1870 and 1900—a period for which census and other data are available—we conclude that the apparel industry conformed only partially to some of these general trends and models of modernization and structuring in the Canadian manufacturing sector during the late nineteenth century. Indeed, it seems to have been unusual in its labour force, capital structure, organization, entrepreneurial recruitment, responsiveness to tariffs and general growth trends.

The manufacture of clothing was already a considerable business in Toronto by mid-century. Canada's census of 1851 registered 468 tailors, tailoresses, seamstresses and other clothing workers in the city, and although there are no official measures of the value of output, the numbers of retail and wholesale clothiers operating in the city during the 1850s suggest that it was substantial.[17] And while there is no evidence of even approximate proportions of Canadian-produced and imported clothing sold by local retailers, a high proportion of it was probably of Canadian manufacture, because the provincial trade figures record only tiny quantities of clothing imports.[18] In the 1850s at least one Toronto apparel manufacturer began using sewing machines,[19] presumably to increase production and reduce labour costs. As early as 1851 Toronto had over 10 percent of all clothing workers in Canada West, and nearly 12 percent in 1861.[20] Moreover, by 1861 clothing was Toronto's major employer of labour.[21] Growth continued over the next 10 years and by 1871 Toronto was producing 11.5 per cent of the value of Canada's apparel production.[22]

By this early stage, there were already four clearly discernible sectors of the industry—menswear, womenswear, furnishings, and furs and hats.[23] Menswear such as workclothes of various kinds included cotton or denim shirts, pants, overalls, boyswear, vests and jackets as well as tailored woollen items like suits and coats. Women's clothing consisted of various millinery goods as well as dresses, woollen suits, coats and mantles and, by the late nineteenth century, sportswear. Furs and hats included decorative pieces, fur hats as well as straw or cloth hats and caps. As furnishings, a wide variety of apparel and accessory goods were produced, such as haberdashery (shirts, ties, suspenders), cotton underwear, corsets, and leather mittens and gloves.

The value of Toronto's clothing production in each census year from 1871 to 1901, is displayed in Table 1. It grew in the 1870s by more than 50 percent, with the most dynamic sector, furnishings, increasing by nearly 750 percent—an astonishing record. However it was in the 1880s that the industry as a whole achieved its most impressive decennial gain. Value for all four sectors rose from $2.6 to $7.6 million, some 190 percent. Most remarkable in this decade was the huge growth of the womenswear sector by about 425

Table 1: Value of Toronto Clothing Production, 1871–1901, by Sector

	Furnishings	Furs and Hats	Menswear	Womenswear	All Sectors
Year			**Value of Production ($'000)**		
1871	50	163	1,341	145	1,699
1881	424	325	1,596	284	2,629
1891	1,602	1,316	3,172	1,487	7,577
1901[a]	1,061	1,188	4,158	2,736	9,143
Period			**Percentage Increase in Value of Production**		
1871 to 1881	748	99	19	9	55
1881 " 1891	278	305	99	424	188
1891 " 1901[a]	-34	-10	31	84	21
1871 " 1891	3,104	707	137	926	346
" " 1901[a]	2,022	629	210	1,787	438

Source: Canada, *Census of Canada...*, III (Ottawa, 1875, 1883, 1894, 1905).

[a]   The report for 1901 applies only to firms with five or more employees. The number of smaller establishments in 1901 is uncertain but there must have been many. Thus statistics for 1901 are underestimates.

percent. By contrast, in the same period production of menswear merely doubled. Yet even that increase is impressive by the standards of the 1870s and particularly by those of the 1890s, when value of production apparently declined in two of the four sectors, furnishings and furs and hats, and seemingly only a modest increase of 21 percent was attained by the industry as a whole. The available 1901 data are limited to firms with five or more employees; thus growth rates for the 1890s are underestimates of uncertain magnitude. Many analysts in the 1890s, however, regarded Toronto's apparel industry as being in a serious slump. Certainly, compared to the golden days of the 1880s it was.

The size of Toronto's clothing industry labour force also increased remarkably during these three decades, particularly during the 1880s and 1890s when, treating the four sectors as one, the number of workers more than doubled in each decade (see Table 2). Indeed, from 1871 to 1901 the increase was at least 684 percent! More notable, however, were the contrasting changes within sectors during the 1890s. Menswear and womenswear grew by more than 230 and 110 percent respectively, whereas the number of workers in furs and hats rose by a modest 33 percent and, it seems, in the furnishings sector fell by 27 percent. Again, because the 1901 census report excludes the smallest firms, the statistics on growth during the 1890s may be regarded as minimum estimates.

The labour force included men and women, as well as small numbers of children, the largest numbers of whom—mostly girls—worked on women's apparel and furnishings. As Table 3 shows, within-sector sex ratios changed significantly during the period 1871–91 only within furs and hats, where the proportion of the work force accounted for by men and boys increased from 28 to 36 percent. Despite this gain, however, the male share of the apparel industry's total labour force declined somewhat, falling from 31 to 25 percent between 1871 and 1891. While in every year females outnumbered males in every sector, sex ratios differed significantly between the two leading sectors. The largest proportion of male workers, nearly 40 percent on average, was in menswear while the smallest, 3 percent, was in womenswear. These imbalances reflect the sexual division of skills within this labour force. Women could most frequently provide the sorts of skilled labour needed in womenswear, most of which was produced for the custom trade in small shops for specific retail outlets. Men, on the other hand, could most frequently supply the somewhat different skills required in the custom trade in other sectors, particularly furs and hats. In addition, because in every sector the making of ready-made clothing was less dependent on the sorts of skilled labour that either sex laid special claim to, employers in the ready-made trade more frequently hired women and girls than men and boys, generally because females' wages were lower than those for males. Consequently, the increase in the production of ready-made clothing towards the close of the century, particularly in menswear, contributed to the modest but steady decline in the relative size of the male labour force in Toronto's apparel industry. An additional factor associated with sex ratios in the industry was the availability of significant numbers of skilled furriers and tailors among the Jewish immigrants arriving in the city during the 1880s (when the Jewish community nearly trebled in size) and 1890s (when it increased by another 100 percent). These individuals may have contributed to the stability of sex ratios in menswear and furnishings, and their presence certainly helps to explain the increase in the male share of employment in furs and hats.[24]

Also significant are the increases in the numbers of firms in every sector and—at least for the period 1871–91—the stability or decline in the average number of workers per firm, especially in those establishments producing womenswear (see Table 4). Many of the latter were tiny tailoring or dressmaking businesses with fewer than five employees—firms excluded from consideration in the published 1901 industrial census tables. As well, value

Table 2: The Toronto Clothing Industry Labour Force, 1871–1901, by Sector

	Furnishings	Furs and Hats	Menswear	Womenswear	All Sectors
Year			Number of Employees		
1871	77	182	1,299	251	1,809
1881	428	290	1,503	483	2,704
1891	1,387	647	2,654	1,677	6,365
1901[a]	1,008	862	8,781	3,532	14,183
Period			Percentage Increase in Number of Employees		
1871 to 1881	456	59	16	92	49
1881 " 1891	224	123	77	247	135
1891 " 1901[a]	-27	33	231	111	123
1871 " 1891	1,701	255	104	568	252
" " 1901[a]	1,209	374	576	1,307	684

Source: Canada, *Census of Canada…*, III (Ottawa, 1875, 1883, 1894, 1905).

[a]   The report for 1901 applies only to firms with five or more employees. The number of smaller establishments in 1901 is uncertain but there must have been many. Thus statistics for 1901 are underestimates.

added (the value of production less the cost of raw materials) per worker increased to 1891, if not also to 1901, in every sector and particularly during the 1880s in furnishings and furs and hats (see Table 4, column 11). The profitability of the industry is difficult to determine from the available evidence, but by subtracting labour and raw material costs (though not rent and other expenses) from the value of production, it is possible to arrive at a rough estimate of gross margin. Gross margin per employee appears to have climbed in every sector up to 1891—dramatically so during the 1880s—and very likely continued to rise during the 1890s, the censored evidence for 1901 notwithstanding (see Table 4, column 13).

Table 3: The Toronto Clothing Industry Labour Force, 1871–91, within Sector by Sex of Employee

Year	Furnishings		Furs and Hats		Menswear		Womenswear		All Sectors	
	M	F	M	F	M	F	M	F	M	F

Number of Employees

1871	14	63	51	131	488	811	8	243	561	1,248
1881	68	360	90	200	553	950	14	469	725	1,979
1891	248	1,139	234	413	1,062	1,592	45	1,632	1,589	4,776

Percentage of Employees[a]

1871	18	82	28	72	38	62	3	97	31	69
1881	16	84	31	69	37	63	3	97	27	73
1891	18	82	36	64	40	60	3	97	25	75

Source: Canada, *Census of Canada...*, III (Ottawa, 1875, 1883, 1894). The report for 1901 provides no statistics by sex of employee.

M   Male
F   Female
[a]   within sector by year

The relative importance of each sector of the industry altered considerably during these three decades. The sectors are ranked below by their share of the value of production in each census year (from Table 1):

Rk	1871		1881		1891		1901	
	Sector	%	Sector	%	Sector	%	Sector	%
1	Menswear	79	Menswear	61	Menswear	42	Menswear	45
2	Furs & Hats	10	Furnishings	16	Furnishings	21	Womenswear	30
3	Womenswear	9	Furs & Hats	12	Womenswear	20	Furs & Hats	13
4	Furnishings	3	Womenswear	11	Furs & Hats	17	Furnishings	12

Although menswear remained the leading sector throughout the period, it declined dramatically in importance relative to the other three, owing largely to the equally dramatic rise in the share of production accounted for by

Table 4: The Toronto Clothing Industry, 1871–1901: Measures of Employment and Productivity

	1	2	3	4	5	6	7	8	9	10	11	12	13
		Employees		Annual Wages		Raw Materials	Production	Value of Production			Value Added[a]	Margin[b]	
Year	Firms	No.	No. per Firm	Total paid $'000	per Empl. $	$'000	$'000	per Firm $	per Empl. $	per Ann. wages $	per Empl. $	per Firm $	per Empl. $
Furnishings (mitts, gloves, corsets, underwear, collars, shirts, ties, suspenders, hosiery)													
1871	1	77	77.0	14.0	182	24.0	50.0	50,000	649	3.57	338	12,000	156
1881	13	428	32.9	74.7	174	262.3	423.9	32,608	990	5.67	378	6,685	203
1891	32	1,387	43.3	324.2	234	575.0	1,601.9	50,059	1,155	4.94	740	21,959	507
1901[c]	17	1,008	59.3	313.7	311	512.2	1,061.2	62,423	1,053	3.38	545	13,840	233
Furs and Hats													
1871	10	182	18.2	28.8	158	86.6	162.5	16,254	893	5.64	418	4,719	259
1881	15	290	19.3	51.1	176	161.1	325.2	21,680	1,121	6.37	566	7,535	390
1891	30	647	21.6	198.1	306	625.0	1,316.4	43,878	2,035	6.64	1,069	16,441	762
1901[c]	24	862	35.9	336.2	390	677.6	1,187.7	49,488	1,378	3.53	592	7,245	202

Table 4: The Toronto Clothing Industry, 1871–1901:
Measures of Employment and Productivity—Continued

	1	2	3	4	5	6	7	8	9	10	11	12	13
Menswear (suits, coats, workwear, boyswear)													
1871	51	1,299	25.5	293.3	226	731.5	1,341.5	26,303	1,033	4.57	470	6,208	244
1881	61	1,503	24.6	349.0	232	849.9	1,595.5	26,156	1,062	4.57	496	6,502	264
1891	216	2,654	12.3	839.2	316	1,539.7	3,172.4	14,687	1,195	3.78	615	3,673	299
1901c	86	8,781	102.1	1,279.2	146	2,239.9	4,157.8	48,347	474	3.25	218	7,427	73
Womenswear (coats, mantles, dresses)													
1871	25	251	10.0	28.4	113	76.3	145.0	5,802	578	5.12	274	1,614	161
1881	72	483	6.7	69.4	144	133.4	284.3	3,948	589	4.09	312	1,131	169
1891	402	1,677	4.2	327.0	195	673.9	1,487.0	3,699	887	4.55	485	1,209	290
1901c	55	3,532	64.2	780.9	221	1,330.6	2,736.4	49,752	775	3.50	398	11,361	177

Source: Canada, *Census of Canada...*, III (Ottawa, 1875, 1883, 1894, 1905).

a value of production – value of raw materials

b value of production – (annual wages paid + value of raw materials)

c The report for 1901 applies only to firms with five or more employees. The number of smaller establishments in 1901 is uncertain but there must have been many. Thus data for 1901 are underestimates.

Data ($) on wages, raw materials, and production are unadjusted for change in the value of the dollar, which generally declined across the period. Canadian wholesale price index (1926=100.0): 1871= 62.0; 1881= 55.5; 1891= 51.5; 1901= 49.0; plate 125 in D. G. G. Kerr, ed., *Historical Atlas of Canada*, 2nd ed. (Toronto, 1966).

Table 5: Value of Clothing Production in Four Leading
Canadian Centres, 1871–1911 ($'000)

By Centre

Centre	Sector	1871 $	1871 %	1881 $	1881 %	1891 $	1891 %	1901 $	1901 %	1911 $	1911 %
Toronto	Menswear	1,341	79	1,596	61	3,172	42	4,158	45	6,647	27
	Womenswear	145	9	284	11	1,487	20	2,736	30	13,002	53
	Furs & Hats	163	10	325	12	1,316	17	1,188	13	2,245	9
	Furnishings	50	3	424	16	1,602	21	1,061	12	2,772	11
	Total	1,699	100	2,629	100	7,577	100	9,143	100	24,666	100
Montreal	Menswear	1,924	45	3,770	49	3,687	46	5,096	53	12,491	59
	Womenswear	535	13	824	11	879	11	801	8	3,889	18
	Furs & Hats	1,704	40	2,051	26	1,668	21	2,231	23	4,284	20
	Furnishings	80	2	1,103	14	1,720	22	1,545	16	486	2
	Total	4,243	100	7,748	100	7,954	100	9,673	100	21,150	100
Hamilton	Menswear	594	76	591	59	138	14	1,705	78	3,452	80
	Womenswear	61	8	158	16	588	62	183	8	181	4
	Furs & Hats	124	16	126	12	76	8	103	5	175	4
	Furnishings	5	1	134	13	154	16	181	8	504	12
	Total	784	100	1,009	100	956	100	2,172	100	4,312	100
Quebec	Menswear	237	31	668	61	831	32	358	37	705	38
	Womenswear	85	11	186	17	570	22	170	18	0	0
	Furs & Hats	455	59	226	21	1,017	39	433	45	1,138	62
	Furnishings	0	0	13	1	206	8	0	0	0	0
	Total	777	100	1,093	100	2,624	100	961	100	1,843	100

womenswear. One reason for this change appears to lie in the inability of menswear to achieve more than a modest increase in margin per employee compared to the other sectors: 23 percent for the period 1871–91 compared to 80 percent in womenswear, 194 percent in furs and hats and 225 percent in furnishings (see Table 4, column 13). Equally important was the advance of womenswear by 1891, when it almost equalled furnishings, and its position well above both furnishings and furs and hats by 1901. It should be recalled that these changes were occurring as sectors were experiencing major increases in their value of production—in the 1880s, for example, furs and hats grew by some 300 percent, womenswear by more than 400 percent (see Table 1).

Toronto's apparel manufacturing industry was experiencing rates of growth between 1871 and 1901 that greatly exceeded those in most Cana-

Table 5: Value of Clothing Production in Four Leading Canadian Centres, 1871–1911 ($'000) — Continued

By Sector

Sector	Centre	1871		1881		1891		1901		1911	
		$	%	$	%	$	%	$	%	$	%
Mens-	Toronto	1,341	33	1,596	24	3,172	41	4,158	37	6,647	29
wear	Montreal	1,924	47	3,770	57	3,687	47	5,096	45	12,491	54
	Hamilton	594	15	591	9	138	2	1,705	15	3,452	15
	Quebec	237	6	668	10	831	11	358	3	705	3
	Total	4,096	100	6,625	100	7,828	100	11,317	100	23,295	100
Womens-											
wear	Toronto	145	18	284	20	1,487	42	2,736	70	13,002	76
	Montreal	535	65	824	57	879	25	801	21	3,889	23
	Hamilton	61	7	158	11	588	17	183	5	181	1
	Quebec	85	10	186	13	570	16	170	4	0	0
	Total	826	100	1,452	100	3,524	100	3,890	100	17,072	100
Furs and											
Hats	Toronto	163	7	325	12	1,316	32	1,188	30	2,245	29
	Montreal	1,704	70	2,051	75	1,668	41	2,231	56	4,284	55
	Hamilton	124	5	126	5	76	2	103	3	175	2
	Quebec	455	19	226	8	1,017	25	433	11	1,138	15
	Total	2,446	100	2,728	100	4,077	100	3,955	100	7,842	100
Furnish-											
ings	Toronto	50	37	424	25	1,602	44	1,061	38	2,772	74
	Montreal	80	59	1,103	66	1,720	47	1,545	55	486	13
	Hamilton	5	4	134	8	154	4	181	6	504	13
	Quebec	0	0	13	1	206	6	0	0	0	0
	Total	135	100	1,674	100	3,682	100	2,787	100	3,762	100

Source: Canada, *Census of Canada...*, III (Ottawa, 1875, 1883, 1894, 1905, 1915).

Data are unadjusted for change in the value of the dollar, which generally declined across the period to 1901. Canadian wholesale price index (1926=100.0): 1871=62.0, 1881=55.5, 1891=51.5, 1901=49.0, 1911=62.0; plate 125 in D. G. G. Kerr, ed., *Historical Atlas of Canada*, 2nd ed. (Toronto, 1966).

dian industries.[25] By 1891 the city was clearly Canada's major production centre for womenswear and women's fashions generally (see Table 5). Equally important is the fact that Toronto's output levels by value rose significantly in relation to those of its chief rival. By 1891 Toronto's production nearly equalled that of Montreal for the industry as a whole and exceeded Montreal's in womenswear by nearly 70 percent. Its pre-eminence in this sector was to become even more pronounced after 1901, whereas Montreal accentuated its strength in menswear.[26] These post-1900 trends towards undisputed sectoral dominance by these two metropolitan rivals were, however, not self-evident to observers in late-nineteenth-century Toronto.[27] In 1889, for example, their view was that Toronto, already ahead in the manufacture of womenswear, was clearly challenging Montreal in menswear, furs and hats and furnishings.

According to the 1871 industrial census of Canada, Toronto had 24 clothing firms with between 5 and 19 employees; an additional 10 clothiers had between 20 and 49 workers, 2 employed 50 to 99 and 2 others had 100 or more.[28] The largest of these firms included Henderson and Bertram's straw hat factory, the menswear manufacturer Livingston, Johnson and Company, and Robert Walker and Sons, which produced both men's and women's clothing. A majority of the manufacturers appear to have been retailers, and contemporary business sketches reveal that most of them produced goods for their own stores on both a custom basis and "for stock," or sale off-the-rack.

Robert Walker and Sons offers an instructive example of the symbiotic relationship which often existed between apparel retailing and manufacturing. Proprietors of an emporium called the "Golden Lion," housed in a huge four-storey building erected in 1867 on Yonge Street, the Walkers sold dry and fancy goods, home furnishings, carpets, as well as an assortment of women's clothing such as mantles, millinery and skirts.[29] Although the firm began by specializing in the manufacture of women's apparel, by the 1880s the Walkers were also producing ready-to-wear men's suits and overcoats as well as boyswear[30] for sale in the Toronto store and in their London branch. In 1871 they reported to census enumerators an output valued at $100,000. Their workforce then numbered 116, including 50 men, 60 women and 6 children.[31] The employment of an unusually high proportion of males indicates that the firm specialized in custom work which required skilled tailors, virtually all of whom were men.

On the other hand, Livingston, Johnson and Company had no retail outlets of its own and produced solely for the wholesale trade. Its labour force of 124, including as many as 100 women, manufactured only menswear, which was worth $110,000 in 1871. It was a much leaner operation than the Walkers', not only because it had a smaller cutting and tailoring staff but also because it operated with a working capital of just $14,000—in comparison to the Walkers' $60,000—and with a fixed capital investment of $2,000, compared to 10 times that for Walkers (who apparently did not distinguish between retail and manufacturing fixed capital).[32] Thomas Lailey's firm on Front Street was similar to Livingston and Johnson's in producing exclusively for the wholesale trade and sold to merchants in Ontario, Quebec, the Maritimes and Manitoba.[33] Its wage bill in 1871 indicated a workforce of about the same size as Livingston's.

Retailing, therefore, did not offer the only access to apparel production in Toronto. Except for shirt and hat manufacturers, of the three major firms turning out ready-made clothing in Toronto, two were exclusively wholesale houses. Hamilton's largest men's clothing manufacturer, William Sanford, sold only at wholesale, as did a number of others. Most of the major Montreal producers in the 1870s also appear to have sold exclusively at wholesale.[34] Thus, while there was a link between the retail and the industrial aspects of the apparel business, it was by no means universal among the largest manufacturers. The enumerators' reports in the industrial census of 1871 suggest that merchant tailors, dressmakers and milliners who catered mainly to the men's and women's custom trade retained modest-sized operations by comparison to those who produced for the wholesale market.[35] However, some retailers of cheaper grades of clothing sometimes manufactured for their own stores, and possibly made a transition to wholesaling later. Indeed some of the larger custom shops may have made up certain categories of garments in advance of orders, possibly leaving them partly unfinished until specific orders were received.

Womenswear manufacturers and merchant tailors generally produced on their own premises. According to one contemporary survey of Toronto businesses, these manufacturers ran medium-sized shops with between 20 to 60 employees. Several of the merchant tailors reported that their made-to-measure trade extended well beyond Toronto by the mid 1880s. P. M. Clark and Son, Tailor's and Gentlemen's Haberdashers on King St. West, boasted that "the trade of the firm extends throughout Ontario, British Columbia and the Northwest, where they have numerous patrons," while R. Score and Son, merchant tailors also located on King St. West, claimed that their custom trade "extends throughout the Dominion."[36] While this commerce in custom clothing was facilitated by upcountry merchants who mailed in their customer's measurements, women's clothing was even more customized and, except for coats and mantles, was produced largely for a local clientele, until the appearance, in 1884, of Eaton's mail order catalogues which included a complete range of women's ready-made clothes, even dresses.

Clothing was a risky business, especially for those who manufactured strictly for the wholesale trade. According to the *Canadian Textile Directory* (a Montreal publication which first appeared in 1885), of 9 Toronto menswear wholesaling manufacturers and dealers in 1885, only 3 had survived until 1889.[37] In that year 30 firms were listed. But, by 1892, 7 of these had disappeared, while 11 new ones, some of them contractors, had emerged. By 1899, 14 of these had vanished; but there were now no less than 68 menswear firms, 26 of them contractors. To be sure, most of those that had vanished were clearly small custom-tailors or shirtmakers whose presence in the trade had obviously been very brief. Judging from the names, we can conclude that most of the Toronto contractors listed in 1899 were Jews, many of them probably experienced tailors, small storekeepers or peddlars who were attracted by the opportunities in this burgeoning industry, able to muster the small amount of required capital for starting up in business and willing to take the risk.

Because of more frequent and radical style changes in women's than in men's apparel, one would expect that there would be even higher rates of failure in the womenswear sector. But for the late 1880s and early 1890s survival rates were much better; virtually all of the manufacturers who were in business in 1889 were listed in the 1892 directory. By the end of that decade, however, the casualty rate for those Toronto womenswear producers—especially the smaller ones—was about 50 percent. Still, new firms abounded and there were now 40 manufacturers, some of whom also produced children's and menswear. Because womenswear was still largely a custom business, there were no contractors listed exclusive to the women's trade, although some of those who produced menswear possibly also turned out women's apparel when they could get the contracts.

Toronto's well-developed financial, transportation, commercial and industrial facilities increased its economic importance within Ontario during the late nineteenth century,[38] and its clear lead in the importation of dry and fancy goods and costlier textiles probably contributed to the huge growth of its apparel industry, especially of women's wear, which used a large variety of silks, muslins and other materials.[39] Moreover, located as it was in about the centre of the woollen textile manufacturing towns of southcentral and southwestern Ontario, Toronto served as the main wool-dealing centre for the fabrics produced in the region.[40] Style consciousness was advanced by the publication in Toronto of several women's magazines which included fashion plates showing Paris, London and New York modes, as well as garment patterns; courses in pattern cutting and design became widely available during these years.[41]

A general decline in the price of fabrics may have contributed to an increase in the availability of cheap ready-to-wear clothing.[42] The extent of the Ontario market for these goods is indicated by the fact that women's clothing manufacturer and retailer Robert Walker maintained a branch store in London, and John Northway enjoyed a very successful business career selling women's tailored and ready-to-wear apparel in several western Ontario towns during the 1880s.[43] As women's ready-to-wear was a newer industry, and one whose product was probably subject to volatile swings in demand, manufacturers saw advantages in locating their operations close to customers. In order to eliminate middlemen's profits, Timothy Eaton, who had produced small amounts of clothing for his store as early as the 1870s, began manufacturing men's shirts, women's underwear and boy's knickerbockers in the late 1880s.[44] This venture was so profitable that, in 1893, he built a large four-storey factory near the store to make women's coats, dresses, capes and skirts; three years later, he erected another building to produce men's wear.[45] In the early 1890s, when deciding where to locate his factory, John Northway opted for Toronto rather than Montreal; even though he imported most of his fine woollens and other inputs—such as trimmings and linings—from Britain, the extra transportation costs were apparently insignificant.[46] Thus, proximity to major markets in Toronto and southwestern Ontario appear to have been crucially important.[47]

Toronto's largest menswear manufacturers were not nearly as big as Montreal's Hollis Shorey nor Hamilton's William Sanford—Canada's clothing tycoons—who employed about 2,000 workers each during the late 1880s.[48] What explains the size of these operations, as well as James O'Brien's of Montreal, is that they were each important suppliers of military and other uniforms to the federal government. Contracts for consignments of uniforms allowed them to benefit from the economies of scale associated with large production runs of coats, tunics and trousers made in standard sizes. Between 1887 and 1895 O'Brien got contracts to produce no less than 24,000 pairs of riding breeches for the Royal North West Mounted Police at $5.55 each.[49] Toronto had only one such contractor, Ed. Boisseau and Company, whose government contracts for supplying uniforms were far less lucrative and not nearly as big as those of his competitors: according to an 1886 publication which listed Toronto's major manufacturers, the largest menswear producer, B. Spain—a merchant tailor—employed only 60 operatives.[50]

Ready-made clothing was also emerging in the late nineteenth century as a major industry in Britain and the United States. But whereas Canadian clothing manufacturing was increasingly concentrated in Toronto and Montreal,[51] the British production was scattered in a number of different centres, some of which—like Leeds and Manchester—specialized in certain lines because of close access to inputs. Leeds clothiers concentrated on men's woollen suits and coats because of the availability nearby of Yorkshire fine woollens, while those in Manchester specialized in cotton shirts, dresses, blouses and underwear production because of the huge output of cotton textiles in the city.[52] Glasgow, the site of a Singer sewing machine factory, was also a centre of clothing production. But ready access to inputs like textiles, as well as to labour and machinery, were not necessarily the only, or perhaps the most critical, factors even in Britain where there were relatively short-hauls to markets. Other factors were the availability locally of sewing machines and cheap local and immigrant Jewish labour; all these things contributed to the development of the Leeds clothing industry.[53] London, which was further away from the Midlands textile centres but the home of a vast pool of cheap immigrant Jewish and other labour, became Britain's leading clothing producer by the early twentieth century with nearly one third of the entire national workforce in this industry.[54] In the United States, large-scale, ready-made clothing production developed in cities like New York, Boston and Baltimore which were growing cities and major regional market centres.[55] Philadelphia was a major clothing centre from the Civil War onwards largely because of the availability of large quantities of woollen and cotton textiles from nearby mills. Yet in this period major clothing manufacturing centres also arose in Rochester, Chicago and St. Louis, all of which were great distances from the major textile-producing or importing centres in the eastern United States, but much closer to major new markets in the mid-West.[56]

Certain economies of location might also have contributed to the emergence of the Montreal or Toronto clothing industries. Whereas some of the woollens for coats, suits and mantles were imported from Britain, as were the many kinds of textiles used in the making of womenswear in the late nineteenth century, Canadian cotton and woollen mills such as Rosamond's at Almonte were beginning to turn out some of the fabrics that were employed in the domestic clothing industry.[57] The increasing use of Canadian-produced textiles is indicated by the fact that importations of cotton cloth in 1890 were worth less than half those of 1871, while woollens and silks remained largely unchanged for that twenty-year period (see Table 6). Sewing machines were readily available from factories in Guelph, Hamilton and Montreal, or from agents selling Singer and other imported goods.[58]

Yet, proximity to critical inputs in Canada, as in Britain and the United States, is only part of the reason for the industry's growth in Montreal and Toronto. The fact that both of these cities were major regional market centres possessing a wide range of commercial facilities and advantages over proximate rival cities is probably of great importance in explaining the growth of the clothing industry in both places. As centres where large wholesalers concentrated, where retailers from the smaller towns in their respective regions came on buying trips, and where many other economic and social opportunities were offered, Montreal and Toronto were perhaps bound to become the major clothing-producing centres in Canada, like New York, Philadelphia and Chicago in the United States. Toronto's dominance in Ontario was recognized even by Hamilton's William Sanford; as early as 1892 he maintained his sales offices in Toronto and, in recognition of the potential in the West, another in Winnipeg, where he competed with sales representatives of Toronto and Montreal menswear producers.[59]

Unlike many other manufacturing industries, especially those which attracted so much notice during Toronto's industrial revolution, clothing production was not becoming centralized in large factories. While small workshops were maintained over or behind a merchant tailor's or milliner's store, the use of a putting-out system generally prevailed. Even the largest manufacturers had small premises, preferring to parcel out the major part of their manufacturing operations to workers who were employed to work at home at piece-rates when seasonal production schedules required it.

Outwork prevailed in apparel manufacturing even though the spread of cheap and efficient "lock stitch" sewing machines by Canadian and American manufacturers led to greatly increased productivity.[60] Improvements in these devices made possible even higher rates and more intricate forms of production. By the 1870s some of them were capable of 2,000 stitches per minute, more than double the capability of the earliest devices. Cutting could now be performed by the long knives—a type of sawing device which made it possible to cut up to 18 thicknesses of cloth.[61] A decade later steam-powered band knives, which could cut 24 thicknesses, became available.[62]

Table 6: Value of Canadian Textile Imports, 1871–1900 ($'000)

Year	Cottons	Woollens	Silks	Clothing[a]
1871	9,077	9,717	2,040	432
1872	10,182	11,735	2,598	540
1873	10,076	11,195	2,267	877
1874	11,182	11,298	2,141	1,082
1875	9,831	19,002	2,219	1,723
1876	7,205	7,763	1,337	1,147
1877	7,404	7,893	1,126	1,307
1878	7,089	7,573	1,410	1,281
1879	6,639	7,063	1,561	996
1880	9,321	6,359	2,200	681
1881	10,204	8,742	2,839	730
1882	11,125	10,161	3,318	931
1883	10,044	10,106	2,916	1,049
1884	7,539	8,408	2,211	906
1885	6,241	9,054	2,305	860
1886	5,780	9,321	2,357	1,053
1887	5,471	11,815	2,888	1,408
1888	4,200	9,842	2,777	1,110
1889	4,246	10,415	2,978	905
1890	3,963	11,017	2,846	1,162
1891	4,029	9,963	2,770	1,255
1892	3,992	10,341	2,456	1,345
1893	4,557	10,946	2,764	1,508
1894	4,002	9,494	2,481	1,337
1895	4,218	7,953	2,231	
1896	4,632	8,671	2,557	
1897	4,051	7,126	1,998	
1898	4,743	7,986	2,651	
1899	5,957	9,803	3,777	
1900	6,475	9,802	3,882	

Source: Tables of trade and navigation of the Dominion of Canada, in Canada, House of Commons, *Sessional Papers* (Ottawa, 1872–1901).

[a]   cottons and woollens

Steam presses now began to replace hand irons, and new devices were introduced for faster button-hole making, pocket stitching and other processes.[63] And while early sewing machines were operated by hand or foot treadle, the invention of the oscillating shuttle led to the use of other sources of power, such as steam and gas engines and, at the turn of the century, electricity to drive these machines.[64]

Paradoxically, however, none of these innovations made it necessary to concentrate all production processes in one location. Indeed, the very cheapness—Singer sold on the instalment plan—and portability of hand- and foot-propelled sewing machines facilitated the diffusion of sewing operations into urban, and even rural, locations where cheap labour was available. Thus, the clothing industry was in many ways an anomaly among late-nineteenth-century manufacturing sectors, which were increasingly characterized by factory production and expanding plant size as a result of technological changes and economies of scale. In contrast to most other industries, the industrial census of 1871 revealed that, aside from a knitting and two straw hat factories, no steam power was used in the Toronto clothing trades.[65]

Most ready-to-wear men's clothing, the cheaper grades in particular, were sewn together in small shops or homes scattered throughout the city, or possibly, in the surrounding countryside by women and men who were paid by the piece, as was the case in Quebec.[66] Long hours, low wages and unsanitary conditions characterized this system.[67] By the 1880s the clothing industry had become synonymous with the "sweating system," a phrase which connoted the misery and exploitation alleged to be prevalent in the industry. While in the 1874 House of Commons investigation into the state of Canada's manufacturing industries it was suggested that the clothiers themselves organized this outwork, the Royal Commission investigation into industrial conditions in 1886 demonstrated that most of the outwork involved in making men's apparel was now being done through independent middlemen known as contractors.[68] Outwork was confined mainly to cheaper grades of menswear, and chiefly to the making of pants and vests; most of the higher quality men's and women's clothing was made in shops run by manufacturers themselves. Although Toronto was apparently not as large a centre for lower quality men's ready-to-wear and uniforms as Montreal and Hamilton, the sweating system intensified as contracting and the use of outworkers spread.[69]

The testimony of various clothing manufacturers in 1874 revealed how production was organized.[70] Of his total workforce, William Sanford explained that only 10 percent, notably the cutters, were employed on his own premises, where it was possible to exercise close supervision and perform the most exact measurements. The remainder of his employees were seasonally employed outworkers, mainly women who sewed up garments at home. Bundles of marked pieces, which had been cut at the factory, were taken home and sewn together by these outworkers who were paid by the piece. The finished goods were then collected, assembled, inspected and pressed before being shipped to retailers. This system, which was common throughout the industry in Britain and the United States as well as in Canada,[71] allowed contractors and manufacturers—many of whom were now really clothing financiers and wholesalers—to avoid the cost of establishing factories and the necessity of complying with the legislation and inspections that governed them. Contractors put up no investment, other than their own skill and labour. Therefore, their numbers proliferated and the competition for orders compelled them to lower their prices and, in turn, force down the wages they paid their workers. In 1882, the commissioners who had been investigating labouring conditions in mills and factories pointed out that wholesale clothiers employed as many as 1,000 workers, each "in private houses and what may be described as workshops which are very difficult to find, sometimes being in the attic of a four storey building, at others in a low, damp basement where artificial light has to be used the entire day."[72] An investigation into the conditions of female labour in Ontario in 1891 revealed that women got only about two thirds of the wages that men received in the wholesale and custom-tailoring trades for the same work.[73]

Two inquiries during the late 1890s into sweating and the production of postal uniforms revealed that the outwork system had become prevalent in Toronto's booming menswear trade. Investigating in 1896, Alexander W. Wright found that a great proportion of the work was done in many private homes across the city, although he noted that separate contractors' shops also existed.[74] Largely on the basis of evidence supplied by a union organizer among Toronto Jewish garment workers, Louis Gurofsky, Wright concluded that "the contracting system tends inevitably to the lowering of wages and degrading the conditions of labour," and that in many contractors' shops "there was great room for improvement." He found that in many Toronto shops sanitary conditions were worse than those in Montreal. More horrifying still was the lot of those competing with the contractors by accepting work at lower rates—the families (many of them Jewish) that undertook the making of pants and vests in their own homes where bedrooms and livingrooms were used as work space. Here conditions were abominable: "Scarlet fever and diphtheria had been known to exist in places where clothing was being made," and "women and children work many more hours daily than would be permitted in shops and factories under the regulation of the [provincial] Acts," even though school laws checked the evil to some extent.[75] The investigation undertaken by William Lyon Mackenzie King two years later into the conditions under which postal uniforms were being produced also exposed some of the sweating system's horrors in Toronto.[76] Despite these revelations, however, the evil continued long afterward, even though both governments and labour unions attempted to eliminate it. Sweating remained for many years a persistent, perhaps endemic, feature in this industry of small workshops, seasonal labour and volatile style changes.[77]

Yet, notwithstanding the notoriety of the sweating system, the data on average wages in the Toronto clothing industry suggest that conditions were improving considerably in every sector through to 1901 (see Table 4, column 5). From 1871 to 1891—years for which the published reports count all employees—the average annual wage per worker across the whole industry increased by a third, from $201 to $265, with increases of 29 percent in furnishings, 40 percent in menswear, 73 percent in womenswear and 94 percent in furs and hats. If the sectoral data for 1871 and 1901 are compared, even larger percentage increases can be seen in furnishings, womenswear and furs and hats: 71, 96 and 147 percent respectively. And, despite the statistic for menswear, average wages probably were up in that sector too. The census report for 1901 excludes an uncertain but assuredly considerable number of workers in small tailoring shops—those with fewer than five employees—who were typically higher-paid skilled tailors and other workers; their exclusion results in a lower than otherwise annual wage per worker, particularly as the employees of many of the firms which were counted were outworkers employed under the contracting system, with its associated evils of sweated labour and low wages. Of course, the menswear data for 1891 and 1901 also suggest the magnitude of the difference between skilled and unskilled workers' wages in this sector. Still, the general picture is of a decidedly upward trend in yearly wages to at least 1901. Moreover, to 1901, annual wages per employee were improving at higher rates than value-added per employee, suggesting that, despite the exploitation of labour in the industry and contrary to general trends, workers as well as employers may have benefitted to some extent from higher productivity[78] and longer periods of employment to earn higher annual wages, even though hourly or piece rates may not have increased.

While there were a few examples of Canadian tariffs encouraging the relocation of plants by certain shirt manufacturers from the United States to Canada, there are no known cases of American branch plants in this industry. The belief that Canada's clothing industry expanded because of import substitution fostered by tariff protection is open to doubt.[79] As early as 1858, Canadian protectionists had proposed favouring the domestic clothing industry, then centred largely in Montreal, with a duty of 30 percent on finished clothing, the highest level in their whole schedule.[80] But what manufacturers regarded as too low a level of tariff protection had not prevented the emergence of a significant clothing manufacturing industry in Canada by 1871. In 1871 the general rate of 17.5 percent applied and, though several of the manufacturers who appeared before the 1874 inquiry into the state of Canadian manufacturing complained that this was not high enough, one of them admitted that his net profits had amounted to a handsome 25 percent.[81] Others argued that a higher tariff on clothing would help to exclude the British goods or "slops" which, though not up to Canadian standards of style and durability, had captured about one quarter of the Canadian market for ready-made menswear.[82] This was the only foreign competition causing Canadian apparel-makers any serious concern in the 1870s.

The available data on clothing importations raises doubts about the assumptions concerning tariff protection and growth of clothing production. As shown in Table 6, imports rose steadily but the figures do not indicate unusual increases between 1867 and 1874, when tariffs were lower than in preceding and subsequent years. And while imports dropped off after 1879, when the National Policy schedules were established, they recovered and exceeded previous levels by the end of the 1880s. The new rates on fully-manufactured cotton and woollen clothing were set at nearly the highest level, at 30 and 25 percent.[83] Yet imports continued to rise steadily, suggesting that these items were probably goods either at the top of the market, such as high-fashion women's apparel, top quality men's suits, military uniforms or those very cheap and unstylish British goods.[84] Thus, while manufacturers like Thomas Lailey and William Sanford argued for the necessity of high tariffs to ensure the prosperity of their industry,[85] there is no evidence that the tariff mattered significantly.

In fact the degree of effective protection afforded them under the National Policy was substantially less than the specific rates suggest, because of high tariffs on their raw materials.[86] For example, the fine woollens which manufacturers used to produce men's and women's suits and coats was taxed at 23.33 percent.[87] And since the cost of these fabrics amounted to about 48 percent of the value of output, the effective protection was only about 19 percent.[88] Manufacturers argued that this was not enough to exclude the competition from certain British tailoring houses which were sending representatives twice annually to Canada and, they argued, skimming off a significant part of the market. When threatened in 1904 with even higher tariffs on imported fabrics—the result of lobbying by Canadian textile manufacturers—clothiers like John Northway howled with outrage that their competitors would enjoy even more advantages, while the lucrative market among Americans travelling in Canada would be lost.[89] But the fact that in submissions to government, manufacturers were never specific on these matters leaves room for considerable skepticism regarding their arguments about the relationship between high protective tariffs and the growth of this industry.

The rise of the clothing industry contributed to the decline of established commercial structures and to the rise of new ones. A major casualty was the Toronto wholesale drygoods trade.[90] Larger retailers avoided wholesalers as much as possible and manufacturers like John Northway or Timothy Eaton sold the clothes they manufactured in their own stores, while Sanford and others without retail outlets marketed at wholesale at the plant itself, at sales offices or through their own travelling salesmen. Some clothing manufacturers in this era sought to combat "ruinous competition" and protect "living profits." Montreal's manufacturers got together in 1884 to try to regulate competition by agreeing to send out their salesmen only twice a year at specified dates with spring and fall samples. A number of cloak producers organized themselves within the Canadian Manufacturers' Association in 1903 to standardize cloak designs, size of discounts, employment policies and other matters in the interests of "orderly marketing" but apparently without success.[91] Markets, apparently, were much too volatile and capital-threshold levels for entry into the apparel trades were far too low to keep out the hungry interlopers. By the turn of the century the Canadian appetite for stylish ready-made clothing was stimulated not only by mail-order catalogues, but also by the daily press, which ran increasingly large retail store advertisements featuring a wide variety of ready-to-wear men's, women's and children's attire for every season in numerous styles and fabrics.[92]

In a period that saw the rise of a great many smokestack factories, Toronto's leading industry, the manufacture of clothing, continued to be characterized by a large number of small shops, relatively simple technology, low capital requirements, direct links to the retail sector and the use of outworkers as the largest component of its labour force. Despite its great importance in the Toronto industrial scene, however, clothing manufacturing had a lower profile than many other industries, apparently because its production was scattered in many small locations. Its entrepreneurs were often tailors able to apply increasingly outmoded craft skills to the mass production of ready-made clothes, lesser merchants or, by the end of the century, immigrant Jews. Although those conditions had prevailed since the early 1870s, it was not until the end of the century that the sweatshop conditions would attract public notoriety. Large clothing factories where the production of a specific item of apparel could be carried through from beginning to end—what came to be called manufacturers' "inside shops"—were not developed until the 1890s when Eaton's and other manufacturers were able to exploit the emerging mass market demands for uniformity, promptness and reliability.[93] And even though Eaton's ran its own factories for certain lines, it also contracted out the production of other items.[94]

Far from demonstrating the kinds of centripetal characteristics which, it has been asserted recently, were typical of Toronto's major industries in 1871, clothing was not industrialized "with large concentrations of workers, extensive mechanization, and an elaborate division of labour."[95] Consistently showing up as one of Toronto's leading industries in every decennial census between 1871 and 1901, apparel manufacturing demonstrates a pronounced contrary trend towards centrifugality and disaggregation into smaller units with small average workforces, limited amounts of mechanization and relatively little discernible division of labour. And because it did not generate economies of scale and technological innovations which created declining marginal costs or barriers to entry, the industry offered plenty of room for small-scale entrepreneurs to try their luck. Thus, even though the clothing industry was characterized by a new and advancing technology and expanding markets, it did not experience anything like a "managerial revolution." Instead of guidance from a "visible hand," the clothing industry experienced something akin to the frantic ride of a roller coaster which dipped, climbed and weaved, while brave or foolhardy entrepreneurs leaped aboard, some to survive—for a while—and others to plummet immediately to the ground below.[96]

The small shops that continued to proliferate in all sectors of clothing production, even though some factories had begun to appear in the early twentieth century, provided a beckoning entrepreneurial frontier for newcomers, notably the Jews who were slowly emerging during the 1890s as a significant force as both workers and contractors. Meanwhile, the general locus of the industry was beginning a gradual shift westwards towards its permanent home in the city's Spadina district, an area being settled by the Jewish immigrants arriving in the city after 1900.[97]

Although exhibiting most of its historic characteristics, the apparel industry in early-twentieth-century Toronto was no longer completely hidden among the smokestacks. Its new proud symbols were the impressive multi-storied structures, each housing several manufacturers, that dotted the skyline of lower Spadina Avenue and the nearby blocks of King, Queen and Adelaide, indicating a spatial reorganization which reflected the changing social geography of the city.[98] Meanwhile, by 1930, down on the waterfront next to the city's baseball stadium, stood David Dunkelman's massive new factory and headquarters of Tip Top Tailors.[99] Yet, symbols aside, the industry remained a highly volatile one, where entrepreneurs requiring no more than a few thousand dollars as start-up capital seemed ever willing to try their luck. Whether housed in those giant structures or in tiny shops on adjoining streets, firms emerged and disappeared with bewildering speed.[100] All the while, they continued to exhibit sweatshop conditions, an indication that the changes which had taken place had not completely altered the inherent characteristics of Toronto's greatest industry.

I am happy to acknowledge financial support for my research from the Social Sciences and Humanities Research Council, Queen's University and the Multiculturalism Directorate of the Secretary of State. I received helpful comments on an earlier draft of this paper from David Keane, an anonymous appraisor, Peter George, Keith Johnson, Viv Nelles, Donald Swainson and Brian Young.

1   Donald C. Masters, *The Rise of Toronto, 1850 to 1890* (Toronto, 1947), 216–17.

2   For a penetrating analysis of the effects of industrial growth on the social landscape of Toronto, see Peter Goheen, *Victorian Toronto, 1850 to 1900: Pattern and Process of Growth* (Chicago, 1970).

3   See the illustrations in Graeme Mercer Adam, *Toronto: Old and New*... (Toronto,1891), *passim*.

4   A. Gordon Darroch, "Early Industrialism and Inequality", *Labour/Le Travailleur* 11 (1983), 31–61. The same point is made in a recent study of industrialization in Philadelphia by Bruce Laurie and Mark Schmitz, "Manufacture and Productivity: The Making of an Industrial Base, Philadelphia, 1850–1880", in Theodore Hershberg, ed., *Philadelphia: Work, Space, Family and Group Experience in the Nineteenth Century, Essays Toward an Interdisciplinary History of the City* (New York, 1981), 43–92, especially 51; Laurie and Schmitz point out (pp. 43, 87) that although scale economies existed in only a few industries, "traditional and transitional forms of production existed along with factories as late as 1880."

5   Gordon W. Bertram, "Historical Statistics on Growth and Structure in Manufacturing in Canada, 1870–1957", in Canadian Political Science Association, *Conferences on Statistics 1962 & 1963—Papers*, ed. by J. Henripin and A. Asimakopulos (Toronto, 1964), 93–146, especially 112–13; Gregory S. Kealey, *Toronto Workers Respond to Industrial Capitalism, 1867–1892* (Toronto, 1980), Tables I.14, I.15, 308–9.

6   Toronto's share of the clothing industry, 1871–1901:

Year	Value ($'000) of Production			Toronto as % of	
	Toronto	Ontario	Canada	Ontario	Canada
1871	1,699	7,289	14,807	23.3	11.5
1881	2,629	13,737	26,713	19.1	9.8
1891	7,577	24,339	43,898	31.1	17.3
1901	9,143	17,769	36,540	51.5	25.0

Source: Canada, *Census of Canada...*, III (Ottawa, 1875, 1883, 1894, 1905). The report for 1901 applies only to firms with five or more employees.

7   Bertram, 112–13.

8   A. E. Musson, *The Growth of British Industry* (New York, 1978), 230, has noted a similar comparative neglect of the clothing industry's history in Britain. While more substantial, the historiography of the industry in the United States still lacks a systematic national study. The most thorough work is Jesse E. Pope, *The Clothing Industry in New York* (Columbia, Mo., 1905). For a recent analysis see Peter Fraser, "Combined and Uneven Development in the Men's Clothing Industry", *Business History Review* 57 (1983), 522–47.

9   See R. P. Sparks, "The Garment and Clothing Industries—History and Organization", in *Manual of the Textile Industry of Canada* (Toronto, 1930), 107–32; J. M. S. Careless, *Toronto to 1918: An Illustrated History* (Toronto, 1984), ch. 4, *passim*. For a detailed analysis by industrial sector of the urbanization of manufacturing in central Canada, including York County, see Edward J. Chambers and Gordon W. Bertram, "Urbanization and Manufacturing in Central Canada, 1870–1890", in Canadian Political Science Association, *Conference on Statistics 1964—Papers on Regional Statistical Studies*, ed. by Sylvia Ostry and T. K. Rymes (Toronto, 1966), 225–40.

10 Guy Steed, "Historical Geography of the Canadian Clothing Industries: 1800–1930s", research note 11, Department of Geography and Regional Planning, University of Ottawa (Ottawa, 1976); Alan Wilson, *John Northway: A Blue Serge Canadian* (Toronto, 1965); Mercedes Steedman, "Skill and Gender in the Canadian Clothing Industry, 1890–1940", in Craig Heron and Robert Storey, eds., *On the Job: Confronting the Labour Process in Canada* (Kingston, 1986), 152–76.

11 On the spatial concentration of manufacturing see James M. Gilmour, *Spatial Evolution of Manufacturing: Southern Ontario, 1851–1891* (Toronto, 1972). The late-nineteenth-century mergers and plant relocations that resulted in the domination of agricultural implements manufacturing by the Massey-Harris company are examined in Peter Cook, *Massey At the Brink: The Story of Canada's Greatest Multinational and Its Struggle to Survive* (Toronto, 1981), ch. 2. Duncan McDowell, *Steel at the Sault: Francis H. Clergue, Sir James Dunn, and the Algoma Steel Corporation 1901–1956* (Toronto, 1984), 7–22, discusses the effects of technological changes on the nascent Canadian iron and steel industry of the 1890s.

12 Alfred D. Chandler Jr., *The Visible Hand: The Managerial Revolution in American Business* (Cambridge, 1977), 8.

13 Ibid., 6.

14 Michael Bliss, *A Living Profit: Studies in the Social History of Canadian Business, 1883–1911* (Toronto, 1974).

15 Fraser, 523, 535. These sectors were the primary, which was advanced, stable, factory-centred and based on demand at the bottom of the business cycle, and the secondary,

which was backward and less sophisticated, volatile and dependent upon the variable component of demand.

16 G. W. Bertram, "Economic Growth in Canadian Industry, 1870–1915: The Staple Model", in W. T. Easterbrook and M. H. Watkins, eds., *Approaches to Canadian Economic History* (Toronto, 1967), 74–98.

17 Canada [United Province], *Census of Canada, 1851–2*, I (Quebec, 1853), 504–25. See also National Archives of Canada [hereafter NAC], MG 28–III, R. G. Dun and Co. Collection, Canada, vols. 26–27, *passim* [mfm., from originals in the Baker Library, Graduate School of Business Administration, Harvard University].

18 See tables of trade and navigation in appendices and sessional papers [various numbers], in Canada [United Province], Legislative Assembly, *Session Papers* [title varies] (Quebec and Toronto, 1850–65), *passim*.

19 Kealey, 39–40.

20 Canada [United Province], *Census of 1860–1861*, I (Quebec, 1863), 557–75.

21 Ibid.

22 See note 6.

23 See Eileen Collard, *Clothing in English Canada, Circa 1867 to 1907* (n.p., n.d.) and K. B. Brett, *Women's Costume in Ontario, 1867–1907* (Toronto, 1966).

24 Stephen Speisman, *The Jews of Toronto: A History to 1937* (Toronto, 1979), 71. Salo Baron argues that for social and religious reasons Jewish communities in Eastern Europe included large numbers of tailors. In 1897 Jews in the Russian Pale of Settlement were represented most fully in the clothing industry. See Salo Baron, *The Russian Jew Under Tsars and Soviets* (New York, 1976), 81, 88, and Henry Tobias, *The Jewish Bund in Russia: From its Origins to 1905* (Stanford, 1972), 8. Thus, in Toronto as in other North American centres, the textile and clothing industries lent themselves well to Jewish enterprise.

25 Bertram, "Economic Growth", 86–87, demonstrates that of 23 industry groups only tobacco and paper products experienced faster rates of growth than clothing in value-added as a percentage of total value-added in the manufacturing sector between 1870 and 1900. Moreover, clothing rose from seventh to third place in rank by value of output during the same period.

26 N. Maurice Davidson, "Montreal's Dominance of the Men's Fine Clothing Industry" (M.A. diss., University of Western Ontario, 1969), 10–29.

27 See the Ontario evidence in Canada, Royal Commission on the Relations of Labour and Capital in Canada, *Report* (Ottawa, 1889) [hereafter RCRLC], 832.

28 The reliability of the 1871 industrial census, which provides an invaluable and detailed Canadian industrial portrait, might legitimately be questioned, as this was the first census conducted by the new Dominion government. Efforts were made to make the returns as uniform and reliable as possible. See "Introduction", in Canada, Dept. of Agriculture, *Census of Canada, 1870–71*, I (Ottawa, 1873), xii, where it is made clear that enumerators had received detailed instructions in collecting and entering information on the schedules; for the text of the instructions, see Canada, Dept. of Agriculture (Census Branch), *Manual Containing "The Census Act," and the Instructions to Officers Employed in the Taking of the First Census of Canada, (1871)* (Ottawa, 1871).

29 J. Timperlake, comp., *Illustrated Toronto: Past and Present* (Toronto, 1877), 334.

30 H. E. Stephenson and Carlton McNaught, *The Story of Advertising in Canada: A Chronicle of Fifty Years* (Toronto, 1940), 83.

31 NAC, RG 31, Statistics Canada, Census Records, Ontario, 1871 [hereafter MSS Census 1871], mfm. C–9971, dist. 47 Toronto East, subdist. A, St. Lawrence Ward, sched. 6, p. 14, row 4.

32 Ibid., p. 13, row 4.

33 Lailey's name does not appear in MSS Census 1871 but his firm is probably the one listed as a "Clothing, Mantle and Millinery Factory", ibid., p. 18, row 4. See also Timperlake, 330–31.

34 Canada, House of Commons, *Journals* (1874), app. 3, "Select Committee to inquire into the extent and condition of the Manufacturing interests of the Dominion", 12–63 [hereafter "Select Committee"].

35 MSS Census 1871, mfm. C–9969–73, *passim*.

36 *Industries of Canada: Historical and Commercial Sketches of Toronto and Environs, etc.* (Toronto, 1886), 101, 197.

37 *Canadian Textile Directory* [hereafter CTD] (Montreal, 1885), 193–94; (Montreal, 1889), 236–37; (Montreal, 1892), 316–17; (Montreal, 1899), 373–74.

38 Masters, *passim*. Assumptions concerning Toronto's metropolitan status in the late nineteenth century have been challenged recently by Jim Sentance, "Reconsidering Toronto's Emergence as a Metropolis: Some Evidence From the Census", *Urban History Review* 13 (1984), 9–18.

39 Careless, 115.

40 Sparks, 132.

41 Collard, 5.

42 Paul H. Nystrom, *Economics of Fashion* (New York, 1928), 275, 294.

43 See Wilson, 28–52.

44 Linda Shapiro, ed., *Yesterday's Toronto, 1870–1910* (Toronto, 1978), 66–67.

45 Mary-Etta Macpherson, *Shopkeepers to a Nation: The Eatons* (Toronto, 1963), 27.

46 Wilson, 65–68.

47 In examining the growth of London's clothing industry, the historical geographer P. G. Hall explained that close and frequent contact with its market was imperative "because of the importance of individual fit and the capriciousness and unpredictable trends of style." P. G. Hall, *The Industries of London Since 1861* (London, 1962), 52.

48 RCRLC, 829; *The Canadian Biographical Dictionary and Portrait Gallery of Eminent and Self-Made Men, Ontario Volume* (Toronto, 1880), 434–40, especially 437.

49 NAC, MG 26–J–4, William Lyon Mackenzie King Papers, Memoranda and Notes, vol. 27, C18021–31.

50 *Industries of Canada*, 123.

51 Steed, 47–48; Gilmour, 143, points out that all consumer-goods industries in Ontario concentrated in the area that emerged as the manufacturing belt to a much higher degree than he expected.

52 Musson, 230.

53 Joan Thomas, *A History of the Leeds Clothing Industry*, Yorkshire Bulletin of Economic and Social Research, Occasional Paper, no.1 (n.p., n.d.), 14–15.

54 Hall, 39. On the rise of Jewish participation in the London clothing industry see Robert S. Wechsler, "The Jewish Garment Trade in East London 1875–1914: A Study of Conditions and Responses" (Ph.D. diss., Columbia University, 1979).

55 On New York, see Pope and B. M. Selekman et al., *The Clothing and Textile Industries in New York and Environs* (New York, 1925); Philip Scranton, *Proprietary Capitalism, The Textile Manufacture at Philadelphia, 1800–1885* (New York, 1983), 281–83, 335–36. For contemporary descriptions of Philadelphia's ready-made clothing industry see Edwin T. Freedley, *Philadelphia and Its Manufacturers* (Philadelphia, 1858), 220–25.

56 Chicago became a leading national centre for the production of high quality men's ready-to-wear suits and coats; see Bessie L. Pierce, *A History of Chicago, 1871–1893*, I (Chicago, 1957), 171–74; Robert James Myers, *The Economic Aspects of the Production of Men's Clothing (With Particular Reference to the Industry in Chicago)* (Chicago, 1937).

57 Elizabeth Price, "The Changing Geography of the Woollen Industry in Lanark, Renfrew and Carleton Counties, 1830–1911" (M.A. diss., University of Toronto, 1979), 51 and *passim*. See also Richard Reid, "The Rosamond Woolen Company of Almonte: Industrial Development in a Rural Setting", *Ontario History* 75 (1983), 266–89.

58 Martha Eckman Brent, "A Stitch in Time; The Sewing Machine Industry of Ontario, 1860–1897", *Material History Bulletin* 10 (1980), 1–31.

59 CTD (Montreal, 1892), 315; (Montreal, 1899), 371. Toronto did not compete with Montreal for the Maritimes market for manufactured goods until after 1911; Larry D. McCann, "Metropolitanism, Canadian-Style: Urban Dominance and the Economy of the Maritimes, 1867–1929", paper presented to the Canadian Historical Association, Vancouver, June 1983, 10.

60 The initial rejection in 1852 of sewing machines by the Toronto tailors employed at Walker and Hutchinson did not succeed in preventing the widespread adoption of this new technology throughout the industry; Conyngham C. Taylor, *Toronto "Called Back" From 1887–1847* (Toronto, 1887), 75. Kealey, 322, provides a list of tailors' strikes in the 1870s and 1880s but no discussion of their origins and outcome. The evolution of the Canadian sewing machine industry well deserves a systematic study. From the 1860s Singer had an efficient distribution network operating in Canada; Andrew B. Jack, "The Channels of Distribution For an Innovation: The Sewing Machine Industry in America, 1860–1865", *Explorations in Entrepreneurial History* 9 (1957), 113–41.

61 William C. Browning, "The Clothing and Furnishing Trade", in Chauncey M.Depew, ed., *One Hundred Years of American Commerce, 1795–1895* (New York, 1895), 561–65.

62 Martin Popkin, *Organization, Management and Technology in the Manufacture of Men's Clothing* (New York, 1929), 7, 336–85.

63 Ibid., 336–85. A Montreal company was chartered in 1884 to manufacture and distribute button-holing equipment; see NAC, RG 68–IV–A, Dept. of the Registrar General, Originals of registered documents, Documents, mfm. C–4009, pp. 414–16.

64 Margaret Wray, *The Women's Outerwear Industry* (London, 1957), 17.

65 MSS Census 1871, mfm. C–9969–73, *passim*, include returns on two straw hat and one knitwear manufacturers who used steam power. The British clothing trades also used very little steam power in 1870; Raphael Samuel, "The Workshop of the World: Steam Power and Hand Technology in mid-Victorian Britain", *History Workshop* 3 (1977), 19.

66 W. L. Mackenzie King, *Report to the Postmaster-General on the Methods Adopted in Canada in the Carrying Out of Government Clothing Contracts* (Ottawa, 1898), 11.

67 In the 1840s, Charles Kingsley reported on the evils of the London outwork system in his essay "Cheap Clothes and Nasty", while Henry Mayhew wrote lurid exposes for the London *Morning Chronicle* on the extent of the exploitation and degradation that outwork created among London clothing workers. See Henry Mayhew, *London Labour and the London Poor* (New York, 1967).

68 RCRLC, 628.

69 Ibid.

70 "Select Committee", *passim*.

71 James A. Schmeichen, *Sweated Industries and Sweated Labour: The London Clothing Trades, 1860–1914* (Urbana, 1984), 7–23.

72 Canada, House of Commons, *Sessional Papers* (Ottawa, 1882), no. 42, "Report of the Commissioners appointed to enquire into the working of Mills and Factories of the Dominion, and the labour employed in them", 4.

73 Jean T. Scott, *The Conditions of Female Labour in Ontario* (Toronto, 1891), 23.

74 Canada, House of Commons, *Sessional Papers* (Ottawa, 1896), no. 61, "Report Upon the Sweating System in Canada…", 6 [hereafter "Sweating System"].

75 Ibid., 9.

76 King, *passim*.

77 See, for example, Paul Harrison, *Inside the Inner City: Life Under the Cutting Edge* (London, 1983), 42.

78 G. Kealey and B. Palmer argue that wages as a percentage of value added were relatively stable in Ontario between 1871 and 1901; "The Bonds of Unity; the Knights of Labor in Ontario, 1880–1900", *Histoire sociale/Social History* 14 (1981), 369–411, especially 377. A. Gordon Darroch, "Occupational Structure, Assessed Wealth and Homeowning during Toronto's Early Industrialization, 1861–1899", ibid. 16 (1983), 381–410, argues that "inequality among [Toronto's] occupational groups was at its height in 1871, early in industrialization, declined with industrial expansion but then increased as the city entered the twentieth century," 399.

79 See Sparks, 114–18; Careless, 111. D. F. Barnett, "The Galt Tariff: Incidental Or Effective Protection?", *Canadian Journal of Economics* 9 (1976), 389–407, demonstrates that the 1859 tariff changes affected the apparel and other tertiary industries least.

80 Jacob DeWitt et al., *Letters to the People of Canada on Canadian Manufactures* (Montreal, 1858), 14; *The Canadian Merchants' Magazine and Commercial Review* 2 (1858), 289–97.

81   "Select Committee", 35. This testimony from William Muir, a Montreal wholesale clothier, did not specify what this was a percentage of.

82   Ibid., 14, 19.

83   Orville J. McDiarmid, *Commercial Policy in the Canadian Economy* (Cambridge, Mass., 1946), 162.

84   Canada's militia imported virtually all of its uniforms from Britain until the late 1880s, when local manufacturers finally succeeded in convincing authorities that work of the same quality could be done in Canada; Norbert H. Black, "The Search For Canadian Sources: Supplying the Militia, 1867–1905", graduate seminar paper, Department of History, Queen's University (March 1986) [mss. in possession of author].

85   Dominion National League, *Country Before Party* (Hamilton, 1878), 19–21, and *Proceedings of a Special Meeting of the Manufacturers' Association of Ontario, Held at St. Lawrence Hall, 25 & 26 November, 1875* (Toronto, 1876), *passim*. The Montreal fur goods manufacturer E. K. Greene was a leading spokesman of protectionists in Quebec; see Ben Forster, "The Coming of the National Policy: Business, Government and the Tariff, 1876–1879", *Journal of Canadian Studies* 14 (1979), 39–49, especially 43.

86   Clarence L. Barber, "Canadian Tariff Policy", *Canadian Journal of Economics and Political Science* 21 (1955), 513–30; see 523–24 for an explanation of the important distinction between the formal or published tariff rates and the *effective* or real level of protection.

87   NAC, RG 36–17, Fielding Tariff Inquiry Commission 1898–1906 [hereafter FTIC], vol. 1, p. 793.

88   In these calculations I have employed the ratios of costs of materials, miscellaneous expenses, wages, salaries and interest on capital to values of products, reported for clothing in *Census of Canada, 1901*, III (Ottawa, 1905), xlix. These average 48 percent.

89   FTIC, John Northway to W. S. Fielding, 10 June 1904.

90   Brenda K. Newell, "From Cloth to Clothing: The Emergence of the Department Stores in Late Nineteenth Century Toronto" (M.A. diss., Trent University, 1984), 173. See also Ian M. Drummond, "The Revolution in Ontario Commerce, 1867–1940", 3, 8 [mss. in possession of author].

91   *Montreal Star*, 19 Apr. 1884. NAC, MG 28–I, Canadian Manufacturers' Association Papers, vol. 39, Cloak Manufacturers' Association Minutes, 17.

92   Paul Rutherford, *Victorian Authority: The Daily Press in Late Nineteenth-Century Canada* (Toronto, 1982), 123.

93   Fraser, 537, dates the emergence of the modern clothing factory or "inside shop" in the United States from 1905.

94   "Sweating System".

95   Kealey, 29. Gordon Darroch, "Early Industrialization", 53, points out, however, that Kealey's statistics indicate "there were very few exceedingly large shops…and hundreds more traditional workplaces."

96   Interview with C. Laviolette, executive secretary, Canadian Men's Clothing Manufacturers' Association, Montreal, 7 July 1977. Statistics on the women's clothing sector show that an average of 18.6 percent of manufacturers failed every year between 1916 and 1929. Sparks, 130.

97   See Daniel Hiebert, "The Emergence of the Spadina District in Toronto", paper presented to the Canadian Association of Geographers, Winnipeg, 1983, and "Ethnicity and the Urban Experience: The Spatial and Social Mobility of Jews in Toronto, 1901–1931", paper presented to the Canadian Association of Geographers, Nanaimo, 1984.

98   Edward K. Muller and Paul A. Groves have made a useful analysis of this kind of transformation in nineteenth-century Baltimore, "The Changing Location of the Clothing Industry: A Link to the Social Geography of Baltimore in the Nineteenth Century", *Maryland Historical Magazine* 71 (1976), 403–20.

99   Ben Dunkelman, *Dual Allegiance* (Toronto, 1978), 7–8.

100 Sparks, *passim*; Canada, Royal Commission on Price Spreads, *Report* (Ottawa, 1935), 109–12. See also Louis Levine, *The Women's Garment Workers: A History of the International Ladies' Garment Workers' Union* (New York, 1924), viii.

"Friendly Atoms in Chemistry": Women and Men at Normal School in Mid-Nineteenth-Century Toronto

ALISON PRENTICE

Jane A. Cruise enrolled in the Ontario Normal School in Toronto in the autumn of 1869. Miss Cruise, then 16, was a Toronto resident, member of the Church of England, and graduate of the model school for girls associated with the provincial teacher-training institution. Not surprisingly given her age, she had no prior experience of teaching school, a fact which distinguished her from many of her fellow students, especially the men. Jane Cruise completed two sessions at Toronto Normal, leaving with a first-class certificate in the spring of 1870, whereupon she was immediately snapped up by the Toronto Public School Board. She went to work at Toronto's Victoria Street School for an annual salary of 140 dollars. Within a year she had been transferred to the Elizabeth Street School and had received a substantial raise.[1]

In some ways the experience of Jane Cruise was typical of urban Ontario elementary school teachers for both her period and her sex. By the time she entered the Normal School in 1869, hundreds of young city women had passed through the 22-year-old institution. Often they stayed for more than one half-year session and, if they won certificates, more often than not they ended up teaching for an urban school board. What makes Jane Cruise special is the fact that 15 years after her first appointment in a Toronto school she joined forces with seven of her Public School Board colleagues to found an innovative female organization, the embryo Women Teachers' Association of Toronto.[2] All of the eight founding members of the WTA had been to the Provincial Normal School. But in this they were not unique, for by the 1880s so too had the vast majority of their fellow workers in the city's public schools.[3]

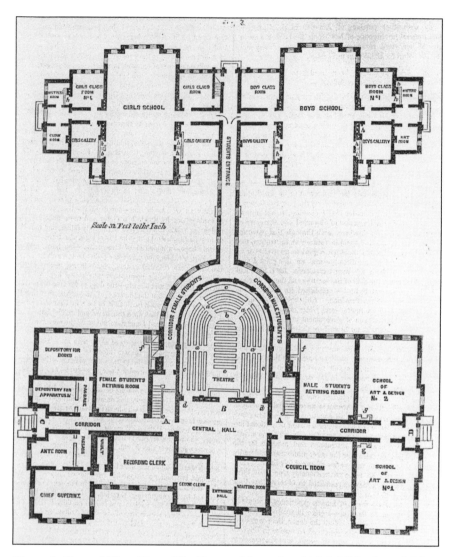

Figure 1: Ground Floor Plan of the Toronto Normal and Model Schools and Education Offices, **Journal of Education of Upper Canada** *4 (July 1851), 100*

What were the purposes of the institution that trained Jane Cruise? Who were the women and men who attended it and what were the experiences of the female and male students at this early teacher-training school? An exploration of these questions sheds light on an important early experiment in the advanced schooling of women.[4] But it also has much to tell us about regional variation in the history of an interesting educational institution. The Normal School in Toronto was very much the product of a teacher-training movement with ties reaching far beyond Ontario, and even North America, to western Europe. But inevitably it was also a product of a particular place. Both as an educational and as a social institution, it was moulded by, reflected and ultimately exerted a powerful influence on the culture of schooling in Toronto and across the province.

The school brought into being by Upper Canada's chief superintendent of schools, Egerton Ryerson, and his supporters in the mid 1840s was designed with a particular and in some ways unique set of goals in mind. Unlike most American normal schools,[5] which were located in small towns, Upper Canada's was situated in a city that was rapidly becoming the province's economic centre and would soon be its permanent political capital as well. From this vantage point Toronto Normal was clearly intended to play a metropolitan role. Although the school first opened in temporary quarters in the fall of 1847, it was the dedication of the imposing stone structure on Gould Street, between Church and Victoria, which was to become its home in 1852, that provided the occasion for Ryerson and other leading men of the times to elaborate on this theme. To Egerton Ryerson, the new institution was more than just a model for the province. The school he was to watch over so closely in the years that followed was, he claimed, the very "personi-fication" of public instruction in Upper Canada. But it was the chief justice of Upper Canada, John Beverley Robinson, who put forward most clearly the idea of the school as a centre of metropolitan influence. The effect, he be-lieved, could not be instantaneous; but very quickly a "dispersion" or "multiplying" process would occur. "Each well informed and well trained teacher will impart what he has learned to many." The many, in turn, would gradually help to raise the general standard of intelligence throughout the province.[6]

In Upper Canada the initiators of teacher training under the auspices of the state looked for inspiration to a number of sources. They were accused of imposing on the province a questionable and potentially dangerous Prus-sian approach to the task of teacher education—and Prussian schools had indeed made a lasting impression on Ryerson, as they had on the founders of similar state schools in New England. But the institution that appears to have impressed Ryerson most on his exploratory travels in the United States and Europe was the Irish national school for training teachers in Dublin. Almost within a year of his appointment as the chief superintendent's clerk in the Education Office, the young John George Hodgins had been dis-patched to the Dublin school to spend a term there learning the ropes. The first headmaster engaged for Toronto, Robert Rintoul, was headmaster of the model school attached to Dublin Normal. Unable to make the journey to Upper Canada because of family illness, he was replaced by Thomas Robertson, then chief inspector of the Irish national school system. In addi-tion, during a formative year prior to the opening of Upper Canada's school, Ryerson and Hodgins evidently sought advice from their Irish mentors.[7]

Within a year of their school's opening, however, the Upper Canadian authorities broke with their Irish model in one crucial respect. Although the Dublin school was an exclusively male institution and although Ryerson, when outlining his plans for Toronto's school in 1846, referred only to the "young men" who would be trained there under his supervision,[8] Upper Canada's training school remained a single-sex institution for but one session. When the second session began in 1848 women were admitted along with the men. If there was a debate on the question of admitting women, evidence of it has yet to be uncovered. We know only that the authorities who controlled the Normal changed their minds about who should or could attend. The pressures they bowed to may well have been economic; co-education was introduced in many other nineteenth-century North American post-elementary institutions at least partly to make up for insufficient male enrolment and help defray escalating costs.[9] There may also have been pressure from the families of potential female students. Clearly there were Upper Canadian women who wanted to attend Toronto Normal and who, in the case of the more youthful among them, had families or guardians who welcomed the opportunity to enrol their daughters or female dependents in the school for one or more terms.

Letters of inquiry written by and on behalf of applicants of both sexes[10] reveal much about the economic circumstances and motives of interested families as well as of the women and men who made their way to the school's doors during its first decades. Parental letters sometimes hint at serious family hardships. Elizabeth Spohn, writing on behalf of her son Gloward in 1860, was probably a widow although she did not say so. Robert Heron of Canfield, perhaps concerned that his remaining years as a schoolmaster were few, requested information not only about the school on behalf of his child but also about teachers' pensions. Samuel Horner of Brockville pointed out that the schoolmistress daughter whom he wished to send to the Normal was currently unemployed. This made for a difficult situation since his family was large and, after 20 years of teaching school, he was in feeble health.[11]

Even more telling are the letters of people who wrote on behalf of siblings, wards or acquaintances. G. W. Desvoung sought information on behalf of his housekeeper's niece, who came from a large family and whose father was a cripple. James Gamble sought entry for his ward, Mary Elizabeth Brown. He argued that Mary Elizabeth, although only 15 years old, was "very steady in her habits" and had made "great progress" at the female seminary in Picton. The problem was that her mother was dead and her father did not look after her; soon she would have to provide for herself. Perhaps the most poignant communications of this sort were those seeking admission for older women and men who were clearly in distressed circumstances. An Irish immigrant wrote describing the "utter destitution" into which the death of her father had precipitated his children. She and her sister intended to move to Toronto and to support their brother's studies at the Normal School by their work as dressmakers.[12]

Although correspondents most frequently spoke of economic problems facing future pupil-teachers or their families, more than a few referred to another category of difficulty: physical disability. Where manual labour was painful or impossible, teaching may have seemed the best or even the only path towards a measure of independence in life. A local superintendent wrote in 1859, for example, on behalf of a young teacher who was lame in both feet and had to walk on crutches. He noted that it was the belief of the young man's father that no lame person could be admitted to the school. Evidence on the point is, of course, ambiguous. Ansel Randall, who had been a student six years earlier, had a lame leg and an arm amputated below the elbow. On the other hand, a letter by Ryerson written a year before Randall was admitted expresses concern that a proposed candidate's mind might be "so far affected by his body" that he would not be able to advance with the class. The degree of disability was obviously important, as was the idea of keeping up. It would not do, Ryerson wrote, for an institution which ought to be efficient and sought after to become "the resort of invalids."[13]

The letters of inquiry which came directly from prospective students are equally revealing. Most of the writers were already teachers; many expressed concerns similar to those of the less directly interested correspondents. Quite a few of those writing on their own behalf, however, felt called upon to give more elevated reasons for wanting to enter the Normal. Isaac Barefoot, a teacher on the Grand River Indian Reserve, wished to acquire a "more extended knowledge of education" and of "the school's system of teaching." George W. Ross wrote of the teacher's need, if he wished to be genuinely qualified, to be "thoroughly versed" in whatever he undertook to teach. Arthur Purkis referred to "the valuable method of imparting instruction so nobly inaugurated" by Ryerson, and without which no teacher could hope to "succeed in his profession."[14]

Some teachers wanted to attend the Normal School even though they already had long experience in the classroom. Such was J. Taylor of Collins Bay, who had taught for 12 years, part of the time as second master of the Kingston Grammar School but chiefly in his own private establishment. He and a great many other teachers probably shared the motive of R. O'Brien, who wrote in 1853 of his wish to return for a second term in the hope of getting a provincial certificate. This valuable paper would exempt him from the "ordeal" of going before a county board of public instruction to be examined for a teaching certificate "on the occasion of almost every change of locality." That teachers should move constantly from one school section or county to another was not the wish of the Education Department but it was clearly the method of proceeding preferred by many rural teachers in the nineteenth century. O'Brien noted in his letter that any "pecuniary loss" incurred as a result of attending the Normal would be more than repaid by the "consoling fact" that he would never again have to face a county board examination. O'Brien was unusual in expressing such a sanguine view of the costs. Far more often, prospective students who commented on fees expressed concern about the financial outlay involved in coming to Toronto.[15]

Another unknown that caused anxiety to the parents, guardians and friends of prospective pupil teachers was the moral atmosphere of both the school and the city in which it was situated. A local superintendent inquired in 1858 on behalf of a father who had expressed special interest in the safety of the boarding arrangements. Another wrote on behalf of a "rich farmer" who was anxious to know how much attention Dr. Ryerson was able to pay to the young men in his charge. So confident in Ryerson's all-seeing eye was this correspondent that he had not waited for a reply; he had already "assured" the farmer that the young men received "all necessary attention." Prospective students also worried that they might not be able to keep up with the classes. Others were concerned about the declaration, required on entry, that they would devote themselves to teaching. Did this mean a commitment for the rest of their lives? James C. McDonald of Oxford County frankly admitted that he intended to teach for only a few years. Alma Sophia Allingham, on the other hand, saw her future very differently. She wrote from Hawkestone to find out what requirements might exist specifically for female teachers who aspired to first-class certificates. Allingham already had a county certificate but, unlike many rural teachers, she did not wish to be an itinerant. On the contrary she saw the provincial certificate leading to the certainty of "a good permanent engagement."[16]

If Alma Allingham was aware that women might be treated as special cases, members of religious minorities had similar perceptions. Philip H. How was a teacher in Orillia who reported that people were prejudiced against him because he did not believe that Sunday was the sabbath. Would his religious views prevent him from attending the school? That local prejudice against hiring Roman Catholics might be a problem was certainly the belief of Jeremiah Gallivan. In the first of a series of letters to Ryerson, Gallivan reported that although he had already been trained at Dublin Normal, Thomas Robertson had "very candidly" informed him that the training would not be of much use to him because he was a Roman Catholic and would be in the Normal for a long time before he would get "a call." In a subsequent letter, Gallivan, noting that he had now become a Protestant, presumed that this difficulty no longer applied.[17]

Clearly the waters of religious feeling were considerably muddied in Gallivan's case by his stated intention to spend less than a full session at the Normal. On this issue, which appears to have been a matter of internal dispute, Robertson was adamant. He maintained that it would be impossible to guarantee any student's knowledge of the "Canadian" system of instruction after only a few weeks' attendance. The discussion of Gallivan's case did not end the question, for March 1863 found Robertson writing again to Ryerson to reiterate his view that late admission was both "inconvenient" and "mischievous." It was hard enough to take the class through the program in one session. In April 1864 he repeated his stand against pupil-teachers attending less than a complete term. Whatever students' literary accomplishments, the school's masters needed time to form an opinion about their "personal habits, general tone of mind, & style, or...capabilities in communicating knowledge."[18]

The fact that inquiries and discussion continued on this issue is evidence of how unaccustomed many Upper Canadians still were to the idea of a fixed school term or year. At the Normal School this appears to have settled down to a year consisting of two five-month sessions, one beginning in January, the second beginning in August.[19] But the rigid attendance schedules that reformist schoolmasters and mistresses were so anxious to enforce, in the interests of introducing a methodology that involved covering a given course or teaching an entire class "simultaneously," were still considered inappropriate and unnecessary in many rural school sections. Indeed teachers frequently wrote to say that they could not arrive at the beginning of the Normal School session because their current teaching position did not "finish" on time.[20]

The irritation felt by applicants who were forced to adjust the timing of their lives to the school's fixed schedule was minor compared to that experienced by those who, for various reasons, were compelled to leave in mid-session or whose applications were rejected. One can only wonder at the feelings of a Bathurst District student who left during the first session. A terse note in the school's register records his shortcomings: "Reads badly spells worse. No geog arith bad No geomt No Algebra. Gone 27 May incompetent."[21] Possibly in response to this and similar cases and the high drop-out rate experienced in the Normal's early years, entrance examinations were in place by the early 1850s. The humiliation involved for some would-be students who failed to gain entry emerges in a letter written to Ryerson by a deeply offended parent in 1852. Peter Sammons of Welland believed that his boy had been sent home for failing to answer the questions put to him in geography, a subject he had never studied. Sammon accused the "great men" of Toronto of trifling with people's feelings and pocketbooks. The school, after all, was supposed to be "for the education of young men, not for those that have their education finished." John Fraser wrote in 1864 to defend a rejected daughter, Emma, who in his view had not been examined fairly. Fraser was a critic of some force, for two of Emma's sisters had attended the Normal, not only passing with honours but obtaining first-class certificates. Fraser had in fact prepared seven of his children to be teachers and clearly was unhappy to have this one crushed in spirit by losing her place in the school.[22] He believed that the real reason for rejecting large numbers of students in 1864 was overcrowding and the need to reduce enrolments.[23]

Certainly Fraser's complaint came at a period when the percentage of applicants who failed to pass the entrance examinations had been at a fairly high level for several sessions. Overall, the school seems to have rejected no more than 10 percent of the women and men who applied for admission during its first two decades. But the rejection rate for women jumped to 20 percent during a brief period in the early 1850s and rose again in the late 1850s for both sexes, staying relatively high until the mid 1860s (Table 1). Presumably these higher rates and, indeed, what happened to Emma Fraser reflected the higher admission standards adopted in 1859. Depressed eco-

Table 1: Toronto Normal School, 1847–71: Admissions and Attendance by Sex

Session	Women					Men				
	Applicants	Admitted		Left Early[a]		Applicants	Admitted		Left Early[a]	
	n	n	%[b]	n	%[c]	n	n	%[b]	n	%[c]
1–5 1847–50	138	125	90.6	36	28.8	488	419	85.9	158	37.7
6–10 1850–53	257	209	81.3	45	21.5	392	354	90.3	108	30.5
11–15 1853–56	380	347	91.3	56	16.1	260	248	95.4	73	29.4
16–20 1856–58	379	360	95.0	50	13.9	422	405	96.0	104	25.7
21–25 1859–61	427	356	83.4	61	17.1	504	436	86.5	127	29.1
26–30 1861–63	395	346	87.6	63	18.2	440	376	85.5	91	24.2
31–35 1864–66	464	427	92.0	94	22.0	382	347	90.8	99	28.5
36–40 1866–68	427	391	91.6	86	22.0	269	249	92.6	85	34.1
41–45 1869–71	504	474	94.0	83	17.5	378	364	96.3	118	32.4
1–45 1847–71	3,371	3,035	90.0	574	18.9	3,535	3,198	90.5	963	30.1

Source: Statistical tables in *Annual Report of the Chief Superintendent of Schools* [title varies] (Quebec, Toronto [place varies], 1862–72). Education Dept. officials included persons re-applying for admission or attending a second or subsequent session in calculating each session's totals.

n number of persons

[a] withdrew from classes before the end of the session

[b] n as a percentage of total applicants in the period

[c] n as a percentage of total admitted in the period

nomic conditions in the late 1850s may also have contributed; hard times may have encouraged unqualified persons to apply in proportionately larger numbers. By the late 1860s, however, either the harsher mood had passed or the weaker candidates were no longer applying to the same extent. Between 1864 and 1871 both women and men achieved admission rates of over 90 percent once again.[24]

This did not mean that all those who won entry in any given session managed to remain for the entire school term. Indeed the drop-out rate was high: 25 percent of all students "left early" during the first 45 sessions from 1847 to 1871 (Table 1). And there was a major difference between the female and male students: in all but 5 of the first 45 sessions, proportionately fewer women than men left early. Taking the 1st to 45th sessions as a whole, the rate for the women was 19 percent compared to 30 percent for the men.

Why did students drop out in mid-session? Clearly concerned about the problem, school authorities attempted to keep track of the reasons. From 1850 to 1854 comments were recorded reasonably consistently in the school register; these are extant for 189 individuals. In addition, a special report survives dealing with 25 students who did not complete the session ending in April 1855.[25] For six tenths of the 73 women and seven tenths of the 141 men in these combined groups the reasons are clear (Table 2). Ill health, whether of themselves or a member of their family, was the most common cause, being cited by approximately 40 percent of both sexes. Discipline-related causes came next for the men and "incompetence" for the women, but each sex had some in each category. Hardly any of the women left in mid-session to take a school but 11 percent of the men who gave reasons had been lured away to teaching positions. Finally, students left because they were too young, were "needed elsewhere," or were simply "dissatisfied." Perhaps some shared the views of A. McCharles, who reminisced many years later about his decision to leave the school. McCharles had been promoted from the second- to the first-class department as a result of his success on the entrance examination, but in the six weeks that followed he had learned absolutely nothing that was new to him "except the name of a little branch of the Danube River."[26]

When the winnowing process was completed in any given session, the decrease in the numbers of male students must have been discernible. Less noticeable at the time but more significant in the long run was the gradual overall decline in the numbers, both relative and absolute, of men compared to women who applied and were accepted into the school in the first place (Table 1). The men dropped quickly from the numerical pre-eminence they clearly enjoyed during the first ten terms; after 1853 they barely averaged one half of the student body. By the mid and late 1860s women were consistently entering the school in larger numbers than the men, as well as persisting more effectively once they got there.

The tendency to persist, that is to complete the session, may have been related to whether the student had any previous teaching experience. And here another important contrast can be seen between the women and men

Table 2: Toronto Normal School, 1850–54 and 1855: Reasons for Leaving Early (before the end of the session)

Reason	Women			Men		
	Rank	n	%	Rank	n	%
A: Known						
Illness/"alleged" illness/death of student or family member	1	19	44	1	36	36
"Incompetence"	2	14	33	3	14	14
"Dissatisfied"/"Wanted at home"/ "Own convenience"	3	5	12	4	12	12
Discipline-related problem(s)	4	3	7	2	16	16
"To take a school"	5.5	1	2	5	11	11
"Want of funds"	5.5	1	2	7	3	3
"Too young"	–	0	0	6	7	7
Total Known		43	100		99	100
B: Not Given or Unclear		30			42	
Total		73			141	

Source: Archives of Ontario, RG 2–H–1, vol. 10, Toronto Normal School Registers, sessions 1850–54; RG 2–C–6–C, Incoming General Correspondence, "List of students who left during the session", 18 Apr. 1855.

n   number of students leaving early
%   n as percentage of total for whom a reason is known

attending the Normal during its first two decades. The women were much less likely than the men to have taught school before they sought teacher training. Indeed, the gap appears to have widened slightly over time. In the Normal's first decade a little over 35 percent of the women had previously taught school, whereas around 61 percent of the men had already been teachers. During the second decade the proportion of former teachers among the women dropped to 28 percent while that for the men rose to 73 percent, nearly three quarters of all the men who enrolled.[27]

The tendency to persist seems also to have been related to the student's age. Students' ages on entry are recorded in the school's registers. An examination of two cohorts of pupil-teachers, a group of 311 women and 384 men who attended between 1850 and 1854 and a second group of 484 women and 480 men who attended between 1869 and 1872, reveals that the women in the first cohort tended to be slightly older than those in the second, the difference in median ages being 1 year (Table 3). A different pattern is revealed with the men. Those in the first cohort were essentially neither older nor younger than those in the second; the median age in each cohort was 21 years. The most dramatic contrasts, however, are those between the women and the men. Moreover, the major differences between the sexes in the first cohort are not merely repeated in the second; they are if anything larger. In both cohorts the women were generally at least 2 years younger than the men. Well over one third of the women were in fact younger than 18. Less than six percent of the male students were this young in the 1850–54 cohort; indeed, in 1851 the rules stipulated that boys under 18 were no longer eligible to attend.[28] Only three such cases slipped through the admission net between 1869 and 1872.

Both the metropolitan purposes of Ontario's first training school and the political controversy surrounding its capture by the city of Toronto[29] suggested the need to draw a representative group of pupils from the four corners of the province and, after their training, to send them back again to their respective communities, both to spread the word and to ensure that the school was useful to the province as a whole and not just to its leading urban centre. But if this was the ideal, the reality was that the Normal's pupil-teachers were not as representative of the provincial population as either the school's founders or some hinterland residents might have wished.

The women, far more often than the men, came from York County and its neighbouring counties of Ontario and Peel (Table 4). The tendency of the school to draw on the local region diminished over time, especially in the case of the men, but the women coming from the three central counties in any two- or three-year period hovered around 50 percent of all female students, dropping below 40 percent only once, in the last period examined, 1869–71. The vast majority of these women came from York County, a good many from Toronto. An examination of the registers, in which students' places of origin are recorded more precisely than in the printed annual reports of the chief superintendent of schools, reveals that some 29 percent of the women who attended in the 1850–54 cohort came from one of the province's five cities,[30] compared to only 12 percent of the men (Table 5). Most of the city women were in fact from Toronto. By 1869–72 women of city origin were, at 28 percent, as numerous as before among female entrants, but male city dwellers now comprised less than 3 percent of all male students.[31]

Table 3: Toronto Normal School, Students' Ages on Entering their First Session, 1850–54 and 1869–72

Session	Age	Women		Men	
		n	%	n	%
6, 7, 9–13	19 and younger	188	61.2	136	36.0
1850–54[a]	20–24	89	29.0	145	38.4
	25 and older	30	9.8	97	25.7
	Total	307	100.0	378	100.0
	Mean (sd)	19.5	(4.6)	22.1	(5.1)
	Median	19.0		21.0	
41–47	19 and younger	325	67.1	165	34.4
1869–72	20–24	125	25.8	212	44.2
	25 and older	34	7.0	103	21.5
	Total	484	100.0	480	100.0
	Mean (sd)	19.1	(3.3)	22.4	(5.4)
	Median	18.0		21.0	

Source: Archives of Ontario, RG 2–H–1, vols. 10–11, Toronto Normal School Registers.

Age	age on entry to the student's first session, in years
n	number of students entering their first session
%	n as percentage of total within period
sd	standard deviation
[a]	excludes 4 women and 6 men whose ages are not recorded

The number of urban female and male students taken together was always disproportionately large relative to the province's urban population. Urban Upper Canada accounted for only 10 percent of the provincial population in the periods under study but produced from 15 to 20 percent of the Normal School's students.

No doubt responding to criticism of the over-representation of Toronto and York County, the authorities took measures to attract students from the city's rural hinterland. The dates of Normal School sessions were advertised in provincial newspapers and, almost from the beginning, pupil-teachers from out of town received subsidies to help defray their lodging expenses. Although the sums paid did not cover the full cost of room and board, they clearly made it possible for some students to attend who otherwise would have been unable to.[32] In addition, all pupil-teachers received their text-

Table 4: Toronto Normal School, 1847–71: Students' Geographical Origins, the Counties around Toronto

Session	Sex	York			York, Peel & Ontario			Canada West (all counties)	
		n	%Co	%CW	n	%Co	%CW	n	%Co
1–5	Women	50	28.7	40.0	74	30.1	59.2	125	23.0
1847–50	Men	124	71.3	29.6	172	69.9	41.1	419	77.0
6–10	Women	80	53.7	38.3	93	49.2	44.5	209	37.1
1850–53	Men	69	46.3	19.5	96	50.8	27.1	354	62.9
11–15	Women	154	77.0	44.4	173	69.8	49.9	347	58.3
1853–56	Men	46	23.0	18.5	75	30.2	30.2	248	41.7
16–20	Women	164	64.3	45.6	173	58.4	48.1	360	47.1
1856–58	Men	91	35.7	22.5	123	41.6	30.4	405	52.9
21–25	Women	162	62.8	45.5	180	55.6	50.6	356	44.9
1859–61	Men	96	37.2	22.0	144	44.4	33.0	436	55.1
26–30	Women	156	70.3	45.1	174	61.3	50.3	346	47.9
1861–63	Men	66	29.7	17.6	110	38.7	29.3	376	52.1
31–35	Women	205	82.0	48.0	217	74.3	50.8	427	55.2
1864–66	Men	45	18.0	13.0	75	25.7	21.6	347	44.8
36–40	Women	157	82.6	40.2	173	76.9	44.2	391	61.1
1866–68	Men	33	17.4	13.3	52	23.1	20.9	249	38.9
41–45	Women	142	83.5	30.0	170	75.9	35.9	474	56.6
1869–71	Men	28	16.5	7.7	54	24.1	14.8	364	43.4

Source: Statistical tables in *Annual Report of the Chief Superintendent of Schools* [title varies] (Quebec, Toronto [place varies], 1862–72).

n sum of the number of students attending each session, including in each session those attending their second or subsequent session; thus for each period n likely exceeds the number of discrete students in attendance during the period

%Co n as percentage of all women and men from the county/counties in the period; percentages may not total 100.0 due to rounding error

%CW n as percentage of the total of the *same sex* from Canada West in the period

Table 5: Toronto Normal School, 1850–54 and 1869–72: Students' Geographical Origins, Toronto, Other Cities and Beyond in Canada West

Session	Sex	Toronto			Other Cities[a]			Beyond the Cities[b]			Canada West	
		n	%	%CW	n	%	%CW	n	%	%CW	n	%
6–7, 9–13	Women	80	67.2	25.7	10	62.5	3.2	221	39.5	71.1	311	44.7
1850–54	Men	39	32.8	10.2	6	37.5	1.6	339	60.5	88.3	384	55.3
	Total	119	100.0	17.1	16	100.0	2.3	560	100.0	80.6	695	100.0
41–47	Women	79	91.9	16.7	52	91.2	11.0	343	42.3	72.4	474	49.7
1869–72	Men	7	8.1	1.5	5	8.8	1.0	468	57.7	97.5	480	50.3
	Total	86	100.0	9.0	57	100.0	6.0	811	100.0	85.0	954	100.0

Source: Archives of Ontario, RG 2–H–1, vols. 10–11, Toronto Normal School Registers.

a   Hamilton, London, Kingston and Ottawa

b   nine tenths (92.5 percent in 1851, 91.8 percent in 1871) of Ontarians resided beyond the five cities; *Census of the Canadas, 1851–52* , I (Quebec, 1853), *Census of Canada, 1870–71* , I (Ottawa, 1873)

n   the number of students in attendance during the period; those attending a second or subsequent session in the period were counted only once toward the period total

%   n as a percentage of the total *n* for the indicated city, cities or area in the period

%CW   n as a percentage of the total of the *same sex* from Canada West in the period; percentages may not total 100.0 due to rounding error

books on loan from the school. To supplement these measures, local councils were urged to sponsor and help finance candidates from their regions. Yet, although these measures did succeed in altering the composition of the school to some extent, complete regional representation remained elusive.[33]

Nor was the student body fully representative when it came to religion, for an overwhelming majority of the pupil-teachers were Protestants. There was, moreover, little fluctuation in the denominational composition of the school during its first two decades. By 1870, of the 6,069 students, female and male, who had registered up to that date, some 35 percent had been Methodists, 28 percent Presbyterians, 17 percent Anglicans and 7 percent Baptists. Roman Catholics, who comprised about 17 percent of the provincial population, accounted for only 4 percent of the Normal's pupil-teachers.[34] This Protestant and nonconformist bias in the student body is not surprising given the Methodism of the provincial school system's chief superintendent, Egerton Ryerson, and the political and religious prejudices of the times.

What is surprising, perhaps, is the fact that members of the Roman Catholic minority came to the school at all and managed to survive the discouragement that, if Jeremiah Gallivan was right, they apparently experienced there. There is some evidence that the reaction they encountered was not simply a response to their religion, for it seems that Irish Roman Catholics in particular were made to feel uncomfortable at Toronto Normal. But still they came, although their numbers were very small.[35]

The varying welcome offered by the school to different groups of Upper Canadians raises the question of social class. The government school system's mission in the province involved the development of a "respectable" class of teachers; presumably, to attract respectable students from the middling classes was also a goal of its flagship in Toronto. Did it succeed? Unfortunately, the school's registers give little direct information of the social backgrounds of those admitted. But a study of manuscript census returns for four Toronto wards in 1861, 1871 and 1881 shows that many city teachers, an increasing number of whom were Normal School graduates, came from relatively modest households.[36] Evidence of the modest social origins of the Normal's students may also be found in the registers from 1869 to 1872, in which were recorded the schools previously attended by the pupil-teachers. Once again a pronounced difference is apparent between women and men. Of the 423 male students for whom this information is recorded, 24 percent had come from grammar or secondary schools and slightly less than 4 percent from academies or private schools. The remaining 71 percent had only a common-school education. In contrast, just 48 percent of the 484 women reported a common-school training. Like the men, 4 percent had been to academies or private schools. However, 33 percent had been to a grammar or secondary school and 13 percent had a model-school background. Altogether, roughly one quarter of the men and one half of the women in the 1869–72 sessions had been exposed to something more, or other, than common schooling before they came to the Normal. On the other hand, almost three quarters of the men and the other half of the women had *not* had the benefit of any post-elementary or special schooling.[37]

All the evidence suggests that the Normal School which mid-nineteenth century educators and their students created in Toronto had multiple functions. It clearly served as a mecca for Protestant, especially nonconformist, individuals of both sexes, experienced teachers as well as neophytes, who wished to be trained in the official techniques of teaching that the school promoted. Secondly, it attracted men from all over the province who were already teachers and hoped to obtain the school's stamp of approval in order to ease their passage through the state system. One way in which they could achieve this was by winning a permanent certificate which was good anywhere in the province and enabled its holder to by-pass certification exams at the county level. At least some of the women students, especially those who had already taught school, were older than average and came from outside the Toronto region, probably had motives similar to these men.

But there was clearly another group, the majority of whom were women, who were attending the school for a different purpose: namely to obtain a post-elementary education or *additional* advanced schooling during their adolescent years. Although it was rare for anyone to attend for more than two years, many young women did attend for more than one session. And there is no doubt that the curriculum reflected not only the school's mission to upgrade its students in terms of their basic knowledge of subjects but also a strong interest on the part of the students themselves to acquire that knowledge.

Studies of other nineteenth-century North American normal schools have demonstrated the extent to which, especially in the American mid-West, they typically doubled as colleges or incipient secondary schools and served local populations in pursuit of an education higher than that available in regional common schools.[38] Evidently the Normal School in Toronto was no exception. Although the school's authorities tried hard to fulfill their provincial mandate, the Normal, at least in its first two decades, was much used by Toronto area families who saw in teacher training an avenue to the advanced schooling of their adolescent children, particularly their daughters, at the state's expense.

What was the experience of the women and men at the school during the early years? The evidence is inevitably scattered and incomplete,[39] yet an impression of how the school affected the first pupil-teachers and even a story of sorts can be pieced together. From the minutes of the provincial Board of Education and its successor, the Council of Public Instruction, the school's registers and the correspondence of the Education Office, we catch tantalizing glimpses of the Normal School, its staff and its students. More information can be gleaned from the records made by the staff of the Normal's female and male model schools, where its students did their practice teaching; from a long, informative letter to his wife by a married student who attended in 1853; and from the classroom notes of a woman who was a student in 1869.[40] Finally, there are two unique sources from a later period: a celebratory volume marking the school's 50th anniversary in 1897; and a novel that denigrates the Normal but celebrates at least some of its students, published long after his time at the school by Robert Barr, a journalist who had been a student in 1873.[41]

From these diverse sources there emerges a picture of an institution considerably troubled from time to time by its role as an innovator in the realm of co-education. There emerges also a sense that the lives led by women and men at the school may have been dissimilar in many respects and that the uses made of their education later on differed substantially as well. Finally, there is revealed at least a hint of the potential for social and intellectual liberation that even the relatively restricted opportunities at the school could mean for some of the women who experienced them.

Concern about the safety and propriety of the co-educational experience was characteristic of Toronto Normal from the beginning and was expressed most concretely perhaps in the school's physical layout (Figure 1). Separate entrances for women and men were provided to the main building, as well as to the lecture theatre. East and west corridors around the theatre enabled students to reach the model schools where they practice-taught without meeting members of the opposite sex. "By this arrangement," the architect explained, "it will be seen that except when actually in the presence of the Master, the male and female students will be entirely separated." When a museum was installed in the main building, appropriate separation was evidently impossible and so it was arranged that female and male students should visit the museum on different days.[42]

There are suggestions that segregation by sex may have been less strictly enforced when the school occupied temporary quarters prior to 1852. Certainly a group of male students who complained about the rules in the summer of 1853 felt that those prohibiting social intercourse between women and men had become more restrictive. But the evidence is contradictory. The fact that Thomas Graham was suspended in 1849 for tickling Jane Stephens during lectures and John Meighen in 1850 for using the ladies' entrance to the lecture room clearly indicates that fairly severe restrictions were in force from very early on. On the other hand, suspensions and expulsions do seem to have escalated in 1852 and during the first half of 1853. During the ninth session William Irvine of Kingston was sent away for "attempting to communicate with the female portion of the class and conducting himself in general unsteadily." Emily Clark was twice suspended, once for failing to inform the authorities of advances made to her by male students, a second time for encouraging such advances. Griffin Lanon got into trouble for speaking to "some of the ladies in the hall," having entered it by mistake before they had left. Lanon's refusal to apologize for remarks he made in response to their comments and laughter was termed "subversive of all order and discipline" by Headmaster Thomas Robertson.[43]

The attempt to prevent communication between women and men was by no means confined to school premises. Elizabeth Douglas was suspended for speaking to a fellow student on the boat when travelling home for vacation. Mary Tobias received a warning after walking with a male student in the late evening; after doing so a second time, she left the school to avoid expulsion. In the tenth session two more young women and two young men left or were dismissed for walking out together, a single male student more simply for "violation of rules" regarding female students, and one man and one women for writing letters to students of the opposite sex.[44]

It was no doubt the atmosphere created by these dismissals that motivated a mother to write, somewhat apologetically, to Robertson in May 1853, requesting that her young and homesick daughter be permitted to "converse occasionally" with some male relatives who attended the school. By late summer, feeling was running so high that the subject of male-female relations at the Normal provoked discussion in the press. This in turn gave students the courage to protest collectively; the 13th of August found the "male portion of the class" petitioning against regulations newly tacked onto the wall of their waiting room. The grounds of their protest were the "imposing, reproaching and insulting tenor" of these rules which, their petition implied, were harsher than earlier regulations. Expressing "utter contempt" for "outrageously inconsistent and needless restrictions" which seemed to prohibit "intercourse with females in the City of any kind," the petitioners withdrew their obedience to the discipline of the school until their "social rights, liberty, freedom and position as students" had been restored and acknowledged. By way of a coda, the writers of the petition expressed their appreciation of various city periodicals whose editors had spoken out in favour of Normal students' "personal rights." Certainly, support for student protest extended beyond the boundaries of the school and even of the city. By the 26th of August the "barbarous" rules of the Normal School had become the subject of editorial comment not only in Toronto but as far away as Niagara.[45]

By that time Egerton Ryerson had already written to the *North American* outlining the position of the school. Arguing that students were expected to devote all their time to preparing for their "noble profession" and that the spending of public money on this enterprise required that they study "without distraction," the chief superintendent also called attention to the fact that many of the students were away from home for the first time and that the rules were intended to sooth the nerves of "anxious parents and friends." Ryerson went on to dispute the assertion that Normal School women as well as men were opposed to them; on the contrary many of the "young ladies" were "thankful for the relief and advantage" that the rules provided. Finally, Ryerson's letter made the point that the regulations were far from new, having existed "since the first day" that women students had been admitted to the school.[46]

August ended with the leaders of the protest, under threat of suspension, apologizing for the tone of their complaint. They expressed their acceptance of the rules in the light of explanations that had been conveyed to them verbally, and also their hope that the offensive wording might be reconsidered. Ryerson, for his part, provided a written explanation to the effect that the rule most objected to was intended to "prevent the visiting of improper places and the formation of improper intimacies in the city, but not to interfere with the relations and usages of social life." The students were forgiven, but the resolution of this blowup did not immediately prevent further difficulties. September found Ryerson writing to a parent to explain that his daughter had been suspended for flirting with young men, an act still considered "subversive of the discipline" of the school. By April 1855 Robertson was able to report to the chief superintendent that there had been no discipline cases for some time; relative calm seems to have been established. However, in 1860 three women and two men were suspended for walking together and then denying it "with the most unblushing effrontery," and three more were asked to leave permanently in 1863 for writing anonymous letters to members of the opposite sex.[47]

If the rules against women and men communicating caused distress and hardship to some, at least one woman graduate at the school's 50th anniversary celebrations felt called upon to make light of them as she recalled the "darker" side of the school's early days. It was true, this career teacher reminisced, that the women and men at the Normal were not allowed to speak to one another. But, she noted, the rules said nothing about singing or the giving of gifts. Enamoured swains serenaded their loves and gave them fruit; and "eyes looked love to eyes that spake again." The same Thomas Robertson who disciplined his wayward students so sternly, an early model school teacher recalled, also took homesick pupil-teachers yachting and entertained them in his home with tea, cakes and "exquisite music" provided by his wife and daughters.[48] Clearly, social interaction between the sexes was not totally out of the question. The issues were, rather, control of this interaction and its respectability.

The relations between female and male students were, of course, not the only source of conflict between students and school authorities. In the majority of discipline cases the students involved were men, disciplined for failing to do the required work, for cheating, for fighting with each other, for striking Model School pupils, or because they became embroiled in altercations with the masters. As well, there seems to have been an increase in incidents involving academic honour as examinations became more intense and competitive. There is also clear evidence that from the beginning some male students had difficulty accepting Normal School discipline because they felt beyond the age of reprimand. As one of these pointed out, he was "rather old to be trifled with." Of five male students of the early 1850s who are recorded in the registers as having left because they felt "aggrieved" at being corrected by the masters or because they were "dissatisfied," one was 20, one was 25, two were 26 and one was 36 years old.[49] The presence of these older male students and the disparities in average ages in a school in which one third of the women were under 18 must also have affected both sides in the battle over communication between the sexes.

Clearly, too, the lion's share of discipline cases, whatever their cause, involved students from out of town, rather than those living with their families in Toronto. We have seen that the Upper Canadians broke with the Dublin Normal School model in accepting women into their school. A second break with the Dublin model occurred in the matter of how out-of-town students were accommodated. In the year that the school opened, Ryerson apparently sought information about the Irish school's "training houses." The result was a long letter to Hodgins from one T. C. Young outlining in some detail how Dublin Normal supervised the daily lives of its students. Each house, Young noted, was controlled by a superintendent who assisted the resident pupil-teachers in their evening lesson preparations and saw to the correctness of their out-of-school behaviour and to their conformity to the written rules of the institution. Apparently gathering from the original inquiry that there was resistance to the idea of properly supervised student residences in Toronto, Young issued a strong warning against boarding the pupil-teachers in ordinary houses in the city. "The result will be bad," he predicted. "Living about the town, they will be subject to the worst of influences, and their Course of training will be to some a Course of idleness and to others a Course of vice—to all a state of great temptation." It was in spite of this advice that the Upper Canadian Normal School's founders chose to place their boarding students in ordinary, unsupervised Toronto homes.[50] And from the beginning, even though all lodging houses had to be approved by school authorities, there were difficulties.

By the spring of 1848 it had come to the school's attention that some students were living in taverns. On the 30th of June of that year, the rule that students receiving a lodging subsidy could board only in approved houses was reiterated, with the added warning that this did not include taverns or hotels. By mid-December it was decided that each boarding house should have a student monitor and that the masters should inspect the houses every alternate week, reporting on their condition to the chief superintendent. The houses continued to give trouble, however. In August 1850 a rural school trustee informed Ryerson that a former Normal School student had carried away his daughter-in-law and was living with her "in sin" in one of the approved boarding houses.[51]

It must have been cases like this and accusations of the importuning of female students by fellow male boarders that led to the decision to accept only sexually segregated boarding houses for the women students who required accommodation while attending the Normal. But even this regulation did not eliminate all problems. And it is clear that the inspection of boarding houses became an increasingly onerous task for the masters. In 1855 they were asked to explain why they had reduced their boarding-house visits to once a month, and by 1857 there were new rules. Henceforth, no houses were to be licensed unless they provided for a minimum of two persons per bedroom and a sizable sitting room for the use of the teachers-in-training.[52] Concern about students boarding in disreputable houses continued to be expressed in the late 1850s and into the 1860s. After an outbreak of typhoid fever which took the lives of two students in 1866, acting Headmaster John Sangster reported that several of the licensed houses were "filthy" and that others were in "low and depraved" neighbourhoods. Sangster recommended that the bad houses be struck off the list and that new ones should be inspected before the school accepted them as suitable for student boarders. By this time he was beginning to question the wisdom of shared rooms as well as raising the issues of cleanliness and the suitability of surroundings.[53]

Although student health was clearly a worry to the authorities, with overcrowding and small, ill-ventilated rooms eventually becoming a major concern, the overriding focus of the masters' reports on the boarding houses prior to the mid 1860s was the issue of sexual morality.[54] The Thomas Graham whose first misdemeanour was tickling a female student was suspended once again when accused of entering the bedroom of his landlady's daughter with "a criminal intention." In 1852 school authorities had to deal chiefly with male students fighting with each other in the boarding houses but by January 1853 male-female relations were once again the issue. A Mrs. Walker reported that three of her female boarders were going to evening church services five or six times a week, leaving the house long before the services started. February brought the case of a male boarder caught sending obscene valentines to "females living in the neighbourhood," while in June Ichabod Bowerman was arraigned for leaving a verse on a scrap of paper at one of the girls' houses. Robertson perceived this as a "deliberate infringement of the rules" and argued that chaos would ensue if students like Bowerman were not expelled permanently. In August, on the heels of the public furor about the Normal School's rules, Robertson was investigating the conduct of Mary Ann Wilson, accused by a neighbour of receiving visits from young men "at unseasonable hours" in a house that she shared with her two sisters. By September there were further complaints, again from neighbours, about undue "levity" at one of the female students' boarding houses.[55]

By the mid 1850s the second master, William Ormiston, had less to say about particular cases and more on the general problem of providing adequate supervision. There were too many boarding houses; they were too scattered; and visiting them even once a month was becoming difficult. There was a need for a better class of houses. Moreover, establishments willing to take women were scarce. In the late 1850s specific questions of sexual morality emerged once again as the focus but concern seems to have been somewhat less pronounced than formerly. The masters wrote to Ryerson of students sharing rooms, of female boarders suspected of visiting male boarding houses, and "slight infractions" involving students staying out after hours. There was only minimal anxiety when school authorities received complaints, some anonymous, of serious problems in houses run by proprietors said to be "of bad character." Nor was there great alarm about two female students from different houses who frequently spent the night with each other. Still, if Robertson argued that this involved no impropriety, he was nevertheless concerned that the visits had been "the subject of comment" and reported that he had taken measures to prevent their recurrence. A tendency by housekeepers to ignore the rule prohibiting male boarders in female students' houses provoked a stronger response. In future, guilty proprietors were to be struck off the list permanently.[56]

By 1863 Robertson may well have been tiring of the effort to control the boarding houses. Four young men sharing one room with only two beds elicited comment but no concern. One house had permitted much visiting of women students by young men but was now closed to boarders; somewhat philosophically, Robertson observed that there had been "upon the whole very little of this sort of visiting going on" and that it would be "mischievous" to attempt to enforce a rule that female students "should never receive any visits whatever." Watchfulness and personal influence were the answer, Robertson concluded, as experience had already proven. In 1866, following the typhoid epidemic mentioned earlier and a subsequent investigation of dirty conditions in some approved houses, John Sangster, Robertson's successor as headmaster, eliminated a number of houses. He cited as his reasons: health problems; overcrowding, "i.e., having one or more sleeping apartments and no sitting room or insisting upon placing two beds in one room"; selling liquor on the premises; keeping cows; proximity to houses of ill fame; and refusing to permit inspection. The acceptable houses, 11 for women and 27 for men, were classified according to the nature of their facilities and their locality.[57]

Perhaps the final word on boarding houses belongs to the students. If male students in 1853 exhibited concern for the right to govern their own social lives, they also recognized that they were a valuable commodity, not least to proprietors of lodging houses. Ansel Randall, in a long letter to his wife about his first days at the school in the notorious summer of 1853, recorded his successful battle with his landlady for his right, as a Normal boarder, to free laundry. He had also insisted on his right to sleep without either a bedfellow or roommate and argued his way to better food. In addition, Randall wrote about his experiences at the school. On the opening day, he reported, the "laws" of the institution had been read out and students presented with 49 pages of lessons to read the first night, considerable labour in his view. The work, it was confirmed on the second day, was to be prodigious—"we have got to work and no mistake"—and the rules were to be strictly enforced. Classes began at 6:30 a.m.; the boarding house curfew was 9:30 p.m. Woe betide the student who failed to keep these rules, as well as those governing day-to-day social encounters:

> We...cannot Speak, Bow or Wink at one of the Female Students—nor spit about the School Rooms or even premises occupied by the Buildings. Now if we violate the least of the Rules given...or fail of being at the Rooms at the time the Roll is called we are <u>Expelled</u> without further ceremony.[58]

If we learn from Randall's account that both the workload and rules were to be taken seriously, we must turn to a later source for the flavour of typical classes. In notes that she took in 1869, Maria Payne focussed particularly on the need for order in classrooms. "Do not suppose you can let them grow inattentive and then straighten them in a minute," she wrote. "There must be perfect order in a school. This is the prime requisite to teaching....'[59] That controlling the class and preventing the least inattention on the part of the pupils were the chief issues in practice teaching is also the message of Model School registers from the period. The critic-teachers' assessments of students' work were chiefly negative. Most pupil-teachers were judged 3rd, 4th or 5th rate and it was only grudgingly admitted that the one or two ranked 2nd class might eventually become competent members of their profession. The Model School masters and mistresses found that Normal School trainees "lacked energy" and were "lifeless in manner." They were also not "watchful" and failed to command the constant and total attention of the pupils.[60]

It is from the lively pen of Robert Barr, a Normal School student in 1873, that we get the most complete and detailed picture of what the battle for this attention might mean. Barr was given only a 3rd-class ranking by the Boys' Model School principal, James Hughes, yet judged to be in "complete control of his class." He was also assessed as "sharp" or even "a little too sharp."[61] Little did his critic-teacher know how sharp. Forty years later Barr, by then a well-to-do journalist living in England, had harsh words for his old school, a "pork-packing factory" which rushed students in and out, "scraped off" some but not much of the ignorance in the process, and "flung" them upon a "defenceless Province." Fortunately for us, Barr decided in middle age to write a comic novel focussing on the adventures of four young Normal School students in the early 1870s. Entitled *The Measure of the Rule*, Barr's book deals only in part with the disciplinary problems encountered by teachers-in-training in the Boys' Model School and the alternately violent, woolly-headed or downright nasty masters with whom pupil-teachers of both sexes had to contend. The focus and real interest of his novel are the friendships that inevitably developed between not just a few but, he implies, a great many of the female students and their fellow male pupil-teachers. The girls of the school are portrayed as initially law-abiding but ultimately determined to disobey the rules in order to spend time with their young men, much to the discomfort of the masters, one of whom mounts a vicious campaign to discredit the rule-breaking students. The day is saved by the efforts of the warm-hearted if violent-tempered headmaster, an entirely human individual who is only too aware that the women and men of the Normal School are, "like the two friendly atoms in chemistry; compelled towards each other by forces [they] may not comprehend, and are unable to resist."[62] The fact that in the end no one is expelled is important, it turns out, in the case of only one of the four main characters, a young man who must obtain a teaching position in order to support the fellow student who will be his bride. The latter, who is happy to escape the suitor chosen by her family, will not teach—she will become a wife instead. Nor will the novel's hero or his love; they both go to Europe, he to become an artist, she to accompany an autocratic and unyielding father. The father, fortunately, is also fond of art and finally allows his daughter to marry the artist, her one-time Normal School lover.

In Barr's novel patriarchy is by no means totally triumphant. Yet the women in this book exist only in the shadow of the rambunctious and career-oriented men who are the tale's main protagonists. They move from the orbit of their families, in the most important case a widowed father, to the patriarchal authority of the school. If they reject the latter, it is because they are busy attaching themselves to future husbands. The "rule" of the book's title is found wanting, but it is hard to know to what extent "the dear girls" within its covers are liberated by their experience at the Normal. Perhaps the best sense of this is in the book's promise of a future in potentially egalitarian marriages chosen by the "girls" themselves. The Normal School represented for these young women at least the freedom to reject husbands who were not of their own choosing.

Turning from fiction to fact, we find evidence that the school might have seemed liberating in another sense for the women who attended. At the end of each session, beginning in the early 1850s, the headmaster sent to the chief superintendent a list of students who had been awarded certificates, indicating the intended destination of each graduate. The majority of these lists have been preserved[63] and from them it is possible to get some idea of where the students who received certificates went after leaving the school (Table 6). More than half of all the women named on the lists extant from the 1850s and 1860s intended to live in one of Upper Canada's five cities. The city they preferred was Toronto. Although the proportion of female students entering from Toronto did not exceed 26 percent in the two periods studied intensively, 1850–54 and 1869–72 (Table 5), 40 percent of female graduates between 1853 and 1867 gave that city as their intended destination (Table 6). This was in sharp contrast to the experience of male graduates. Increasingly the men who left with certificates were headed for destinations other than Toronto or, for that matter, any other Ontario city. If 37 percent of the men went to a city in the 1850s, by the middle 1860s only about 11 percent were choosing to do so. Normal School training and certification thus provided very different opportunities and led to contrasting futures for the women and men who graduated in the school's first decades. Although some men won assistantships or principalships in the cities—and these positions were increasingly important for career teachers—the majority found the Normal a gateway to preferment in the schools and school systems of rural and small town Ontario.

Brief biographical sketches of many who graduated in the Ryerson era are printed in the Normal's jubilee volume published in 1897; these reveal areas of both contrast and similarity. Quite a few of the men appear to have ended up in business, in farming or in professions other than teaching. Some women shared in the return to rural or small town roots but many of these left teaching when they married. Nevertheless, there were others who stayed in the occupation as single women, widows or, in a few cases, wives. A tiny number shared with their male fellow graduates the move into medicine. One of Ontario's leading suffragists, Dr. Emily Stowe, was part of this group.[64]

Why were the future paths of female and male graduates of the Normal School generally so different? At least part of the answer lies in the different openings available to them. Expanding opportunities in university education and professional training for men contrasted, in the third quarter of the nineteenth century, with very limited opportunities for women. Rural and small town inspectorates and principalships and, where available, similar jobs in cities would increasingly provide new career paths for male graduates, as did growth in the medical and legal professions, in government service and in business. For women, there was but one major new opportu-

Table 6: Toronto Normal School, 1853–67:
Intended First Destination after Graduation
of Students Winning Certificates

Session	Sex	Toronto			Other Cities[a]			Beyond the Cities[b]			Canada West	
		n	%	%CW	n	%	%CW	n	%	%CW	n	%
10, 13–14,	Women	95	49.0	38.8	42	82.4	17.1	108	36.9	44.1	245	45.5
18–21	Men	99	51.0	33.8	9	17.6	3.1	185	63.1	63.1	293	54.5
1853–59	Total	194	100.0	36.1	51	100.0	9.5	293	100.0	54.5	538	100.0
23–28, 30	Women	116	64.4	43.3	32	97.0	11.9	120	30.5	44.8	268	44.2
1860–63	Men	64	35.6	18.9	1	3.0	0.3	274	69.5	80.8	339	55.8
	Total	180	100.0	29.7	33	100.0	5.4	394	100.0	64.9	607	100.0
31–38	Women	151	83.4	37.6	79	96.3	19.6	172	39.0	42.8	402	57.1
1864–67	Men	30	16.6	9.9	3	3.7	1.0	269	61.0	89.1	302	42.9
	Total	181	100.0	25.7	82	100.0	11.6	441	100.0	62.6	704	100.0

Source: Archives of Ontario, RG 2–C–6–C, Incoming General Correspondence, lists of students who were to receive certificates and their intended first destinations; students who attended additional sessions and obtained another, higher-ranking certificate were counted on each occasion by Education Dept. officials in compiling these lists.

[a]   Hamilton, London, Kingston and Ottawa

[b]   nine tenths (92.5 percent in 1851, 91.8 percent in 1871) of Ontarians resided beyond the five cities; *Census of the Canadas, 1851–52*, I (Quebec, 1853); *Census of Canada, 1870–71*, I (Ottawa, 1873)

n   sum of the numbers of certificants in each session in the period

%   n as a percentage of the total *n* for the indicated city, cities or area in the period

%CW   n as a percentage of the total of the *same sex* from Canada West in the period; percentages may not total 100.0 due to rounding error

nity and that was to join an urban school system, as these systems were expanding. It is significant that the records show women typically earning lower-level certificates than their male counterparts. We know, as well, that slightly lower levels of work were required of women seeking first- and second-class certificates than were required of men.[65] Not surprisingly, then, the women who joined city school systems were generally hired as "assistants" to teach the lower grades whereas the men joined chiefly as senior members of the developing administrative hierarchies. At the end of the Normal's first decade in 1858, none of the 9 headmasters and male assistants but 11 of the 26 women assistants teaching for the Toronto School Board had

Normal School certificates. By 1881 nearly all of the women (134 of 137) but only slightly over half (15 of 26) of the men were graduates of the school.[66] At first inclined perhaps to spurn the products of Toronto Normal,[67] the board had done an about-face. The provincial school had become, at least in part, a place of preparation for Toronto's own teachers and especially for its female assistants.[68]

As one of Toronto Normal's most successful graduates, Dr. Emily Stowe was one of those most likely to express positive feelings about her experience at the school. On the occasion of its jubilee celebration Stowe pointed out that, in Canada, the Normal was not only "the first to open the doors to women's higher education" but also "the first to recognize equality in the ability of the sexes to compete in the halls of learning, and the first to establish a system of co-education."[69] Stowe's position was both inaccurate and exaggerated; "higher education" as it was understood in the mid-nineteenth century had been available to young Upper Canadian women in a number of private academies a decade or more before the Normal admitted women. Some of the academies and some provincially funded grammar schools were, moreover, already co-educational by 1847.[70] Nevertheless, her point of view cannot be dismissed out of hand. For many young women of Stowe's generation, the Normal School in Toronto provided an opportunity to escape the restrictions of rural or small town life and to seek respectable education and employment in cities. For some it may have represented the chance to choose a mate for themselves; for a few, like Emily Stowe, it led to further advanced education and independence through a career in medicine.[71]

An important aspect of both women's and men's experience at the Normal was that they were taken seriously as students and as prospective teachers. Yet Egerton Ryerson represented both his times and the school in his special attitude to those women whose teaching careers would be brief. These "young ladies," he said, would be teachers all their lives in their roles as mothers.[72] And, in fact, the futures of female students in the public labour force were taken less seriously than those of male students. The certificate examinations for women were less rigorous and relatively fewer women than men were granted the top certificates. In addition, as inhabitants of segregated boarding houses or as young women living at home with their families, female students' lives were more restricted. Certainly it was only the male students, as far as we know, who articulated a sense of their rights as Normal School students and as individuals. For although women and men alike had to deal with the authoritarian character of the school's government, the women were younger and had less previous experience as teachers. If the rules bore more heavily on them because of their youth, they may also have accepted patriarchal regulation more easily for the same reason.

The training at the Normal School in Toronto was, for both men and women, training in the most intense kind of city-living the province could provide.[73] It was also training in segregation by sex, which prepared Normal students for the sex-based hierarchies of rank and pay they would encounter in urban school boards, such as Toronto's, by the third quarter of the nineteenth century.[74] Normal-School-trained teachers in Ontario had been taught that their job was to be "watchful" and to keep control. They had learned to function in a competitive environment in which there were a number of negative forces: unpleasant landladies, disorderly pupils and, above all, the watchful and sometimes nit-picking male authorities who governed the school. On the other hand, these authority figures were often kind; some may have looked the other way when Normal School students fell in love. Or, if they were homesick, the headmaster might take them sailing and home for tea, cakes and music.

Female Normal students were not only younger than the men, they tended to come more often from cities and the central counties of the province. If the women went to live in cities and especially Toronto upon graduation, male graduates went far more often to rural areas or the smaller towns. But whatever their sex and their futures, the message that Normal School graduates were meant to carry to the schools of Ontario and elsewhere was the same. This was the message that the training they had received—in urban living, in segregation by sex, and in competitive and authoritarian modes of school government—was the very best training and that it ought to be a model for their future work in the schools, wherever they might be.

Yet this was not the only message they received. Paul Mattingly has called attention to the importance of looking at the disjunctures between intention and result in the development of educational institutions.[75] Some women and perhaps some men learned things at Toronto Normal that were not part of the original plan. Emily Stowe felt that the place had opened doors that had previously been shut to women. And if many or even most of the women graduates who taught school internalized the Normal's messages about hierarchy and women's second-class status in a world governed by men, not all did so. As we noted at the beginning, in 1885 Jane Cruise and seven other female Normal School graduates employed by the Toronto Public School Board rebelled, indicating that on the question of their status and rights they had begun to have doubts. In meeting separately from the men and forming their own Women Teachers' Association, they demonstrated that sexual segregation was a two-edged sword. It limited opportunities for women and emphasized their difference from men. But at the same time it gave them a base from which to organize a collective resistance and a weapon in their fight for better treatment as women.

I am greatly indebted to Nancy Kiefer and Beth Light for their assistance in coding, entering into the computer, and analyzing the records of the Normal School and the Toronto Board. Their work created the database which made it possible to reconstruct the individual and collective experience of teachers like Jane Cruise. I would also like to thank Nancy Kiefer and

Donna Varga Heise for their extremely useful work on the tables, David Keane for invaluable help with both tables and text, and Bruce Curtis, whose generous sharing of his own research in the education records at AO made my own work much easier. The Ontario Institute for Studies in Education and the Social Sciences and Humanities Research Council of Canada provided the financial support which made possible this research and writing.

1   Archives of Ontario [hereafter AO], RG 2–H–1, Upper Canada/Ontario Education Dept., Teacher Education, Normal and Model School Records, vols. 10–11, Toronto Normal School Registers of Students 1847–59 and 1863–73 [hereafter Register–10, Register–11 and, collectively, Registers]; *Annual Report of the Toronto Public School Board* [hereafter ARTPSB] Toronto, 1851–72).

2   *The Story of the Women Teachers' Association of Toronto* (Toronto, 1932), 10. The group first met in 1885; its original members in addition to Jane Cruise were Amelia Sims, Minnie Emery, Mary Gunn, Annie Carey, Jessie Semple, Harriet Johnston and Annie Gray. The early history of the WTA is explored in my preliminary study, "Themes in the History of the Women Teachers' Association of Toronto, 1892–1914", in Paula Bourne, ed., *Women's Paid and Unpaid Work: Historical and Contemporary Perspectives* (Toronto, 1985). See also Wendy Bryans, "Virtuous Women at Half the Price: The Feminization of the Teaching Force and Early Women Teacher Organizations in Ontario" (M.A. diss., University of Toronto, 1974); Pat Staton and Beth Light, *Speak with their Own Voices* (Toronto, 1987); and Harry Smaller, "Teachers' Protective Associations: Professionalism and the 'State' in Nineteenth Century Canada" (Ph.D. diss., University of Toronto, 1988), ch. 7.

3   *ARTPSB* (Toronto, 1870–80).

4   The practice of age grading, that is, of assigning pupils to classes partly on the basis of their ages, and the construction of secondary and tertiary curricula that would eventually result in a clear separation between university level institutions and high schools, developed concurrently with or in some cases following the founding of the first teacher-training schools. Joyce Senders Pederson, "The Reform of Women's Secondary and Higher Education: Institutional Change and Social Values in Mid and Late Victorian England", *History of Education Quarterly* [hereafter HEQ] 19 (1979), 61–91, provides an informative discussion of aspects of this transition as it occurred in Great Britain.

5   Jurgen Herbst, "Nineteenth-century Normal Schools in the United States: A Fresh Look", *History of Education* 9 (1980), 219–20. Drawing in particular on his knowledge of the history of mid-western American normal schools, Herbst argues persuasively for a regional approach as well as one which pays more attention to students' goals. For a discussion of the importance of a regional perspective in the history of teachers, see Marta Danylewycz, Beth Light and Alison Prentice, "The Evolution of the Sexual Division of Labour in Teaching: A Nineteenth Century Case Study", *Histoire sociale/ Social History* 16 (1983), 81–109.

6   *The Normal School for Ontario: Its Design and Functions* (Toronto, 1871), 71, 74. For details about the construction and opening of the school, see Susan E. Houston and Alison Prentice, *Schooling and Scholars in Nineteenth Century Ontario* (Toronto, 1988), ch. 6.

7   *Toronto Normal School Jubilee Celebration* (Toronto, 1898), 28; AO, RG 2–B, Upper Canada/Ontario Education Dept., General Board of Education (Second) and Council of Public Instruction [hereafter GBE/CPI], vol. 2, Minutes of Proceedings 1846–58, pp. 25–28, 6 Apr., 29 June, 7 July 1847; RG 2–C–6–C, Upper Canada/Ontario Education Dept., Dept. of Public Instruction, Incoming General Correspondence 1841–76 [hereafter Incoming–C], T. C. Young to J. George Hodgins, 3 June 1847.

8   J. George Hodgins, comp., *Documentary History of Education in Upper Canada* (Toronto, 1894–1910) [hereafter DHEUC], VI, 259, Egerton Ryerson to Governor General Charles Metcalfe, 9 May 1846.

9   Jill Conway has explored this question with particular reference to Oberlin College, which accepted women in the 1830s, and other American colleges which did so during and after the Civil War, in "Perspectives on the History of Women's Education in the

United States", *HEQ* 14 (1974), 2–12. For the Canadian scene see Donna Yavorsky Ronish, "Sweet Girl Graduates: The Admission of Women to English-Speaking Universities in Canada in the Nineteenth Century" (Ph.D. diss., University of Montreal, 1985); Paula J. S. LaPierre, "Separate or Mixed: The Debate over Co-Education at McGill University" (M.A. diss., McGill University, 1983); Nancy Ramsay Thompson, "The Controversy over the Admission of Women to University College" (M.A. diss., University of Toronto, 1974); and Margaret Gillett, *We Walked Very Warily: A History of Women at McGill* (Montreal, 1981).

10   Incoming–C contains some 300 boxes of letters; for this study I read those from the first two decades of the school's existence. Except where indicated all Incoming–C correspondence cited below is addressed to Ryerson.

11   Incoming–C: E. Spohn, 22 Aug. 1860; R. Heron, 29 Sep. 1860; S. Horner, 23 Aug. 1861.

12   Ibid.: G. Desvoung, 10 Jan. 1860; J. Gamble, 3 Nov. 1853; A. Green, 23 July 1861.

13   Ibid.: J. Eckford, 31 Dec. 1859. Thomas Fisher Rare Book Library (Toronto), Rare Books and Special Collections Dept., General MSS. Coll., Ansel B. Randall to Eliza Randall, 22 May–2 June 1853, holograph letter, 14 pp. [hereafter Randall letter]. GBE/CPI, vol. 1, Letterbook A, Ryerson to Rev. James Baird, 10 Sep. 1852, draft letter [loose insert].

14   Incoming–C: I. Barefoot, 6 Sep. 1859; G. Ross, 28 June 1860; A. Purkis, 17 Mar. 1863 (#2336); S. Fox, 26 June 1860; W. Leith to Hodgins, 3 Dec. 1860.

15   Ibid.: J. Taylor, 1 Dec. 1860; R. O'Brien, 5 Jan. 1853; S. Ferguson, 18 Nov. 1858; A. Ouellet, 24 Dec. 1858; G. Crane, 26 Mar. 1860. On the mobility of nineteenth-century teachers see Houston and Prentice, *Schooling and Scholars*, ch. 6.

16   Incoming–C: A. Parth, 1 Apr. 1858; M. Poole to Hodgins, 1 Oct. 1849; B. Way, 23 July 1860; H. McColl, 27 Feb. 1860; J. McDonald, 15 Dec. 1860; A. Allingham to Thomas Robertson, 13 June 1862.

17   Ibid.: P. How, 9 Apr. 1860; J. Gallivan, 31 Oct. [received] and 9 Nov. 1859, the latter with comments to Ryerson by Robertson, 17 Nov. 1859.

18   Ibid.: Robertson, 23 Mar. 1863 (#2421), 22 Apr. 1864 (#3157). See also RG 2–C–1, Upper Canada/Ontario Education Dept., Dept. of Public Instruction, Outgoing General Correspondence 1842–60 [hereafter Outgoing–1], vol. 18, Letterbook T, Ryerson to D. G. Sullivan, 30 Jan. 1857, in which Ryerson declared that one full session was the shortest acceptable period of attendance.

19   *Annual Report of the Chief Superintendent of Schools* [hereafter ARCSS] (Toronto, 1858), 125; the terms are 8 Jan. to 22 June and 8 Aug. to 22 Dec.

20   Incoming–C: W. Eljorshire, 8 Apr. 1856, is an example.

21   Register–10.

22   Incoming–C: P. Sammons, 10 Dec. 1852; J. Fraser, 14 Mar. 1864 (#2376), 4 Apr. 1864 (#2867); D. McNaughton, 14 Mar. 1864 (#2441); John Sangster, 17 Mar. 1864 (#2376), in which Sangster, the mathematics master, defended his conduct respecting Emma Fraser's examination.

23   Overcrowding, if a factor, may well have been due to the loss of space occasioned by parts of the building falling into disrepair by the late 1850s, a problem much complained of by Sangster when he became headmaster in the mid 1860s. It was only after Confederation that the government, in the person of the Ontario Works Dept., began effective repairs.

24   Incoming–C: Robertson, 29 June 1859. Three cohorts of students were also examined for which surviving records provide exceptionally complete coverage of the applicant pool or students in attendance. The first consists of applicants and students of sessions 6, 7 and 9 to 13 (1850–54); for this group acceptances and rejections were not indicated. In the second group, applicants of sessions 20 to 24 (1858–60), 80 percent of the women and 85 percent of the men were accepted; and in the third group, made up of applicants and students of sessions 41 to 47 (1869–72), the rates were 97 percent for the women and 95 percent for the men. Compiled from Registers and Incoming–C, admissions lists dated 20 July 1858, 18 Feb. and 17 Oct. 1859, 27 Feb. and 8 Sep. 1860. Registers are lacking for sessions from 1859 to 1863 and beyond Feb. 1873. The admissions lists are also an incomplete series.

25 Registers–10; Incoming–C: "List of students who left during the session", 18 Apr. 1855.

26 A. McCharles, *Bemocked of Destiny* (Toronto, 1908), 49.

27 Percentages calculated from statistical tables in *ARCSS*. Sessions 1 to 20 define the first decade (1847–1858); sessions 21 to 40, the second (1859–1868). Data in the Registers show a similar but less radical shift and a slightly narrower gap between women and men. Sessions 6, 7 and 9 to 13 (1850–54): almost 40 percent of the women and 59 percent of the men are recorded as having taught before. Sessions 41 to 47 (1869–72): about 32 percent of the women and 60 percent of the men are so listed. Register-based calculations exclude students attending their second or any subsequent session; such students were apparently not eliminated from the statistical tables in *ARCSS*.

28 The age of admission for men was officially raised to 18 in 1851; see "Revised Terms of Admission into the Normal School, 1851", *DHEUC*, X, 20. See also GBE/CPI, vol. 1, Letterbook A, pp. 120, 141, Ryerson to Rev. M. Fawcett, 1 Aug. 1851, and to L. Allan, 20 Mar. 1852. The youth of the women who attended Hockerill College, an English training school for female teachers, in the mid-nineteenth century is also emphasized in Michael Heafford, "Women Entrants to a Teachers' Training College, 1852–60", *History of Education Society Bulletin* (GB) 23 (1979), 14–29. Hockerill's women may have been slightly older than Toronto's female students; the "vast majority" were from 17 to 20. In 1857 Hockerill raised its age of admission to 17.

29 Francis Hincks, speaking at the ceremony to celebrate the opening of the new buildings in 1852, referred to regional opposition to the school arising from jealousy of Toronto; *The Normal School for Ontario*, 69. For an example of the early opposition, see "Memorial to the Legislature of the Gore District Council against the Common School Act of 1846", *DHEUC*, VII, 115.

30 Toronto, Hamilton, London, Kingston and Ottawa.

31 A regional comparison reveals a similar female-male pattern. The central counties (Peel, York and Ontario) accounted for 40 percent of the female but only 28 percent of the male students in the first cohort (1850–54), and 26 percent of the women compared to 12 percent of the men in the second (1869–72). Calculated from Registers. Place of origin was not recorded for almost 3 percent of the first cohort and just over 8 percent of the second.

32 Ansel Randall, writing to his wife during 22 May–2 June 1853, noted that some students in his session had dropped out because the subsidy had been reduced; Randall letter. Commentary on the subsidies and complaints about their inadequacy may be found in GBE/CPI, vol. 1, Letterbook A, p. 146, Ryerson to R. Cooper Esq., 7 May 1852; Incoming–C: R. Elliot, 17 Nov. 1849; W. Schuler to A. Allen, 15 Feb. 1850. Schuler's letter dealt with the need for local model schools to train teachers; Allen was superintendent of schools for Wellington County.

33 By the 1870s it was clear that additional measures were called for. A second normal school was opened in Ottawa in 1875 and by 1879 the Ontario Dept. of Education had decided to pay travel expenses of students who came to either school from out of town. See *DHEUC*, VI, 238, and AO, Pamphlet Coll., Adam Crooks, *Speeches* (1879), 37.

34 Registers.

35 Over the census years 1852, 1861 and 1871, Roman Catholics averaged about 17 percent of the population in Upper Canada/Ontario. Canada, Dept. of Agriculture, *Census of 1871*, IV *Censuses of Canada...to 1871* (Ottawa, 1876). Perhaps the most famous Roman Catholic to attend the school during this period was Mary Harris—"Maria Harris" in the 1859 register. After working in the United States as a teacher, wife and mother, and seamstress, Mary Harris became the famous labour agitator "Mother Jones." See "Mary Harris Jones", in Edward T. James, ed., *Notable American Women, 1607–1950: A Biographical Dictionary* (Cambridge, Mass., 1971), II, 266–88.

36 Marta Danylewycz and Alison Prentice, "Teachers, Gender and Bureaucratizing School Systems in Nineteenth Century Montreal and Toronto", *HEQ* 24 (1984), 75–100.

37 Register–11. Seven (1.5 percent) of the men claimed to have been entirely "self taught". Ten women (2 percent) are recorded as coming from separate schools or convents. Similar conclusions have also been reached about the modest class backgrounds of

women and men who trained to be teachers in England and British Columbia. See Frances Widdowson, *Going Up Into the Next Class: Women and Elementary Teacher Training, 1840–1914* (London, 1983); John Calam, "Teaching the Teachers: Establishment and Early Years of the B.C. Provincial Normal Schools", *BC Studies* 61 (1984), 38–39; Peter Searby, *The Training of Teachers in Cambridge University, 1879–1939* (Cambridge, 1982), 13–14.

38 Herbst, "Nineteenth-Century Normal Schools", and Jeff Wasserman, "Wisconsin Normal Schools and the Educational Hierarchy, 1860–1890", *Journal of the Midwest History of Education Society* 7 (1979): 219–27.

39 No student diary or extensive correspondence by students of Toronto Normal has been uncovered. For a diary of a student attending an American normal school in 1839, see Nancy Hoffman, ed., *Woman's "True" Profession: Voices from the History of Teaching* (Old Westbury, N.Y., 1981), 64–74.

40 GBE/CPI, vol. 1, Letterbook A; vol. 2, Minutes; Registers; Incoming–C; Outgoing–1; AO, RG 2–C–2, Upper Canada/Ontario Education Dept., Dept. of Public Instruction, Drafts of Outgoing Correspondence 1843–75 [hereafter Outgoing–2]; AO, RG 2–H–1, Upper Canada/Ontario Education Dept., Teacher Education, Normal and Model School Records, vols. 12–13, Provincial Model School Training Registers, Toronto, 1871–74 [hereafter Model School Register]; AO, Education Papers Collection, MU 975, box 5, Maria Payne, Normal School notebooks 1869 [hereafter Payne notebooks]; Randall letter.

41 *Jubilee Celebration*; Robert Barr, *The Measure of the Rule* (Toronto, 1907; reprint ed. with intro. by Louis K. Mackendrick, Toronto, 1973).

42 *DHEUC*, X, 14; Edwin C. Guillet, *In the Cause of Education: Centennial History of the Ontario Educational Association, 1861–1960* (Toronto, 1960), 61–62.

43 Incoming–C: W. Abercrombie and A. Lawder, 13 Aug. and A. Lawder, 18 Aug. 1853; GBE/CPI, vol. 2, Minutes, pp. 175, 235 and 266, 18 Dec. 1849, 7 May, 18 June 1851; Register–10, sess. 5–6, 9, 1850, 1852; Incoming–C: G. Lanon to Robertson, 12 and 14 Jan., and to Ryerson, 14 Jan. 1853; Robertson, 14 Jan. 1853.

44 Register–10, sess. 9–10, 1852–53.

45 Incoming–C: Jane Burns to Robertson, 30 May 1853; Abercrombie and Lawder, 13 Aug. 1853; "Barbarous Rules of Toronto Normal Schools", *Niagara Chronicle* (Niagara-on-the-Lake), 26 Aug. 1853.

46 Outgoing–2, box 2, Ryerson to the editor of the *North American* (Toronto), 13 Aug. 1853.

47 Incoming–C: Lawder, 18 Aug.; Robertson, 19 Aug. 1853; Outgoing–2: box 2, Ryerson to Lawder, 30 Aug., and to W. Higgins, 28 Sep. 1853; Incoming–C: Robertson, 18 Apr. 1855, 28 July 1860, 28 Oct. 1863 (#5457).

48 *Jubilee Celebration*, 17, 32.

49 Register–10, sess. 5–6, 1850; 9, 1852; Incoming–C: Robertson, 8 Apr. 1852; D. Knox to Robertson, 9 Apr. 1852; H. Hind, 12 and 13 Apr. 1852; Robertson, 9 (#2088) and 14 Mar. 1864 (#2375), 2 Jan. 1866 (#25); T. Callbary, 17 Apr. 1866 (#3667); Lanon, 11 Jan. 1853; Register–10, sess. 7, 1851; 9–10, 1852–53.

50 Incoming–C: Young to Hodgins, 3 June 1847. Ryerson had earlier expressed reservations about boarding halls and may have believed that they were morally dangerous. He argued that Normal students should live as they were most likely to live "in the course of their profession" rather than "secluded from the domestic circle and congregated together" in a communal residence. *DHEUC*, VII, 99. I discuss Ryerson's attitude to boarding halls in my "Education and the Metaphor of the Family: The Upper Canada Example", in Michael B. Katz and Paul H. Mattingly, eds., *Education and Social Change: Themes from Ontario's Past* (New York, 1975), 110–32.

51 GBE/CPI, vol. 2, Minutes, pp. 54, 76, 30 June, 15 Dec. 1848. For reports from the masters on the state of the boarding houses, see Incoming–C: H. Hind, 6 Dec. 1848; Robertson, 20 and 24 Jan. 1849. An exception to the rule prohibiting residence in taverns and hotels was made for S. Buckland, who received assistance while boarding with an innkeeper—his mother; ibid., p. 72, 20 Nov. 1848. The trustee's complaint is in Incoming–C: P. Tobin, 13 Aug. 1850.

52　GBE/CPI, vol. 2, Minutes, pp. 292, 440, 28 Feb. 1855, 26 Nov. 1857. Both of these regulations seem to have been honoured more in the breach than obeyed.

53　Incoming–C: Robertson, 20 Apr., 17 Oct. 1859; W. Hughes, 10 Aug. 1859; Sangster, 9 June 1866.

54　In December 1863 there were 31 female and 69 male student boarders. See Incoming–C: Robertson, 29 Dec. 1860, 28 Dec. 1863 (#6245).

55　Ibid.: Robertson to Hodgins, 27 and 30 Apr., 5 May 1851; Robertson, 11 May 1851; T. Graham to Hodgins, 24 May 1851; Robertson, 13 July, 21 Aug. 1852, 18 Jan., 18 Feb. 1853; P. Blaicher to Robertson, 17 Feb. 1853; Robertson to Hodgins, 5 Mar. 1853; Robertson, 9 June 1853; I. Bowerman, 15 June 1853; Robertson, 31 Aug., 15 Sep. 1853; Register–10, sess. 9–10, 1852–53.

56　Incoming–C: W. Ormiston, 19 Mar., 2 Apr., 3 Aug. 1855, 22 Jan. 1856; Robertson, 8 Apr. 1856; W. Watt, 15 July 1858; Robertson, 20 Apr., 17 Oct. 1859; W. Hughes, 10 Aug. 1859; Robertson, 13 Apr. 1860, 5 Nov. 1861.

57　Ibid.: Robertson, 23 Mar. 1863 (#2422); Sangster, 9 June (#4508), 3 Aug. 1866 (#5736).

58　Randall letter.

59　Payne notebooks.

60　Model School Registers, boxes 12, 13.

61　Ibid., box 12.

62　Barr, *Measure*, 24, 152.

63　Incoming–C: certificate lists survive for sess. 10, 13, 14, 18–21 (1853–59), 23–28 (1860–62), 30–38 (1863–67).

64　*Jubilee Celebration*, 100–198.

65　This comparison of certificate levels is based partly on impressionistic evidence. However, taking only the 361 women and 226 men for whom Toronto is given as their destination on the 22 surviving certificates lists, the disparity is beyond doubt: 32 percent (116) of these women and 52 percent (118) of these men held first-class certificates. On certificate requirements, see *The Common School Acts of Upper Canada* (Toronto, 1853), 102.

66　Incoming–C: Frederick Cumberland [Toronto School Board Trustee], 15 Jan. 1859. A March 1858 report by the Toronto superintendent lists 2 additional female asssistants with Normal School certificates, for a total of 13; Incoming–C: G. A. Barber, 14 May 1858. *ARTPSB* (Toronto, 1881).

67　This is the implication of a letter on the subject of the status of Normal graduates in the Toronto system in 1858, although the point was debated. See Incoming–C: F. Cumberland, 5 Jan. 1859; and "Dr. Ryerson and the Toronto Board of School Trustees", *Globe* (Toronto), 5 Jan. 1859.

68　Research conducted by Susan Laskin for the education plates of *The Historical Atlas of Canada*, vol. 2, shows that Normal School graduates, compared to all practising common-school teachers in Ontario, were overrepresented in the central counties in 1861 and 1866, the two years analysed. In 1866, for example, 30 percent of all such teachers employed in York and Brant counties had Normal School certificates; the proportion was even higher, 44 percent, in Wentworth County. In most of the remaining counties, especially those distant from the centre, Normal School graduates comprised well under one quarter of all active common-school teachers, and less than one in ten in a majority of cases. Data courtesy Historical Atlas of Canada Project, funded by the Social Sciences and Humanities Research Council of Canada.

69　*Jubilee Celebration*, 25.

70　Academies aspiring to provide advanced schooling for young women included the Upper Canada Academy and the Burlington Ladies' Academy, popular in the 1830s and 1840s. If one includes Grantham Academy in St. Catharines, the opportunities provided by academies date from the 1820s. The opening of some grammar schools to girls also appears to date from the late 1820s. Their status in those schools became the subject of heated debate in the mid 1860s. See Houston and Prentice, *Schooling and Scholars*, ch. 10.

71 American studies calling attention to the possibly liberating effects for some women of nineteenth-century educational and teaching experiences include Ann F. Scott, "The Ever Widening Circle: The Diffusion of Feminist Values from Troy Female Seminary, 1822–1872", *HEQ* 19 (1979), and Geraldine J. Clifford, "Teaching as a Seedbed of Feminism", paper presented at the Fifth Berkshire Conference on Women's History, Vassar College, Poughkeepsie, New York, June 1981. See also my "Towards a Feminist History of Women and Education", in Neil McDonald, ed., *Approaches to Educational History* ([Winnipeg], 1980), 39–64.

72 *Jubilee Celebration*, 24.

73 Marta Danylewycz called attention to the way in which convents in nineteenth-century Quebec acted as conduits for the transition from rural to urban life for women who opted to leave after their noviciates, as well as for many of the students of convent boarding schools; "Through Women's Eyes: The Family in Late Nineteenth Century Quebec", paper presented to the Canadian Historical Association, Montreal, June 1980.

74 See Danylewycz and Prentice, "Teachers, Gender and Bureaucratizing School Systems", and my "The Feminization of Teaching", in Susan Mann Trofimenkoff and Alison Prentice, eds., *The Neglected Majority: Essays in Canadian Women's History*, (Toronto, 1977), 49–65.

75 Paul H. Mattingly, "Structures over Time: Institutional History", in John H. Best, ed., *Historical Inquiry in Education: A Research Agenda* (Washington, D.C., 1983), 46.

J. M. S. Careless—Curriculum Vitæ

Birthplace

        Toronto, Ontario, 17 February 1919

Education

        University of Toronto Schools
        University of Toronto (Trinity College), B.A. 1940
        Harvard University, A.M. 1941, Ph.D. 1950

War Service

1943	Assistant to the Naval Historian, Naval Service Headquarters, Canadian Department of National Defence, Ottawa
1944–45	Special Assistant, Department of External Affairs, Ottawa and the Atlantic theatre

Academic Appointments

1945–	University of Toronto, Department of History
	1945–49 Lecturer
	1949–54 Assistant Professor
	1954–59 Associate Professor
	1959–67 Professor and Chair
	1967–77 Professor
	1977–84 University Professor
	1984– University Professor Emeritus
1966–	University of Toronto, Massey College
	1966–85 Senior Fellow
	1978–82 Senior Southam Fellow
	1985– Senior Fellow Emeritus
1968	University of Edinburgh, George Brown Lecturer
1968–69	University of Victoria, Visiting Professor
1971	University of London, Special Lecturer
1977	Ohio State University, Edwin Kennedy Lecturer
1978	Australian National University, Visiting Senior Research Fellow
1987	University of Toronto, D. G. Creighton Lecturer; University College, Toronto, Tetzel Lecturer
1988	McMaster University, Messecar Visiting Professor
1989	University of Manitoba, W. L. Morton Lecturer

Academic Awards

1942–43	Sheldon Travelling Fellow, Harvard University
1955–56	Rockefeller Foundation Award, studies in England
1958	Carnegie Fellowship, administered by the Canadian Humanities Council, studies in Australia
1978	Visiting Senior Research Fellow, Australian National University

Distinctions

1962	Fellow, Royal Society of Canada
1981	Officer, Order of Canada
1987	Officer, Order of Ontario

Other Awards

1954	Governor General's Award, Non-Fiction, in history
1960	University of British Columbia Medal for Biography
1962	Tyrrell Medal for Canadian History, Royal Society of Canada
1964	Governor General's Award, Non-Fiction, in history
1965	Award, American Assoc. of State and Local History Societies
1968	Cruikshank Medal, Ontario Historical Society
1985	City of Toronto Book Award
1986	Award of Merit, Canadian Historical Association
1987	National Heritage Award, Environment Canada

Honorary Degrees (D.Litt. or L.L.D.)

1979	Laurentian University
1981	Memorial University
1982	University of Victoria
1984	Royal Canadian Naval College (Royal Roads), McMaster University and University of New Brunswick
1986	University of Calgary

Activity in Historical and Cultural Associations

1948–58	Co-Editor, *Canadian Historical Review*
1950–	Member and member of the Executive (various years), Canadian Historical Association and Ontario Historical Society
1954–75	Member, and co-Chair 1961–72, Ontario Archaeological and Historic Sites Board
1957–79	Historical Consultant, Canadian Broadcasting Corporation
1959–60	President, Ontario Historical Society
1961–66	Advisor, historical series, National Film Board
1962–	Member and member of Section committees (various years), Royal Society of Canada
1963–73	Trustee, Ontario Centennial Centre for Science and Technology
1967–68	President, Canadian Historical Association
1969–73	Member, Ontario Commission on Post-Secondary Education
1971–	Trustee, and Chair 1982–, Ontario Historical Studies Series; Member, Advisory Board, *Acadiensis*

1972–85	Member, and Chair 1980–85, Historic Sites and Monuments Board of Canada
1975–81	Director, and Chair of the Historical Committee, Ontario Heritage Foundation; Member, Management Board, University of Toronto Press; Member, Editorial Advisory Board, *Urban History Review*
1976–79	Associate, Canadian Theatre History Research Programme
1976–	Director, and Chair to 1982, Multicultural History Society of Ontario
1977–78	Advisor, series on French-English relations in Canada, National Film Board
1977–80	Historical Consultant, Urban Series, National Museum of Man
1981–85	Member, National Advisory Board, *The Canadian Encyclopedia*
1985–87	Member, Canadian Studies Committee, Shastri Indo-Canadian Institute
1986	Special Advisor, Historic Sites and Monuments Board of Canada
1987	Co-Chair, Policy Review Conferences, Ontario Heritage Foundation

J. M. S. Careless—Select Bibliography

1945

"Confederation", "The United States to 1860", "The United States Since 1860", "Modern Britain", "Canada's Armed Forces", "Newfoundland", "Ottawa", "Royal Military College", *The Canadian Book of Knowledge* (Toronto). And subsequent editions, various years, to 1960

1948

"The Toronto *Globe* and Agrarian Radicalism, 1850–67", *Canadian Historical Review* 29 (1) March, 14–39

Review of *The Rise of Toronto* by D. C. Masters, *Canadian Journal of Economics and Political Science* 14 (2) May, 275–76

1949

Review of *This New Canada* by M. McWilliams, *Canadian Historical Review* 30 (2) June, 170–71

1950

"The Diary of Peter Brown", *Ontario History* 42 (3) July, 113–51

"Mid-Victorian Liberalism in Central Canadian Newspapers, 1850–67", *Canadian Historical Review* 31 (3) September, 221–36

"Who Was George Brown?", *Ontario History* 42 (2) April, 57–66

Review of *Our Canada* by A. G. Dorland, *Canadian Historical Review* 31 (1) March, 75–76

Review of *The Mohawk* by C. Hislop and *The Mackenzie* by L. Roberts, *Canadian Historical Review* 31 (1) March, 77–78

1951

"History and Canadian Unity", *Culture* 12 (2) June, 117–24

"Letters in Canada, Social Studies, II: The Land and the People", *University of Toronto Quarterly* . Review articles on regional works, annually to 1960

Review of *The Valley of the Lower Thames: 1640 to 1850* by F. C. Hamil and *The Physiography of Southern Ontario* by L. J. Chapman and D. F. Putnam, *Canadian Historical Review* 32 (3) September, 276–77

1952

"1925–1939: II", in A. Watson, ed., *Trinity 1852–1952* (Toronto), 153–67. Essay on student life

1953

Canada: A Story of Challenge (Cambridge and Toronto, rev. eds. 1963, 1970, 1985; Japanese ed. Tokyo, 1978)

Canada and the Commonwealth (Toronto). Co-author with G. W. Brown, C. R. MacLeod and E. P. Ray

1954

Canada and the Americas (Toronto). Co-author with G. W. Brown, G. M. Craig and E. P. Ray

"Canadian Nationalism—Immature or Obsolete? ", Canadian Historical Association, *Report*, 12–14

"Frontierism, Metropolitanism, and Canadian History", *Canadian Historical Review* 35 (1) March, 1–21

Review of *Our Sense of Identity: A Book of Canadian Essays* by Malcolm Ross, *Canadian Historical Review* 35 (4) December, 353

Review of *Three Centuries of Robinsons: The Story of a Family* by Julia Jarvis, *Canadian Historical Review* 35 (2) June, 157–58

"W. K. Rolph" [Obit.], *Canadian Historical Review* 35 (1) March, 92

1955

Canada and the World (Toronto). Co-author with G. W. Brown, G. M. Craig and E. P. Ray

1956

Review of *Pioneer Public Service: An Administrative History of the United Canadas, 1841–1867* by J. E. Hodgetts, *Canadian Historical Review* 37 (4) December, 365–66

1957

"The Independent Member for Kent Reports, 1853", *Canadian Historical Review* 38 (1) March, 41–51

"Letters from Thomas Talbot to John Beverley Robinson", *Ontario History* 49 (1) Winter, 25–41

"The Political Ideas of George Brown", *Canadian Forum* 36 February, 247–50

Review of *Daylight Through the Mountain: Letters and Labours of Civil Engineers Walter and Francis Shanly* by F. N. Walker, *Canadian Historical Review* 38 (4) December, 335

Review of *Sam Slick in Pictures: The Best of the Humour of Thomas Chandler Haliburton*, ed. Lorne Pierce, illus. C. W. Jefferys, *Canadian Historical Review* 38 (1) March, 77

1958

Review of *The Grand Trunk Railway of Canada* by A. W. Currie, *Canadian Historical Review* 39 (4) December, 339–40

1959

Brown of The Globe, I: *The Voice of Upper Canada, 1818–1859* (Toronto)

"George Brown", in R. L. MacDougall, ed., *Our Living Tradition, Second and Third Series* (Toronto), 31–54

Review of *Galloping Head: The Life of the Right Honourable Sir Francis Bond Head, 1793–1875* by Sydney Jackman, *Canadian Historical Review* 40 (2) June, 168–69

Review of *Problems of Wartime Co-operation and Post-War Change, 1939–1952* by N. Mansergh, *American Historical Review* 64 (4) July, 941–42

1960

"George Brown and the Mother of Confederation, 1864", Canadian Historical Association, *Report*, 57–73

1962

"Government and Historical Resources in Canada", in Canada, Northern Affairs and Natural Resources, Second Seminar on the Development of Canadian Historical Resources, *Report* (Ottawa). Veritype

Review of *The Idea of Continental Union: Agitation for the Annexation of Canada to the United States, 1849–1893* by D. F. Warner, *Canadian Historical Review* 43 (2) June, 153–54

1963

Brown of the Globe, II: *Statesman of Confederation, 1860–1880* (Toronto)

1964

"Introduction", in Morris Zaslow, ed., *The Defended Border: Upper Canada and the War of 1812* (Toronto), 1–8

1966

"Metropolitanism and Nationalism", in
Peter Russell, ed., *Nationalism in Canada*
(Toronto), 271–83

1967

*The Union of the Canadas: The Growth of
Canadian Institutions, 1841–1857*,
Canadian Centenary Series (Toronto)

"Confederation Conferences", "Durham",
"Elgin", "Ewart", "Devonshire",
"United Canada, 1841–1867", *The
Encyclopedia Americana* (New York).
And subsequent editions, various
years, to 1972

"Introduction", in his and R. C. Brown, eds.,
The Canadians, 1867–1967 (Toronto),
xiii-xix. Co-author with R. C. Brown.
Republished with the historical essays
as *Part One of The Canadians, 1867–1967*
(Toronto, 1968)

1968

"Culture", in Mark Satin, ed., *Manual for
Draft-Age Immigrants to Canada*
(Toronto), 57–60

"Hooray for the Scars and Gripes", in A.
Purdy, ed., *The New Romans* (Edmonton), 132–34

"Introduction", in *The Pioneers: The Picture
Story of Canadian Settlement*, Canadian
Illustrated Library (Toronto), 8–14.
Also volume co-author with W. J.
Eccles, C. M. Johnston, W. S. MacNutt,
M. A. Ormsby and L. H. Thomas

"Somewhat Narrow Horizons", Canadian
Historical Association, *Report*, 1–10

Review of *British Columbia and Confederation*,
ed. W. G. Shelton, *British Columbia
Library Quarterly* 32 (2) October, 27–28

Review of *My First Seventy-Five Years* by A.
R. M. Lower, *Canadian Historical Review*
49 (3) September, 278–79

1969

"Aspects of Metropolitanism in Atlantic
Canada", in Mason Wade, ed.,
*Regionalism in the Canadian Community,
1867–1967* (Toronto), 117–29

" 'Limited Identities' in Canada", *Canadian
Historical Review* 50 (1) March, 1–10. An
earlier version of this paper was read at
a joint session of the American and
Canadian Historical Associations,
Toronto, December 1967

"The Lowe Brothers, 1852–70: A Study in
Business Relations on the North Pacific
Coast", *BC Studies*, No. 2 Summer, 1–18

"Nationalism, Pluralism and Canadian
History", *Culture* 30 March, 19–26.

1970

"The Development of the Winnipeg
Business Community, 1870–1890",
Royal Society of Canada, *Proceedings
and Transactions*, 4th Series, Vol. 8,
239–54

"Donald Creighton and Canadian History:
Some Reflections", in John S. Moir, ed.,
*Character and Circumstance: Essays in
Honour of Donald Grant Creighton*
(Toronto), 8–21

"George Brown and Confederation",
Historical and Scientific Society of
Manitoba, *Transactions*, 3rd Series, Vol.
26, 79–87

"Ralph Flenley" [Obit.], Royal Society of
Canada, *Proceedings and Transactions*,
4th Series, Vol. 8, 71–72

"The *Review* Reviewed or Fifty Years with
the Beaver Patrol", *Canadian Historical
Review* 51 (1) March, 48–71

1971

"The Historian and Nineteenth-Century
Bibliography: A Personal Estimate",
Bibliographical Society of Canada,
Papers 10, 73–84

"Introduction" and "The 1850s", in his, ed., *Colonists and Canadiens, 1760–1867* (Toronto)

Review of *Empire and Nation: Essays in Honour of Frederick H. Soward*, eds. Harvey L. Dyck and H. Peter Krosby, *International Journal* 26 Winter, 274–76

Review of *Montreal: A Brief History* by J. I. Cooper; *Montreal: From Mission Colony to Great World City* by L. Roberts; *Nineteenth Century Cities: Essays in the New Urban History*, eds. S. Thernstrom and R. Sennett; *Illustrated Historical Atlas of the County of York, Canadian Historical Review* 52 (2) June, 177–80

1972

"The Business Community in the Early Development of Victoria, British Columbia", in David. S. Macmillan, ed., *Canadian Business History: Selected Studies, 1491–1971* (Toronto), 104–23

"D. G. Creighton: John A. Macdonald" and "H. A. Innis: The Fur Trade in Canada", in Byron Dexter, ed., *The Foreign Affairs Fifty-Year Bibliography*, (New York), 412, 417

"George Bennett", "George Brown", "David Christie", *Dictionary of Canadian Biography*, X: *1871 to 1880* (Toronto), 49, 91–103, 168–71

"Localism or Parochialism in Canadian History?", *B.C. Perspectives* 2, 4–14

1973

"Aspects of Urban Life in the West, 1870–1914", in Anthony W. Rasporich and Henry C. Klassen, eds., *Prairie Perspectives, II: Selected Papers of the Western Canadian Studies Conferences, 1970 and 1971* (Toronto), 25–40

"Metropolitan Reflections on 'Great Britain's Woodyard' " [Review of *"Great Britain's Woodyard": British America and the Timber Trade, 1763–1867* by A. R. M. Lower], *Acadiensis* 3 (1) Autumn, 103–9

1974

The Learning Society, Report of the Commission on Post-Secondary Education in Ontario (Toronto). Volume co-author and editor of members' "Reservations"

Urban Development in Central Canada to 1850, Canada's Visual History Series (Ottawa)

"Some Aspects of Urbanization in Nineteenth-Century Ontario", in F. H. Armstrong et al., eds., *Aspects of Nineteenth-Century Ontario: Essays Presented to James J. Talman* (Toronto), 65–79

"Urban Development in Canada", *Urban History Review* 3 (1), 9–13

1975

"Two River Empires: The St. Lawrence and the Mississippi", *American Review of Canadian Studies* 5 (2) Autumn, 28–47

"Waspishness and Multiculture", in K. J. Laidler, ed., *Preserving The Canadian Heritage*, Royal Society of Canada (Ottawa), 141–50

1976

"A History of the Provincial Lunatic Asylum", *City Magazine* 2 (3/4) Summer, 42–44

"Peter Brown", "John Roaf", *Dictionary of Canadian Biography*, IX: *1861 to 1870* (Toronto), 88–89, 663–65

1977

"A Few Acres of Snow", Canadian Museums Association, *Gazette* 2. Evaluation of the permanent Canadian Historical Exhibit, National Museum of Man

"In Praise of Vacant Lots", *The Globe and Mail*, 19 February, 7

Review of *Canada Before Confederation* by R. C. Harris and J. C. Warkentin and *Illustrated Historical Atlas of Peterborough County, 1825–1875*, ed. A. O. C. Cole, *Canadian Historical Review* 58 (1) March, 68–70

1978

The Rise of Cities in Canada before 1914, Historical Booklets Series, Canadian Historical Society (Ottawa)

1979

George Brown, The Canadians Series (Toronto)

"The Concept of Canadian Studies and the Multicultural History Society of Ontario", in Historical Society of Mecklenburg, *German-Canadian Yearbook* (Toronto), 1–5

"Metropolis and Region: The Interplay between City and Region in Canadian History before 1914", *Urban History Review* , No. 3–78 February, 99–118

"Riel Just Bad Hollywood", *The Sunday Sun* (Toronto), 22 April, 24. Review of CBC Television dramatic production

Review of *Victoria: A Primer for Regional Architecture* by Martin Seggar, *B.C. Historical News* 12 (4), 36–37

1980

"Dominium Day, 2084", University of Toronto Information Services, *The Graduate* 7 (4) March/April, 16–18

"How We Celebrate Dominion Day—Canada Day—July 1st", *The Globe and Mail*, 1 July, 8

"Limited Identities—Ten Years Later", *Manitoba History* 1 (1), 3–9

"The New Fathers of Confederation", *The Toronto Star*, 6 September, B–1

"One Hundred Years after George Brown, What is his Legacy?", *The Globe and Mail* , 9 May, 7

"The Place, the Office, the Times, and the Men", "Robert Baldwin", and "Epilogue", in his, ed., *The Pre-Confederation Premiers: Ontario Government Leaders, 1841–1867*, Ontario Historical Studies Series (Toronto), 3–31, 89–147, 315–19

"Submarines, Princes and Hollywood Commandos, or At Sea in B.C.", *B.C. Studies*, No. 45 Spring, 3–16

Review of *Mirrors of the New World: Images and Image-Makers in the Settlement Process* by J. M. Powell, *Australian Journal of Politics and History* 26 (2), 319–20

Review of *The Jews of Toronto* by S. Speisman, *Canadian Jewish Historical Society Journal* 4 (1) Spring, 95–98

1981

"The Myth of the Downtrodden West", *Saturday Night* May, 30–34, 36

Review of *A Canadian Millionaire: The Life and Business Times of Sir Joseph Flavelle, Bart., 1858–1939* by Michael Bliss, *Révue d'histoire de l'Amérique Française* 34 (4) March, 627–30. In French, trans. M. Caya

1982

"James Lesslie", *Dictionary of Canadian Biography*, XI: *1881 to 1890* (Toronto), 516–19

"Reflections on the Individual in Canadian Society", *Expression* 3 (4) Winter, 5–9

1984

Toronto to 1918: An Illustrated History, History of Canadian Cities Series (Toronto)

"The First Hurrah: Toronto's Semi-Centennial of 1884", in Victor L. Russell, ed., *Forging a Consensus: Historical Essays on Toronto* (Toronto), 141–54

"The Life of a New City: Toronto, 1834",
Empire Club of Canada, *Addresses
1983–1984* (Toronto), 285–97

1985

"Corn Laws", "George Brown", "Learned
Societies", "Metropolitan-Hinterland
Thesis", "Province of Canada", "Rep
by Pop", "Royal Society of Canada",
"Toronto", *The Canadian Encyclopedia*
(Edmonton)

"The Emergence of Cabbagetown in
Victorian Toronto", in Robert F.
Harney, ed., *Gathering Place: Peoples and
Neighbourhoods of Toronto, 1834–1945*
(Toronto), 25–46

"J. B. Conacher: A Personal Appreciation",
in Bruce L. Kinzer, ed., *The Gladstonian
Turn of Mind: Essays Presented to J. B.
Conacher* (Toronto), ix-xv

"Upper Canada and Confederation", in
Nick and Helma Mika, comps., *The
Shaping of Ontario: From Exploration to
Confederation* (Belleville), 241–47

1986

"Canada before 1800", in Charles Humber,
ed., *Canada: From Sea Unto Sea* (Mississauga), 84–107

Review of *Shocked and Appalled: A Century of
Letters to The Globe and Mail*, ed. Jack
Kapica, *Canadian Historical Review* 67
(3) September, 440–41

1987

Review of *Canada, 1900–1945* by Robert
Bothwell, Ian Drummond and John
English, syndicated in Thomson
Newspapers Inc., December

Review of *The Orangeman: The Life and Times
of Ogle Gowan* by Don Akenson,
syndicated in Thomson Newspapers
Inc., January

1988

"The Aftermath of Rebellion", in D. Duncan
and G. Lockwood, eds., *1837 Rebellion
Remembered* (Toronto), 151–64

1989

*Frontier and Metropolis in Canada: Regions,
Cities and Identities to 1914* (Toronto).
The 1987 Creighton Lectures, Univer-
sity of Toronto

The Editors & Contributors

Frederick H. Armstrong * is a professor in the History Department, University of Western Ontario. He has published extensively in the political and social history of nineteenth-century Ontario.

Peter Baskerville is an associate professor in the Department of History, University of Victoria, and author of *The Bank of Upper Canada: A Collection of Documents*.

Tony Hall * is an associate professor in the Department of Native American Studies at the University of Lethbridge. He was formerly a member of the Department of Native Studies, University of Sudbury.

J. K. Johnson is a professor in the History Department, Carleton University, and has published a number of studies on Upper Canadian élites.

David Keane * is a research associate in the programs for educational and faculty development of the Faculty of Health Sciences, McMaster University.

Kenneth McNaught is a professor emeritus in the Department of History, University of Toronto. Among his many works is *The Pelican History of Canada*.

Graeme Patterson * is an associate professor in the History Department, University of Toronto. He has published a number of papers on politics, élites and political ideology in early Upper Canada.

Alison Prentice * is a professor in the Department of History and Philosophy of Education, Ontario Institute for Studies in Education. She is a co-author with Susan E. Houston of *Schooling and Scholars in Nineteenth-Century Ontario*.

Colin Read * is a professor in the History Department at Huron College, University of Western Ontario, and president (1989–1990) of the Ontario Historical Society.

Paul Romney * is author of *Mr. Attorney: The Attorney General for Ontario in Court, Cabinet, and Legislature, 1791–1899*, as well as several articles on Ontario's nineteenth-century social, political and legal history.

Neil Semple * is a former archivist at the United Church Archives, and has published several papers on the history of Methodism in nineteenth-century Ontario.

Allan C. Smith * is an associate professor in the Department of History, University of British Columbia. He has published several studies on nineteen-century Ontarians' social attitudes and cultural values.

Malcolm Thurlby is an associate professor of Visual Arts, Faculty of Fine Arts, York University, and associate dean of Graduate Studies at York.

Gerald Tulchinsky * is a professor in the Department of History, Queen's University. He is currently researching the history of the Jews in Canada.

William Westfall * is chair of the History Department at Atkinson College, York University. He is a co-editor with Roger Hall and Laurel Sefton MacDowell of *Patterns of the Past: Interpreting Ontario's History* and author of *Two Worlds: The Protestant Culture of Nineteenth-Century Ontario.*

* Ph.D. work supervised by Maurice Careless

Acknowledgements

Maps and Pictures

Credit	Page
after maps by RC Harris and J Warkentin, DGG Kerr, G Craig, and R Langman.	10.
after maps by RC Harris and J Warkentin, and DGG Kerr.	11.
JMS Careless.	13,23,33,37.
Archives of Ontario	71,77,78,79,139,175,235, 286.
United Church of Canada Central Archives.	95,111.
AWN Pugin, *Contrasts...*, 2nd edition (London, 1841).	122.
W Westfall and M Thurlby	124,128,129,130,132,133, 134,135,136,137, 141.
The *Builder*, 11 (1853).	127.
Archives of Ontario (Horwood Collection).	131,138.
Woodland Cultural Centre.	148.
Metropolitan Toronto Reference Library, Baldwin Room.	193.
Metropolitan Toronto Reference Library.	218,237.

Selections from J. M. S. Careless, "Two River Empires: An Historical Analysis," are reprinted with permission of the Association for Canadian Studies in the United States; those from J. M. S. Careless, "Frontierism, Metropolitanism, and Canadian History," " 'Limited Identities' in Canada" and a review of J. I. Cooper, *Montreal: A Brief History,* are with permission of the University of Toronto Press.